THE
MYSTERIES OF MAGIC

*A DIGEST OF THE WRITINGS OF
ÉLIPHAS LÉVI*

WITH BIOGRAPHICAL AND CRITICAL ESSAY

BY

ARTHUR EDWARD WAITE

"Mon livre sera sans portée pour mon siècle . . . . mais que m'importe? J'ai voué ma vie à la vérité, et je le dira pour qui voudra et saura l'entendre. SI CE N'EST PAS DANS UN JOUR, IL SERA DANS UN AN, SI CE N'EST PAS DANS UN AN, CE SERA DANS UN SIÈCLE, MAIS JE SUIS TRANQUILLE CAR JE SAIS QU'ON Y VIENDRA."—*La Science des Esprits*, p. 83.

Copyright © 2018 Read Books Ltd.
This book is copyright and may not be
reproduced or copied in any way without
the express permission of the publisher in writing

British Library Cataloguing-in-Publication Data
A catalogue record for this book is available from
the British Library

Folklore

Folklore, or often, simply 'lore' consists of legends, music, oral history, proverbs, popular beliefs, fairytales, stories and customs included in the traditions of a culture, subculture or group. The English antiquarian William Thoms was the first person to introduce the term 'folklore' specifically, in a letter published in the London journal *The Athenaeum* in 1846. He invented this compound word to replace the various other terms used at the time, including 'popular antiquities' or 'popular literature.' In usage, folklore and mythology usually signify the same thing and there are four general areas of study; artefacts (such as voodoo dolls), describable and transmissible entity (oral tradition), culture, and behaviour (rituals). These areas do not stand alone however, as often a particular element may fit into more than one of these groupings.

While folklore can contain religious or mythic elements, such as the Icelandic skaldic poetry or the Christian stories of Saint George or Saint Christopher, it equally concerns itself with the sometimes mundane traditions of everyday life. Though many argue this is a successful method of demonstrating societal relationships, in the Jungian view, folklore pertains to unconscious psychological patterns; instincts or archetypes of the mind. These folktales may or may not emerge from a religious tradition, but nevertheless speak to deep psychological issues. The familiar folktale, 'Hansel and Gretel' is an example of this fine line. The manifest purpose of the tale may primarily be one of mundane instruction regarding forest safety or secondarily a cautionary tale about the dangers of famine to large families, but its latent meaning may evoke a strong emotional response. This is largely due to the widely understood themes and motifs such as 'the terrible mother', 'death' and 'atonement with the father.'

The critical interpretation of myths and folklore goes as far back as the tales themselves. For instance, Sallustius (a fourth century Roman writer) divided myths into five categories; theological, physical (or concerning natural laws) animastic (or concerning soul), material and mixed. And although Plato famously condemned poetic myth when discussing the education of the young in the *Republic*, primarily on the grounds that there was a danger that the young and uneducated might take the stories of Gods and heroes literally, nevertheless he constantly refers to myths of all kinds throughout his writings. Interest in folkloric story telling continued well into the Renaissance, and notably during the nineteenth century, folktales and fairy tales were perceived as eroded fragments of earlier mythology (famously by the Brothers Grimm and Elias Lönnrot). Mythological themes are also very often consciously employed in literature, beginning with Homer – and the foundational *Iliad* and the *Odyssey*.

Legends are very closely tied to the history of folklore and mythology, but they are generally narratives of human actions that are *perceived* by both teller and listeners to take place *within* human history and to possess certain qualities that give the tale verisimilitude. Whilst legends will not include happenings outside the realm of 'possibility', they often contain miracles - believable in a specific religious context. The Brothers Grimm, the chief collectors of Germanic folk and fairy tales of the nineteenth century, defined legend as specifically historically grounded, as opposed to their own *Märchen*. Legends and folklore often both serve the purpose of romantic nationalism though; in which a people derive their legitimacy from a common culture, language, race and customs.

The telling of stories appears to be a cultural universal, common to basic and complex societies alike. Even the forms folktales take are similar from culture to culture, and comparative studies of their themes and narratives have been successful in showing these relationships. Although folktales are exceptionally similar to myths, mythology does differ slightly in that it will often refer to 'ideology.' They have most famously been analysed by Roland Barthes (1950s, *Mythologies*), who argued that modern culture explores religious experience in many more ways than we realise. He further posited that because it is not the job of science to define human morality, this is where myths (and to some extent folklore) come in – as pseudo-religious experiences attempting to connect the present with a perceived moral past.

There are many forms of contemporary folklore that are so common that most people do not realize they are folklore, such as **riddles**, children's **rhymes** and ghost stories, rumours (including conspiracy theories), ethnic stereotypes and holiday customs. Although myth was traditionally transmitted through the oral tradition on a small scale, the technology of the film industry has enabled filmmakers to transmit myths to large audiences via film dissemination. The basis of modern storytelling in both cinema and television lies deeply rooted in the mythological tradition. The **Disney Corporation** is notorious among cultural study scholars for 'reinventing' traditional childhood myths. While many films are not as obvious as Disney fairy tales in respect to the employment of myth, the plots of many films are largely based on the rough structure of the myth such as the cautionary tale regarding the abuse of technology, battles between gods, and creation stories are often the subject of major film productions. Folklore, myths and legends are very much a part of our life today, and it is hoped that the current reader is inspired to find out more about this fascinating subject.

ARTHUR EDWARD WAITE

Arthur Edward Waite was born in Brooklyn, New York, USA in 1857. His father died when he was very young, and his widowed mother returned to her home country of England, where he was then raised. Waite was educated at a small private school in North London, and St. Charles' College. After school, he became a clerk, and wrote verse in his spare time.

In 1874, the death of Waite's sister saw him become deeply interested in psychical research. He began to read regularly in the Library of the British Museum, studying many branches of esotericism. Not long later, Waite became editor of an occultist magazine called *The Unknown World,* and in 1891 joined Aleister Crowley's Hermetic Order of the Golden Dawn. A decade later, he became a Freemason, and entered the Societas Rosicruciana in Anglia. Waite had a lifelong rivalry with Aleister Crowley, who presented him as a villainous wizard in his novel *Moonchild*.

Waite was a prolific author, and many of his works were well received in academic circles. He wrote occult texts on subjects such as divination, esotericism, Rosicrucianism, Freemasonry, Kabbalism and alchemy; he also translated and reissued several important mystical and occultist works. His works on the Holy Grail rank amongst his finest publications.

However, Waite is best-remembered not for his scholarly work, but for his co-creation of the popular and widely used Rider-Waite Tarot deck, and his authoring of its companion volume, *The Key to the Tarot*. First published in 1909, the Rider-Waite-Smith tarot was notable for being one of the first tarot decks to illustrate all 78 cards fully, in addition to the 22 major arcana cards. The work made him famous, and Waite spent much of the rest of his life lecturing and speaking on the topic of the Tarot. He died in 1942, aged 88.

To

THE SUBLIME SPIRIT OF

ALPHONSE LOUIS CONSTANT,

I Dedicate this Book.

CONTENTS.

	PAGE
BIOGRAPHICAL SKETCH OF ALPHONSE LOUIS CONSTANT .	xi
CRITICAL ESSAY ON HIS WRITINGS	xvii
INTRODUCTION	1
INITIATORY EXERCISES AND PREPARATIONS . . .	22

RELIGIOUS AND PHILOSOPHICAL PROBLEMS AND HYPO-
THESES—

THE HERMETIC AXIOM	33
FAITH	34
THE TRUE GOD	38
THE CHRIST OF GOD	42
MYSTERIES OF THE LOGOS	48
THE TRUE RELIGION	52
THE REASON OF PRODIGIES, OR THE DEVIL BEFORE SCIENCE	60

SCIENTIFIC AND MAGICAL THEOREMS—

ON NUMBERS AND THEIR VIRTUES	66
THEORY OF WILL-POWER	70
THE TRANSLUCID	73
THE GREAT MAGIC AGENT, OR THE MYSTERIES OF THE ASTRAL LIGHT	74
MAGICAL EQUILIBRIUM	79
THE MAGIC CHAIN	83
THE GREAT MAGIC ARCANUM	89

CONTENTS.

THE DOCTRINE OF SPIRITUAL ESSENCES, OR KABBALISTIC PNEUMATICS; WITH THE MYSTERIES OF EVOCATION, NECROMANCY, AND BLACK MAGIC—

INTRODUCTION	94
IMMORTALITY	96
THE ASTRAL BODY	97
UNITY AND SOLIDARITY OF SPIRITS	100
THE GREAT ARCANUM OF DEATH, OR SPIRITUAL TRANSITION	102
HIERARCHY AND CLASSIFICATION OF SPIRITS	109
FLUIDIC PHANTOMS AND THEIR MYSTERIES	113
ELEMENTARY SPIRITS AND THE RITUAL OF THEIR CONJURATION	118
NECROMANCY	128
MYSTERIES OF THE PENTAGRAM AND OTHER PANTACLES	136
MAGICAL CEREMONIAL AND CONSECRATION OF TALISMANS	143
BLACK MAGIC, AND THE SECRETS OF THE WITCHES' SABBATH	154
WITCHCRAFT AND SPELLS	164
THE KEY OF MESMERISM	177
MODERN SPIRITISM	181

THE GREAT PRACTICAL SECRETS, OR REALISATIONS OF MAGICAL SCIENCE—

INTRODUCTION	194
THE *MAGNUM OPUS*	196
THE UNIVERSAL MEDICINE	206
RENEWED YOUTH	211
TRANSFORMATIONS	214
DIVINATION	222
ASTROLOGY	226
THE TAROT, THE BOOK OF HERMES, OR OF THOTH	242
ETERNAL LIFE, OR PROFOUND PEACE	265

CONTENTS. ix

EPILOGUE—
1. THE VISION OF THE WANDERING JEW . . . 271
2. THE FAREWELL TO CALVARY 274
3. THE REIGN OF THE MESSIAH 277
4. THE FINAL VISION 279

SUPPLEMENT—
THE KABBALAH 283
THAUMATURGICAL EXPERIENCES OF ÉLIPHAS LÉVI—
EVOCATION OF APOLLONIUS OF TYANA . . . 309
GHOSTS IN PARIS — THE MAGICIAN AND THE
MEDIUM—ÉLIPHAS LÉVI AND THE SECT OF
EUGÈNE VINTRAS 313
THE MAGICIAN AND THE SORCERER—SECRET HIS-
TORY OF THE ASSASSINATION OF THE ARCH-
BISHOP OF PARIS 326

NOTES 342

BIOGRAPHICAL AND CRITICAL ESSAY.

DESPITE the wide reputation in his own country and the growing European celebrity of the great French Kabbalist and occultist, who, in the third quarter of this century, published his immortal elucidations of the Mysteries of Magic for the instruction of France and the world, under the Hebraistic pseudonym of Éliphas Lévi Zahed, the materials for a biography of Alphonse Louis Constant are meagre and unsatisfactory in the extreme. He was born in an obscure street of Paris, and was the son of a shoemaker in a small way of business, and apparently in the poorest circumstances. The exact date of his birth I am unable to state, but it was at the beginning of the century, and probably at or about the year 1809. He was delicate in his childhood,* and received no regular education, "but his aptitude for learning, and his avidity for picking up stray bits of knowledge were so great that at last the neighbours used to talk of him as 'the clever lad.'" † This precocity introduced him to the notice of the Curé of his parish, who obtained him a gratuitous education at the Seminary of Saint Sulpice, where he entered on his studies for the priesthood, and in addition to proficiency in the two languages of classical antiquity which would be expected of an ordinary ecclesiastic, he became "a first-rate Hebrew scholar." Thus in this probationary period, he laid the foundations of that Kabbalistic knowledge which eventually led him through the darkest paths of esoterism to his reconciliation of religion and science. Grave doubts on matters of doctrinal belief presented themselves at an early period to his mind, but they were probably the result of an acquaintance with Voltairian free-thought, which is the basis of his occult philosophy, rather than of a juvenile initiation into the mysteries of magical art. His friend and disciple, the famous chiromancist Desbarrolles, speaks of his religious

* Desbarrolles—*Mystères de la Main*.   † *Theosophist*, Jan. 1886.

exaltations, and of those doubts and scruples which led him to relinquish the sacerdotal career when on the point of engaging himself definitely and irrevocably therein. On this point we are indebted to Madame Gebhard for the following curious story:—

"Before his last vows were taken he was sent as a punishment to an old out-of-the-way monastery, it having been discovered that he had on several occasions, while preaching in some country villages, given expression to opinions which were not considered consistent with the Catholic faith. He was kept a prisoner in this monastery for some months. His food was very scanty, consisting of little more than bread and water. He had a large room allotted to him on the ground floor; the roof was vaulted, bare cold stones formed the floor, and the furniture consisted of a pallet bed, one chair, and a table.

"This part of the monastery was said to be haunted, and he once related a very curious anecdote in connection with it. One night being in the dark (for he was not allowed a light), he heard sounds as if an immense number of people were marching across the end of the room; they seemed to come in at one door and go out at another, though in the day-time he had never found any second mode of ingress or egress.

"After passing many agitated and unpleasant hours, he slept, and on awakening towards dawn saw the figure of a monk sitting by his side. He was startled, thinking it was a ghost, when the apparition said to him, 'Do not fear; I am not a denizen of the other world, but a real living man.' This monk proved a good friend to him, for from that day he was better treated, received sufficient food, was given a smaller and more comfortable room, and had even books lent to him, and writing materials placed at his disposal."

Whatever may be otherwise thought of this story, the imprisonment of Louis Constant was not of a very rigorous kind; the description of his original cell corresponds, except in the matter of size, to those which are in daily use among many monks of unblemished orthodoxy, and it is difficult to see how a young cleric who had not taken final vows, and could have been only in minor orders, was permitted to perambulate the country preaching independently, in defiance of all the law and order so scrupulously observed in these matters by the whole of the Latin Church.

BIOGRAPHICAL AND CRITICAL ESSAY.   xiii

Even the preaching of deacons who have taken irrevocable vows, is a wholly exceptional thing. Nevertheless, as a friend and a pupil of Éliphas Lévi in the advancing years of his life, Madame Gebhard had good opportunities to ascertain the facts of the case, and, of course, her authority is very high.

That delightful little pastoral story, *Le Sorcier de Meudon*, which Éliphas describes as "*à peu près notre biographie*," * apparently gives us an idealised picture of the writer's monastic experiences. The Frère Lubin of that story is the young Alphonse Louis Constant. Maître François Rabelais, "*le Frère Médecin*," personifies the occult sciences, and surely it is a device of no ordinary genius to embody the sublime wisdom of the Magi, which supplies to all "the most efficacious consolations and the most salutary counsels," in "*la personne sacrée du joyeux curé de Meudon*," that supreme "magician of the gay science in a century of furious fanaticism and insane extravagance." *

Éliphas Lévi at length returned to the world; as in so many candidates for the Catholic priesthood, it was probably the scruples to which Desbarrolles refers as much as the doubts which interfered with his vocation. It does not appear that he was on bad terms in after life with his ecclesiastical superiors, for in the year 1850 I find him contributing to that noble and marvellous series of cheap theological encyclopædias projected by the Abbé Migne, his voluminous and interesting "Dictionary of Christian Literature," which is a perfectly orthodox work, though it avoids dangerous and debateable subjects. His renunciation of the sacerdotal career was followed by a runaway marriage with "a beautiful young girl of sixteen," who was the exquisitely-sketched Madeline, "*la gentille et blonde petite jouvencelle*" of the "*Sorcier de Meudon*." The parents of the young lady, who had originally refused their consent, became afterwards reconciled to the match in spite of this escapade, but "the union," says Madame Gebhard, "was unfortunately not a happy one; they lost their two children at an early age, and one morning Éliphas woke up to find that his wife had left him for ever. He sought consolation in books, and gave himself up altogether to the occult sciences."

* *Le Sorcier de Meudon*. Preface.

b

This tragical finale to a hasty and ill-considered match is also commemorated in the novel I have referred to. Frère Lubin is rewarded for the infidelity of his wife by the inspiration of the poet, and this gift of song again typifies the occult sciences under a new aspect, for the power of the Magus is wholly in his discernment of the natural analogies between God, man, and the universe, as was divined by Saint Martin, the disciple of Pasqualis Martinez, in his mystical "*Tableau.*" Éliphas Lévi possessed, moreover, in an eminent degree the two-fold endowment which we find in great poets, namely, profound knowledge of the human heart, and keen insight, with the power of discerning correspondences, which is a part of poetical insight.

After this heartless desertion of her husband, Madame Constant (whose maiden name I have been unable to discover) is said to have supported herself by sculpture. She was not only very handsome but extremely talented; and she exhibited at the salon several busts, which she had herself sculptured, under the name of Madame Claude de Vingmy. Some time after the Franco-German war she is said to have married a Monsieur Ronère, who was at that time a member of the French Parliament. Of her history subsequent to this event I can find no information.

A divinatory calculation in the *Dogme de la Haute Magie* throws a vague glimmer of light on certain epochs in the life of the author.

"In 1825 family life came to an end for me, and I was definitively engaged in a fateful path which conducted me to knowledge and misfortune. In 1843 I travelled as a pioneer addressing the common people, and persecuted by ill-intentioned individuals,—in a word, I was honoured and proscribed.* In 1847, I was violently separated from my family, and great sufferings for mine and me resulted from this separation. In 1851 I had employment, which was moderately but sufficiently remunerative, with some embarrassment of position."

In 1853 Éliphas Lévi repaired to London, where his reputation as an occultist had preceded him, and where he

---

* He was apparently engaged in a political propaganda, and was on one occasion imprisoned for a couple of weeks, on account of some newspaper article against the (? Imperial) Government.

performed his celebrated ceremonial evocation of Apollonius of Tyana.* Some passages in the writings of Éliphas Lévi suggest that he made the acquaintance of the late Lord Lytton, and the absolute identity between the mysterious *vril* of "The Coming Race" and the universal force of the Astral Light, is conclusive as to the great novelist's acquaintance with the works of his Kabbalistic contemporary. I, therefore, addressed an inquiry to the present Earl of Lytton, and I am indebted to his courtesy for the information which follows.

His lordship is almost certain that his father was personally acquainted with M. Constant, of whose works there is a copy at Knebworth, presented, he thinks, by the author. He is under the impression that Éliphas Lévi made the acquaintance of the late Lord Lytton either at Paris or at Nice. Among the papers at Knebworth there is a letter from M. Constant on the existence of a universal force, and the requisite conditions of its employment for the evocation of spiritual visions and presences. The letter is only dated "Sunday, 10 April," the date of the year is wanting, and from the style it would appear to be addressed either to a stranger, or to a very distant acquaintance.

The *Dictionnaire de la Littérature Chrétienne* was published in 1851. It had been preceded by some obscure efforts, such as the *Evangile de la Liberté*, written, I imagine, in conjunction with Alphonse Esquiros, the fantastic author of "The Magician," and one of Louis Constant's earliest friends.† The *Dogme et Rituel de la Haute Magie* were issued separately in 1854 and 1856, but there is internal evidence to show that they existed originally as a whole, and were afterwards separated in a somewhat arbitrary manner, and not without detriment to their general coherence. These volumes, which set their author in the foremost rank of occultists, were followed by the *Histoire de la Magie*, a work of the first interest, written on a philosophical plan, but manifesting already a wide diver-

---

* See "Thaumaturgical Experiences," chapter i.
† "The Last Incarnation," by A. Constant of Geneva, has been translated from a copy of the French original, which the owner supposed to be unique, and has been published at Springfield, Ill., U.S.A. This is an unknown work by Lévi, advocating Socialistic principles. Some of its legends were subsequently embodied in *La Science des Esprits*.

gence in the views of its author. In 1861 appeared a second edition of the *Dogme et Rituel*, with a long prefatory dissertation embodying the later opinions just referred to, and scarcely consonant with the work to which it was prefixed. *La Clef des Grands Mystères* was published in the same year in which also the admirers of Éliphas Lévi were delighted by the appearance of the *Sorcier de Meudon*. In 1862 the first series of the *Philosophie Occulte* was issued under the title of *Fables et Symboles*, and consisted of poetical apologues, containing rather more of the gold of wisdom than is generally to be met with in the ore of the fabulists, together with an occult and philosophical commentary which is full of the keen insight and characteristic ingenuity of its author. The second series followed in 1865; this was *La Science des Esprits*, a defence of the symbolical spirit of the Christian gospel against the spirits of table-rapping, for, as Madame Gebhard tells us, Éliphas Levi had "a horror of Spiritualism, and used to say that mediums and spiritualists were like children playing with lighted matches near a barrel of powder, which any moment might explode and destroy them." His horror, however, was exaggerated, and originated, partially at any rate, in the indignation of an initiated thaumaturge at such a general invasion of the realm of prodigies by the *profanum vulgus* of unqualified investigators. The physical and moral deterioration accompanying the indiscriminate use of mediumistic gifts was, however, in itself a justification for the author's denunciations, and *La Science des Esprits* will take rank among the most interesting of his productions. It was followed by a silence of ten years, and in 1875 the gifted spirit of Alphonse Louis Constant passed to the next stage of its eternal progress.

We are indebted to Madam Gebhard for the following portraiture of her revered teacher:—" He was of a short and corpulent figure; his face was kind and benevolent, beaming with good nature, and he wore a long grey beard which covered nearly the whole of his breast. His apartment resembled a *bric-à-brac* shop, with specimens of the most beautiful and rare old china, tapestry, and valuable paintings. In one of the rooms there was an alcove in which stood a bed, covered with a gorgeous quilt of red velvet heavily embroidered with gold; the curtains were also of red velvet bordered with massive gold fringe, and a red velvet step stood before this magnificent couch, having a soft cushion also of red and gold laid on the top of it. . . . He lived a quiet and retired life, having few friends. . . . His habits . . . were simple, but he was no vegetarian. . . . He had a wonderful memory, and a marvellous flow of language, his expressions and illustrations being of the choicest and rarest character. . . . Never," says this lady in her interesting but too brief narrative, " did I leave his presence without feeling that my own nature had been uplifted to nobler and better things, and I look upon Éliphas Levi as one of the truest friends I ever had, for he taught me the highest truth which it is in the power of man or woman to grasp."

The hand of Éliphas Lévi was engraved by Desbarrolles in his *Mystères de la Main;* it has the highest psychical and philosophical peculiarities; it indicates " irresistible attractions towards sensual gratifications followed immediately by aspirations towards ascetical life "—pride and the most complete indifference alternately ruling his behaviour —" and that fatality which, through all his days, impelled him towards the secret sciences, for which he was created and of which he bears all the signs, by successively depriving him of whatever could attach him to actual life, and in the end of his most cherished affections."

In the *Dogme et Rituel de la Haute Magie,* Éliphas Levi claims to be in possession of a secret which has once, at least, revolutionised the world; he claims to have discovered a force by which all miracles divine and diabolical have been, and may still be, performed, to possess the key of prophecies, to have traced the exoteric doctrines of all theogonies to one primal and universal dogma. He has recovered the claviculæ of Solomon, and has " opened without difficulty every door of the ancient sanctuaries where absolute truth seemed to slumber;" he has unravelled the transcendent secrets which mediæval adepts concealed under the more or less equivocal expressions of the *Magnum Opus,* the philosopher's stone, the quadrature of the circle, the universal medicine, and the transmutation of metals. He has discovered, in fine, " the secret of human omnipotence and of indefinite progression—he is, in one word, the master of the absolute.

Now, in attempting to estimate the value of this gigantic claim, and of Éliphas Lévi's contributions to the elucidations of occult science, we are brought face to face with the fact, that after posing as an initiate in possession of the Great Arcanum, he has done his best to stultify himself by attempting to pose also as a faithful and humble child of the Catholic Church, and this without abandoning his previous position. Such a course has naturally led him into flagrant contradictions, which cannot but scandalise his students in proportion to their personal earnestness, and is calculated to make many reject his claims to secret knowledge as utterly unfounded.

We must not, however, be misled by appearances; the subtlety of the human intellect delights in the attempt to establish a harmony between things which are essentially opposite and a division between things which are similar. Moreover, the discoveries of science are unaffected by the recantations of any Galileo. I shall, therefore, begin boldly by stating the inconsistencies of Éliphas Lévi, to ascertain how far they really modify his claims; I shall next consider those claims, and afterwards briefly define the nature of his true greatness.

The *Dogme et Rituel de la Haute Magie* establishes or seeks to establish the following points with regard to religious belief:—

1. The domain of faith is the infinity of the unknown.
2. To expressly define anything which we may believe to exist in this domain is to formulate the unknown, and, of course, is absurdity.
3. The laws of human reason should control the imagination in its excursions into the domain of the unknown.
4. All our conceptions concerning this region must be characterized by a sublime vagueness.
5. God is an explanatory hypothesis of the human mind —an aggrandized conception of himself which man sets on the throne of infinity.
6. There is an underlying principle in all so-called revelations, and this principle is the doctrine of analogy—viz., that there is a correspondence between things seen and things unseen; earth is the shadow of heaven, man a reflec-

tion of divinity, a spiritual sun corresponds to the physical sun, &c.

7. The reasonable religion which results from this doctrine, and which is the only indefectible Catholic faith, is unsuited to the multitude for whom fables and nurse tales are necessary.

8. Therefore the secrets of Nature are dressed up by means of allegory in the guise of dogmas, and are presented to the multitude as innocuous substitutes for truths which are dangerous to the profane.

9. The doctrine of analogy is the basis of magic, which is the only formidable enemy of hierarchic religions, because by revealing the allegories of dogmas it makes these "*le mensonge de la vérité et la vérite du mensonge,*" and thus utterly destroys that claim of absolute truth which every religion makes in regard to its doctrines. Every religion, therefore, condemns magic.

10. The initiate knows the significance of all symbolism and all forms of worship, and he may practise or abstain from them without compromising sincerity or good faith.*

It is plain that this teaching aims a death-blow at exoteric theologies; it reduces all their dogmas, small and great, to the same level as the puppets of the Pilgrim's Progress. They are "shows that show." Now, the life of theological faith is in the assumption of the absolute, as opposed to the symbolical, truth of its dogmas. It follows also from the philosophy of the *Dogme et Rituel*:

1. That no intelligence from the unseen world has ever come down among men to make known the mysteries of the unseen world.

2. That no God has ever really become incarnate in humanity to prove God more than a reasonable hypothesis, or that man has been created after God's image and not God after the likeness of humanity.

3. That no church possesses or has ever possessed a direct mission from above to teach and define truths concerning the eternal world.

4. That it is legitimate for one who is initiated into the secret of the transfiguration of dogmas, that is, the evolution

---

* "He (the initiate) knows the reason of all symbolism and all forms of worship; he dares to practise or abstain from them without hypocrisy or impiety, and he is silent on the one dogma of supreme initiation."—*Dogma*, p. 219.

of all theologies from the one assumption of pseudo-Hermes, to revolutionise heaven and earth by the creation of a new dogmatic symbolism, provided the moment be opportune.

Now, what should be the position of such a thinker towards the hierarchic religion of his country, towards the dominant orthodoxy of the moment? In the eleventh chapter of the *Dogme de la Haute Magie* he describes himself as a "*savant pauvre et obscur*" who has recovered Archimedes' lever, and who offers it gratuitously to those who by their exalted social position will be able to use it effectually. "This knowledge has come to me too late for myself, and I have lost in its acquisition the time and resources which might have enabled me to make use of it." That is to say, Éliphas Lévi cannot himself accomplish another divine revolution in the world, he is devoid of an adequate initiative for the propaganda of a loftier symbolism, very properly, therefore, he refrains from devising small insurrections or futile departures in sectarianism. He publishes his books that he may, if possible, make new priests and new kings for the *Regnum Dei* of the age to come, but personally, and in his private character, he submits to the reigning religion, whose dogmas he, moreover, considers to be the most perfect allegorical drapery which has yet been woven round the secrets of Nature.

This is perfectly intelligible, and cannot be reasonably objected to. But though an individual does right in conforming to the constitution of his country despite its imperfections, and does not thereby compromise his sincerity, however transparent such imperfections may be to him, yet if in gratuitously undertaking to champion the cause of that constitution, he should obstinately shut his eyes to its shortcomings, and even endeavour to hide them, he would undoubtedly place himself in an equivocal position, disinterested though his motives might be. We should not, therefore, expect Éliphas Lévi, who has openly proclaimed the common disabilities of all exoteric theologies, whose books are of a most revolutionary character, who undertakes to put into the hands of his readers a key to every religious symbol, so that they can worship anywhere with equal sincerity or refrain from any form of worship without impiety, we should not expect him to come forward as the uncompromising champion of a special form of dogmatism, bent at the risk of all kinds of self-contradiction, on re-

BIOGRAPHICAL AND CRITICAL ESSAY.   xxi

establishing what he has previously demolished. This, however, is actually the case. The results of the *Dogme et Rituel* being such as I have stated, he becomes in his subsequent works the declared champion of the Roman orthodoxy, endeavouring to unsay what he has said against her, yet without confessing that he has changed his views, and without any apparent consciousness of his fundamental discrepancies, some of which I shall now lay before the reader to substantiate my statements. I am forced to select those which present a sharp contrast, but no quotations, and no contrasts of a verbal kind, can give an adequate idea of the writer's radical change of front.

THE LATIN CHURCH AND DEMONOLOGY.

"The Church, in her exorcisms, has consecrated the belief in all these things (diabolical compacts, &c.), and we may say that black magic and its prince of darkness are a true, living, terrible creation of Roman Catholicism, that they are, in fact, its special and characteristic work, for priests do not invent God. Moreover, true Catholics cling from the bottom of their hearts to the preservation and regeneration even of this *magnum opus*, which is the philosophers' stone of the official and positive cultus."—*Rituel*, p. 233.

The *Histoire de la Magie*, on the contrary, describes the Church as most reserved on the subject of Satan, and admires this reservation (p. 196). Good Christians do not even name him, and religious moralists recommend the faithful not to think about him, but to direct their minds to God. Instead of representing the Church as answerable for the creation of the mediæval Satan, he refers the importance assumed by this phantom to the *penchant* of diseased imaginations and weak heads for things monstrous and horrible (p. 290). Finally, instead of representing black magic as the creation of the Roman Church, the *Histoire* represents it as the work of sectarians and dissidents.

PAPAL INFALLIBILITY AND THE KABBALISTIC KEYS.

"The Gnostic revelations have separated the Church from the supreme truths of the Kabbalah, which contains all the secrets of transcendental theology. Thus the blind have become leaders of the blind, and great obscurities, great lapses, and deplorable scandals have resulted ; afterwards the sacred books whose keys are entirely Kabbalistic, from Genesis

"The loss of the Kabbalistic Keys could not involve that of the infallibility of the Church, ever assisted by the Holy Spirit, but it has caused great obscurities in exegesis, and has made the majestic images of Ezekiel's prophecy and St John's Apocalypse completely unintelligible."—*Histoire*, p. 222.

to the Apocalypse, have become so unintelligible to Christians that their pastors have rightly judged it needful to forbid their perusal to simple believers."—*Rituel*, p. 143.

Comment here is hardly needed. It is preposterous to accredit blind leaders with infallibility; if they be infallible, they are not blind. Notice, also, that the loss of the Kabbalistic Keys, according to the *Rituel*, not only makes Ezekiel and the Apocalypse unintelligible, but also the whole Bible.

CONNECTION OF PAGAN AND CHRISTIAN SYMBOLISM.

On p. 16 of the *Rituel* we are assured that Christian symbolism was created from the débris of all worships which had been overcome by the "queen of the world"—that is, by Rome.

In the *Histoire*, on the contrary, we are told that it is wrong to accuse Christianity with having borrowed what was most beautiful in the old worships. "Christianity — last form of universal orthodoxy—has preserved all that belonged to her, and has rejected nothing but dangerous observances and futile superstitions" (p. 159).

ST PAUL AND MAGICAL BOOKS.

"The successive phases of fanaticism have almost brought men to despair of scientific or religious rationality. St Paul burned the books of Trismegistus; Omar burned the disciples of Trismegistus and St Paul. O persecutors! O incendiaries! O scoffers! when will ye finish your work of darkness and destruction?"—*Rituel*, p. 327.

"We read in the Acts of the Apostles, that St Paul collected at Ephesus all the works which treated of 'curious arts' and burned them publicly. Doubtless the goëtic or necromantic works of the ancients are here referred to. The loss is much to be regretted, for even from the monuments of error gleams of truth and scientifically valuable information may be frequently obtained."—*Histoire* (p. 181).

What is remarkable here is the suggestive toning down; instead of the fanaticism, persecution, and incendiarism of a frantic iconoclast, who is accredited with destroying *the sublime works of Hermes*, we have a mild invitation to regret the loss of some books on *black magic*. Éliphas Lévi had not, however, made his last remarks on this subject; it seemed good to him that previous discrepancies should be further accentuated. "Was St Paul a barbarian? Did he commit outrage on science when he burned the books of the hierophants? No; he consumed the winding-sheets that death might be forgotten" (*La Clef des Grands Mystères*, p. 79). Therefore, fanaticism, persecution, and incendiarism do not constitute barbarism, and the works of the hierophants, the works of "thrice-great" Hermes, are the pestiferous cerements of the sepulchre! And this is from a writer who tells us that "the supreme and absolute science is magic"!

CHRISTIANITY AND NEOPLATONISM.

On p. 65 of the *Dogme*, the author speaks of positive Christianity at length triumphing over the sublime dreams and gigantic aspirations of the Alexandrian school, and daring publicly to fulminate its anathemas against this philosophy."

The *Histoire*, while acknowledging that the school of Plato diffused a great light in Alexandria, says that "Christianity, after three centuries of struggle, had assimilated all that was true and durable in the doctrines of antiquity" (p. 223). What is noticeable here is the complete change of attitude; instead of the audacity of fledgling faith we have the lawful appropriation of hardly-won spoils.

BIBLICAL MIRACLES.

"Let us start by declaring that we believe in all miracles, because we are convinced and certain, even by our own experience, of their complete possibility. *There are some which we do not attempt to explain, but which we consider to be none the less explicable.* From the greater to the lesser, from the lesser to the greater, the consequences are identically connected and the proportions progressively rigorous" (*Rituel*, p. 33). That the Biblical miracles are referred to in the passage I have italicised is, of course, evident, but Éliphas Lévi does subsequently explain them. "When Moses struck the rock, he did not create a source of water; he revealed it to the people, occult science having previously made

"Be far from us the notion of attributing to magic the miracles of this man (Moses), inspired by God" (*Histoire*, p. 83). Here the contradiction is complete and irretrievable; but even were there no contradiction, what are we to think of a writer who, on p. 327 of the *Rituel de la Haute Magie*, informs us that by the use of the treatise of Trithemius—*De Septem Secundeis* — one may easily surpass the prevision of Isaiah or Jeremiah, yet would see the intervention of Deity to assist in the production of parasitic insects? Little, however, is the dependence to be placed on what is said in either case, for in his very next book—*La Clef des Grands Mystères*, p. 214—we find the author attributing the same Mosaic proit known to himself by means of the divining-rod" (*Dogme*, p. 181) —that is, by an instrument of diabolical magic from the standpoint of accredited Catholic theologians. digies to science and address— by implication, it is true. He also explains why the magicians of Pharaoh cried, "Miracle!" when they were beaten, namely, that it is more soothing to the vanity of a charlatan to consider himself overcome by the intervention of supermundane power than by the superior chicanery of a *confrère*. Finally, the "*Histoire de la Magie*" declares to us that Moses and the magicians of Pharaoh both made use of one instrument in the performance of their prodigies, and that this instrument was the Great Magical Agent of the Astral Light. Therefore the miracles of Moses are to be explained by magic since they are explained by the magical hypothesis of the Astral Light. (*Histoire*, pp. 19, 20.)

The most glaring contradiction which Éliphas Lévi's new views on matters of belief have occasioned, is the last of its kind which I shall cite, though quotations might be continued much further.

IMMORTALITY.

"One of the great benefits of magnetism is that it renders evident, by incontestable facts, the spirituality, unity, and immortality of the soul. Spirituality, unity, and immortality once proved, God would be manifested to all intelligences and all hearts."—*Histoire*, p. 22.

"The immortality of the soul, being one of the most consoling dogmas of religion, must be reserved for the aspirations of faith, and will consequently never be proved by facts accessible to the criticism of science."—*Histoire*, p. 529.

Immortality is proved by incontestable facts, says the one passage; it can never be proved by facts, says the other. This is the universal science! This, too, between the pages of the same book—ludicrous instance of obstinate determination to sit at the same time on the throne of science and the footstool of childlike faith in the decisions of the dominant sacerdotal orthodoxy!

It is time, however, to ascertain what influence has been exercised by this singular change of views on Éliphas Lévi's previous estimation of the facts, theories, and possibilities of magical science, as this is the point which will more nearly concern the ordinary student of occultism. The author of the *Dogme et Rituel de la Haute Magie* comes before us as one speaking with authority on the existence of elementary spirits, fluidic phantoms, the survival of the astral body after the decease of the physical organism, and after the departure of the divine spirit; he comes before us as one who has personally practised white or permissible necromancy, as one who has evoked, seen, and touched, has beheld clearly and distinctly, an apparition in the Astral Light, and has thus proved the terrible efficacy of magical ceremonies. He comes before us as one who is in possession of "the first book of humanity," "the keystone of the whole edifice of occultism," the inspiring instrument of all revelations, and "the most perfect method of divination," one indeed which "may be employed with complete confidence." This is the marvellous Tarot. Let us briefly consider these claims in the light of his later books.

La Science des Esprits tells us that angels and demons alike are purely hypothetical or legendary beings, which must be relegated to the domain of poetry, since they can never belong to that of science (p. 6). It also tells us that satyrs and ghouls, and three-headed monsters, "and *all the rest of the darksome phantasmagoria* are nightmares of madness" (p. 314). The *Histoire* had already characterised the occult doctrine of fluidic phantoms as hypothesis (p. 114); it now appears as the hypothesis of insanity. The former distinction between white and black necromancy is entirely ignored, and the whole practice is bodily characterised as "a crime against nature."* The spiritists are told that their mediums evoke the dead, and that necromantic evocation is "the blackest of the sciences of the abyss, the most accursed of sacrilegious operations."† All that can be said is that Éliphas Lévi has himself committed this unnatural crime and frightful sacrilege, for no one can consider it permissible to perform what is detestable and accursed under the plea of scientific experiment. It is the Tarot itself, to which he was indebted for all his science, which, however, fares the worst. That "true key to the oratorical art and to the great art of Raymund Lully," that "secret of the trans-

* *La Science des Esprits*, p. 245.   † Ibid., p. 299.

mutation of darkness into light," that "first and most important of all the arcana of the *magnum opus*, is declared to be an instrument which cannot be consulted without danger and without crime.* It is a method of divination, divination is a compact with vertigo, vertigo is falsehood, evil, and hell itself.† This is the instrument to which Éliphas Lévi owes his universal science, this is "the occult and sacred alphabet" composed of ideas and numbers, and which realises the mathematics of thoughts.‡ Again, in regard to the faculty of vision in the Astral Light, the *Dogme et Rituel de la Haute Magie* is loud in the praise of the lucidity of the supreme adept, and we are told that the Kabbalists who speak of the world of spirits "have simply recounted what they have beheld in their evocations, visions, and intuitions in what they have denominated *the light of glory*." § *La Science des Esprits*, on the contrary, tells us that "the things which are beyond this life may be conjectured on in two manners, either by the calculations of analogy, or by the intuitions of extasis, in other words, by reason or madness. The sages of Judea chose reason, and have left us their magnificent hypotheses in books which are generally ignored." ‖ The falsehood, folly, and wickedness of all visionary exaltation of the imagination and mind of man is insisted on continually in the later books. And then in regard to the soul's eternal destiny the contradictions are both numerous and notable; on this point, however, the Jewish Kabbalists seem to be as little in harmony with one another as Éliphas Levi is with himself. I have referred to these contradictions in the Notes, so here I need only remark that whereas the *Dogme et Rituel* both direct us to conquer our individual immortality by achieving in the isolation of self-conquest, and by resisting and eradicating the propensities of Nature, a personal and imperishable life, the *Histoire* tells us that life is "a universal communion," and that it is in this communion that immortality is to be found. The isolation of self is death by self-condemnation, and an eternity of isolation would be eternal death.¶

It is unnecessary to continue these contrasts; the discrepancies of less importance are too numerous for tabulation, and as they arise, one and all, from the author's

---

* *Histoire de la Magie*, p. 466.   † *La Science des Esprits*, p. 298.
‡ *La Clef des Grands Mystères*, p. 3.   § *Dogme*, p. 260.
‖ *La Science des Esprits*, p. 125.   ¶ *Histoire de la Magie*, p. 40.

BIOGRAPHICAL AND CRITICAL ESSAY.   xxvii

change of front towards the Catholic religion, or else from his grotesque and sometimes comic detestation of modern spiritualism, my purpose is already served, and I shall conclude this portion of my subject by determining as far as possible the sincerity or otherwise of such a change. That it was dictated by no motive of personal gain or interest will be readily believed, but that it was sincere it is impossible to maintain, and the author himself in one of those side-lights which he is in the habit of occasionally flashing on some of his paradoxical positions,* informs us that it is "*la haute convenance*" which actuates him, and with ludicrous inconsequence he contradicts his own submission to the decisions of the hierarchy by sowing broadcast through the books which contain them the most audacious contradictions of orthodox teaching on vital and fundamental questions of current religious belief. He says, "Be it well understood that our scientific revelations pause before faith, and that, as Christian and Catholic, we submit our work entirely to the supreme judgment of the church." † Then he at once proceeds to discuss the personality of Satan. "All that has a name exists," he says; of course, he means us to add, "even if it be in name only." "The devil," he continues, "is named and personified in the Gospel, and he may, therefore, be considered as a person." This admission is due, however, to his complaisance as a Christian. "Let science speak, or reason, which is the same thing." So science speaks, and does not hesitate to inform us that if such a personification must be taken seriously, the devil would be the most absolutely dead and deceived of all beings; in other words, "the affirmation of his existence would imply an evident contradiction." The devil, however, is a blind force abused by malicious intelligence, and the Lucifer of the heterodox—read orthodox—legend is "a rash, monstrous, and impious conception." Such is the commentary of reason on the personifications of the Gospel; such is Éliphas Lévi's commentary on his own concessions to the ideal code of "*la haute convenance*."

Again, he informs us that "every definition of God which is hazarded by human intelligence is a recipe of religious

---

* For instance, the statement that "the ancient sanctuaries had their secrets which have not come down to us" is a curious commentary on some of the same writer's anterior claims.
† *Histoire*, p. 14.

empiricism, by means of which superstition will sooner or later be able to fabricate a devil." The assertion may be absolutely true in the overwhelming majority of instances, but does it not raise a smile when we consider the logical result of such a doctrine on the rage for theological definition, which is a chief characteristic of the Roman Church? The submissions of Éliphas Lévi are, in fact, thoroughly disingenuous, and how he could have imagined they would deceive any one—that is, any one worth deceiving—it is impossible to conjecture. He will never convince a reasonable man that it is necessary to believe in dogmas on the authority of Rome, when he has told us that all dogmas are the puppets of allegory, and that the key of their mystery is discoverable by any one who searches with sufficient diligence, and, of course, in the right direction. *La haute convenance* may keep us silent whenever it is expedient; it may even prompt us to perform the outward duties of "the official cultus," but it will not justify us in wilfully substituting the veil of symbolism for the truth it hides; it will not prevent us from speech in season, nor will it cause us to come forward as gratuitous champions of the evanescent orthodoxy of the moment. We are definitely assured, even in the later books, that religious dogma is merely a nurse-story, but "provided that it is ingenious and morally beneficial, it is perfectly true for the child."* Nothing, however, can be expected from grown men but a certain mild and kindly interest in the folk-tales of their childhood. They will not tell children that there are no such things as fairies, but it would be utterly preposterous to parade their absolute submission to the fables and saws of their grandmothers. It does not improve matters to tell us that orthodoxy in religion is respect for the hierarchy,† for this is a definition which the hierarchy would be certainly the first to reject. Orthodoxy in religion is absolute faith in the truth of hierarchic teaching. I have a great respect for Mr Gladstone, but I have no faith in his foreign policy. Moreover, the veneration of Kabbalistic *illuminati* and possessors of the universal science for the *haute raison* of "blind leaders," is a little paradoxical in sound, and is hardly more dignified in the one than it is complimentary to the other. If any of my readers be inclined to prefer the positivism of Latin dogma to the some-

* *Histoire*, p. 31. † *Histoire*, p. 34.

what nebulous poetics of indefinite religious aspiration, I should be the last to endeavour to dissuade them, but let them ground their judgment on the involuntary apologists of the Abbé Migne, and not on the gratuitous defences of Éliphas Lévi. He has told us to respect the Church in her old age, and this we will cheerfully, but we do not feel called on to identify ourselves with that old age. The point missed throughout all the author's arguments on the importance of the hierarchy in matters of religion is that authority may abdicate its right to rule.* On his own showing, a hierarchic cultus can become effete, and then may be rightly replaced.† If Christian dogmas are to undergo a final transfiguration, as Éliphas Lévi desires, this transfiguration must begin as a *cultus illicitus*, as Christianity itself began. It is equally erroneous to assert that articles of belief are not legitimate objects of discussion.‡ It is the duty of an intelligent Christian man, when he is requested to receive a new article of faith, to examine what is offered him, to compare it with the opinions of antiquity, with other doctrines which he already adheres to, and with his notions of God and Nature, unless from previous consideration he be absolutely convinced that the authority which propounds the novelty is wholly divine and infallible. Such a conviction is, of course, outside the pure rationalism of Éliphas Lévi's philosophy; his arguments in defence of the Church of his childhood are, therefore, bad as well as disingenuous; they originate in false notions of expediency, and in a kind of pseudo-chivalry which seems to have overtaken their author by fits and starts. § As it is difficult to believe that they could have deceived himself, we might be justified in concluding from the evidence in hand that Éliphas Lévi's description of the writings of the demonologist Bodin has a peculiar application to his own, and that, in fact, " they are profoundly Machiavelian, and strike at the root of the institutions which they appear to defend." He calls *La Clef des Grands Mystères*, which is full of these paradoxical submissions, " a

---

* See *e.g.*, *Histoire*, p. 136.   † *Ibid.*, p. 160.   ‡ *Ibid.*, p. 183.
§ " If thy mother, the Church, be sleeping with disordered garments, cover her with thy mantle, walking backwards, if necessary, to do so. To retrograde thus is to advance."—*La Clef des Grands Mystères*, p. 364. Éliphas Lévi did not practise what he preached, or he could not have written as he has written.

mystification or a monument;" it is probably a monumental mystification.

What would appear to be most genuine in the virtual retractations of Éliphas Lévi are those which concern the occult sciences, and they are merely a natural revulsion from the transcendental charlatanry and poetic exaggerations of the *Dogme et Rituel*. Those volumes, the most suggestive and beautiful in their way which have ever been contributed to the elucidation of magical mysteries, are the product of an enthusiasm which beheld all the vistas of occultism through the rose-hued medium of a light which was certainly never on the land or sea of the known actualities of mysticism; and the romantic assertions of the inspired visionary who produced them, in the evanescent ecstasy consequent on his supposed solution of all problems, scientific, philosophical, or religious, are successively though stealthily toned down as the true theosophical adept emerged into scientific realism from the wonder-world of the neophyte.

Let it be once for all plainly understood before proceeding further that I do not accuse Éliphas Lévi of wilful falsification anywhere. There is the gold of wisdom on every page of his unparalleled books, and to me they have been gain inestimable; but the natural enthusiasm consequent on his extraordinary discoveries has occasionally carried him away, and I believe myself to deserve well at the hands of all students of occultism by pointing out where facts do not warrant his assertions, and where his earlier assertions are qualified by his own later and maturer statements.

The basis of Éliphas Lévi's philosophy and of all magic is declared to be the single assumption which is contained in the great Hermetic axiom: That which is above is equivalent to that which is below, and that which is below is equivalent to that which is above. This is the introductory statement of the celebrated "Table of Emerald," which claims to be the work of Hermes Trismegistus, but which cannot be traced in history to a more considerable antiquity than the seventh century of the Christian era.[*] The ultimate basis of Éliphas Lévi's teachings is not, however, to be found in any single dogma, but in Voltairian free-thought, and he has read Voltairian principles into the

[*] Figuier, *L'Alchemie et les Alchemistes*, p. 42.

theurgic and theosophic obscurities of Kabbalistic writings. He is a pure rationalist who has adopted the hypothesis of the Kabbalah as the most trustworthy calculus of probabilities concerning an unseen world with which there is no real communication from either side in life. He considers God to be a hypothesis only, "*très probablement nécessaire*," and the question of personal immortality falls within the same category. Revelation in the true sense of the word—not in the sense of sacerdotal charlatanism—is so much out of the question that it does not strike our author as a possibility which need be seriously discussed, and the divinity which he attributes to Jesus Christ is the divinity of the natural man, who by sacrifice of self, and by passing into the region of symbolism, identifies himself, humanly speaking, with God, that is, with the human conception of Deity. It is evident that the simple naturalism of these assumptions, however much it may be supplemented by Kabbalistic reasonings whose hypothetical nature he allows, can never provide us with an absolute religious certitude, which he promised in the *Dogme et Rituel*, nor with a universal science, which he has also promised us, and so, as a fact, it proves, for the magical science of Éliphas Lévi is essentially one of power—the power of an emancipated will over wills which are not emancipated, the power of a self-controlled and self-containing man over the ill-governed passions of the multitude, the power of an intelligence which is initiated into the doctrine of the transfiguration of dogmas over the innumerable children of credulity, the power of the enlightened man over his proper self, and his unlimited power over nature. The secrets contained in his books are concerned with the development and direction of these energies for the progression of humanity at large, for the elevation of those who possess them, and for the multiplication of natural resources. The occult doctrine of revelation by analogy and correspondences in the three intelligible worlds finds in Éliphas Lévi its only lucid exponent, and yet there is little doubt that, with the characteristic ingenuity of the symbolist, he has read into "the universal dogma" a far more extensive meaning than it possessed for the author of "the admirable symbol." For the traditional Hermes it was simply an assertion which modern science is slowly and painfully working up to by the *à posteriori* method, that there is only one substance of which all material things are transitory modifications. *Quod superius sicut quod inferius*, and conversely, but for what? Not to establish a system of correspondence between the known and the unknown, but *ad perpetranda miracula rei unius*, that is, the *magnum opus* of metallic transmutation. The doctrine of universal analogy as the basis of progressive revelation is a noble and beautiful hypothesis which eminently recommends itself to reason, and once properly understood it would be an inexhaustible fountain of purest inspiration for the poetry of the age to come; it transforms the whole visible universe into one grand symbol, and the created intelligence of man becomes a microcosmic god whose faculties are in exact though infinitesimal proportion with the uncreated and eternal mind. Apart from direct revelation, it would be truly "the sole possible mediator between the seen and the unseen," establishing the grounds of faith in the rationality of a single assumption, and harmonising the positivism of physical science with the religion of legitimate aspirations towards the infinity of the unknown. But the possibility of direct communication with the invisible worlds, based on the claim of the ages, is of solemn and palmary importance, and is not to be excluded from consideration by the exigencies of any hypothesis; so when the hypothesis of universal analogy in the hands of Éliphas Levi practically rejects this possibility, it is right to point out that his doctrine of correspondences is a pure assumption, which, from his own rationalistic standpoint, is utterly unproveable, and the possible fact of communication between the seen and the unseen is a preferable object of investigation to a plausible theory. The doctrine, moreover, supposes operations which are intellectually inconceivable. "Measure a corner of creation, make a proportionally progressive multiplication, and all infinity will multiply its circles filled with universes, which will pass in proportional segments between the ideal ever-extending branches of your compass."* Mathematics and reason alike contradict this statement; the multiplication of the finite will produce only the finite. But even if the operation were possible, what would follow from this romance of arithmetic? What is meant to follow is this: *that the knowledge of a part gives the knowledge of the whole.* Not always! If the circumference of a circle be so enormous

* *Histoire de la Magie*, p. 7.

BIOGRAPHICAL AND CRITICAL ESSAY.   xxxiii

that in its visible portion we can perceive no curve, we shall never know the extent of that circle. The best argument in favour of the hypothesis, though it may seem paradoxical to say so, is that it gives full and complete expression to the inevitable anthropomorphism and materialism of the human mind, which "idealises itself to conceive God," and idealises the world around it to conceive the eternal world. The impossibility of doing otherwise is the best excuse for doing so, and we may take refuge with Leibnitz in the veracity of the *causa causarum*, which will not doom us to permanent intellectual deception. The doctrine of analogy may be taken, therefore, as a great help provided by natural necessity, but do not let us exalt it into the sole guide and mediator! Let us seek rather to establish the philosophy of the transcendental on a basis of psychic fact. Assumptions, however plausible, are no better evidence of things unseen than faith which is now considered insufficient.

Passing, at length, from the assumptions of Éliphas Levi to his matter and method, it will be seen that, in accordance with the traditions of occultism, he has surrounded his teachings with enigmas and mysteries. I have not felt justified in removing these veils, which serve a purpose, but I have endeavoured to arrange them so that the secrets which they are supposed to hide will scarcely escape the student. It will be evident to any one that the true adepts of a divine science would never really enclose dangerous or "indicible" arcana in anagrams and word-puzzles, which exert only the ingenuity of the inquirer, and give absolutely no guarantee of the moral or other qualifications of those who solve them. These ingenuities are the stock-in-trade of the thaumaturge, "*pour égarer les profanes.*" The *verbum inenarrabile* of the Neo-Platonists, the Tetragrammaton, Ararita, and Agla of the Hebrews, the "*nom occulte du grand Arcane*," are mysteries of no importance in themselves. They are signs and pantacles which of themselves have no virtue or significance. A universal science may be resumed in a single figure, but the figure of itself will never give the universal science to an uninitiated student; the volumes devoted to the philosophy of the Magi by Eliphas Lévi reveal the secrets of magic to the careful inquirer without the false lights of double meanings and the delusive elucidations of cryptograms. When we are told that the revelation of the Great Arcanum would revolutionise earth and heaven, it is the heaven of human conceptions which is referred to, the *Quod Superius* of the Hermetic formula, according to the interpretation of Éliphas Lévi. The *bouleversement* in question is the application of the secret doctrine to the creation of a new sequence of theological ideas, and Éliphas Lévi is the illuminated pioneer who has opened up the way for such a change.

An excessively scarce pantacle of Trithemius, described in the *Histoire de la Magie*,* is declared by Éliphas Lévi to contain the final secret and indicible formula of the Great Arcanum. " This pantacle is composed of two triangles—one white and one black—which are joined at the base. Beneath the inverted apex of the black triangle there is a fool crouching, painfully twisting his head, and looking with a grimace of terror at his own image reflected in the obscurity of the black triangle, while a man in knightly garments, in the vigour of maturity, with a steady glance and a strong yet pacific attitude of command, is balanced on the apex of the white triangle, within which are the letters of the divine tetragram."

Éliphas Lévi provides the exoteric explanation as follows:—" The wise man depends on the fear of the true God, while the fool is crushed by his terror of the false god made in his own image." Its esoteric significance is as follows:—Uninitiated humanity creates God by a blackened, magnified, and distorted resemblance of itself which it reflects on the illimitable background of stupidity and ignorance, then it crouches and shivers in the presence of the monstrous phantom. The adept also creates God, not however, by reflecting his likeness on infinity, but the conception of his power and knowledge, figured by a symbol. This conception is reflected on the white triangle, that is, on the unknown world enlightened by the analogies of science. The initiate is represented as poised above this triangle, not only because the hypothesis which he has formed becomes the source of his intellectual and moral stability, but because the creation of this hypothesis is a theurgic act, and the intellect is above that which it creates. The initiate is, therefore, God for the profane, he is the actual finite deity who stands on earth for the hypothe-

* Pp. 345, 346.

tical, infinite God, and he has the right of life and death over any particular conception of divinity which may at any time dominate the crowd of men. The end of magic is thus the *creation of the gods* and the evolution of the Deific conception in the *élite* of humanity. From the Christian standpoint all this is outrageous blasphemy, but it is the outcome of Éliphas Lévi's philosophy. If any proof were wanting it would be supplied by the following passage :—" Jehovah is he who overcomes nature (understand human nature to be included) as we tame a rebellious horse and makes it proceed where we will." * This is the absolute, indicible,† theurgic secret. Here Jehovah cannot mean the all-creating God, to whom everything that exists must be necessarily in complete subjection, and who cannot be described as overcoming by force what lies in the hollow of his hand. Jehovah here is the God-creating man, the self-conqueror, who by the *création de soi-même* has power over the chaos of human passion and over the blind forces of nature. The Great Magic Arcanum is thus in its primary phase the secret of the power of a completely emancipated mind over the slaves of superstition and ignorance. The unique Athanor, the philosophic and moral alchemy, is the transmutation of darkness into light, in the intellectual order, of gross matter into gold refined, of ignorance into knowledge, of dead substances into substances quickened by the energies of veritable life, of the mere animal into the conscious man, and of man into God. " The stone becomes a plant, the plant an animal, the animal a man, and man greatens into Deity." " *Quand l'homme grandit Dieu s' éleve.*"

The Great Magic Agent is a good working hypothesis to conciliate science and religion by a natural explanation of all prodigies, and to direct qualified investigators to the discovery of a universal force. But we must bear in mind that although the exuberant dogmatism of the *Dogme et Rituel de la Haute Magie* couches all statements concerning it in extremely authoritative language, it is a hypothesis and a hypothesis only, as the author himself admits at a

---

* *La Clef des Grands Mystères,* p. 219.
† It is of course an absurdity to speak of any secret as really indicible. According to the *Dogme de la Haute Magie,* every idea has its form, that is, its expression, and no idea is conceivable without its corresponding expression in speech. It may be imprudent, difficult, or wicked to proclaim it publicly, but there are no inexpressible ideas.

later stage of his revelations. "The secret agent of the *magnum opus* ... is Magnetised Electricity. The union of these two words does not reveal us much, nevertheless they *perhaps* enclose a force which can revolutionise the world. We say *perhaps* out of *philosophic benevolence*, for on our part, *we do not doubt* the high importance of this great Hermetic Arcanum."* The parts which I have italicised, are conclusive, as regards the hypothetical nature of the force which Éliphas Lévi believed himself to have discovered in the alchemical allegories, and the most he can assert concerning it is a supreme personal conviction. This force he usually terms the Astral Light, a name which is borrowed from Saint-Martin and the French mystics of the eighteenth century. It is an unfortunate one, because, in the first place, he does not pretend to determine the real nature of the agent he denominates, and, in the second place, because it is eminently liable to multiply false analogies. The metaphorical use of the word "light" in philosophy has been a source of very serious misconceptions precisely on this score.† The preservation of the images of all forms in the universal agent, which is the mirror of visions, supplies the author with his natural explanation of all kinds of apparitions, including those which are seen in necromantic evocations. It is invented to conciliate the reality of such visions with the futility of their general results, "for the supposed spirits reveal nothing of the life beyond." Modern Spiritualism has amply supplied this deficiency, though its mediums seem eminently liable to the control of Ananias. With regard to the magical experiences of Éliphas Lévi, we shall do well to remember that the conservation of the images of objects in the Astral Light is a hypothesis, but the evocation of Apollonius is a fact, and though the sceptical philosophy of the Magus degraded his own prodigy, the serious student will perhaps find therein something more than a mere "pathological fact," or the "*rêve d'un homme éveillé.*"‡ ... The Great Magic Agent, like the Arcanum by means of which it is directed, is, at least in one of its phases, a moral force. The power which is promised to the emancipated and enlightened mind is dominion over

---

* *La Clef des Grands Mystères*, p. 207.
† Balmes' *Fundamental Philosophy*, vol. i.
‡ *Dogme*, p. 273.

Azoth, the domain of Magnesia, and the secret of quickening the dead substances of the alchemical symbolists. But, unlike electricity, steam, &c., this mysterious Azoth cannot be directed by a man of science working in secret and possessing only his knowledge and his instruments. He must form the magic chain; he must be able to set in motion and direct a current of enthusiasm in unenlightened humanity. It is not, therefore, primarily a physical force. The hopes, the fears, the caprices, the weaknesses, the imaginations of the crowd, in a word, its FREEWILL, these are the monster to be conquered, these are the blind force which equally lends itself to good or evil. The ill-directed force of will, the undirected strength of passion, the blind and mad enthusiasm and the savage excesses of fury, the natural sense and instincts, the crude reasoning powers, and the plastic conscience of humanity, these are Azoth, these are the *matière première* of the *magnum opus* of universal reconstruction; these are the mysterious force whose equilibrium is social life, progress, civilisation, and whose disturbance is anarchy, revolution, barbarism, from whose chaos a new equilibrium at length evolves, the cosmos of a new order, when another dove has brooded over the blackened and disturbed waters. This is the force by which the world is upset, the seasons are changed, by which the night of misery and misrule may be transfigured into the day of Christ —

"*Dies venit, dies tua,
In qua reflorent omnia*"—

into the era of a new civilisation, when the morning stars sing together, and all the sons of God utter a joyful shout.

With regard to the Tarot, we may at once set aside its subsequent condemnation by Éliphas Lévi as utterly unserious, but as magic art depends on no special form of divination and on no single assumption, but on the experimental methods of science, we need not fear to moderate, if necessary, the importance he originally attributed to it. When hypothesis, which is necessarily tentative, arrays itself in dogmatism, and assumes the terminology of history, and when history supplies the lacunæ in its materials from the imaginative realms of hypothesis, neither brilliant talent, nor even some inherent probability, can make the result worthy of serious consideration. This, however, is Éliphas Lévi's method of proving the immense antiquity of the Tarot. He begins by stating that it is perhaps more ancient than the book of Henoch.* Outside the erudition of Dr Kenealy, no modern scholarship attributes any more remote antiquity to the latter work than the fourth century B.C. But Éliphas Lévi believes the Tarot to be the work of Hermes Trismegistus,†

> "Who uttered his oracles sublime,
> Before the Olympiads in the dew
> Of the early dawn and dusk of time."

And the book of Henoch is by implication of the same primeval epoch. Afterwards he speaks of the Tarot variously as the hieroglyphic work of Hermes, the Claviculæ of Solomon, &c.; it is declared to have existed certainly before Moses and the prophets, and throughout the whole *Dogme et Rituel* this assumption is continued, its justification being reserved till the final chapter, when he promises to demonstrate that it is "the primitive book." ‡ This demonstration is simply a series of ingenious suppositions which beg successively every important question. Thus he assumes that it was reserved only for the high priests, that it was identical with the divinatory instrument invented by Michas, and described in Philo, that after the destruction of Jerusalem its figures were drawn on ivory, parchment, copper, and finally on cards, and thus has the Tarot come down to us. All this, of course, is romancing. Court de Gebelin in his *Monde Primitif*, vol. viii., is content with the attempt to establish its Egyptian origin and divinatory utility. Modern Egyptology has not corroborated his opinions on the former point, and the Egyptians do not seem to have been a card-playing nation. The facts, therefore, as opposed to the hypothesis are these—that a hieroglyphic game and instrument of divination, having some quasi-Egyptian figures, but of unknown origin, was discovered by a French antiquary at the close of the last century. Its name Tarot suggests a connection with Tora, "the sacramental name which the Jews give to their inspired book."§ Its twenty-two trump cards recall the twenty-two letters of the Hebrew Alphabet, the twenty-two

---

* *Dogme*, p. 68. † *Ibid.*, p. 84. ‡ *Ibid.*, p. 234.
§ *La Clef des Grands Mystères*, p. 321.

chapters of the mystical book of the Apocalypse, &c. In the sixteenth century William Postel, the Kabbalist, in his *Clavis Absconditorum à Constitutione Mundi*, inscribes on the circlet of his symbolic key the four letters T A R O, but arranged in such a manner that it is uncertain how they should be read, and he writes of a hieroglyphic book which he calls the Genesis of Henoch. Finally, Éliphas Lévi solemnly testifies—1. That without the Tarot the magic of the ancients is a sealed book. 2. That it alone gives the true interpretation of the magic squares of the planetary genii as they are represented by Paracelsus. 3. That the rabbinical notary art is at bottom nothing else but the science of the Tarot signs, and their complex and various application to the divination of all secrets. 4. That he himself has opened all the doors of the ancient sanctuaries and ascertained the significance of all symbols by the means of this instrument. All this deserves our most serious attention, and the publication of a Tarot which shall be accurate in all its figures is much to be desired. If there be any key existing to the symbolism of the ages, besides that which is provided by internal evidence and analogy, the Tarot may be that key, but take notice, that according to the same author, " Magnetic intuitions alone give force and reality to all Kabbalistic and astrological calculations, puerile perhaps and completely arbitrary if they are made without inspiration, by frigid curiosity, or in the absence of a determining force of will."* This is the conclusion of a chapter which treats of the Tarot and of magical astrology. The Tarot is, therefore, like all instruments of divination, "a pretext for self-magnetisation." Elsewhere he declares it to require "the assistance of a good medium."* What has unlocked the secrets of universal symbolism to Éliphas Lévi is not the bald symbolism of the Tarot, but the intuitions of his own gifted mind and his power of discerning analogies. In the creation of allegorical hieroglyphs there is in them so much meaning as the intelligence of their contriver can infuse, but in their interpretation there is so much meaning as the inspiration of the student can extract. The significance of symbols, therefore, varies in essence and extent with each individual, and their absolutely correct interpretation is eminently difficult to arrive at in a labyrinth of plausible

* *Histoire*, p. 156.

possibilities. While, therefore, acknowledging to its full extent the extreme interest attaching to the Tarot, it will be well to suspend our judgment with regard to its history, and to attribute the prodigies it works in the main to the clairvoyance of its consulters.

The practical magic of Eliphas Lévi traces thaumaturgic art to its purely natural genesis. His universal medicine is a moral specific based on the philosophy of the interaction of mind and body, with special reference to the science of prestige in its application to curative purposes. The *magnum opus* of so-called metallic transmutation is the application of will-power to the modification of those natural substances which are the *matières mortes* of the philosophers. The condemnation of much that is included in the scope of magical practices is a solemn warning to psychic investigators. Éliphas Lévi doubtless lived to find, as did Cornelius Agrippa before him and as others will probably after, that there is much which is vain and futile in the pursuits of occult science, that evocation in the universal glass of visions is fatiguing in practice, and after the first few times generally barren in result, that the mysteries of the life beyond are seldom if ever revealed to the lucidity of clairvoyants, that the magical creation of gold is a conquest wrung from nature by the heart's blood of the alchemist as hardly as it is commercially manufactured in the grinding mills of the competition of social life. The indiscriminate condemnation of spiritualism has a side of truth, but it originates in the exclusiveness of the adept. Just as the great Roman orthodoxy looks with suspicion and distrust on all independent religious speculation, on all "lay theology," just as she denounces most miraculous phenomena occurring outside her own spiritual jurisdiction, so does Éliphas Lévi regard with contempt and dislike all magical wonders produced outside the *sanctum regnum* of initiation. He is right in so far as initiation provides precautions against the dangers of psychical research. But whatever may be thought of modern spiritualism in its intellectual and moral aspects, it has proved the existence of spiritual natures within and without us, so that it is not in hypothesis but in fact that our conviction may be grounded.

I have reached the extreme limits of this criticism and must briefly sum up. The Great Arcanum is the secret of will-ability. It is the secret of the subjection of the sphinx of human liberty, the serpent of passionate desire, the Baphomet of superstitions, not by their destruction but by making all and each perform unconsciously the will of the adept. The science of Éliphas Lévi is the science of power and prestige. But the great secret is the will and the great agent is enthusiasm with its ten thousand illusions, by which cataclysms are caused and by which the world is renewed. That this science should be occult is comprehensible, for to reveal the arcana of leadership to those who are led is to take the reins out of the hands of the charioteers and cast them to the winds. Those who are seeking an absolute religious certitude will not get the help they may have expected from Éliphas Lévi as a possessor of "the universal science." His system reduces God to a sensible and rational hypothesis, and it gives no proof of the soul's immortality. It does not direct us to the eternal truth, but it tells us how we may reign over superstition and by superstition.* Some of us, however, are seeking God and the soul ; we have no wish to pose as deities in the presence of our benighted fellow-creatures, we have no ambition to be adored as gods. Doubtless, we could present to may sections of humanity a nobler notion of Deity, but it would be of our own conceiving, and conscience forbids us to impose on others an idea which has been developed within us as an eternal truth with us; we cannot undertake to lead humanity until we have established a certainty for ourselves, and the Hermetic doctrine of correspondences is not a certainty—it is a dogma.

Still less have we any desire to reign over superstition or by superstition, which we detest with our whole hearts, and with which we will have no connection either as masters or servants. But a debt of indefinite magnitude we still owe to the writings of Éliphas Lévi, whose true greatness is first and foremost in the supreme elevation of his beautiful moral philosophy. He has taught us to conciliate those opposing forces, physical and spiritual, whose equilibrium is life and immortality; to harmonise the "liberty of individuals with the necessity of things," and the divine privileges of self-devotion. In the second place, the true greatness of Éliphas Lévi is in his bold attempt to establish a harmony between religion and science by revealing to reason the logical necessity of faith, by proclaiming to faith the sanctity of natural reason, and by a rational

* *Dogme*, p. 217.

explanation of all prodigies. He has taught us to venerate religion, but also to make way for science, and in a century of doubt and disillusion he has endeavoured to create, without the help of miracle or revelation, a reasonable hope for man in an unseen world and an eternal future.

In the third place, the true greatness of Éliphas Lévi consists in his revelation for the first time to the modern world of the great Arcanum of will-power, which comprises in one word the whole history and mystery of magical art. Doctrine and theory are nothing—all magic is in the will, that secret of universal power in heaven and on earth. "God is but a great will pervading all things by reason of its intentness," says Glanvil, and man by the same faculty can raise himself from the circle of necessity into the circle of creative providence; as a part of the Grand Totality, which is the super-personal God, he can create and adapt in his turn. The transmutation of the philosophical metals is not a chemical process, or, rather, it is a process of transcendental and mystical chemistry by the application of the purified and emancipated will to the psycho-chemical instrument of a diaphanous imagination. Any neophyte who expends more than the thirty thalers of Khunrath the Teutonic adept over the accomplishment of the *magnum opus*, deserves no part in the *Regnum Dei* of the life to come, for he misunderstands the first principles of the Hermetic philosophy.

The question of will-power is closely connected with the greatest danger of modern Spiritualism. The medium submits himself to the will of an unseen individuality with no guarantee about the consequences. The adept in will-ability seeks, on the contrary, to establish his intellectual dominion over all the powers of the air by the force of invincible determination, and to attract by the sympathy of kindred inspiration, kindred faith, kindred greatness, kindred moral elevation, the intelligences of a higher order whom he cannot indeed command, but whom he may draw towards him.

When, in addition to what I have enumerated, we remember that Éliphas Lévi has originated a new departure in Kabbalistic exegesis, that his interpretations have infused new life into old symbolism, and that his doctrine of the transfiguration of dogmas — whatever may be its ultimate value—casts much light on comparative theology, it is sufficient for one incarnation, and with a certain modification of meaning we need have no hesitation in proclaiming him an initiate of the first order and the prince of the French adepts.

A word must be added on the method of this translation. I have not confined myself within the barren limits of a slavish literalism, because the references in the original to the various subjects treated of are scattered over the pages of six large volumes, and their collation and arrangement, which I have taken great pains to accomplish as harmoniously as possible, in the present digest have necessitated adaptation and èlimination. Moreover, in spite of innumerable beauties of thought, in spite of a fresh, animated, and unconventional style, with occasional passages of really splendid eloquence, the originals as a whole are diffusive and tautological. Large portions of Éliphas Levi's works are no more connected with magic, as ordinarily understood, than the theosophical speculations and fire-philosophy of Berkeley's Siris are connected with the virtues of tar-water. The substance of these portions will be found under the title of Religious and Philosophical Problems, at the beginning of this book. I have struggled to eliminate discrepancies from this digest, but some of necessity remain which I trust the discernment of my readers will attribute to their true cause. A certain faculty of interpretation should also be brought to bear upon several extreme statements. I have undertaken this criticism in the interest of no system, but in the cause of truth, and I now recommend what follows to earnest and determined seekers for the supernatural as a light to guide them amidst the aberrations of mysticism and the dangers of magical practices. The noble and generous spirit of Éliphas Levi has passed behind the veil, and has doubtless achieved the immortality he aspired to, and the Absolute which he sought in life. May the Benediction of AGOTH be upon him, and the Crown of Life reward him, and from his throne

"Built beyond mortal thought
Far in the Unapparent,"

may his approval follow this translation, which I have undertaken in the cause of that Synthesis of Religious Belief of which he was the pioneer and the prophet!

INTRODUCTION.

BEHIND the veil of all the hieratic and mystical allegories of ancient dogmas, behind the shadows and fantastic ordeals of all initiations, beneath the seal of all sacred writings, amidst the ruins of Nineveh or of Thebes, on the crumbling stones of ancient temples, and on the scorched visage of the Sphinx of Assyria or Egypt, in the monstrous or marvellous paintings which translate for the faithful of India the sacred pages of the Vedas, in the strange emblems of our old alchemical works, in the initiatory ceremonies adopted by all secret societies, we find the traces of a doctrine which is everywhere the same and everywhere carefully concealed. Occult philosophy seems to have been the nurse and godmother of all intellectual forces, the key of all divine obscurities, and the absolute mistress of society, in those ages when it was exclusively reserved for the education of priests and of kings.

It reigned in Persia with the Magi, who one day perished, as the masters of the world do perish, because they abused their power; it endowed India with the most wonderful traditions, and with an incredible wealth of poetry, of grace, and of terror in its emblems; it civilised Greece to the sounds of the lyre of Orpheus; it concealed the first principles of every science and of all intellectual progress in the daring calculations of Pythagoras; fable was replete with its marvels, and history, when it undertook to estimate this unknown power, confused itself with fable. It shook or established empires by its oracles, made tyrants grow pale on their thrones, and governed all minds by curiosity or fear. For this science, saith the crowd, there is nothing impossible: it commands the elements, knows the language of the stars, and directs the course of the planets; the moon at its voice falls blood-red from the sky; the dead rise up and articulate into ominous words the night-wind which sighs through their skulls. Mistress of love or of hate, this science can bestow at will on human hearts either paradise or hell   It disposes at pleasure of all forms, and with ease distributes either beauty or ugliness. By turns it changes, with the wand of Circe, men into animals and animals into men ; it even dispenses life or death, and can confer wealth on its adepts by the transmutation of metals, and immortality by its quintessence and elixir compounded of gold and light. Such was magic from Zoroaster to Manes, from Orpheus to Apollonius of Tyana, when dogmatic Christianity, at length victorious over the sublime dreams and gigantic aspirations of the Alexandrian school, dared to fulminate publicly its anathemas against this philosophy, and thus compelled it to become more secret and mysterious than ever.

Subsequently, strange and alarming reports began to circulate in respect of the initiates or adepts; these men were everywhere surrounded with a baleful influence. They slew or sent mad those who permitted themselves to be carried away by their persuasive eloquence, or by the prestige of their knowledge. The women whom they loved became vampires, their children disappeared at their nocturnal gatherings, and folks spoke shudderingly and in whispers of their sanguinary orgies and abominable banquets. Bones had been discovered in the vaults of ancient temples, shrieks had been heard in the night ; the harvests withered and flocks languished when the magician went by. Diseases which defied medical skill made occasionally their appearance in the world, and always, it was said, beneath the venomous glance of the adepts. Finally, a universal shout of reprobation rose up against magic, whose very name became a crime, and the hatred of the rabble was expressed in this outcry—" To the flames with the sorcerers ! " as some centuries earlier it had been vociferated—" To the lions with the Christians ! "

Now, the multitude conspires only against veritable powers ; it has not the knowledge of what is true, but by instinct it knows what is strong. It was reserved for the eighteenth century to deride alike Christianity and magic, even while infatuated with the homilies of Rousseau and the fascinations of Cagliostro. Notwithstanding, the basis of magic is science, as the foundation of Christianity is love, and in the gospel symbolism we find the incarnate Logos adored in his childhood by three Magi, who are

INTRODUCTION. 3

conducted by a star—the triad and the sign of the microcosmos—and receiving from them gold, frankincense, and myrrh—a second mysterious triplicity, beneath whose emblem the highest kabbalistic secrets are allegorically contained. Tradition further applies to these Magi the title of kings, because initiation into magic constitutes a true kingdom, and because the grand Art of the Magi is called by all adepts the *royal art*, or holy kingdom, *sanctum regnum*. The star which led them is that Blazing Star whose symbol is to be met with in all initiations. For the alchemists, it is the sign of the quintessence; for the magicians, the great Arcanum; for the Kabbalists, the sacred and mysterious Pentagram.

Christianity, therefore, owes no hatred to magic, but human ignorance has ever stood in awe of the unknown. The science was forced to hide itself to avoid the zealous assaults of a blind love; it clothed itself in new hieroglyphics, dissimulated its aims, disguised its hopes. Thus was the jargon of the alchemists created, that continual deception for the uninitiated who are covetous of gold, and a living language only for the true followers of Hermes.

Singular fact! In the sacred books of the Christians are included two works which the infallible Church does not pretend to understand, and never ventures to explain —the prophecy of Ezekiel and the Apocalypse—two kabbalistic claviculæ, doubtless reserved by heaven for the commentaries of magian kings, books which for faithful believers are sealed with seven seals, yet are perfectly clear to the infidel who is an initiate of the occult sciences.

There exists also another book, but this, though in a certain sense it is popular and circulates everywhere, is of all the most hidden and unknown, because it is the key of all the rest; it is in circulation without being known by the public; where it is, no one expects to discover it, and should anyone suspect its existence, he would a thousand times over vainly waste his time if he sought it under any but one form. This book, more ancient perhaps than that of Enoch, has never been translated, and it exists only in primitive characters, on single leaves, like the tablets of antiquity. A distinguished scholar has revealed, though no one appears to have noticed it, not exactly its secret but its antiquity and extraordinary preservation; another scholar, though of a genius more fantastic than judicious, passed thirty years in the study of this book, and has barely divined its importance. It is, in truth, a monumental and phenomenal work, strong and simple as the architecture of the Pyramids, durable, therefore, as are those; a book which epitomises all sciences, and whose infinite combinations can solve all problems; a book which speaks by evoking thought, the inspirer and controller of all possible conceptions, the masterpiece perhaps of the human mind, and undoubtedly one of the finest things which antiquity has bequeathed to us, a universal *clavicula*, whose name was understood and explained by the learned *illuminé*, William Postel; a unique text, whose first characters alone ravished into ecstasy the devotional spirit of St Martin, and might have restored reason to the sublime and unfortunate Swedenborg. We shall treat of this work later on, and its mathematical and exact explanation will be the completion and crown of our conscientious undertaking.

The original alliance between Christianity and the science of the Magi, once satisfactorily proved, will be a discovery of no small importance, and we do not doubt that the result of a serious study of magic and the Kabbalah will lead earnest minds to the reconciliation, till now regarded as impossible, of science and dogma, of reason and faith.

Before proceeding further, let us precisely define magic. Magic is the traditional science of the secrets of Nature which comes to us from the Magi. It unites in a single science all that is most certain in philosophy and most infallible and eternal in religion. It provides the human mind with an instrument of philosophical and religious certitude as exact as mathematics, and accounting for the exactitude of mathematics themselves. Consequently, the Absolute does exist in the order of intelligence and of faith. The Supreme Reason has not left human understanding to vacillate at hazard. There is an incontestable truth; there is an infallible method of knowing that truth, and, by its knowledge, those who adopt it as the rule of their conduct can endow their will with a sovereign power, which will make them masters of inferior things and of all wandering spirits, that is, arbiters and monarchs of the world.

If this be the case, why is this supreme science still unknown? How are we to assume in a dark and clouded sky the existence of so brilliant a sun ? . . . The supreme science has been always known, but only by the flower of intelligences, who have understood the necessity of being silent, and biding their time. If a skilful surgeon succeeded, in the middle of the night, in opening the eyes of a man born blind, how would he make him understand before morning the existence and nature of the sun ? Science has its nights and mornings, because it endows the intellectual world with a life which has its regulated movements and progressive phases. Yes, the supreme and absolute science is magic, the science of Abraham and Orpheus, of Confucius and Zoroaster. Its doctrines were engraved on stone tables by Enoch and Trismegistus. Moses purified and *reveiled* them —this is the sense of the word *reveal*—when he made the holy Kabbalah the exclusive heritage of the people of Israel and the inviolable secret of its priests. The mysteries of Eleusis and of Thebes preserved among the nations some symbols already mutilated, and whose mysterious key was lost among the instruments of an ever increasing superstition. Jerusalem, the destroyer of her prophets, and so often prostituted to the false gods of the Assyrians and Babylonians, had at length, in her turn, lost the sacred word, when a Saviour announced to the Magi by the holy star of initiation appeared to rend the threadbare veil of the old temple, and to endow the church with a new tissue of legends and symbols which always conceal from the profane, and always preserve for the elect, the same eternal truth.

We have said that the Church, whose special attribute is the custody of the keys, does not claim to have those of the Apocalypse, or of Ezekiel's visions. For Christians, and in their opinion, the scientific and magical keys of Solomon are lost. It is, nevertheless, certain that, in the sphere of intelligence, governed by the LOGOS, nothing which is written perishes. What men cease to understand simply ceases to exist for them, at least as a Logos ; it then enters the domain of enigma and mystery.

Moreover, the antipathy, and even open hostility, of the official Church against everything which is included within the scope of magic, is connected with causes which are necessary and even inherent in the hierarchic and political constitution of Christian sacerdotalism. The Church ignores magic, because ignore it she must or perish ; she none the less recognises that her mysterious founder was saluted in his cradle by three Magi, that is, by hieratic ambassadors from the three divisions of the known world, and the three analogical worlds of occult philosophy.

In the Alexandrian School, magic and Christianity nearly join hands under the auspices of Ammonius, Saccus, and Plato. The doctrine of Hermes is found almost in its entirety in the writings attributed to Dionysius the Areopagite, which are valuable for science, as they consecrate the union of the initiations of the old world with the Christian revelation, by joining a perfect comprehension of transcendental philosophy with the most complete and irreproachable orthodoxy. Synesius, one of the greatest philosophers, and the greatest poet, of the first Christian centuries, sketches the plan of a treatise on dreams which deserved later on to be annotated by Cardan, and composes hymns which might do duty as the liturgy of the Swedenborgian Church, could a church of the illuminated possess a liturgy. With this period of fervent abstractions and impassioned logomachy must also be connected the philosophical reign of Julian, called the Apostate, because in his youth he made an unwilling profession of Christianity. Everyone knows that Julian was guilty of being an unseasonable hero of Plutarch, and was, so to speak, the Don Quixote of Roman chivalry, but what everyone does not know is this, that Julian was an *illuminé* and initiate of the highest order, that he believed in the unity of God, and in the universal doctrine of the Trinity, that, in a word, he regretted nothing in the ancient world but its magnificent symbols and its too alluring images. Julian was no pagan, he was a gnostic seduced by the allegories of polytheism, and who had the misfortune to find the name of Jesus Christ less sonorous than that of Orpheus. The Emperor paid in his own person for his tastes as an academician, philosopher, and rhetorician, and having afforded himself the gratification and the spectacle of expiring like Epaminondas with the sentiments of Cato, he had, in public opinion, which already was wholly Christian, anathemas for his funeral oration, and a disgraceful epithet for his subsequent celebrity.

Let us skip the small things and small personages of the Bas-Empire, and pass on to the Middle Ages. . . . Stay, take this book and read the seventh page, then be seated on this mantle I have spread, and with the corner of which we will cover our eyes. . . . Your head whirls, does

INTRODUCTION.

it not? and the earth seems to spin beneath your feet? Hold tightly, and do not look round. . . . The vertigo ceases, we have reached our journey's end. Stand up and open your eyes, but be careful to make no sign and to pronounce no Christian word. We are in a landscape of Salvator Rosa. It is a troubled waste, reposing after a tempest. The moon shines no longer in the sky, but can you not discern small stars dancing in the heather? Do you not hear about you the flight of monstrous birds, who seem whispering strange words in their passage? Approach stealthily this cross-road among the rocks! A hoarse and funereal trumpet is heard; lurid torches burn on every side; a disorderly assembly surges round an empty seat; all look round them in expectation, then suddenly fall prostrate and mutter—"He is here! He is here! 'Tis himself!" A goat-headed prince comes forward with bounds; he ascends the throne, turns round, and, stooping, presents to the assembly a human posterior, which everyone approaches, black taper in hand, to salute and to kiss; then he stands up with a discordant laugh, and distributes to his favourites gold, secret instructions, occult medicines, and poisons, Meanwhile, fires are lighted, in which fern and aloe-wood are burning pell-mell with human bones and the fat of executed criminals. Druidic priestesses, crowned with vervain and wild parsley, immolate unbaptized children with golden knives, and prepare revolting love-feasts. Tables are garnished, masked men seat themselves beside half-naked females, and a bacchanalian banquet begins; nothing but salt is wanting, which is the symbol of wisdom and immortality. Wine flows in streams, leaving stains like those of blood; obscene proposals and extravagant caresses begin, and behold the whole assembly is intoxicated with wine, wickedness, indulgence, and singing! They rise in confusion, and hasten to form infernal rings. . . . Then come all legendary monsters, all phantoms of nightmare. Enormous toads blow the flute backwards and whistle, with paws pressing their flanks; limping scarabs mingle in the dance, crabs play the castanets, crocodiles make Jew's harps of their scales, elephants and mammoths come in the guise of Cupids, and foot it in the dance; then the distracted circles break and disperse; each merrymaker draws shrieking after him a dishevelled female. The lamps and candles formed of human fat go out smoking in the gloom. . . . Cries are heard here and there, peals of laughter, blasphemies, and rattlings in the throat. . . . Let us be gone, rouse up, do not cross yourself! See, I have brought you safely home, and now you are at rest in your bed! You are a little fatigued, perhaps even a little shattered, by your journey and your night; but you have beheld something which most people speak of without knowledge; you are initiated into secrets as terrible as that of Triphonius—you have been present at the Sabbath! It remains for you now to preserve your reason, to keep yourself in wholesome fear of the law, and at a respectful distance from the Church and her stakes.

Would you behold something less fantastic and of greater reality? You shall assist at the punishment of Jacques de Molay and his accomplices or brothers in martyrdom. . . . Do not err, however; confound not the guilty and the innocent! Did the Templars in reality worship Baphomet? Did they offer a humiliating salutation to the buttocks of the goat of Mendes? What was that secret and mighty association which imperilled both Church and State, and which thus was destroyed without a hearing? Judge nothing hastily! They are guilty of a great crime; they have permitted the sanctuary of antique initiation to be seen by the profane; they have once more gathered and shared the fruits of the knowledge of good and evil. The sentence which condemns them comes from a higher source than the Pope or King Philippe le Bel. " In what day soever thou shalt eat of this fruit thou shalt die the death," said God Himself, as we read in the Book of Genesis.

What then is taking place in the world, and why do priests and kings tremble? What secret power threatens both tiaras and crowns? You perceive certain madmen who are reported to be concealing the stone of the philosophers beneath the rags of their wretchedness. They can change earth into gold, and they are destitute of food or habitation. Their brows are circled by a nimbus of glory and a shadow of disgrace. One has discovered the universal science and seeks death vainly as a refuge from the agonies of his triumph—it is the Majorcan Raymond Lully. Another cures imaginary diseases by fantastic remedies, and gives a formal denial beforehand to the proverb which asserts the uselessness of a cautery on a wooden leg—it is the marvellous Paracelsus, always drunk and always lucid, like the heroes of Rabelais. Here is William Postel writing naïvely to the fathers of the Council of Trent, because he has discovered the absolute doctrine concealed from the foundation of the world, and is burning to share it with them. The council does not even do so much as disturb itself on the maniac's account, does not deign to condemn him, and proceeds to the examination of the grave questions of efficacious grace and sufficing grace. He whom we see perishing poor and abandoned is Cornelius Agrippa, the least magician of all, but one whom the uninitiated persist in mistaking for the greatest sorcerer, because he was sometimes a satirist and mystifier. What secret do these men bear with them into their tombs? Why are they admired without being understood? Why are they condemned without being heard? Why are they initiated into those terrific secret sciences which the Church and society are afraid of? Why are they proficient in what others know nothing of? Why do they disguise what every one longs to learn? Why are they invested with a terrible and unknown power? The occult sciences! Magic! These are the words which will reveal all, and give food for further thought! *De omni re scibili et quibusdam aliis.*

And what then was magic? What then was the power of these men so proscribed and so spirited? If thus strong, why did they not vanquish their enemies? If they were weak and beside themselves, why did people do them the honour of being afraid of them? Is there a magic, is there a secret science, which is truly a power, as we have declared, and which performs prodigies fit to be compared with the miracles of authorized religions. To these two palmary questions we reply by a sentence and by a book. The book shall justify the sentence, which is this—Yes, there has existed, and there still is, a potent and true magic; all that legends have related of it was fact, but, in this instance, and contrary to what commonly happens, the popular exaggerations have been not only beside but below the truth. Yes, there is a formidable secret whose revelation has once already revolutionized the world, as the religious traditions of Egypt, epitomized symbolically by Moses at the beginning of Genesis, attest. This secret constitutes the fatal knowledge of good and evil, and its result, when divulged, is death. Moses represents it under the emblem of a tree which is in *the centre* of the terrestrial paradise, and which is connected by its roots with the tree of life; the four mystic rivers rise at the foot of this tree, which is guarded by the fiery sword and by the fourfold Biblical sphinx, the cherub of Ezekiel. . . . Here I must pause, and I already fear that I have said too much.

Yes, there is a unique, universal, imperishable dogma, powerful as supreme reason, simple like everything great, intelligible like all that is universally and absolutely true, and this dogma has been the father of all others. Yes, there is a science which confers on man prerogatives apparently superhuman. I find them enumerated as follows in a Hebrew manuscript of the sixteenth century.

"These are the privileges and power of the man who holds in his right hand the Keys of Solomon, and in his left the Branch of the Blossoming Almond:—

"*Aleph.* He beholds God face to face, without dying, and convrsees intimately with the seven genii who command the whole celestial army.

"*Beth.* He is superior to every affliction and to every fear.

"*Ghimel.* He reigns with all heaven, and is served by all hell.

"*Daleth.* He disposes of his own health and life, and can equally influence the health and life of others.

"*He.* He can neither be surprised by misfortune, nor overwhelmed by disasters, nor vanquished by his enemies.

"*Vav.* He knows the reason of the past, present, and future.

"*Dzain.* He holds the secret of the resurrection of the dead, and the key of immortality.

"Such are the seven transcendent privileges. Those which rank next are as follows:—

"*Cheth.* To find the stone of the philosophers.

"*Teth.* To possess the universal medicine.

"*Jod.* To know the laws of perpetual motion, and the demonstration of the quadrature of the circle.

"*Caph.* To change into gold not merely all metals, but also the earth itself, and even the refuse of the earth.

"*Lamed.* To subdue the most savage animals, and to know the words which paralyse and charm serpents.

"*Mem.* To possess the numerical art which gives the universal science.

INTRODUCTION.

"*Nun.* To speak learnedly on all subjects without preparation and without study.

"Finally, the seven least privileges of the Magus are these:—

"*Samech.* To pierce at a glance the depths of men's souls and the secrets of women's hearts.

"*Gnain.* To force Nature to give in to him whenever it may please him.

"*Phe.* To foresee all future events which do not depend on a superior free arbiter, or on an indiscernible cause.

"*Tsade.* To give at once and to all the most efficacious consolations and the most salutary counsels.

"*Coph.* To triumph over adversities.

"*Resch.* To conquer love and hate.

"*Schin.* To possess the secret of wealth; to be always its master, and never its slave; to know how to enjoy even poverty, and never to fall into abjectness or wretchedness.

"*Thav.* Add to these three septenaries that the wise man governs the elements, stills tempests, cures diseases by the touch, and resuscitates the dead.

"But there are some things which Solomon hath sealed with his triple seal. The initiates know it is enough! As for others, whether they laugh, believe, or doubt, whether they threaten or are afraid, what matters it to science or to us?"

Such, in fact, are the consequences of occult philosophy, and we are in a position to brave an accusation of folly, or a suspicion of charlatanry, when we assert that all these privileges are real. The object of our entire work on occult philosophy is to prove this.

The philosophical stone, the universal medicine, the transmutation of metals, the quadrature of the circle, the secret of perpetual motion are, therefore, neither mystifications of science, nor insane dreams; they are terms which are to be interpreted in their veritable sense; they express the various applications of a single secret, the several qualities of a single operation which is more generally defined by the appellation of the *magnum opus*.

These are the secrets of occult philosophy; such magic appears to us in history; let us now consider it in its books, its initiation, and its rites.

The key of all magical allegories is found in the tablets we have referred to, and which we believe to be the work of Hermes. Round this work, which may be called the keystone of the whole edifice of the secret sciences, are grouped innumerable legends, which are either its partial translation or its commentary endlessly renewed under a thousand different forms. Sometimes these ingenious fables are arranged symmetrically, and form a great epic which is characteristic of an epoch, though the crowd knows neither how nor why. Thus the fabulous history of the Golden Fleece epitomises, while it veils, the Hermetic and magical doctrines of Orpheus, and if we refer only to the mysterious poetry of Greece, it is because the sanctuaries of Egypt and India to some extent overwhelm us with their wealth, and our choice is embarrassed in the midst of so many riches. The Golden Fleece is the spoil of the sun, it is light appropriated to the use of men; the great secret of magical achievements—initiation, in fine—is what the allegorical heroes go in search of into Asia. This fable joins Hermetic magic with the Greek initiations. The celestial ram, whose fleece must be obtained in order to be the sovereign of the world, is the symbol of the *magnum opus*. The Argonautic ship built of the prophetic oaks of Dodona, the speaking vessel, is the bark of the mysteries of Isis, the ark of seeds and renovation, the coffin of Osiris, the ovum of divine regeneration. The adventurer, Jason, is the man called to initiation; he is only a hero in audacity, he has all the weakness and fickleness of humanity, but he leads forth with him the personifications of every power. Hercules, who signifies brute force, can by no means concur in the enterprise, and he strays from the path in pursuit of unworthy love; the rest reach the country of initiation, in Colchis, where some Zoroastrian secrets were still preserved; but how was their key to be obtained? Science is again betrayed by a woman. Medea delivers to Jason the arcana of the *magnum opus;* she sacrifices the kingdom and the life of her father, for it is a fatal law of the occult sanctuaries that the revelation of their secrets entails death to those who are unable to preserve them. Medea informs Jason of the monsters he must do battle with, and how he can vanquish them. First, there is the terrestrial and winged serpent, the astral fluid, which must be seized and condensed; its teeth must be drawn and sown in a plain, which has been previously dug up by yoking the oxen of Mars to the plough. The dragon's teeth are the acids which dissolve the metallic earth, prepared by a double furnace and by the magnetic forces of the earth. Then a fermentation and, as it were, a strife takes place, the impure is devoured by the impure, and the brilliant fleece becomes the recompense of the adept.

So ends the magic romance of Jason; that of Medea follows, for Greek antiquity has sought to include in this fable the epic of the secret sciences. After Hermetic magic comes the Goëtic, with parricide, fratricide, infanticide, sacrificing everything to their passions, and never enjoying the fruit of their crimes. Medea betrays her father, like Cham; assassinates her brother, like Cain. She poniards her children, poisons her rival, and reaps only the hatred of the man whose love she sought. One is astonished to see that Jason, when master of the Golden Fleece, is none the wiser for it; but it must be remembered that he owes the discovery of its secrets to treason. He is not an adept like Orpheus, he is a robber, like Prometheus. What he sought was not knowledge, but wealth and power. Therefore he died wretchedly, and the inspiring and sovereign properties of the Golden Fleece can be understood by none save the disciples of Orpheus.

But we are anxious to approach the Thebäid, that appalling synthesis of all dogma, present, past, and to come, that infinite fable, so to speak, which touches, like the deity of Orpheus, the two extremities of the cycle of human life. Singular fact! The seven gates of Thebes, defended and assaulted by seven heroes who have sworn upon the blood of victims, have the same meaning as the seven seals of the sacred book, explained by seven genii, and attacked by a seven-headed monster, after being opened by a living but immolated lamb, in the symbolic work of St John. The mysterious origin of Œdipus, who was found suspended from a tree, like a bleeding fruit, recalls the symbols of Moses and the narratives of Genesis. He makes war on his father and slays him unawares—tremendous prophecy of the blind emancipation of reason devoid of knowledge; then he comes into the presence of the sphinx! The sphinx—that symbol of symbols, the everlasting enigma of the uninitiated, the granite pedestal of the science of the sages, the devouring and silent monster whose unmoving form expresses the unique dogma of the great, universal mystery, the living palladium of humanity, the symbolic key of the science of nature, whose metaphysic is represented by the Pyramids!* How is the tetrad changed into the duad and explained by the triad? In more common but more emblematic words, what is that animal which has four feet in the morning, two at noon, and three in the evening? Speaking philosophically, how does the dogma of elementary forces produce the dualism of Zoroaster, and how is it summarised by the triad of Pythagoras and Plato? What is the ultimate significance of allegories and numbers, the final word of all symbolisms? Œdipus replies with a simple and terrible word, which destroys the sphinx and crowns the diviner King of Thebes—the solution of the enigma is Man! . . . Unfortunate! He has discerned too much, yet not with sufficient perspicuity, and he will soon atone for his calamitous and incomplete clairvoyance by a voluntary blindness. Then will he vanish in a storm, like all civilisations which shall at any time divine the solution of the sphinx's enigma without understanding its whole purport and mystery. All is symbolical and transcendental in this gigantic epic of mortal destinies. The two hostile brothers signify the second part of the great mystery divinely completed by the sacrifice of Antigone; then the last battle, the brothers destroyed by one another, Capaneus slain by the lightning he defies, Amphiaraüs swallowed by the earth, are so many allegories which fill those who can penetrate their triple hieratic meaning with astonishment by their truth and their grandeur.

The secret book of antique initiation was not unknown to Homer, who sketches its plan and chief figures on the shield of Achilles with minute precision. But Homer's graceful fables seem to have soon obscured the simple abstract truths of primeval revelation. Man clings to the form and lets the idea slide into oblivion; signs lose their power in their multiplication. Magic also became corrupted at this period, and descended to the most infamous enchantments among the sorcerers of Thessaly. The crime of Œdipus produced its deadly fruits, and the knowledge of good and evil erects evil into a sacrilegious divinity. Men grown tired of light take refuge in the darkness of material substance; the conception of that void which is filled by Deity seems to them greater than God, and thus hell is created.

* See Note 1.

Whenever in the course of this work we make use of the consecrated words God, Heaven, and Hell, let it be once for all plainly understood that we depart as much from the meaning which is attached to these terms by the profane as initiation is remote from ordinary thought. God for us is the AZOTH of the sages,* the efficient and final principle of the *magnum opus*. We shall explain later on what is obscure in these words.

Returning to the fable of Œdipus, the crime of the Theban king was that he did not understand the sphinx, that he destroyed the scourge of Thebes without being pure enough to complete the expiation in the name of his people. A pestilence in consequence soon avenged the death of the sphinx, and the king, forced to abdicate, sacrificed himself to the terrible manes of the monster, who is more living and voracious than ever when it has passed from the domain of form into that of idea. Œdipus discerned what man was, and he put out his own eyes for not having seen what God was. He divulged half of the Great Magic Arcanum, and, to save his people, it was necessary that he should take the other half of the awful secret into exile and the tomb.

After the colossal fable of Œdipus we find the graceful poem of Psyche, of which Apuleius was certainly not the inventor. The Great Magic Arcanum reappears herein under the image of the mysterious union between a god and a weak mortal, who is abandoned naked and alone upon a rock. Psyche must remain ignorant of the secret of his ideal royalty, and if she behold her husband, she must lose him. Here Apuleius annotates and interprets the allegories of Moses, but did not the Elohim and the gods of Apuleius alike issue from the sanctuaries of Memphis and Thebes? Psyche is the sister of Eve, or rather, she is Eve spiritualised. Both desire to know and lose innocence for the honour of the trial. Both deserve to descend into Hades, one to carry away the antique box of Pandora, the other to seek and to crush the serpent's head, the symbol of time and evil. Both commit the crime which must be expiated by the Prometheus of ancient days and the Lucifer of the Christian legend, the one delivered by Hercules, the other conquered by the Saviour.

After the wonderful golden ass of Apuleius, we find no

* See Note 2.

more magical epics. Science, overcome in Alexandria by the fanaticism of the murderers of Hypatia, became Christian, or, rather, concealed itself in the guise of Christianity with Ammonius, Synesius, and the pseudonymous author of the works of Dionysius the Areopagite. In such times it was needful to excuse miracles by the semblance of superstition, and knowledge by an unintelligible language. Hieroglyphic writing was revived, pantacles and characters were invented which epitomized a whole doctrine in a sign, a whole chain of tendencies and revelations in a sentence. What was the aim of these aspirants to knowledge? They sought the secret of the *magnum opus*, or the philosophers' stone, or the secret of perpetual motion, or the area of the circle, or the universal medicine, formulæ which frequently preserved them from persecution and hatred by taxing them with insanity, but which each gave expression to some aspect of the great magic secret, as we shall prove later on. This absence of magical epics continued till the Romance of the Rose, that profound work in trivial guise, a revelation of the mysteries of occultism as learned as that of Apuleius. The rose of Flamel the alchemist, of Jean de Meung, of Dante, and, we may add, of Apuleius himself, flourished on the same rose tree. The Romance of the Rose and the Divine Comedy are the two opposite sides of the same achievement—initiation through independence of the intellect, satire on all contemporary institutions, and the allegorical formulation of the great secrets of the Rosicrucian Society. The rose, which from time immemorial has been the symbol of beauty and life, of love and pleasure, expressed in a mystical manner all the protestations of the Renaissance. It was the flesh revolting against the oppression of the spirit, it was nature declaring herself to be, like grace, the daughter of God, it was love refusing to be stifled by the celibate, it was life desiring to be barren no longer, it was humanity aspiring to a natural religion, full of love and reason, founded on the revelation of the harmonies of existence of which the rose was for initiates the living and blooming symbol. This symbol is borrowed from the transcendent Kabbalah, and it is time that we should consider that immense and secret source of universal philosophy.

The Bible, with all the allegories it contains, only expresses the religious knowledge of the Hebrews in an incomplete and veiled manner. The book we have before spoken of, and whose hieratic characters we shall explain, that book which William Postel calls the Genesis of Enoch, certainly existed before Moses and the prophets, whose doctrine, fundamentally identical as it is with that of the ancient Egyptians, had also its exoterism and its veils. When Moses spoke to the people, says the sacred book, allegorically, he placed a veil over his face, and he removed it before addressing the Deity—such is the cause of those pretended Biblical absurdities which so much exercised the satirical genius of Voltaire. The books of the Bible were committed to writing only to recall tradition, and they were inscribed in symbols unintelligible to the profane. The Pentateuch and poems of the prophets were, moreover, merely elementary works, whether as regards doctrine, ethics, or liturgy. The true secret and traditional philosophy was not committed to writing till a later period, and then under still less transparent veils. There originated in this manner a second Bible, unknown, or rather misunderstood, by the Christians, and which they denominate a collection of monstrous absurdities (for here the believers talk like the sceptics with whom they are confounded in a common ignorance), while we affirm it to be a monument which harmonises all the sublimity ever attained or imagined by religious and philosophical genius, a treasure encompassed by thorns, a diamond concealed in a gross and opaque stone—our readers will have divined already that we refer to the Talmud.

How strange is the destiny of the Jews! those scapegoats, martyrs, and saviours of the world, that long-lived, courageous, and hardy race, which persecutions have ever preserved intact, because it has not yet accomplished its mission! Do not our apostolical traditions affirm that, after the decay of faith among the Gentiles, salvation will again come forth from the house of Israel, and that then the crucified Jew will surrender the empire of the world into the hands of His Father?

On penetrating into the sanctuary of the Kabbalah, one is seized with admiration at the sight of a doctrine so simple and at the same time so absolute. The necessary union of ideas and signs, the consecration of the most fundamental realities by primitive characters, the trinity of words, letters, and numbers; a philosophy simple as the alphabet, pro-

B

found and infinite as the Logos; theorems more luminous and complete than those of Pythagoras; a theology which may be epitomized by counting on the fingers; an infinity which can be held in the hollow of an infant's hand; ten numerals and twenty-two letters, a triangle, a square, and a circle—such are the elements of the Kabbalah, such are the primary principles of the written word, shadow of that spoken Logos which created the world!

All truly dogmatic religions have issued from the Kabbalah and return therein; whatever is scientific and grandiose in the religious dreams of all *illuminati*—Jacob Bœhmen, Swedenborg, Saint Martin, and the rest—has been borrowed from the Kabbalah; all masonic associations owe their secrets and their symbols thereto. The Kabbalah alone consecrates the alliance of universal reason and the Divine Word; it establishes, by the counterpoise of two forces in apparent opposition, the eternal balance of existence; it reconciles reason with faith, power with liberty, knowledge with mystery; it has the keys of the present, past, and future.

To be initiated into the Kabbalah, it is insufficient to read and digest the writings of Reuchlin, Galatinus, Kircher, or Mirandola; it is needful also to study the Hebrew writers in the collection of Pistorius, the Sepher Jezirah above all, and then the philosophy of love by Leon the Israelite. We must also master the great book of Sohar in the collection of 1684, entitled *Cabala Denudata*, the treatise on Kabbalistic Pneumatics, and that of the Revolution of Souls; then enter boldly into the luminous obscurity of the whole dogmatic and allegorical substance of the Talmud; after which we shall understand William Postel, and confess in an undertone that, his exceedingly premature and over-generous dreams of female emancipation set aside, this famous and erudite *illuminé* was not such a maniac as is pretended by those who have not read him.

We have sketched rapidly the history of occult philosophy, we have indicated its sources and briefly analysed its principal books. Magic power is composed of two things —a science and a force. Without the force the science is nothing, or, rather, it is a danger. Give knowledge to power alone, such is the supreme law of initiations. So the great Revealer says, "The kingdom of Heaven suffereth violence, and the violent only shall bear it away."

The gate of truth is closed, like the sanctuary of a virgin; he must be a man who would enter. All miracles are promised to faith, but what is faith except the audacity of a will which does not falter in the darkness, and which advances towards the light through all trials, and overcoming all obstacles?

It is unnecessary here to repeat the history of old initiations; the more dangerous and terrible they were, the greater was their efficacy, and thus the world had true men to govern and instruct it in those days. The priestly art and the kingly art consisted above all things in trials of courage, discretion, and will-power. There were noviciates similar to those of the priests, who under the name of Jesuits are so unpopular in our own day, but who would still be the rulers of the world had they a truly wise and intelligent leader.

After spending our lifetime in the search for the absolute in religion, science, and justice, after revolving in the circle of Faust, we have arrived at the first doctrine and the first book of humanity. There do we pause, there have we discovered the secret of human omnipotence and of indefinite progress, the key of all symbolisms, the first and final doctrine; and we have comprehended the significance of that sentence, so often repeated in the Gospel, "the kingdom of God." *

To provide a fixed point as a fulcrum for human activity is to solve the problem of Archimedes, by realising the use of his famous lever. This is what was done by the great initiates who convulsed the world, and they could only have accomplished it by means of the Great and Incommunicable Secret. Moreover, as a guarantee of his renewed youth, the symbolic phœnix never reappeared to the world without having solemnly consumed the ashes and proofs of his anterior life. Thus, Moses caused all those who had known Egypt and her mysteries to die in the desert; thus, St Paul at Ephesus burned all books which treated of the occult sciences; thus, finally, the French Revolution, that daughter of the great Johannite Orient, and the ashes of the Templars, spoliated the churches and blasphemed the allegories of the divine cultus. But all doctrines and all restorations proscribe magic, and doom its mysteries to the flames or oblivion. This is because every cultus or

* See Note 3.

philosophy is a Benjamin of humanity, which lives by the death of its mother, because the symbolic serpent revolves ever by devouring its own tail, because a void is necessary as a condition of existence to every plenitude, a negation for each affirmation; it is the eternal realisation of the phœnix allegory.

Two illustrious scholars have already proceeded me in the path I travel, but they have, so to speak, passed the night there, and have had no beacon. I refer to Volney and Dupuis; to Dupuis above all, whose immense erudition has produced only a negative work. He has seen astronomy alone in the origin of all religions, mistaking thus the symbolic cycle for doctrine, and the calendar for legend. He lacked a single branch of knowledge—that of true magic which comprises the secrets of the Kabbalah. Dupuis has passed through the sanctuaries of eld, like the prophet Ezekiel through the plain covered with dry bones, and he has perceived death only, for he did not know the word which collects the virtue of the four winds of heaven, and which can make a living people of all that vast charnel-house by crying to the ancient symbols—"Arise! take up a new shape, and walk!"

What no one has therefore been able or has dared to do before us, it is time that we should have the boldness to attempt. Like Julian, we would rebuild the Temple, and do not conceive that we shall thereby give the lie to a wisdom which we adore, and which Julian himself was worthy to adore also, had the rancorous and fanatical doctors of his time permitted him to understand it. The Temple for us has two pillars, on one of which Christianity has inscribed its name. We have, therefore, no wish to attack Christianity; far from it—we would interpret and fulfil it. Understanding and will have alternately exercised their power in the world; in our own days religion and philosophy still wage war, but must end by agreeing. The provisional object of Christianity has been the establishment by obedience and faith of a supernatural or religious equality among men, and the petrifaction of intelligence by faith, in order to provide a fulcrum for virtue, which came to destroy the aristocracy of knowledge, or rather, to replace that aristocracy already destroyed. Philosophy, on the contrary, has laboured to bring back men by liberty and reason to natural inequality, and to substitute *savoir-*

faire for virtue by inaugurating the reign of industry. Neither of these two courses has been complete and sufficing, neither has led man to perfection and happiness. What is now being dreamed of, almost without daring to hope it, is an alliance between these two forces long considered contrary, and there is good reason for desiring their union; these two great energies of the human soul are no more opposed to one another than the male sex is opposed to the female; doubtless, they are different, but their apparently contrary appearances come only from their aptitude to meet and unite.

We propose nothing less than a universal solution of all problems, the explanation of the philosopher's stone, perpetual motion, the secret of the *magnum opus*, and the universal medicine. Men will charge us with insanity, as they did the divine Paracelsus, or with charlatanism, as they did the great and unfortunate Agrippa. If the stake of Urban Grandier be extinguished, the inexorable proscriptions of silence and calumny remain. We do not defy them, but we are resigned to them. We have not sought of ourselves the publication of this work, and we believe that if the time be come for speaking, speech will produce itself, through us or through others. We shall, therefore, remain calm and wait.

INITIATORY EXERCISES AND PREPARATIONS.

THOU who art holding this book in thy hands and dost undertake to read it, who art thou? On the pediment of a temple which was dedicated by antiquity to the god of light, there might be read this inscription—" Know thyself!" I give the same advice to every man who is seeking to approach science.

Magic, called by the ancients the *sanctum regnum*, the holy kingdom, or the kingdom of God, *regnum Dei*, exists but for kings and for priests—art thou a priest? art thou a king? The priesthood of magic is no common sacerdotalism, and its royalty has nothing to dispute with the princes of this world. The kings of science are the priests of truth, and their dominion is concealed from the multitude, like their sacrifices and their prayers. The kings of science are men who have attained truth, and whom the truth has made free, according to the formal promise of the most mighty of all the initiators.

Whosoever is the slave of his passions or of worldly prejudices can never be initiated, can never, at least till he reforms, attain that height. Whosoever loves his own opinions, and fears to lose them; who looks with disfavour on new truths, and who is not disposed to doubt all things rather than admit anything on hazard, should close this book, which is useless and dangerous for him; he will understand it badly, and it will vex him; but should he, peradventure, divine its whole significance, far more will he be troubled thereby.

If thou art attached to anything in the world more than to reason, truth, and justice; if thy will be uncertain and fluctuating either in good or evil; if logic alarm thee, if naked truth make thee blush, if thou art hurt when received errors are assailed, condemn this work out of hand.

Whosoever aspires to wisdom, and to solve the great enigma of nature, must be the inheritor and despoiler of the sphinx; he must have its human head to possess the word, the eagle's wings to achieve the heights, the bull's flanks to furrow the depths, and the lion's talons to make room on the right and on the left, both before and behind. Thou, therefore, who dost aspire to initiation, art thou learned like Faust? Art thou impassible like Job? No; is it not so? But thou canst become so by willing it. Hast thou vanquished the vortices of vague thoughts? Art thou free from uncertainties and caprices? Dost thou accept pleasure only when thou willest it, and dost thou will it only when it is legitimate? No; is it not so? It is not always thus; but it may become so by determining thereon. The sphinx has not only a man's head, but also the breasts of a woman—canst thou resist feminine attractions? No; is it not so? And here thou dost laugh in replying, parading thy moral weakness for the glorification of the vital and physical power within thee. Be it so, however! I allow this homage to be paid to the ass of Sterne or Apuleius; that the ass has its merits I dispute in no way; it was sacred to Priapus, as the goat was to the god of Mendes. But leave it for what it is, and decide if it shall be thy master, or if thou wilt be master of it. He alone can truly possess the pleasure of love who has conquered the love of pleasure. To be able to make use of anything, and to abstain from doing so, is to be twice able. By thy passions the woman enchains thee; be master of thy passions and thou wilt enchain her. The greatest injury which can be inflicted on a man is to call him a coward. Now a coward is one who neglects the care of his moral dignity to obey the instincts of nature blindly. In presence of danger it is, as a matter of fact, natural to be afraid, and why then is it a shameful thing? Because honour has laid down as a law that we should prefer duty to inclination or fear. What is honour from this standpoint? It is the universal fore-consciousness of immortality, and the valuation of the means which can lead to it. The final victory that man can achieve over death is to conquer the relish of life, not by despair but by a nobler hope which is comprised in faith, for all that is honourable and beautiful, by the consent of the universal world.

To learn self-conquest is, therefore, to learn how to live, and the austerities of stoicism were no idle boast of liberty. To yield to the forces of nature is to follow the current of collective life and to be the slave of secondary causes. To resist and overcome nature is to achieve for oneself a personal and imperishable existence; it is to set oneself free from the vicissitudes of life and death. Every man who is prepared to die rather than renounce truth and justice is veritably living, for he is immortal in his soul. The end of all ancient initiations was to find or form such men. Pythagoras exercised his disciples by silence and all kinds of self-denial; in Egypt the neophytes were tried by the four elements; in India it is well known to what incredible austerities the faquirs and brahmins devote themselves in order to attain the realm of free-will and divine independence. All the macerations of asceticism are borrowed from the initiations of the ancient mysteries, and they have ceased because those eligible for initiation, no longer finding initiators, and the leaders of conscience having become in the long run as ignorant as the profane, the blind have grown weary of following the blind, and no one has been willing to submit to trials which issued but in doubt and despair—the path of light was lost.

We must not enter rashly the domain of the transcendental sciences, but once on the road, we must reach their goal or perish. To doubt is to lose reason, to pause is to fall, to go back is to fling one's self into an abyss. The operations of science are not devoid of danger. Their result may be madness for those who are not established on the base of the supreme, absolute, and infallible reason. They may over-excite the nervous system, producing terrible and incurable diseases. When the imagination overawes and alarms itself, they may produce swoons and even death by cerebral congestion. We, cannot, therefore, too strongly dissuade from attempting them all nervous and excitable people, women, young persons, and all who are unaccustomed to complete self-control and the command of fear. In like manner, nothing is more dangerous than to make magic a pastime, or a diversion at parties, as some make it. Even magnetic experiments performed under such conditions will only fatigue the subject, mislead opinions, and perplex science. We cannot with impunity make sport of the mysteries of life and death; and things which are serious should be treated seriously and with the greatest reserve.

Never yield to the temptation to convince by producing

phenomena. The most astounding effects would be no proof to one who is not convinced beforehand. They can always be attributed to ordinary prestige, and the Magus will be considered as a more or less skilful rival of Robert Houdin or of Hamilton. To demand prodigies as a ground of faith in science, is to show one's self unworthy or incapable of knowledge. SANCTA SANCTIS. Moreover, never boast of the works you have performed, even if you have raised the dead. The Great Master ever recommended silence to the sick whom he healed, and had this silence been faithfully preserved, the Initiator would not have been crucified before the completion of his work. Remember the grand symbol of Prometheus, and hold thy peace! All the Magi who have made known their achievements have died violently, and some have been reduced to suicide, like Cardan, Schroeppfer, and others.

Magical operations are the exercise of a power which is natural, though superior to the common forces of nature. They are the result of a science and a discipline which exalt human will above its normal limits. The supernatural is but the natural in an extraordinary or exalted state; a miracle is a phenomenon which astounds the multitude because it is unexpected. The marvellous is that which amazes; it is an effect which surprises those who are unacquainted with its cause, or who assign it a cause disproportioned to such a result. Nothing is miraculous except for the ignorant, but as there is scarcely any absolute knowledge among men, the wonder-world can still exist, and it does so for every one. Let us start by declaring that we believe in all miracles, because we are convinced and certain, even by our own experience, of their entire possibility. There are some which we do not attempt to explain, but which we consider to be no less explicable. From the greater to the lesser, from the lesser to the greater, the consequences are identically connected, and the proportions progressively rigorous. But in order to work miracles we must be outside the ordinary conditions of humanity—we must either be exalted by wisdom or excited by folly, either above all passions or else beside them through ecstasy or frenzy. Such is the first and most indispensable preparation of the operator. Thus, by a providential and necessary law, the magician cannot exercise omnipotence except in an inverse proportion to his material interest;

the alchemist makes so much the more gold as he is so much the more resigned to privations, and esteems that poverty which protects the secrets of the *magnum opus*. The adept whose heart is unimpassioned will alone dispose of the love and the hatred of those whom he would make the instruments of his knowledge; the mythos of Genesis is eternally true, and God permits the tree of science to be approached by such alone as are sufficiently self-denying and strong not to covet its fruits.

Let those, therefore, who seek in magic the means to satisfy their passions, pause in that deadly path, where they will find nothing but death or madness. This is the significance of the vulgar tradition that the devil finished sooner or later by strangling the sorcerers. The Magus must, therefore, be impassible, moderate and chaste, disinterested, impenetrable and inaccessible to every kind of prejudice or fear. He should be devoid of bodily defects, and tested by all contradictions and all afflictions. The first and most important of all magical works is to secure this exceptional superiority.

We have said that the ecstasy of passion may produce the same results as absolute superiority, and this is true so far as regards the issue but not as regards the control of magical operations. Passion forcibly projects the vital fluid and imprints unforeseen movements on the universal life-agent, but it cannot so easily restrain what it has launched, and its destiny then resembles that of Hippolytus carried away by his own steeds, or of Phalaris tortured himself by the instrument he had invented for others. Human will, realised by its acts, is like the cannon-ball which recoils before no obstacle. When projected with violence it passes through it or is lost in it, but if it proceed with patience and perseverance it is never lost; it is like the wave which returns incessantly and ends by undermining the rock. Man can be changed by habit, which, according to the proverb, becomes his second nature. By means of persevering and graduated athletic exercises, the energies and agility of the body are developed or created in an astonishing degree. It is the same with the soul's powers. If you would reign over yourselves and over others, learn how to will!

How can we learn to will? This is the first arcanum of magical initiation, and it was to make the very inmost depth of this secret understood, that the ancient custodians of the sacerdotal art surrounded the approaches to the sanctuary with so many terrors and illusions. They believed in no will till it had stood its tests, and they were right. Power can only manifest itself by achievement. Idleness and forgetfulness are the enemies of will, and this is why all religions have multiplied observances and made their cultus difficult and full of minutiæ. Are not those children the favourites of their mothers, who have cost them the most suffering and anxious care? So does the strength of religion consist exclusively in the inflexible will of those who follow it. As long as there is one faithful believer in the holy sacrifice of the mass, there will be a priest to celebrate it for him, and so long as there is one priest who daily says his office, there will be a pope in the world. Observances which are apparently the most insignificant, and in themselves foreign to the end which they propose, conduce to that end notwithstanding, through education and the exercise of will. The peasant who each morning rises at two or three o'clock and goes far from home to gather a sprig of the same herb before the sun rises, may perform innumerable prodigies by simply carrying this herb about him, for it will be the sign of his will, and thereby will become all that he wants it to be in the interests of his desires.

To accomplish anything we must believe in our ability to accomplish, and this faith must be at once translated into action. Faith has no tentative efforts; it begins in the certainty of finishing, and works calmly as though it had omnipotence at its disposal and eternity before it. Thou, therefore, who hast introduced thyself to the science of the Magi, what dost thou ask thereof? Dare to formulate thy desire, whatever it be, then set to work immediately, and cease not to act in the same manner and for the same end; what you wish for will take place, and has already begun for you and by you. Sixtus V., while tending his sheep, said:—"I determine to be pope." Thou art a mendicant and dost seek to make gold. Set to work, *and never give in*—I guarantee thee, in the name of science, all the treasures of Flamel and Raymond Lully.

What is the first requisite? To believe in one's ability, and then to act. But how act? Rise daily at the same hour and at an early hour, bathe summer and winter before daybreak, in a fountain; never wear soiled clothes, wash them yourself if necessary; exercise yourself by voluntary privations, that you may be better able to bear involuntary ones; finally, impose silence on all desires save that of achieving the *magnum opus*.

"What! By washing daily at a fountain I shall make gold?" will be asked.

"You will work in order to make it."

"This is a jest."

"No, it is an arcanum."

"How can I avail myself of an arcanum which I do not understand?"

"Believe and act; you will understand afterwards."

A sluggard will never be a magician. Magic is an exercise of all hours and moments. The operator of great works must be absolute master of himself, must know how to subdue the allurements of pleasure, appetite, and sleep, must be as insensible to renown as to reproach. His life should be a will directed by one thought and served by entire nature, which will be made subservient to his mind in his own organs, and by sympathy in all the universal forces which correspond to them. Every faculty and sense should share in the work, nothing in the priest of Hermes has the right to be idle; understanding must be formulated by signs and summarised by characters or pantacles; the will must be determined by words, and words must be fulfilled by acts; the magical idea must be translated into light for the eyes, harmony for the ears, perfumes for the sense of smell, savours for the mouth, and shapes for the touch; the operator, in a word, must realise in his whole life what he seeks to realise in the exterior world; he must become a magnet to attract the desired thing, which, when he shall be sufficiently magnetic, will come of itself, and without him thinking of it.

It is important that the Magus should know the secrets of science, but he can do so by intuition and without study. Hermits who dwell in the habitual contemplation of nature frequently divine her harmonies, and in their simple good sense are often more learned than doctors, whose natural perceptions are distorted by the sophistry of the schools. The true practical magicians are found almost always in the country, and are frequently uncultured persons and simple shepherds. There are also certain physical organisations better adapted than others to the revelations of the

INITIATORY EXERCISES AND PREPARATIONS. 29

occult world; there are sensitive and sympathetic natures with whom intuition in the Astral Light is, so to speak, innate. Certain afflictions and certain complaints may modify the nervous system, and make it, without the concurrence of the will, a more or less perfect apparatus for divination, but these are exceptional phenomena, and generally magic power must and can be acquired by perseverance and application. There are also certain substances which produce ecstasy and provoke the magnetic sleep. There are some which place at the disposition of the imagination all the liveliest and most highly coloured reflections of the elementary light; but the use of these is dangerous, for they commonly produce stupefaction and intoxication. They are employed notwithstanding, but in rigorously calculated quantities and in wholly exceptional cases.

He who desires to devote himself seriously to magical exercises, after having ensured his mind against all hallucination and terror, should purify himself outwardly and inwardly for the space of forty days. The number forty is sacred. In Arabic ciphers it is composed of a circle, image of the infinite, and a 4 which resumes the triad by unity. In Roman numerals, arranged in the following manner, it represents the sign of the fundamental dogma of Hermes, and the character of Solomon's seal :—

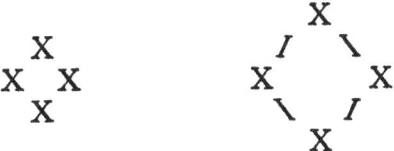

The purification of the Magus consists in abstinence from gross enjoyments and from strong liquors, and in regulating the period of sleep. This preparation has been indicated and represented in every cultus by a time of penitence and trial which precedes the symbolic festivals of life-renewal.

The most scrupulous cleanliness of person must be observed, as we have said; the poorest can find springwater. Garments also must be carefully washed, as well as the furniture and utensils made use of. All slovenliness is evidence of negligence, and negligence is mortal in magic. The air must be purified at rising and retiring with a perfume composed of the resin of laurels, salt, camphor, and sulphur, and the four sacred names * should at the same time be pronounced in turning successively towards the four cardinal points. The operations that are accomplished must be divulged to no one; mystery is the rigorous and indispensable condition of the whole science. The curious must be baffled by the simulation of other occupations and researches, such as chemical experiments for commercial purposes, hygienic prescriptions, the search after some natural secrets, etc., but the decried name of magic must never be pronounced.

The Magus should live in seclusion, and be approached with difficulty. Attachments and friendships are needful to him, but he should select them with care, and preserve them at all costs. He must concentrate his energies within him, and choose his points of contact; but in proportion as he is uncouth and unapproachable at first, so will he be subsequently popular and sought after, when he has magnetised his chain, and determined his position in a current of ideas and of light. He should have another profession besides that of a magician, for magic is not a trade. A poor and laborious life is so favourable to practical initiation that the greatest masters have sought for it, even when the wealth of the world was at their disposal. To devote oneself to ceremonial magic, one must be free from disturbing pre-occupations, must be able to obtain all the instruments of the science, and if necessary know how to make them oneself; an inaccessible laboratory must also be ensured, where there will be no fear of ever being surprised or troubled.

The sight of hideous objects and of deformed persons must be avoided as far as possible; the Magus should not eat with those whom he does not esteem, and must live in the most uniform and methodical manner. He should have the most exalted self-respect, and should consider himself a dethroned sovereign, who consents to existence that he may recover his crown. Being amiable and well-behaved towards everyone, he should never permit himself to be absorbed in social relations, and should withdraw from circles where he does not possess some initiative.

He who devotes himself to the works of science should daily take some moderate exercise, and forbear from vigils unduly prolonged, should avoid poisonous emanations, the

* See Note 4.

INITIATORY EXERCISES AND PREPARATIONS. 31

vicinity of stagnant water, and indigestible or impure food. He should above all divert himself daily from magical preoccupations by mundane cares or toils, whether artistic, industrial, or even manual. In order to see clearly we should not be always looking, and he who spends his life in shooting at a single mark will cease in the end to strike it. A precaution, which must be equally borne in mind, is never to experiment when ill.

It is also an essential condition that the Magus should know how to equilibriate forces and restrain the ardour of individual impulse. This is represented by the eighth figure of the keys of Hermes, where a female is seated between two pillars, holding in one hand an upright sword, and in the other a balance. To equilibriate forces, they must be simultaneously maintained, and made to act alternately, a twofold operation which is represented by the use of the balance, and also by the double cross of the pantacles of Pythagoras and of Ezekiel, where the crosses are equilibriated by each other, and the planetary signs are in permanent opposition. Thus Venus equates the works of Mars, Mercury tempers and accomplishes those of the sun and moon, Saturn balances Jupiter. It was through this antagonism of the ancient gods that Prometheus — that is, the genius of knowledge—contrived to enter Olympus and steal the celestial fire.

Need I speak more plainly? The milder and calmer thou art, the more will thy wrath be effectual; the more aggressive thou art, the higher will be the worth of thy meekness; the more skilful thou art, the better wilt thou profit by thine intelligence, and even by thy virtues; the more indifferent thou art, the easier will it be to make others love thee. This is matter of experience in the moral order, and is rigorously realised in the sphere of action. Undivided human passions inevitably produce an effect contrary to their unbridled longing. Extreme love creates antipathy, blind hatred counteracts and chastises itself, vanity leads to abasement and the cruellest humiliation. So the Great Master revealed a mystery of positive magical science when He said:—" If thine enemy hunger, feed him, if he thirst, give him drink, for in so doing thou shalt heap coals of fire upon his head."

It may be urged that such a forgiveness is hypocritical and strongly resembles a refined revenge, but it must be remembered that the Magus is sovereign. Now, a monarch never avenges himself, he has the right to punish; when he exercises this right he does his duty, and is inexorable as justice. Let it be also borne in mind, so that no one may pervert the meaning of these words, that the point in question is the chastisement of evil by good, and the opposition of mildness to violence. If the exercise of virtue be a scourge to vice, no one has a right to beg that vice may be spared, or that pity be extended to its shame and its sufferings.

Finally, the Magus can and should accomplish the duties and observe the rites of the cultus to which he belongs. Now, of all religions the most magical is that which realises the greatest number of miracles, which grounds the most inconceivable mysteries on the most conclusive reasons, whose lights are equal to its shadows, which popularises the miraculous, and incarnates God in men by faith. This religion has always existed in the world, and under various names has been always the dominant religion. It has, at the present moment, among the nations of the earth, three apparently hostile forms, which will eventually unite for the constitution of a Universal Church. I refer to the Russian orthodoxy, to Roman Catholicism, and to a final transformation of the religion of Buddha.

We believe it to have been sufficiently made clear by what precedes that our magic is opposed to Goëtic and necromantic magic. Ours is at once an absolute science and an absolute religion, which should not destroy and swallow all opinions and all religions, but regenerate and direct them, by reconstituting the circle of initiates, and thus providing the blind masses with wise and clear-headed leaders.

The intellectual and social chaos in the midst of which we are perishing originates in the neglect of initiation and its mysteries and trials. The essential law of nature, that of initiation by achievement and by laborious and voluntary progress, has been fatally misconstrued. To raise up a tottering and foundering society, the hierarchy and initiation must be re-established. The task is difficult, but the whole intelligent world already feels the necessity of undertaking it, and this work is an appeal to all still living to reconstitute life in the very centre of decomposition and death.

RELIGIOUS AND PHILOSOPHICAL PROBLEMS.

I.—THE HERMETIC AXIOM.

THE synthesis of all religions is in the unity of a single dogma, which is the affirmation of existence, and its equality with itself, which constitutes its mathematical value. There is only one dogma in magic, and it is this: The visible is the manifestation of the invisible, or, in other terms, the perfect Logos is, in things which are appreciable and visible, in exact proportion with those which are inappreciable to our senses and invisible to our eyes. The Magus raises one hand towards heaven and points with the other to earth, and he says :—" Above, immensity! below, immensity also! Immensity is equivalent to immensity." This is true in the order both of the seen and the unseen.

The ancient sages, of whom Trismegistus is the organ, formulated the unique dogma in the following terms :— "That which is above is as that which is below, and that which is below is as that which is above." In other words, the form bears proportion to the idea, which is the sole *raison d'être* of all forms; the shadow is the measure of the body calculated with its relation to the luminous ray. The depth of the scabbard corresponds to the length of the sword; negation is proportional to the contrary affirmation; production is equal to destruction in the movement which conserves life; and there is no point in infinity which cannot be the centre of a circle whose circumference expands and indefinitely recedes into space.

The tradition of the Kabbalah rests wholly on this one magical dogma—that the visible is for us the proportional measure of the invisible. Measure a corner of creation, and make a progressive, proportionate multiplication, when all infinity will multiply its circles, filled with universes, which will pass in proportional segments between the ideal and increasing branches of your compass. Therefore, this primeval, unique, magical, kabbalistic, and immovable dogma indicates correspondences and analogies, and is, in fact, that of revelation by analogy in the three intelligible worlds. Analogy is the final word of science and the first of faith. It is the sole possible mediator between the seen and the unseen, between the finite and infinite. It is the key of all the secrets of nature and the only Logos of all revelations. It invests the Magus with every natural power; it is the quintessence of the philosophers' stone, the secret of perpetual motion, the quadrature of the circle; it is the Temple based on the two pillars JAKIN and BOHAS, it is the key of the grand secret, it is the root of the Tree of Life, it is the knowledge of good and evil. To find the exact scale of analogies in things which are cognizable by science is to establish the grounds of faith and seize the rod of miracles. Metallic transmutation is performed spiritually and materially by the positive key of analogies. Everything in magic is predetermined by this universal dogma, in virtue whereof the possibility of true evocations can be satisfactorily proved. It is this dogma which is eternally reproduced in the symbolism of all religious forms, and by it we know that the innate virtue of things has created words, and that there exists an exact proportion between ideas and words, which are the first forms and articulate realisations of ideas.

II.—FAITH.

FAITH is the firm adhesion of the soul to its reasonable and necessary hypotheses, and this faith may itself be called reason. The obstinate adherence of the mind to impossible and unreasonable hypotheses is superstition, fanaticism, folly.

Faith is the confidence of the human soul in a higher reason than its own reason. It, therefore, exalts the intelligence of man instead of degrading it. The expanse of heaven begins where the peaks of the mountains finish. I cannot believe the reverse of what I know, and I cannot know the opposite of that which I believe, without at once

renouncing either my faith or knowledge. The object of faith is, therefore, necessarily hypothetical, but the object of rational faith is necessary hypothesis. Where science pauses faith begins, and it is defined by St Paul in the following terms :—*Accedentem ad Deum oportet credere, quia est et inquirentibus se remunerator sit.*
To enlarge the sphere of science is apparently to defraud faith, but it is in reality to extend its domain in proportion, for it widens its basis. Faith is superstition and madness if reason be not at its base. We must believe in causes whose existence reason compels us to admit on the evidence of effects which are known and appreciated by science. Any faith which does not illuminate and extend reason is a superstition; any dogma which denies the life of the understanding and the spontaneity of free-will is also a superstition. To believe is to acquiesce in what we do not now know, but which reason assures us beforehand that we shall know, or, at least, recognise, some day. Faith is the supplement to reason in the darkness which the latter leaves both before and behind her. It emanates from reason, but must not be confounded with it. Its apparent opposition to reason is the strength of both, for it establishes their distinct and separate provinces, by fructifying the negative side of the one with the positive side of the other. What has caused all religious errors and confusions is the ignorance of the great law of the analogy of contrary things ; we have sought to make religion a philosophy and philosophy a religion ; we have endeavoured to subject the things which are of faith to the critical methods of science, which is quite as ridiculous as to subject science to the blind submissions of faith. To reason upon faith is to destroy faith, whose object is beyond reason. Faith is aspiration towards the infinite; it is not the stupid credulity of astonished ignorance. It is the consciousness and confidence of love ; it is the cry of reason, which persists in the denial of the absurd, even in the presence of the unknown. It is a sentiment as necessary to the soul as breathing is to life, it is the heart's dignity, it is the reality of enthusiasm. It does not consist in the affirmation of this or that symbol, but in true and constant aspiration towards the truths which are veiled by all symbolisms. To deny a religion, or even all religions, rather than adhere to formulæ which the conscience reproves, is a courageous

and sublime act of faith. Every man who suffers for his convictions is a martyr for faith. He may explain himself badly, but he prefers truth and justice before all else; do not let him be condemned without a hearing!

To believe in the supreme truth is not to define it, and to declare our belief in it is to admit the possibility of things beyond our knowledge. To define and circumscribe the object of faith is to formulate the unknown. Professions of belief are statements of human ignorance and aspiration, while scientific theorems are monuments of human conquests. Man can realise that which he believes in the measure of that which he knows, and in virtue of that which he does not know; and he can accomplish all that he desires in the measure of that which he believes, and in virtue of that which he knows. Analogy is the final word of science and the first of faith; it is the sole possible mediator between the finite and the infinite, between the visible and invisible. Dogma is the ever-ascending hypothesis of a presumable equation. For the ignorant, it is the hypothesis which is the absolute affirmation, and the absolute affirmation which is hypothesis. Science has its necessary hypotheses, and he who seeks to realise them ennobles science without restraining faith, for on the other side of faith is infinity.

Faith is greater than all religions, because it determines less than any of them the articles of belief. A definition of faith is, at most, the settlement of the terms of a common hypothesis, for it is impossible to divine the unknown except by the supposed and supposable proportions which it bears to the known, and thus analogy, the one and only dogma of the ancient Magi, has been and ever will be the begetter of all others. No specialised dogma constitutes more than a persuasion which belongs to a particular community, but faith is a sentiment common to humanity at large. The more we argue with a view to definition, the less we believe; an additional dogma is an opinion which a sect appropriates to itself, and, in some sense, abstracts from universal faith. Let the sectarians cast and recast their dogmas; let the superstitious elaborate and formulate their superstitions, let the dead bury their dead, and believe in the inexpressible truth, in the Absolute which reason admits without understanding, and which we perceive without knowing! Believe in the Supreme Reason! Believe in infinite love, and commiserate the stupidities of the schools and the barbarisms of false philosophy!

Moral equilibrium is the concurrence of science and faith. It no more belongs to a theologian to affirm a mathematical absurdity, or deny the demonstration of a theorem, than to a *savant* to cavil, in the name of science, for or against dogmatic mysteries. An article of faith is not a subject for dispute, it is believed or not believed in, but it is of faith precisely because it excludes the examination of science. When the Count Joseph de Maistre asserts that our present stupidity will one day be the cause of as much astonishment as the barbarism of the Middle Ages, he, doubtless, alludes to those so-called strong minds who are daily saying:—"I will believe when the truth of dogma shall be scientifically proved to me." That is to say, I will believe when nothing remains to believe in, when dogma, as such, shall have ceased to exist, having become a scientific theorem, or, in other words, I will not admit the infinite till it be explained, determined, circumscribed, and defined for me, in a word, till it has been limited. I will believe in the infinite when I know there is no infinity, in the immensity of ocean when I have seen it sealed up in bottles. But, good folks, what has been clearly proved to you, you believe no longer, for you know it!

Faith is a divination by intelligence and love, directed by the indices of Nature and reason. It is, therefore, the essence of the things which are of faith to be inaccessible to science, doubtful for philosophy, and indefinite for certitude. Faith is the hypothetical realisation and conventional settlement of the final ends of hope. It is the adherence to the visible sign of things unseen.

Sperandarum substantia rerum
Argumentum non apparentium.

Science is purely human, and faith cannot reasonably affirm itself to be divine unless it be immensely collective. It is this collectiveness which deserves for opinions the name of religion, that is, the moral bond which unites men to one another. An isolated belief does not deserve the name of faith, which signifies confidence. Scientific truth is proved by exact demonstrations, truth in religion by the unanimity of belief and the sanctity of works, which are the proof of faith. To defy all social authority, and only put trust in one's self, is insanity. The Catholic believes in the Church because the Church represents for him the *élite* of believers. It is this which justifies the faith of the charcoal-burner, who not only should be a believer in matters of religion, but also in matters of science. Shall he deny or contest the genius of Newton because he cannot understand his theorems? I am no expert in painting, but I submit willingly to the judgment of great artists, who, not being experts in exegesis, in theology, and in Kabbalah, would be unreasonable if they did not, in such matters, defer to the opinion of those who have made the transcendental sciences a special study.

This, then, is the foundation of faith. It is the confidence of those who do not know in those who do; and as the formulation of beliefs should borrow from science the grounds of its hypotheses, as we cannot reasonably believe in what science shows to be false, as it is necessary that science should at least admit the possibility of such hypotheses, as the hypotheses of faith are such that science confesses itself permanently unable to transform them into axioms or theorems, it follows that in matters of belief, above all, authority is needful, and that this authority should be collective, hierarchic, and universal; in other words, catholic.

III.—THE TRUE GOD.

THE idea of God is a psychological, real, universal, incontestable fact. Logic or reason, the Logos of supreme power, is God. This reason, this universal logic, illuminates all rational souls. It is the great soul of all souls, the immovable centre round which intelligences gravitate like star-dust. To believe that there does not exist an intelligent cause in being, is the most rash and absurd of creeds —a creed, because it is the negation of the indefinite and undefinable; rash, because it is isolating and desolating; absurd, because it supposes the most complete nothingness in place of the most complete perfection. To believe in the reason of God, and in the God of reason, is to render atheism impossible. Idolaters have made atheists. When Voltaire said that "if God did not exist he must be invented," he felt rather than understood the necessity of God. Does the Deity exist in reality? We do not know; we believe it, but have no certainty; if we were certain we should not believe, we should know it. We hope and desire that He does exist, and this is the cause of our faith, which, thus formulated, is reasonable faith, for it admits the doubt of science; and, in fact, we only believe in what seems probable, but which we cannot ascertain. To think otherwise is to rave, to speak otherwise is to talk like fanatics or *illuminés*.

God, in philosophy, cannot be more than a hypothesis, but it is a hypothesis imposed by good sense and reason, a hypothesis so necessary, that without it all theorems become absurd or doubtful. God is the absolute object of human faith. Is the Universal Being a blind machine which eternally evolves intelligences by chance, or a providential intelligence which directs forces for the amelioration of spirits? The first supposition is repugnant to reason, and, therefore, science and reason should defer to the second.

For the initiates of the Kabbalah, God is the absolute unity which creates and animates numbers, and for them the unity of human intelligence proves the unity of God. Mathematics cannot demonstrate blind fatality, since they are the expression of that exactitude which is the character of the most supreme reason. The man who denies God is as fanatical as he who defines Him with assumed infallibility, and the blasphemy is as great in both. Every definition of God is a receipt of religious empiricism, by whose means superstition will be sooner or later enabled to fabricate a devil. God is commonly defined by enumerating all that He is not, for He is necessarily the most unknown of all beings; He can only be defined in the inverse sense of our experiences, He is all that we are not, He is the infinite opposed to the finite by a contradictory hypothesis. Man realises that he is made in the image of God when he has conceived the Deity by enlarging to infinity his conception of himself. Understanding God as man the infinite, man says to himself, I am God the finite. He makes God, by analogy, from less to greater. Absolute magical science bids us, nevertheless, and before all things, believe in God, and adore without seeking to define Him, for a God defined is in some sense a finite God. The less we define God, the more are we forced to believe in Him. God is that which we shall be eternally learning to know, and, consequently, that which we shall never know. The greatest of all mysteries is this existence of Him, for whom alone there is no mystery. Containing the infinite, which is essentially incomprehensible, He is Himself the infinitely and eternally insoluble mystery; that is to say, He is in all appearance that pre-eminent absurdity which Tertullian believed in. *Credo quia absurdum.* Necessarily absurd, since reason must for ever renounce attaining it; necessarily credible, since science and reason, far from proving that it does not exist, are absolutely and necessarily forced to permit the belief that it does, and to adore it themselves with closed eyes, for this absurdity is the infinite source of reason.

God, nevertheless, cannot subsist without some supreme and inevitable reason, and it is this reason which is the absolute, it is in this that we should fix our faith, if we seek a substantial base for it. St Thomas has said :—" A thing is not just because God wills it, but God wills it because it is just." If he had logically deduced all the consequences of this beautiful thought, he would have found the philosophers' stone, and instead of being only the Angel of the Schools, he would have been their reformer.

From the idea which men conceive of God, have always proceeded their notions of power, whether spiritual or temporal, and the word which expresses Divinity having been in all ages the formulation of the absolute both in revelation and natural intuition, the meaning which is attached to this word has been invariably the dominant idea of every religion and philosophy, as of all politics and ethics. Divinity, one in its essence, has two essential conditions for the fundamental bases of its being—necessity and liberty. To conceive in God, liberty without necessity is to imagine an omnipotence without rule or reason, it is to enthrone the ideal of tyranny in heaven. Such was the most pernicious error of the Middle Ages in many mystical and enthusiastic minds. To conceive in God necessity without liberty, is to suppose an infinite machine, of which we are, unfortunately for us, the intelligent wheels. To obey or be broken, such would be our eternal doom, and we should be knowingly obeying something which would command without knowing why; unhappy wanderers should we be, shut up in waggons which a terrible locomotive carries at full steam on the road to the abyss. This pantheistic, materialistic, and fatalist doctrine is at once the absurdity and calamity of our century. But the laws of supreme reason *necessitate* and rule *liberty* in God, who is *necessarily* wise and reasonable.

We have said that in the heaven of human conceptions it is humanity that creates God, and men think that God has made them in His likeness because they represent Him in theirs.* But let us now dare to affirm that there exists an immense fact, equally appreciable by faith and by science, a fact which renders God in a certain sense visible on earth, an incontestable fact and one of immense significance; it is the manifestation in the world, from the epoch of the Christian revelation, of a spirit unknown to the ancients, a spirit evidently divine, more positive than science in its works, more magnificently ideal in its aspirations than the highest poetry, a spirit for which it has been necessary to create a new name, wholly unheard of in the sanctuaries of antiquity, and which in religion, both for science and faith, is the expression of the absolute. This word is CHARITY, and the spirit which we speak of is called the *spirit of charity*, which is God in His earthly manifestation. Before charity, faith prostrates itself, and science bows down overcome, for it is evidently something greater than humanity; it is stronger than all passions, it triumphs over suffering and death; it reveals Deity to every heart, and seems already to fill eternity by that realisation of its legitimate hopes which it commences here below. By the spirit of charity Jesus, expiring on the Cross, triumphed over the anguish of the most frightful torments; by the spirit of charity twelve artizans of Galilee conquered the world; it is by charity, in fine, that the folly of the Cross has become the wisdom of nations, because all noble hearts have felt it a more sublime and worthy thing to believe with those who love and who sacrifice themselves, than to doubt with the egotists and slaves of self-indulgence!

* See Note 5.

IV.—THE CHRIST OF GOD.

THE author of this book calls once more on the Oriental Magi to come forward and acknowledge that Divine Master whose cradle they saluted, the supreme initiatior of all the ages.

All His enemies have fallen, all those who condemned Him are dead, those who persecuted Him are asleep for ever, but He is eternally alive. The envious have combined against Him, they have agreed on one single point; the promoters of discord have united to destroy Him, they have crowned themselves kings and proscribed Him; they have become hypocrites and accused Him, judges, and have pronounced His sentence of death; they have become executioners and destroyed Him; they have forced Him to drink hemlock, they have crucified Him, they have stoned Him and burned Him; His ashes they have cast to the wind; then they have grown white with terror, for He is standing erect before them, accusing them by His wounds, and overwhelming them with the radiance of His scars.

They planned His destruction in the manger at Bethlehem, and He is alive in Egypt! They carry Him to a mountain that they may cast him down it; the mob of His murderers surrounds Him, and rejoices already over His inevitable destruction. Is not that He who is dashed to pieces on the crags of the precipice? They grow livid and turn to one another, while He, calm and smiling with compassion, passes through the midst of them and disappears.

Behold another mountain, which they have dyed with His blood! Behold a cross and a sepulchre! Soldiers are guarding His tomb! Madmen, that tomb is empty, and He whom you looked on as dead is walking quietly between two travellers on the road to Emmaus!

Where is He? Whither doth He go? Warn the masters of the world! Tell Cæsar that his power is threatened! By whom? By a pauper who has no stone to lay his head on, by a man of the people condemned to the death of a slave. What insolence or what folly! But it matters not; all the power of the Cæsars is arrayed, cruel edicts proscribe the fugitive, everywhere scaffolds are erected, arenas open swarming with lions and gladiators, torrents of blood are poured out, pyres are lighted, and the Cæsars, who believe they are victorious, dare add another name to those they rehearse on their trophies; then they die, and their own apotheosis dishonours those deities whom they thought to defend. The hatred of the world confounds Jupiter and Nero in a common contempt; temples, which servility has turned into tombs, are demolished above the ashes of the proscribed, and over the *débris* of idols, over the ruins of empires, He only, He whom the Cæsars denounced, whom so many satellites hunted down, so many executioners tortured, He only survives, alone reigns, alone is victorious!

His own disciples, notwithstanding, soon misuse His name. Pride enters the sanctuary, those who should proclaim His resurrection seek to perpetuate His death, that they may feast like the crows on his ever-reviving flesh. Instead of imitating Him in His sacrifice, and shedding their blood for their children in faith, they imprison Him in the Vatican, as on a second Caucasus, and become the vultures of this divine Prometheus. But of what consequence is their evil dream? They can only confine His image; He himself is always free, proceeding from exile into exile, and from conquest to conquest; for, though a man may be thrust into prison, no one can make captive the Word of God. Speech is free, and nothing can suppress it. This living Logos is the sentence of the wicked, and so they seek to destroy it, but it is they only who perish, and the word of truth survives to pass judgment on their memory!

Orpheus may have been destroyed by the bacchantes; Socrates may have quaffed the poisoned draught; Jesus and His apostles may have perished in the utmost tortures; John Hus, Jerome of Prague, and a thousand others, may have been burned; Saint Bartholomew's Day, and the massacres of September may have had in turn their victims; the Russian Emperor has still his Cossacks, Knouts, and the wilds of Siberia at his command; but the spirit of Orpheus, of Socrates, of Jesus, and of the other martyrs will survive for ever their deceased persecutors; it will survive amidst overthrown institutions and perishing dominions, for it is that Divine Spirit, the Spirit of the only Son of God, which St John represents in his Apocalypse, standing in the midst of the seven golden candlesticks, because He is the centre of all lights, holding seven stars in His hand, like the seed of a whole new heaven, and sending down His word on earth under the symbol of a two-edged sword.

When the wise in their discouragement slumber during the night of doubt, the Spirit of Christ is abroad and watching. When the people, weary of the labour which sets them free, rest and fall asleep in their chains, the Spirit of Christ is awake, and it protests. When the blind partisans of sterilised religions prostrate themselves in the dust of ancient temples, and crouch slavishly in a superstitious terror, the Spirit of Christ is erect and praying. When the strong become weak, when virtue is corrupted, when everything bends and sinks down in search of a shameful pasturage, the Spirit of Christ is erect, gazing heavenward, and awaiting the hour of His Father.

The word Christ signifies priest and king pre-eminently. The Christ-initiator of modern times appeared to create new kings and new priests by means of knowledge, and, above all, by charity. Man, being unable to conceive anything superior to his own nature, idealises himself in order to conceive God. Christ, by His sublime thoughts and admirable virtues, has realised this ideal. It is, therefore, in Jesus Christ that we must study God, and as the mediator is also the prototype and model of humanity, it is in Him still that we must study man, considered exclusively from the spiritual point of view. The whole science of spirits is thus summed up in Jesus Christ. Angels and demons are purely hypothetical or legendary beings; let them remain in the region of poetry, they cannot belong to science. Let us content ourselves with men, let us study Jesus Christ, and let us seek God!

The Gospel is the Spirit of Jesus, and this Spirit is divine. That is our profession of faith, plainly formulated, on the divinity of Jesus Christ. "My words are spirit and life," said this sublime initiator, "and here the flesh profiteth nothing." The Gospel is the history of His Spirit; it is not the chronicle of His flesh. Man according to the flesh, God according to the Spirit, He is dead and He is arisen. "If you live by My Spirit," He said to His apostles, "your flesh shall be My flesh, and your blood My blood;" and these pre-eminently spiritual things, materialised through the density of barbarous theologians, have provided us with bleeding hosts and anthropophagus communions. The time has come for us to confound no longer the spirit with the flesh. When the Spirit of Jesus Christ shall be understood, that spirit which the Church invokes and adores under the names of spirit of knowledge, spirit of understanding, spirit of power, spirit of initiative, or of counsel, and, consequently, spirit of liberty, we shall no longer seek oracles from sleep, from catalepsy, from somnambulism, or from table-turning.

Logic or reason, the Logos of supreme power, is God. This reason, this universal logic enlightens all rational souls; it shines in the obscurities of doubt; it pierces, penetrates, rends the darkness of ignorance, and the darkness cannot grasp or imprison it. This reason speaks by the mouth of sages, it is synthetized in a single man, who, for this cause, has been called the Logos made flesh, or the great incarnate reason. The miracles of this man were miracles of light. He taught men that true religion is philanthropy; he shewed them that it was not in one city, nor on one mountain, nor in the Temple, that God must be sought, but in spirit and in truth. His doctrines were simple like his life. Love God, that is, spirit and truth, above all things, and thy neighbour as thyself; this, said He, is the whole law.

In this manner He opened the eyes of the blind, caused the deaf to hear and the lame to walk. The wonders which He worked on minds have been recounted in the allegorical form so familiar to the Easterns. His speech became bread which multiplied itself, His moral force a foot which walked upon the waves, and a hand which stilled storms. These legends increased with the ever-growing admiration of His disciples. They are charming stories, similar to those of the Thousand and One Nights, and it was worthy of the barbarous ages which we imagine have passed by, but which have not yet ended, to take these graceful fictions for gross and material realities, to debate anatomically the virginal motherhood of Mary, to institute in the hands of Jesus an invisible and miraculous bakery for the multiplication of loaves, and to see a globular and serous blood flowing from the white and pure hosts which protest against blood, and which announce for ever the completion of sacrifice.

The Gospel is the symbol and expression of the great aspirations of humanity which are as ancient as the world, and the ideal legend of the perfect man. The conception of an incarnation or manifestation of God in man is found in all the dogmas of olden sanctuaries. That the Gospel is a symbolic book, the Apostles have not concealed from us. St John says:—" There are also many other things which Jesus did, which if they were written everyone, the world itself, I think, would not contain the books that should be written." Now, the field of history is limited, but that of allegory is immense, and if St John did not mean to indicate by these words the true scope of the Gospel, he would have uttered an absurdity. But when the Apostles were silent, the evidence spoke sufficiently. Is there any need, for example, to prove to reasonable people that the devil, that is, the fictitious personage who represents evil, did not actually and bodily carry away Jesus to a mountain so high that He could behold from thence all the kingdoms of the world? The Gospel is full of similar histories composed in harmony with the genius of the Hebrews, who always surrounded their secret doctrine with enigmas and images, and in harmony with the genius of Jesus Himself, who, according to the Evangelists, scarcely ever spoke without parables.

Must it be said that under all these allegories the person of the historical Christ disappears and is destroyed? Must we think, with Dupuis and Volney, that the personal and human existence of Jesus is as doubtful as that of Osiris, as fabulous as that of the Indian Chrishna, who was also the son of a virgin? Can any one have the temerity to affirm it when Jesus Christ is still living in His works, still present in His spirit, which has already changed, and will certainly transfigure, the whole face of the earth? The existence of Homer has been doubted, but of what Homer? Of the commentators, perhaps, but does this mean that the Iliad and the Odyssey have no existence? Have these divine poems composed themselves? And is it not far from these doubtless admirable works to the living poem of Christianity, to that Iliad of martyrs, wherein gods combat and are overcome by women and children, to that Odyssey of the Church which after so many storms and persecutions arrives, a sublime mendicant, at the threshold of the palace of the Cæsars, launches with victorious arm the javelins which transfix the hearts of her enemies, and takes her seat upon the throne of the world?

The spirit of Jesus exists far more certainly and far more

evidently than the genius of Homer. But this spirit is one of abnegation and sacrifice, for which reason it is divine. The less a man seeks, the more does he find himself. The greater his self-abandonment is, the better he deserves the adoption of heaven. The more he forgets himself, the more will he be remembered. Such, in a few words, are the great secrets of the omnipotence of Christianity, and Jesus, who gave these precepts, has also set the example. The man has passed into the symbol, and it is thus that He has become God. The Gospel tells us that He led His disciples up to a high mountain apart, and was transfigured before them. His face shone like the sun, and His garments became white as snow, that is to say, the man was obliterated in the light of the new revelation, and tradition, completing the legend later on, says that Jesus, when ascending to heaven, left nothing of Himself on earth but His Spirit spread abroad, in all the Church, and the ineffaceable imprint of His feet on the summit of the mountain.

The Gospel is Jesus transfigured; it is the epic of His admirable intelligence, and the wonders of His ethics represented by the most affecting images. Not a word of this book must be expunged, not a letter added, for it is the divine testament of the man who has annihilated Himself for us. Therein let us seek lights for faith and not documents for history, consoling beliefs and not scientific probabilities. When the ancient eastern sculptors represented their deities, they gave them hybrid and monstrous forms to make it known to all that the gods were not men. In the same way the Evangelists by sowing their narrative with facts materially impossible, or formally contradictory, have meant to convey to us that they were not writing a simple history, but a profound symbol, and that here, as in all sacred writings, the letter which kills is a veil of the spirit which alone vivifies.

But this Gospel symbolism does not disprove, as we have said, the historical existence of Jesus. Rousseau declared that the inventor of such a history would be more astonishing than the hero. We fully endorse the sentiment. The Jesus who in His understanding and heart is sufficiently great to create this admirable legend, is superior to him whom the crowd foolishly adore, or still more foolishly deny; He is truly the ever-living incarnation of the Word of Truth, and we hail Him Son of God in all the splendour and in all the fullness of the term.

Alfred de Vigny has said that legend is frequently more true than history, because legend recounts not acts which are often incomplete and abortive, but the genius itself of great men and great nations. It is pre-eminently to the Gospel that this beautiful thought is applicable, for the Gospel is not merely the narration of what has been, it is the sublime revelation of what is and what always will be. Ever will the Saviour of the world be adored by the kings of intelligence, represented by the Magi; ever will He multiply the eucharistic bread, to nourish and comfort our souls; ever, when we invoke Him in the night and the tempest, will He come to us walking on the waters, ever will He stretch forth His hand and make us pass over the crests of the billows; ever will He cure our distempers and give back light to our eyes; ever will He appear to His faithful luminous and transfigured upon Tabor, interpreting the law of Moses and moderating the zeal of Elias.

The miracles of the Eternal are eternal. To admit the symbolism of the Gospel miracles is to intensify their light, is to proclaim their universality and perpetuity. No, these things have by no means passed away, as it is said, they endure eternally. The things which pass away are accidents that pass, the things which divine genius reveals by symbolism are immutable truths.

V.—Mysteries of the Logos.

THAT intelligent power which acts in the universal movement of things we denominate the WORD or LOGOS in a transcendental and absolute manner. It is the initiative of God which can never be ineffectual and can never be arrested before it has attained its end. With God, to speak is to create, and even among men such should be the purport of speech, for true speech is the seed of actions. A projection of intelligence and will can never be barren unless it be an abuse or profanation of its original dignity. This is why the Saviour of men demands a severe reckoning not only for all errant thoughts and thoughts without a legitimate object, but also for idle words, that is, words which have no corresponding action or consequence. A pleasantry, a drollery which causes diversion and laughter is not an idle word.

Jesus, says the Gospel, was powerful in works and in words—the works before the speech—thus He established and proved His right to teach. Jesus began to act and to speak, says another evangelist, and frequently in the primitive language of Holy Scripture an action is called *verbum*. Moreover, in every tongue that which expresses both being and doing is called the VERB, and there is no verb which cannot be supplemented by the verb *to act* through a change in construction. "In the beginning was the Word," says St John. In what beginning? In the first, the absolute *principium* which is before all else—in this beginning—was the Word, that is, action. This is philosophically incontestable, since the first principle, origin, or cause, all which terms are also included in the scope of the word *principium*, is necessarily the first mover. The Logos is not an abstraction, it is the most positive principle in the world, since it proves itself incessantly in deeds. Speech may occasionally be sterile, as in the harvest we find some empty ears of corn, but the Logos is never unfruitful—it is full and productive speech, which its hearers accomplish always, though often without understanding, and seldom without having resisted it. Doctrines most talked of are not those which succeed most. Christianity was a mystery still when the Cæsars were conscious of being ousted by the Christian Logos. A system admired by the world and applauded by the crowd can never be more than a brilliant assemblage of barren verbosity; a system to which humanity, so to speak, submits in spite of itself is A LOGOS.

When a will modifies the world, there is a Logos speaking.

The Word manifested by life is realisation or incarnation. The life of the Word accomplishing its cyclic movement is adaptation or redemption. Do you wish to know the true religion? Seek that which realises most in the divine order, that which humanises God and deifies man, which incarnates the Logos by making Deity visible and tangible to the most ignorant, that, finally, whose doctrine is suitable to all and can be adapted to all; the religion which is hierarchic and cyclical, which has allegories and images for children, a sublime philosophy for grown men, and high hopes and sweet consolations for the old. The Word is the reason of belief, and therein also is the expression of that faith which verifies science.

In the human order, things are as our interior Logos makes them. To believe one's self happy is to be happy; what we esteem grows precious in the ratio of our esteem, and it is thus that magic may be said to change the nature of things. The Word creates forms, which react in their turn on the Word to modify and complete it. Every utterance of truth is the beginning of an act of justice. The question is sometimes asked whether man may not occasionally be driven into evil. Yes, when his judgment is false and his Logos consequently unjust, but we are as responsible for a false judgment as we are for a bad action. What falsifies judgment is the unjust vanity of egotism. The unjust word, not able to realise itself by creation, is realised by destruction. It must destroy or die. If it rested inactive, it would be the greatest of disorders, a permanent blasphemy against truth.

The beauty of speech is a ˙radiation of truth; a true utterance is always beautiful, and a beautiful utterance is invariably true. This is the reason that artistic works are always holy when they are beautiful. What does it signify to me if Anacreon celebrate Bathyllus, provided that I listen in his verses to that divine harmony which is the eternal hymn of beauty? Poetry is pure like the sun; it spreads its veil of light over the errors of humanity. Woe to him who would strip off that veil to investigate deformities! A statue of Nero or Heliogabalus executed like the masterpieces of Phidias would be an absolutely beautiful and absolutely good work. Scandalous statues are statues ill-executed, and bad books are books ill-conceived or ill-written.

Every Logos of beauty is a word of truth, a light formulated in speech, for light is· the instrument of the Word, the shining caligraphy of God on the great book of the night. But in order that the most brilliant splendour may be produced and become visible, it requires a shadow; and in order to the efficacy of creative speech, it has need of contradiction, it must experience denial, derision, and—what is more cruel than either—indifference and oblivion. The grain which is sown in the earth must die before it can germinate. The Logos which affirms and the voice which denies must intermarry, and then practical truth and real progressive speech will issue from their union. Therefore, never let contradiction discourage men of enterprise. A plough is required for the earth, but the earth resists because it is in labour; it defends itself, like all virgins; it conceives and brings forth slowly, like all mothers. Ye, therefore, who seek to sow a new plant in the field of intelligence, understand and respect the bashful resistance of limited experience and reluctant reason. When a new Logos comes into the world it needs bonds and swaddling-clothes; genius has brought it forth, but experience must nourish it. Fear not when it is unbound and apparently perishes; oblivion for it is a healthful repose, and contradictions are its cultivation. When a sun evolves in infinity, it creates or attracts planets; a single spark of developed light is the promise of a universe to space.

All magic is in a word, and this word, Kabbalistically pronounced, is stronger than the powers of heaven, earth, and hell. Nature is commanded with the name of Jod he vau he; the kingdoms are conquered in the name of Adonaï, and the occult forces which comprise the empire of Hermes are all obedient to him who can pronounce, according to science, the incommunicable name of Agla. To pronounce these great names of the Kabbalah according to science, we must do so with full understanding, with a will unchecked by anything, with an activity which nothing can rebuff. In magic, to have said is to have done; the word begins with letters and ends with acts. We do not will anything really except when we will it with our whole hearts—even to the point of destroying our most cherished affections for the sake of it—and with all our strength—even to staking health, fortune, and life on it. It is by absolute self-devotion that faith is constituted and proved. But the man who is armed with such a faith will move mountains.

Plato was the first to proclaim the divinity of the Word, that is, of speech, and he seems to have foreseen the near incarnation of this Logos on earth (for Jesus is the Word incarnate); he announces the passion and death of the perfect just man, condemned by the iniquity of the world. But this sublime philosophy of the Logos was not his invention, it belongs to the pure Kabbalah, and Plato derived it therefrom.

VI. The True Religion.

RELIGION exists in humanity as in love, and it is one like love. Like that also, it exists or does not exist in such or such soul, but, received or denied, it is in humanity; it is, therefore, in life, it is in nature, it is incontestable before science and even before reason. The true religion is that which has always existed, which does, and ever will exist. It alone can be called one, infallible, indefectible, and truly catholic, that is, universal. This religion, of which all others have been successively the veils and shadows, superstitions imitated or borrowed, and false reflections, is that which proves the actual by the actual, truth by reason, reason by evidence and common-sense. It is that which demonstrates by realities the cogency of hypotheses, and which forbids reasoning on hypotheses independently and outside of realities. It is that, whose basis is the dogma of universal analogies, but which never confounds the things of knowledge with those of faith. It can never be *de fide* that two and one make more or less than three, that, in physics, that which is contained is greater than that which contains it, that a solid body, as such, can act like a fluid or a gaseous body—that a human being, for example, can pass through a closed door without dematerialisation or opening. To assert such a thing is to speak like a child or a madman; but it is no less insane to define the unknown and to reason from hypotheses to hypotheses up to the *a priori* denial of evidence for the affirmation of precipitate suppositions. The wise man affirms what he knows, and does not believe in what he is ignorant of, except in conformity with the reasonable and known necessities of hypotheses.

But this rational religion cannot be that of the multitude, for which fables, mysteries, definite hopes, and fears materially induced, are necessary. It is for this reason that the priesthood has been established in the world.

The religion of the Kabbalists is the religion of religions. It is at once wholly hypotheses and wholly certitude, for it proceeds from the known to the unknown by analogy. The Kabbalist recognises religion as a need of humanity, and his prayer can be united to that of all men to direct it by illustrations from science and reason, and to lead it to orthodoxy. If Mary be spoken of, he will reverence that realisation of all that is divine in the dreams of innocence, and all that is adorable in the holy folly of every mother's heart. It is not he who will refuse flowers to decorate the altars of the mother of God, or white banners for her chapels, or even tears for her ingenuous legends! It is not he who will deride the new-born God weeping in the manger, or the bruised victim of Calvary; he repeats, nevertheless, from the bottom of his heart, with the sages of Israel and the faithful believers of Islam, "There is no God but God!" which means for an initiate of the true science, "There is but one Being, and that is Being!" But all that is expedient and touching in beliefs, but the splendour of rituals, the pomp of divine creations, the grace of prayers, the magic of heavenly hopes—are not these the lustre of moral life in all its youth and beauty? If anything could alienate the true initiate from public prayers and temples, if anything could raise his disgust or indignation against all religious forms whatsoever, it is the manifested incredulity of priests or people, want of dignity in the ceremonies of the cultus, the profanation, in a word, of holy things. God is really present when recollected souls and feeling hearts adore Him; He is sensibly and terribly absent when spoken of without light or enthusiasm, that is without intelligence or love.

But so far as sentiments are concerned, association multiplies these by the reunion of those who share them, so that all are electrified by the enthusiasm of all, and ideas produce forms, while forms in their turn reflect and reproduce ideas. These great laws of nature, observed by the ancient Magi, made them see the necessity of a public worship, single, obligatory, hierarchic, and symbolic, like religion in its entirety, splendid as truth, rich and varied as nature, starry as the sky, full of fragrance like earth, of that cultus, in a word, which was later on established by Moses, realised in all its glory by Solomon, and which once more transfigured abides at this day in the great metropolis of St Peter at Rome. Humanity has really never had but one religion and one worship. This universal light has had its uncertain reflections and its shadows, but ever after the night of error we behold it reappear one and pure like the sun.

The magnificence of the cultus is the life of religion, and if Christ chose poor ministers, His sovereign divinity did not wish for poor altars. Protestants have failed to understand that the ritual is an instruction, and that a sordid or despicable god must not be created in the imagination of the multitude. The English, who lavish so much wealth on their own dwelling-places, and who affect to prize the Bible so highly, if they remembered the unparalleled pomp of Solomon's Temple, would find their own churches exceedingly cold and bare. But what withers their cultus is the dryness of their own hearts; and with a cultus devoid of magic, dazzlement, and pathos, how can their hearts be ever informed with life?

Forms of worship are essentially magical. They operate of themselves the religious work, that is, the creative exaltation of the intuitions of faith and visions, whether celestial or infernal. According to their greater or lesser morality, they are a medicine or a poison to the mind. Religions devoid of ceremonies are cold and inefficacious. Protestantism can, therefore, produce only a rare and isolated enthusiasm, being a negation rather than a religious affirmation. It possesses neither the key of prophecies, nor the source of inspirations, nor the rod of miracles. It is incapable of creating God, and will, therefore, never make great saints, which shows how much those people deceive themselves who imagine rational religions, religions devoid of mysteries, mythology, and sacrifices. Mythologies are the fantastic realisations of the religious dogma; superstitions are the sorcery of mistaken piety; but even mythologies and superstitions are more efficacious to the human will than a purely speculative philosophy, exclusive of all exterior observances.

Religion is the magical creation of a fantastic world made sensible by faith. It is the apparent realisation of ultra-rational hypotheses; it is the satisfaction of a craving common to women, children, and all who resemble them. If the Catholic religion be sick of any complaint, it is of having made too many concessions to the reason of the eighteenth century, and it survives only by the remnant of its intolerance. Those who seek to humanise it seek to destroy it, and of this it is fully aware. Should another religion succeed it, it will be inevitably a more unreasonable and, by consequence, a stronger religion, as such. The religious affirmation is the antithesis of the reasonable affirmation, and philosophical harmony results from the analogy of these two contrary things. The Christian who looks on heaven as his true country, walks, morally speaking, with his feet upward and his head downward, and it is thus that heaven becomes a reflection of earth. The union of religion and philosophy must be accomplished by the very fact of their distinction, which permits an alliance between them, as between the two triangles of Solomon's star, as between the sword and sheath, as between the plenum and the void. For this reason the spiritual must be the negative of the temporal, and the royalty of wealth will be always the downfall of sacerdotal power, by destroying the marvellous character of its mission, and exciting the distrust and jealousy of material instincts. For this reason also the temporal power covers itself with ridicule when it interferes with the spiritual, as it will be always suspected of an interested motive. A master is invariably derided who says—"God wills you to obey me." But let a man, truly independent of Cæsar, say to the world—"Obey Cæsar!" and this man will be believed, above all if it be evident that he receives nothing from Cæsar. For the same reason priests cannot marry and remain priests. No one is a prophet in his own home, and jealous wives would demand from their husbands an account of their neighbours' confessions. The ancient Magi were celibates; Pythagoras and Apollonius abstained from women; Paganism itself had its vestals. The abnormal and, in one sense, irrational character of the celibate makes him essentially religious; the world is aware of this, for while it inveighs against the celibacy of the priesthood, it despises wedded priests.

Singular fact! Religion is the most human of all institutions, and philosophy is that which is truly divine in the intellectual life of humanity. Religion is the synthesis of the passions—desire of an infinite good, ambition driven to the delirium of a deific aspiration, despair of a surfeited or unquenchable enjoyment which takes refuge in ecstasy, above all pride—overweening pride—which thinks to humble itself before God, which accuses itself of offending God and disturbing the harmony of the spheres! Philosophy, on the contrary, bold in its doubt, modest in its assurance, believes only in experience, and will owe nothing except to industry. But, as we have already suggested, religion alone and philosophy alone are both erroneous.

At the bottom of the one are ascetical suicide and all the errors of fanaticism, at the bottom of the other the despair of scepticism and the corruption of absolute indifference. Religion and philosophy, like the Eros and Anteros of old mythology, are made to support each other mutually by struggling continually together. The success of Voltaire was necessary to stimulate the pride of Chateaubriand, and without the "Bible Explained" we should never have admired the "Genius of Christianity."

Motion is life, and the law of motion always drives opinion towards extremes, but a proverb says that extremes meet, and the exaggerations of the Comte de Maistre differ little from those of Marat. We are still divided between them, and Fénélon, Vincent of Paul, and Volney are confounded between the two camps in the same estimation and indifference. Men too good and too strong are out of the combat. Truth is set up for competition, but all who attain it are doomed to silence, otherwise the chase would be at an end. "For this," said Christ, "I speak in parables, that seeing they may not see, and hearing they may not understand; otherwise they would be converted and saved."

It is not necessary then that all should be converted, or, to better render it, should turn at the same time from their own way. It is not necessary then that all should be saved, that is, placed by initiation outside the strife of contrary forces. All are called, notwithstanding, but the elect are ever in a minority, that is, the conditions of initiation are such that they can only be fulfilled by a few competitors out of an immense concourse renewing from age to age and continuing till the election and salvation of all.

Neither religion nor philosophy alone make initiates, but the alliance of the two lights united in one only. Then the initiates create at their will both philosophy and religion for the crowd. Fables on one side, rash speculations on the other, between them the science of faith and the faith of science which embrace and join to govern the world. Religion is feminine, and it rules by poetry and love. Scientific progress is male, and it should govern and defend the woman, when needed, by energy and reason. Those who place themselves at Voltaire's extreme and uncompromising standpoint to judge religion must be astonished and indignant to find it still upheld and dominant. In their eyes, as a fact, it is only a degrading

RELIGIOUS AND PHILOSOPHICAL PROBLEMS. 57

series of interested falsehood and imbecile practices, but they judge it as badly as Blessed Margaret Mary Alacoque would judge, if she were still living, the things of progress, science, and liberty. We must always take actualities into account.

Let the rigid puritanism of a celibate philosophy refuse to understand that fables may be told to children, or amiable little falsehoods to soothe them; let it be indignant with nurses and mothers, but Nature will not heed the wrath of the philosopher; a wise man, however, while giving full play to the feminine priesthood, will watch over the choice of fables, will oppose himself to hideous fictions, will deny the existence of the wehr-wolf and of Croquemetaine, and thus will prevent the dawning reason of the child from being enfeebled.

To deceive the people in order to get the better of them, to enslave them and retard their progress, to prevent it even if possible, such is the crime of black magic; to create darkness in order to increase fear, to redouble the obscurity of mysteries, to exact a blind obedience, is the black magic of religions, is the secret of ambitious sacerdotalism, which would substitute the priest for divinity, the temple for religion itself, and observances for virtues. This was the crime of the Magi who all perished in a fatal reaction; it was the crime of the Jewish priests, against whom Jesus protested, and who crucified Jesus.

But to instruct the people progressively by the allegories of dogma and the poetry of mysteries, to ennoble their souls by the grandeur of hope, to win them to wisdom by sublime and ingenious extravagances, is the sacerdotal art in all its purity, is the magic of light, is the Kabbalistic secret of true religion. To avail one's self of blind forces, and to direct them for the construction of the lever of intelligence, is the Great Secret of Magic. To appeal to passions which are the most blind and illimitable in their play, and to subject them to slavish obedience, is to create omnipotence. To place the mind under the dominion of dream, to extend cupidity and fear to infinity, by promises and threats which are thought supernatural, because they are against Nature, to make an army out of the multitude of weak heads and effeminate hearts turned generous through interest or fear, and with this army to achieve the conquest of the world—such is the great sacerdotal dream, and all the secret policy of the pontiffs of black magic. On the contrary, to enlighten the ignorant, to set wills free, to make truth and justice accessible to all, to impose on faith only those hypotheses which are necessary to reason, and thus direct all people to a single, simple, consoling and civilising doctrine, such is divine reality, and it is this which has been published to the world by the Gospel.

But a great misfortune befell Christianity. The betrayal of the mysteries by the false Gnostics—for the Gnostics, that is, *those who knew*, were the initiates of primitive Christianity—caused the Gnosis to be rejected, and alienated the Church from the supreme truths of the Kabbalah, which contain all the secrets of transcendental theology. Thus the people chose the ignorant for their leaders, equality in the sight of faith was proclaimed, the blind became leaders of the blind, great obscurations resulted, great lapses and lamentable scandals. The virtues of the inferior grades being almost impossible in the higher, the chiefs of the priesthood found themselves deficient in the knowledge and the virtues necessary for their elevated dignity. They, therefore, constituted themselves into a caste, to support each other mutually, and attempted to re-establish the old tests, without, however, progressive initiation; so that to subjugate permanently the will of the neophyte, clerical education warps the heart and paralyses the intellect. Thence come all religious abuses, and by consequence those of society. This is why the eloquence of preachers is so cold and inefficacious. How can they cause a law to be loved which they bear themselves like a yoke from their childhood? How can they appeal to hearts whose hearts are sentenced to an eternal silence? The existing priesthood, moreover, makes despairing attempts to maintain the dogmas exposed by the eighteenth century in their previous position. But the veil of Isis cannot be mended, and divinities in patched garments do not inspire confidence. What is needed is a new veil, and popular poetry is already at work on one, for the world is never long without a religion.

The Gnostics were rightly condemned by the Church for divulging the secret doctrines and profaning the mysteries of the Master. Their principles issued from the Kabbalah misunderstood, and they borrowed from the false Kabbalah of India their dreams, which by turns were horrifying and obscene. The Church, therefore, forbade the faithful the study of Kabbalistic science, whose keys should be reserved by the supreme priesthood for itself alone. The false Gnostics thus caused magic to be condemned, but the true science of the Magi is essentially Catholic, because it grounds its entire realisation on the principle of the hierarchy. Now, in the Catholic Church alone is there a serious and absolute hierarchy, and to this we should return as to the sole principle of unity. For this reason, the true adepts have always professed the most profound respect and absolute obedience towards this Church. Henry Khunrath alone was a determined Protestant, but herein he was a German of his period rather than a mystic citizen of the eternal kingdom.

In revealing for the first time to the world the mysteries of magic, we have no wish to revive practices buried beneath the ruins of ancient civilisations, but we proclaim to the humanity of to-day that it also is called to its omnipotent and immortal self-creation by its own works. God has created humanity, but each individual of the race is called to his own self-creation as a moral and consequently immortal being. For ourselves, with all our admiration for the Kabbalah and its secret doctrines which are so full of consolation and hope, we do not think that a new Church can make them the subject of a novel teaching. They belong essentially to occult philosophy, and become condemnable immediately they are divulged.

If we detest with all our heart the crass Pharisaism which has accumulated with the centuries over the pure gold of the sanctuary, we are none the less an partisan of orthodoxy, of authority, and hierarchy; and if our Messianic mission were nothing but a new sectarian departure, if it were not the very foundation of Judaistic science and Christian doctrine, if we did not unreservedly submit to the decision of legitimate authority in all that concerns the bearing and the manner of our instructions, we should have added another dream to those of the Saint-Simoniens and Fourieristes; we should not have recovered true science and eternal truth.

Liberty does not come of itself, it must be seized, says a modern writer; it is the same with science, and this is why the revelation of absolute truth is never of use to the crowd. But at an epoch when the sanctuary is devastated

and in ruins, because its key has been thrown into the
ditch without profit to any one, I have felt myself bound
to pick it up, and I offer it to whomsoever is qualified to
take it; such an one will become in his turn a teacher of
nations and a liberator of the world.

Let the most absolute science, let the highest reasoh,
become once more the patrimony of the leaders of the
people; let the sacerdotal art and the royal art take back
the double sceptre of antique initiations, and the social
world will once more issue from its chaos. Burn the holy
images no longer, demolish the temples no more; temples
and images are necessary for men; but drive the hirelings
from the house of prayer, let the blind be no longer the
leaders of the blind, reconstruct the hierarchy of intelligence
and holiness, and recognise only those who know as the
teachers of those who believe! This book is Catholic, the
magnum opus is a hierarchic and Catholic work, and if our
revelations are calculated to alarm the conscience of the
simple-minded, it is a consolation to think that they will
not read them. We address ourselves to men free from
prejudices, and we have no more wish to flatter irreligion
than fanaticism. But if there be anything in this world
which is essentially unfettered and inviolable, it is belief.
It is our duty by knowledge and persuasion to turn misled
imaginations from what is absurd, but it would invest their
errors with all the dignity and truth of the martyr if we
attempted to threaten or constrain them. So, in religion,
universal and hierarchic orthodoxy, restoration of temples
in all their splendour, re-establishment of all ceremonial
in its primeval pomp, hierarchic teaching of symbolism,
mysteries, miracles, legends for the children, light for the
grown men, who will be far from scandalizing the little
ones in the simplicity of their faith,—such, in religion, is
our whole Utopia; and it is also the desire and the need
of humanity.

VII.—The Reason of Prodigies, or the Devil before Science.

When science and philosophy, reconciled with faith, shall
unite in one all the various symbolisms, then will the
splendours of the ancient worships flourish once more in

the remembrance of men, proclaiming the progression of the human mind in the intuition of the light of God. But of all forms of progress the greatest will be that which, surrendering the keys of nature into the hands of science, shall bind for ever the frightful phantom of Satan, and, by explaining all the exceptional phenomena of the natural world, shall destroy the dominion of superstition and foolish credulity. It is to the accomplishment of this progress that we have consecrated our life, and spent years in the most laborious and difficult researches. We seek to enfranchise the altars by overturning the idols; we desire that the man of understanding should again become the priest and king of nature, and we would preserve, while explaining them, all the images of the universal sanctuary.

For a large number of readers, magic is the science of the devil, as the science of light is the black science. *The devil and science!* It seems that in joining two words so incongruous, the author of this work has revealed beforehand his whole idea. To bring the mystical personification of darkness face to face with light, is not this to destroy the spectre of falsehood by truth? Is it not to disperse the deformed nightmares of the night-time before the brightness of the day? We doubt not that under this impression superficial readers will condemn us unheard. Ill-instructed Christians will think that we are about to sap their fundamental doctrine of ethics by denying hell, while others will inquire what is the use of denouncing those errors which have ceased to deceive anyone. It is important, therefore, that we should state our object clearly, and solidly establish our principles. To the Christians we say first of all: The author of this book is a Christian like you; his faith is that of a Catholic deeply and strongly convinced, therefore his mission is not to deny dogmas, but to combat impiety under one of its most dangerous forms, that of erroneous belief and superstition. He comes to bring forth out of the darkness the black successor of Ahriman, that he may expose in open day his gigantic impotence and formidable misery; he comes to proffer for the solutions of science the antique problem of evil, to dethrone the King of Hades, and abase his head beneath the foot of the Cross. Is not virginal and maternal science, that science of which Mary is the gentle and luminous symbol, predestined also to crush the serpent's head?

To so-called philosophers the author says: Why deny that which you do not understand? Is not the incredulity which asserts itself in the face of the unknown more rash and less consoling than faith? Does the affrighting figure of personified evil make you smile? But moral evil exists, it is a lamentable fact; it reigns in certain souls, it is incarnate in certain men, demons therefore do exist, and the worst of these demons is Satan. Nevertheless, good only is infinite; evil is not so, and for this reason, if God be the eternal object of faith, the devil belongs to science. As a fact, in what Catholic symbol is he mentioned? Would it not be blasphemy to say, "I believe in him"?

I believe in the devil, the most mighty destroyer, disturber of heaven and of earth, and in Antichrist his only son, our persecutor, who will be conceived by an evil spirit, born of a violated virgin, will be glorified, will reign, and will ascend to seat himself on the altar of God, the Father Almighty, from whence he will insult the living and the dead. I believe in the spirit of evil, the synagogue of Satan, the confederacy of the wicked, the perpetuity of sins, the perdition of the flesh and eternal death.

Who will dare to add Amen? Who does not see that the black *Credo* is wholly opposed to the Church's, and that the believer who affirms the one must necessarily deny the other?

The devil is named but not defined in Holy Scripture; Genesis nowhere speaks of a supposed fall of angels, it attributes the sin of the first man to the serpent, the most subtle of the beasts of the field. We know the Christian tradition on this subject, but if this tradition be explainable by one of the greatest and most universal allegories of science, in what way will the solution affect the faith which aspires to God alone and despises the pomps and works of Lucifer?

Lucifer! The Light-Bearer! How strange a name is given to the spirit of darkness! What, is it he who bears light and who blinds weak souls? Yes, doubt it not, for traditions are full of divine revelations and inspirations. " Satan himself transformeth himself into an angel of light," says St Paul. "I have seen Satan fall from heaven like a thunderbolt," says the Saviour of the world. " How art thou fallen from heaven," cries the prophet Isaiah, " bright star who didst herald the morning!" Lucifer is, therefore, a fallen star, a meteor which burns when it no longer illuminates. But is this Lucifer a person or a force? Is it an angel or a lost thunderbolt? Tradition supposes it to be an angel, but does not the Psalmist say, " He makes his angels spirits and his ministers a flaming fire "? The word angel is given in the Bible to all things commissioned of God—messengers or new creations, revealers or scourges, resplendent spirits or dazzling objects. The fiery shafts which the Most High darts from the clouds are the angels of His anger, and this figurative language is familiar to all readers of oriental poetry.

If we define evil as want of rectitude in the being, moral evil as falsehood in acts, as falsehood is crime in speeeh, injustice as the essence of falsehood, the death of moral life, as falsehood is the poison of intelligence, the spirit of evil will then be a spirit of death. Those who hear him are his dupes, whom he poisons, and if the personification of this spirit must be seriously understood, he would himself be absolutely dead and absolutely deceived, that is, the affirmation of his existence implies an evident contradiction. Satan is the personification of all errors, all perversities, and, as a consequence, also all weaknesses. If God may be defined as He who exists necessarily, can we not define His antagonist and enemy as he who necessarily does not exist?

Jesus has said, " The devil is a liar like his father."* Who is the father of the devil? Whosoever gives him a personal existence by living in conformity with his inspirations ; the man who diabolizes himself is the father of the incarnate evil spirit. But there is a rash, impious, monstrous conception, a conception which is traditional, like the pride of the Pharisees, a hybrid creation which has provided the paltry philosophy of the eighteenth century with an apparent argument against the splendours of Christianity. It is the false Lucifer of the heterodox legend; it is that angel proud enough to believe himself God, courageous enough to purchase independence at the price of an eternity of tortures, beautiful enough to be able to adore himself in the flood of divine light, strong enough to reign still in darkness and suffering, and to make a throne of his inextinguishable pyre ; it is the Satan of the heretical and republican Milton ; it is the pseudo-hero of the darksome eternities calumniated by hideousness, disguised in horns and talons which would

* See Note 6.

befit rather his implacable tormentor. It is the diabolical king of evil, as if evil were a kingdom, that devil more intelligent than the men of genius who fear his deceptions, that black light, that darkness which sees, that power which God has not willed and which a mutilated creature could not have created, that prince of anarchy served by a hierarchy of pure spirits, that exile of God who is, like God, everywhere on earth, more visible, more present to the majority, better served than God himself, that conquered one to whom the conqueror gives his children to be eaten, that manufacturer of the sins of the flesh to whom the flesh is nothing, and who can consequently be nothing to the flesh, unless he be a creator and master like God, that immense, realized, personified, eternal falsehood, that death which cannot die, that blasphemy which the Word of God can never silence, that soul-poisoner whom God tolerates in contradiction to His power, or preserves as the Roman emperors preserved Locusta among the instruments of His dominion, that tortured one eyer living to curse his Judge and to withstand Him, since he will never repent.

There is the irreligious phantom which belies religion! Away with this idol which hides our Saviour! Down with the tyrant of falsehood! Down with the black god of the Manichæans! Down with the Ahriman of the old idolaters! Live God alone and His incarnate Logos, Jesus Christ, the Saviour of the world, who beheld Satan precipitated from Heaven! Live Mary the divine mother, who has crushed the head of the infernal serpent! Thus the traditions of the saints and the hearts of all the truly faithful unanimously cry:—To attribute any grandeur whatsoever to the despoiled spirit, is to calumniate divinity; to invest the rebellious spirit with any royalty is to encourage revolt, is to be guilty, at least in thought, of the crime of those who in the Middle Ages were called *sorcerers*. For all the crimes punished formerly by death on the sorcerers of old are real and the greatest of all crimes. They stole fire from heaven, like Prometheus. They bestrode, like Medea, the winged dragons and flying serpent. They poisoned the breatheable air, like the shadow of the manchineel. They profaned holy things, and made even the body of the Saviour subservient to works of destruction and infamy. How is all this possible? Because there exists an agent which is natural and divine, material and spiritual, a universal plastic mediator, a common receptacle of the vibrations of motion and the images of forms, a fluid and a force, which may be called in some way the *Imagination of Nature*. By means of this force all nervous apparatuses secretly communicate together ; thence come sympathy and antipathy, thence dreams, thence are produced the phenomena of second sight and extra-natural vision. This universal agent of Nature's operations is the Od force of the Hebrews and of Baron Reichenbach, it is the Astral Light of the Martinists, and we prefer the latter explanation as more explicit. The existence and possible use of this force is the Great Arcanum of practical magic ; it is the thaumaturgic rod and the key of black magic. The Astral Light magnetizes, heats, lights, touches as with loadstone, attracts, repels, vivifies, destroys, coagulates, separates, breaks, and reunites all things under the impetus of powerful wills. God created it on the first day when He said, "FIAT LUX!" It is in itself a blind force, but can be directed by the leaders of souls, who are spirits of action and energy. This at once explains the whole theory of prodigies and miracles. How, in fact, could both bad and good force Nature to expose her exceptional forces? How could there be both divine and diabolical miracles? How could the reprobate, erring, perverse spirit have in some cases greater power than the spirit of justice, so powerful in its simplicity and wisdom, if we do not assume the existence of an instrument which all can make use of, under certain conditions, on the one side for the greatest good, on the other for the greatest evil?

The magicians of Pharaoh at first performed the same prodigies as Moses ; the instrument they used was, therefore, the same, the influence alone was different, and when they confessed themselves conquered, they proclaimed that for them human power had reached its limits, and that Moses must be possessed of superhuman attributes. Now, this took place in Egypt, mother of magical initiations, in that land where all was occult science and sacred, hierarchic teaching. Notwithstanding, was it more difficult to cause flies to appear than to cause frogs? Certainly not; but the magicians were aware that the fluidic projection by which they fascinated the eyes could not extend beyond certain limits, and that for them already those limits had been surpassed by Moses.

We shall return to the Great Magic Agent at the second division of this work.

SCIENTIFIC AND MAGICAL THEOREMS.

I.—ON NUMBERS AND THEIR VIRTUES.

THE duad is unity reproducing itself to create, and this is why the sacred allegories picture Eve issuing from the very breast of Adam. It is also the number of the Gnosis and the generative number of society and law. One is the cause, two the logos. Unity can only be manifested by means of the duad, for unity itself and the idea of unity already make two. Divinity, which is one in its essence, has two essential conditions as the fundamental basis of its being; these are necessity and liberty. Revelation is the duad—every logos is two-fold and supposes two. The ancients, in their symbols and magical operations, multiplied the signs of the duad, that its law, which is that of equilibrium, might not be forgotten. In their evocations they invariably constructed two altars and immolated two victims, a white and a black one; the operator, holding the sword in one hand and the rod in the other, should have one foot shod and the other bare. But the final hieratic secret of the duad cannot be made known; the reason, according to Hermes Trismegistus, being the stupidity of the vulgar, who would give all the immoral attributes of blind fatality to the sacred necessities of science. We must restrain the multitude, he tells us, by the fear of the unknown, and Christ also has said, "Cast not your pearls before swine, lest trampling them under foot they turn and rend you." The tree of the knowledge of good and evil, whose fruits are deadly, is the image of this hieratic secret of the duad, which, as a fact, if divulged, would not fail to be misconstrued, and the impious negation of that Supreme Arbiter who is the ethical cause of being would be commonly deduced therefrom. It is, therefore, in the essence of things that the revelation of this secret inflicts the

SCIENTIFIC AND MAGICAL THEOREMS. 67

penalty of death, and it is not for all this the Great Arcanum of Magic; but the secret of the duad leads to that of the tetrad, or, more properly, precedes it and is resolved by the triad, which contains the word of the sphinxitic enigma as it should have been discovered in order to save the life, expiate the involuntary crime, and establish the kingdom of Œdipus. The reproduction of unity by the duad necessarily brings us to the conception and dogma of the triad, as we have said, and we pass on to this great number, which is the plenitude and perfect logos of unity.

The triad is the universal dogma, and the basis of magical doctrine. It supposes an intelligent cause, a cause which speaks, and an expressed principle. The Absolute, which is revealed in speech, endows the latter with a significance equivalent to itself, and itself creates a third in the comprehension of this speech. Grammar invariably attributes three persons to the logos or verb. The first is that which speaks, the second that which is spoken to, and the third that which is spoken of. The Infinite Prince in creating speaks of Himself to Himself. Such is the explanation of the Triad and the origin of the dogma of the Trinity. The magical dogma is also triple. That which is above resembles or equals that which is below. Thus two similar things, and the word which expresses their similitude, make three. In magic we have origin, realisation, adaptation; in alchemy, azoth, incorporation, transmutation; in theology, God, incarnation, redemption; in the human soul, thought, love, and action; in the family, father, mother, and child. The triad is the supreme end and expression of love; two seek each other only to become three. *

There are three intelligible worlds which correspond one to another by hierarchic analogy:—The natural or physical world, the spiritual or metaphysical world, and the divine or religious world. From these come the hierarchy of spirits, who are divided into three orders, and in these are always subdivided by the triad. All these revelations are logical deductions from the first mathematical notions of being and number. Unity to become active must reproduce itself. An indivisible, immovable, and unfruitful principle would be a dead and incomprehensible unity. Were God one only, He would be neither Father nor Crea-

* See Note 7.

ior; were He two, there would be antagonism and division n the Infinite; He is triple, therefore, for the creation of the infinite multitude of existences and numbers from Himself and in His image. Thus He is really one in His essence and triple in our conception, by which we also behold Him triple in Himself, and one in our understanding and our love. This is a mystery for the believer, and a logical necessity for the initiate of the absolute and true sciences. The triad issues of itself from the duad; the movement which produces two begets also three. Three is the key of numbers, for it is the first numeral synthesis; it is the triangle of geometry, the first complete and enclosed figure, the generator of an indefinite number of similar or dissimilar triangles.

In the Tetragram, the triad, or He, taken at the beginning of the word, signifies divine copulation, taken at the end it signifies womanhood and maternity. Eve bears a name of three letters, but the primitive Adam is expressed by the single letter Jod, so that the Tetragram Jehovah, יהוה, should be pronounced Java. This leads us to the great and supreme mystery of magic, represented by the tetrad.

The triad resumed by unity, and with the conception of unity, added to that of the triad, produces the first square and perfect number, source of all numerical combinations, and origin of all forms—the quaternary or tetrad, the *tetractys* of Pythagoras, whence all is derived. This number produces the cross and square in geometry. All that exists, whether of good or evil, light or darkness, exists and is revealed by the tetrad. The affirmation of unity supposes the number four, unless this affirmation revolves in unity itself, as in a vicious circle. So the triad, as we have already observed, is explained by the duad and resolved by the tetrad, which is the squared unity of even numbers, and the quadrangular basis of the cube, the unity of construction, solidity, and measure.

The perfect word, that which is adequate to the thought which it expresses, always virtually contains or supposes a tetrad—the idea, with its three necessary and correlative forms, then the image of the thing signified or expressed, with the three terms of the judgment which qualifies it.

A height, a breadth, which the height geometrically divides into two, and a depth separated from the height by

SCIENTIFIC AND MAGICAL THEOREMS. 69

the intersection of the breadth, such is the natural tetrad composed of two lines which are crossed. There are also four movements in Nature produced by two forces which sustain each other by their tendency in a contrary direction. Now the law which rules bodies is analogous and proportional to that which governs minds, and that which governs minds is the manifestation even of God's secret, the mystery of creation. Visible nature reveals the unseen, and secondary causes are proportional and analogous to the manifestations of the First Cause, which is thus always revealed by the cross, that key of the mysteries of Egypt and India, the Tau of the patriarchs, the divine sign of Osiris, the Stauros of the Gnostics, the keystone of the Temple, the symbol of occult masonry, the central point of the junction of the right angles of two infinite triangles.

The Great Magic Agent is revealed by four phenomena, and the secret of its direction is the supreme arcanum of the sublime and ineffable tetrad, which we shall treat of under the title of the Great Magic Arcanum. By the addition of unity to the quaternary, we obtain together and separately the ideas of divine synthesis and analysis, and attain the number five, which is that of the soul represented by the quintessence resulting from the equilibrium of the four magical elements, and the sublime and mysterious Pentagram. The quinary is the religious number, for it is that of Deity joined to that of the woman. In the Tarot this number is represented by the high priest or spiritual autocrat, symbol of human will, that supreme power whose direction decides our eternal destinies.

The number six, or the senary, is that of initiation by trial: it is the number of equilibrium, and the hieroglyphic of the knowledge of good and evil. The number seven, or the septenary, is the sacred number of all theogonies and all symbols, because it is composed of the triad and tetrad. It represents magic power in its whole scope; it is the mind assisted by all elementary forces, it is the soul served by nature, it is the *sanctum regnum* of the *Claviculæ Salomonis*, the great biblical number, the key of the creation of Moses, and the symbol of all religion. The number eight is that of reaction and equilibriating justice. The tetrad joined to the tetrad represents form equilibriating form, creation issuing from creation, the eternal balance of existence; seven being the number of the repose of God, the unity which succeeds represents man, who toils and co-operates with nature in the work of creation. The number nine is that of initiation and prophecy, because, being composed of three times three, it represents the divine idea and the absolute philosophy of numbers, for which reason Apollonius says that the mysteries of the number nine must never be revealed; for this reason, also, it is called the absolute number. The number ten is the number of matter, whose special sign is zero; in the Kabbalistic tree of the Sephiroth, ten represents Malchut, or exterior and material substance. The sin of Adam was materialism, and the fruit which he plucks from the tree represents the flesh isolated from the spirit, zero divided from unity.

II.—Theory of Will-Power.

Axiom 1.

NOTHING can resist the will of man when he knows what is true and wills what is good.

Axiom 2.

To will evil is to will death. A perverse will is the beginning of suicide.

Axiom 3.

To will what is good with violence is to will evil, for violence produces disorder and disorder produces evil.

Axiom 4.

We can and should accept evil as the means to good, but we must never will it or practise it, otherwise we should demolish with one hand what we erect with the other. A good intention never justifies bad means; when it submits to them it corrects them, and condemns them while it makes use of them.

Axiom 5.

To earn the right to possess permanently, we must will long and patiently.

SCIENTIFIC AND MAGICAL THEOREMS. 71

Axiom 6.

To pass one's life in willing what it is impossible to retain for ever is to abdicate life and accept the eternity of death.

Axiom 7.

The more numerous the obstacles which are surmounted by the will, the stronger the will becomes. It is for this reason that Christ has exalted poverty and suffering.

Axiom 8.

When the will is devoted to what is absurd, it is reprimanded by eternal reason.

Axiom 9.

The will of the just man is the will of God Himself, and it is the law of Nature.

Axiom 10.

The understanding perceives through the medium of the will. If the will be healthy, the sight is accurate. God said—"Let there be light!" and the light was. The will says—"Let the world be such as I wish to behold it!" and the intelligence perceives it as the will has determined. This is the meaning of the word *Amen* which confirms the acts of faith.

Axiom 11.

When we produce phantoms we give birth to vampires, and must nourish these children of nightmare with our own blood and life, with our own intelligence and reason, and still we shall never satiate them.

Axiom 12.

To affirm and will what ought to be is to create; to affirm and will what should not be is to destroy.

Axiom 13.

Light is an electric fire, which is placed by man at the disposition of the will; it illuminates those who know how to make use of it, and burns those who abuse it.

Axiom 14.

The empire of the world is the empire of light.

Axiom 15.

Great minds with wills badly equilibrated are like comets, which are abortive suns.

Axiom 16.

To do nothing is as fatal as to commit evil, and it is more cowardly. Sloth is the most unpardonable of the deadly sins.

Axiom 17.

To suffer is to labour. A great misfortune properly endured is a progress accomplished. Those who suffer much live more truly than those who undergo no trials.

Axiom 18.

The voluntary death of self-devotion is not a suicide— it is the apotheosis of free-will.

Axiom 19.

Fear is only indolence of will; and for this reason public opinion brands the coward.

Axiom 20.

An iron chain is less difficult to burst than a chain of flowers.

Axiom 21.

Succeed in not fearing the lion, and the lion will be afraid of you. Say to suffering—"I will that thou shalt become a pleasure," and it will prove such, and more even than a pleasure, for it will be a blessing.

Axiom 22.

Before deciding that a man is happy or otherwise, seek to ascertain the bent of his will. Tiberius died daily at Caprea, while Jesus proved His immortality, and even His divinity, upon Calvary and the Cross.

III.—THE TRANSLUCID.

EVERY individuality is indefinitely perfectible, since the moral order is analogous to the physical, and in the physical order we cannot conceive a point which is unable to dilate and enlarge itself, and radiate in a philosophically infinite circle. What can be said of the entire soul must be also predicated of each faculty thereof. The understanding and the will of man are instruments whose power and capacity are incalculable. But the will and understanding have an auxiliary and instrument in a faculty which is too little understood, and whose omnipotence exclusively belongs to the domain of magic. I speak of the imagination which Kabbalists call the Diaphane or the Translucent.

Imagination is actually as the eye of the soul, and it is therein that forms are delineated and preserved; by its means we behold the reflections of the invisible world, it is the mirror of visions and the apparatus of magical life. Thereby we cure diseases, modify the seasons, ward off death from the living, and resuscitate those who are dead, because this faculty exalts the will and gives it power over the universal agent.

Imagination determines the form of the child in its mother's womb, it gives wings to contagion, and points the weapons of warfare. Are you exposed in a battle? Believe yourself as invulnerable as Achilles, and you will be so, says Paracelsus. Fear attracts bullets, and courage turns them back on their path. It is well known that persons whose limbs have been amputated complain often of pains in the members which they no longer possess. Paracelsus operated on living blood by medically treating the result of a bleeding; he cured headaches at a distance by operating on locks of hair; he forestalled, by the science of the imaginary unity and solidarity of the whole with its parts, all the theories, or rather all the experiences, of our most famous mesmerists. So were his cures miraculous, and he deserved that there should be added to his name of Philip Theophrastus Bombastes that of Aureolus Paracelsus, with the further epithet of divine!

Imagination is the instrument of the adaptation of the

Logos. In its application to reason it is genius, for reason, like genius, is one amidst the complexity of its operations.

The soul can perceive by itself and without the mediation of the corporeal organs, by means of its sensibility and its Diaphane, the objects, whether spiritual or corporeal, which exist in the universe. There is no invisible world, there are merely various degrees in the perfection of organs. The body is the rude representation and perishable coating of the soul. Spiritual and corporeal are words which merely express degrees in the tenuity or density of substance. What we call the imagination in man is the inherent faculty of the soul to assimilate to itself the images and reflections contained in the living light, or Great Magic Agent, which we shall subsequently treat of. These images and reflections are revelations when science intervenes to disclose to us their Logos or light. The man of genius differs from the dreamer and the madman in this only, that his creations are analogous to truth, while those of madmen and dreamers are lost reflections and wandering images. Thus for the sage to imagine is to see, as for the magician to speak is to create.

Demons, souls, and the rest, can therefore be really and truly beheld by means of the imagination; but the imagination of the adept is diaphanous, whilst that of the uninitiated is opaque. The light of truth traverses the one as through a crystal window, and is refracted in the other as in a vitreous mass full of scoriæ and foreign matter.

What contributes most to the errors of the vulgar and the extravagances of the insane are the reflections of depraved imaginations in one another. But the seer knows with an absolute knowledge that the things he imagines are true, and experience invariably confirms his visions. The means by which such lucidity can be acquired will be described in due course.

IV.—The Great Magic Agent, or The Mysteries of the Astral Light.

There exists a force in Nature which is far more powerful than steam, and by whose means a single man, who can master it and knows how to direct it, might throw the world into

SCIENTIFIC AND MAGICAL THEOREMS. 75

confusion and transform its face. This force was known to the ancients; it consists of a universal agent whose supreme law is equilibrium, and whose direction depends immediately on the Great Arcanum of transcendent magic. By the direction of this agent we can change the very order of the seasons, produce in the night the phenomena of day, correspond instantaneously from one end of the earth to the other, discern, like Apollonius, what is taking place at the Antipodes, heal or hurt at a distance, and endow human speech with a universal reverberation and success. This agent, which barely manifests under the uncertainties of the art of Mesmer and his followers, is precisely what the mediæval adepts called the first matter of the *magnum opus*. The Gnostics made it the burning body of the Holy Ghost, and this it was which was adored in the secret rites of the Sabbath or the Temple under the symbolic figure of Baphomet, or of the Androgyne Goat of Mendes.

This ambiant and all-penetrating fluid, this ray detached from the sun's splendour, and fixed by the weight of the atmosphere and by the power of central attraction, this body of the Holy Ghost, which we call the Astral Light and the Universal Agent, this electro-magnetic ether, this vital and luminous caloric is represented on ancient monuments by the girdle of Isis, which twines in a love-knot round two poles, by the bull-headed serpent, by the serpent with the head of a goat or dog, in the ancient theogonies, and by the serpent devouring its own tail, emblem of prudence and of Saturn. It is the winged dragon of Médea, the double serpent of the caduceus, and the tempter of Genesis; but it is also the brazen snake of Moses, encircling the Tau, that is, the generative lingam; it is the Hyle of the Gnostics, and the double tail which forms the legs of the solar cock of Abraxos. Lastly, it is the devil of exoteric dogmatism, and is really the blind force which souls must conquer, in order to detach themselves from the chains of earth; for if their will should not free them from its fatal attraction, they will be absorbed in the current by the same power which first produced them, and will return to the central and eternal fire.

The Great Magic Agent is revealed by four kinds of phenomena, and has been subjected to the uncertain manipulations of profane science under four names—caloric, light, electricity, magnetism. These four imponderable fluids are, therefore, the diverse manifestations of one and the same force, which is that substance created by God before all else, when He said, "Let there be Light!" and there was light. Everything which exists has been evolved from it, and it preserves and reproduces all forms.

The Great Magic Agent is the fourth emanation of the life-principle, of which the sun is the third form (see the initiates of the Alexandrian School and the dogma of Hermes Trismegistus), for the day-star is only the reflection and material shadow of the sun of truth which illuminates the intellectual world, and which itself is but a gleam borrowed from the Absolute. The sun of the divine world is the infinite, spiritual, and uncreated light; this light is, so to speak, verbalised in the philosophical world, and becomes the focus of souls and of truth; then it is incorporated and changed into visible light in the sun of the third world, the central sun of suns, of which the fixed stars are the immortal sparks.

Thus the world's eye, as the ancients called it,* is the mirage of the reflection of God, and the soul of the earth is a permanent glance from the sun which the earth conceives and conserves by impregnation. The moon concurs in this impregnation of the earth by projecting towards her a solar image during the night, so that Hermes was correct when he said, speaking of the Great Agent, "The sun is its sire, the moon its mother." Then he adds, "The wind has borne it in its belly," for the atmosphere is the recipient, and, as it were, the crucible of the solar rays, by means of which there is produced that living image of the sun which penetrates, vivifies, and fructifies the entire earth, determining all that is brought forth on its surface by its continual currents and emanations, which are analogous to those of the sun itself.

The Astral Light, being the instrument of life, naturally settles at living centres; it cleaves to the kernel of planets as to the heart of man (and by the heart we understand, in magic, the great sympathetic), but it identifies itself with the individual life of the existence which it animates. Thus it is terrestrial in its connection with the earth, and exclusively human in its connection with man. We are, in fact, saturated with this light and continually project it to make room for more; by this projection the personal

* See Note 8.

atmosphere of Swedenborg is created. The settlement and polarisation of light about a centre produces a living being; it attracts all the matter necessary to perfect and preserve it, but it is not the immortal spirit, as the Indian hierophants, and every school of Goëtic magic, have imagined. It is by no means the body of the *protoplastes*, as was supposed by the Theurgists of the Alexandrian sect; it is the first physical manifestation of the Divine Breath. God creates it eternally, and man, in the image of the Deity, modifies and apparently multiplies it in the reproduction of his species.

The primordial light, vehicle of all ideas, is the mother of every form, and transmits them from emanation to emanation, merely diminished or altered in proportion to the density of the mediums. All forms correspond to ideas, and there is no idea without its proper and individual form. Secondary forms are reflections which return to the focus of emanated light. The forms of objects being a modification of light remain where the reflection relegates them. Thus the Astral Light or terrestrial fluid is saturated with images or reflections of all kinds, which can be evoked by our soul and submitted to its Diaphane, as the Kabbalists call it; this is the *modus operandi* of all visions. What we call imagination is simply the inherent faculty of the soul to assimilate the images and reflections contained in the living light which is the Great Magnetic Agent. It is by means of this light that statical visionaries place themselves in communication with all the worlds, as so frequently occurred to Emanuel Swedenborg, who was, nevertheless, not perfectly lucid, since he could not distinguish between direct rays and reflections. Clairvoyants merely evoke the images of places in the Astral Light; they do not actually travel to those places, and they can see nothing but what exists in this light, which is latent, and acting on the nerves, enables somnambulists to perceive by means of the nerves only and without the help of radiating light.

The Book of Consciences which, according to the Christian doctrine, will be opened on the Last Day, is nothing more than the Astral Light, in which are preserved the impressions of every Logos, that is, every action and every form. There are no solitary acts and there are no secret acts; all that we truly will, that is, all that we confirm by our deeds, is written in the Astral Light. It is in this light that the forms of those no longer on earth are evoked, and by its means are accomplished the contested but veritable mysteries of necromancy. When summoned by an illuminated reason, these forms are harmoniously manifested; summoned by folly, they appear disorderly and monstrous.

The Astral Light was the instrument of the omnipotence of Adam, and afterwards became that of his punishment, being disturbed by his fall, which intermingled an impure reflection with those primitive images that composed, for his still maiden imagination, the book of universal knowledge. The fall of Adam, according to the initiators, was an erotic intoxication which rendered his generation the slave of the fatal light; all amorous passion is a whirlpool of this light which draws us towards the abyss of death.

The Great Magic Agent, when subordinated to a blind mechanism and proceeding from centres automatically produced, is a dead light which works mathematically according to given impulses or necessary laws. On the contrary, the human light is only fatal to the ignorant; it is subject to the intelligence, subordinate to the imagination, and dependent on the will of man. It is a compound agent, natural and divine, material and spiritual; ever active, ever rich in *sève*, ever alive with ravishing dreams and luxurious images; it may be called, in a certain sense, the Imagination of Nature, as we have said. Blind in itself, and submitted to every will either for good or evil, this *circulus* always renewing an unconquerable life which causes vertigo in the imprudent, this universal seducer, conveys light, yet propagates darkness; it may be named equally Lucifer and Lucifuge; it is a serpent but also a nimbus; it is of the nature of fire, but it may belong equally to the torments of hell and to the incense-offerings dedicated to Heaven. To master it, we must, like the predestined woman, set a foot upon its head.

The Astral Light is the key of all dominion, the secret of all powers, the universal glass of visions, the bond of sympathies, the source of love, prophecy, and glory. To know how to master this agent so as to profit by and to direct its currents is to accomplish the *magnum opus*, to be master of the world, and *the depositary even of the power of God.* The absolute secret of this direction has been possessed by certain men, and can yet be recovered—it is the

Great Magic Arcanum; it depends on an incommunicable axiom, and on an instrument which is the great and unique Athanor of the Hermetists of the highest grade. All magic science consists in the knowledge of this secret. To know it and dare to make use of it is human omnipotence; to reveal it to an outsider is to lose it; to reveal it to a disciple is to abdicate in favour of such disciple, who, from that moment, has the right of life and death over his initiator, and will certainly kill him for fear of dying himself. (This has nothing in common with deeds defined as murder in criminal legislation; practical philosophy, the basis of those laws, denies the facts of bewitchment and occult influences.)

The Great Magic Agent has four properties—to dissolve, to consolidate, to quicken, and to moderate. These four properties, directed by the will of man, can modify all phases of Nature. In making use of the term fluid in connection with this force, we employ a received expression, but we are far from deciding that the latent light is a fluid; everything, on the contrary, leads us to prefer the system of vibrations, in the explanation of this phenomenal force. However this may be, the coming synthesis of chemistry will probably lead our physicists to a knowledge of the universal agent, and then what will hinder them from determining the strength, number, and direction of its magnets? A complete revolution in science will follow, and we shall return to the transcendent magic of the Chaldeans.

V.—MAGICAL EQUILIBRIUM.

THE universe is balanced by two forces which maintain it in equilibrium, those of attraction and repulsion. These forces exist alike in physics, philosophy, and religion. They produce equilibrium in physics, criticism in philosophy, and progressive revelation in religion. The ancients represented this mystery by the strife of Eros and Anteros, by the struggle of Jacob with an angel, and by the equilibrium of the golden mountain, which the gods on one side and the demons on the other hold balanced by means of the symbolic serpent of India. It is also represented by the two cherubim of the ark, by the two sphinxes of the chariot of Osiris, and by the two seraphim, one black and one white. Its scientific reality is proved by the phenomena of polarity, and by the universal law of sympathies and antipathies.

In the soul of the world, which is the universal solar agent, there is a current of desire and a current of wrath. All motion and life consist in the extreme tension of these two forces or principles of universal equilibrium, which are not contrary, though in apparent opposition, for supreme wisdom opposes them one to another. The Great Magic Agent subsists then by two forces, one of attraction and one of repulsion, whence Hermes says that it is continually ascending and descending. By this two-fold force all is created and preserved. It is at once substance and motion; the inherent power which originates its movement is called magnetism, and the movement itself is an uprolling and unrolling which are consecutive and unlimited, or rather simultaneous and perpetual in spiral lines of opposite motions, which never come into collision. It is the same movement as that of the sun which draws and repels at one time all the planets of his system.

Equilibrium is the result then of two forces, but if these were absolutely and permanently equal, equilibrium would be immobility, and consequently the negation of life. Movement is the result of alternated preponderance. The impulse given to one plate of a balance determines necessarily the motion of the other. Thus contraries act upon contraries by correspondence and analogical connection throughout all Nature. All life is composed of an aspiration and a respiration; creation is the supposition of a shadow to serve as a limit to light, of a vacancy to serve as space for the plenitude of being, of a fecundated passive principle to support and realise the potency of the active and generative principle. All nature is bi-sexual, and the movement which produces the phenomena of death and life is a continual generation. To understand the law of this exchange, to know the alternative or simultaneous proportion of all opposite forces, is to possess the first principles of the Great Magic Secret, which constitutes true human divinity. Scientifically, the diverse manifestations of universal motion may be appreciated by electrical or magnetic phenomena. Electrical phenomena above all reveal materially and positively the affinities and antipathies of certain substances. The union of copper with zinc, the

SCIENTIFIC AND MAGICAL THEOREMS.

action of all metals in the galvanic pile, are perpetual and irrecusable revelations. Let the physicists seek and find out, the Kabbalists will explain the discoveries of science. Equilibrium is order, and motion is progress; the science of equilibrium and of motion is the absolute science of Nature; it conducted the initiates to that of universal gravitation about the centres of life, heat, and light. By its means man can produce and direct natural phenomena through a continual self-elevation towards a higher and more perfect intelligence than his own.

The alternate use of contrary forces—warmth after cold, mildness after severity, affection after anger—is the secret of perpetual motion and the prolongation of power; this is instinctively felt by coquettes, who cause their lovers to pass from hope to fear and from joy to sorrow. To operate always on the same side and in the same manner is to overload one side of a balance, and the complete destruction of equilibrium will soon result. Everlasting caressing quickly engenders satiety, disgust, and antipathy, in the same way that constant coldness or severity alienates and discourages affection in the end. In alchemy a fire which is continually the same, and burns without intermission, calcines the first matter and sometimes causes the hermetic vase to explode; it is necessary to substitute at regular intervals the heat of lime or mineral manure for that of fire. And thus in magic the works of wrath or rigour must be tempered by operations of benevolence and love, while if the Magus should keep his will fixed always in the same direction and in the same manner, great fatigue and a species of moral impotence would very soon result. The Magus should not, therefore, live exclusively in his laboratory, amidst his Athanor, his elixirs, and his pantacles. However consuming may be the glance of that Circe called occult power, we must be able to point to it when necessary the sword of Ulysses, and remove in time from our lips the chalice which she offers us. A magical operation should invariably be followed by a rest of equal duration and an analogous diversion, but one contrary in its object. To strive continually against Nature, so that we may overcome and dominate it, is to endanger both life and reason. Paracelsus ventured to do so, but even in the midst of such a struggle he made use of equilibrated forces, and opposed the intoxication of wine to that of the intellect; then he conquered drunkenness by bodily fatigue, and bodily fatigue by fresh intellectual occupation. So was Paracelsus a man of miracles and inspiration, but he consumed his life in this devouring activity, or rather he rapidly wore out and rent its envelope. Men like Paracelsus can use and abuse without fear of anything—they well know that they can no more die than they can grow old.

Nothing disposes us for joy more than grief, and nothing is nearer to grief than joy. So an ignorant operator is astonished that he invariably reaches other results than he proposed himself, because he knows neither how to cross nor alternate his action ; he wishes to bewitch his enemy, and he makes himself ill and wretched. He wishes to make himself loved, and he consumes himself with desire for women who scorn him ; he wishes to manufacture gold, and he exhausts his last resources; his torment is eternally that of Tantalus, the water always flowing back when he stoops down to drink.

To dominate the circle of the Astral Light, we must succeed in getting beyond the reach of its currents, that is, we must attain self-isolation. The torrent of universal life, which is represented in religious dogmas by the expiatory fire of hell, is the instrument of initiation, the enemy to be overcome. It is this which sends to our evocations and to Goëtic conjurations so many larvæ and phantoms ; therein are preserved all those forms whose fantastic and fortuitous assemblage peoples our nightmares with such abominable monsters. To allow one's self to be carried away by the drift of this whirling stream, is to fall into abysses of madness more frightful than those of death ; but to chase the shadows of this chaos and endow them with the perfect forms of thought, is to be a man of genius, is to create, is to have triumphed over hell! The Astral Light directs the instincts of animals, and does battle with the intelligence of man, which it tends to pervert by the luxury of its reflections and the deception of its images; its fatal and necessary action is rendered still more calamitous by the elementary spirits and souls in pain, whose restless wills seek sympathies in our weaknesses, and tempt us less with the intention of destroying us than with the desire to win friends.

To accomplish isolation from the Astral Light, it is insufficient to clothe ourselves in the woollen mantle of

Apollonius;* we must, above all, impose absolute serenity on mind and heart; we must issue from the realm of passions and be convinced of our perseverance in the spontaneous acts of an inflexible will; as fatality is an inevitable concatenation of effects and causes in a given order, so the will is the governing faculty of intelligent forces for the conciliation of the liberty of individuals with the necessity of things. A lucid will can act on the mass of the Astral Light, and, with the concurrence of other wills, which it absorbs and draws after it, can set great and irresistible currents into motion. Every intelligent projection of the will is a projection of the human fluid or light.

To dispose of the Astral Light, we must also understand its two-fold vibration, and the balance of forces which constitutes magical equilibrium—the *senary* of the Kabbalah. This equipoise, considered in its originating cause, is the will of God, in man it is liberty, in matter mathematical equilibrium. Equilibrium produces stability and permanence, liberty gives birth to immortality in man, and the will of God puts in operation the laws of eternal reason. Omnipotence is the most absolute liberty. Now absolute liberty cannot exist without perfect equilibrium. Magical equilibrium is, therefore, one of the first conditions of success in the operations of the science, and must be sought even in occult chemistry by the combination of opposing forces without their neutralisation. By magical equilibrium is explained the grand and primeval mystery of the existence and relative necessity of evil. Moral equilibrium is the concurrence of science and faith, distinct in their forces and joined in their action, to provide the mind and heart of man with that rule which is reason.

V.—The Magic Chain.

THE *magnum opus* in practical magic, after the education of the will and the personal creation of the Magus, is the formation of the magnetic chain, and this secret is truly that of the priesthood and the monarchy. To form the magic chain is to establish a magnetic current of ideas

* See Note 9.

which produces faith and carries away a large number of wills in a given circle of active manifestations. The magnetic current becomes stronger in proportion to the extent of the chain, which, when well-formed, is like a whirlpool drawing in and absorbing all. The chain may be established in three manners—by signs, speech, and contact. It may be established by signs in causing some particular gesture or symbol to be adopted as the representation of a force. Thus all Christians communicate together by the sign of the Cross, masons by that of the square beneath a sun, magicians by the microcosm, made with the five extended fingers. Signs, once accredited and propagated, acquire force of themselves. The sight and imitation of the sign of the Cross sufficed in the first centuries to make proselytes to Christianity. The miraculous medal, as it is called, still performs in our own days a large number of conversions by the same magnetic law. The vision and illumination of the young Jew Alphonse de Ratisbonne is the most remarkable fact of this kind. Imagination is creative not only within us but without us, by means of our fluidic projections.

The magic chain formed by speech was represented among the ancients by the chains of gold which issue from the mouth of Hermes. Nothing equals the electricity of eloquence. Speech creates intelligence of the highest kind in the most grossly-natured crowds. Even those who are out of earshot comprehend by excitement, and are borne away with the mass. Peter the Hermit shook Europe by crying, "God wills it!" One single word of the Emperor electrified his army and made France invincible. Proudhon destroyed socialism with his famous paradox, "Property is robbery!" A chance word is often sufficient to overthrow an authority. Voltaire knew this well—Voltaire, who upset the world by sarcasms. So he who feared neither pope, prince, parliament, nor Bastile, stood in dread of a pun. We are not far from accomplishing the desires of those men whose maxims we repeat.

The third method of establishing the magnetic chain is by contact. Among persons who often come into communication, the head of the current is soon revealed, and the strongest will does not fail to absorb the rest; the direct and positive contact of hand to hand completes the harmony of inclinations, and it is for this reason that it is a mark of sympathy and intimacy. Children, who are prompted instinctively by nature, form the magnetic chain when playing at Prisoner's Base. Then gaiety circulates and laughter ripples. Round tables are also more favourable to festivity than those of any other form. The great circle-dance of the Sabbath, which terminated the mysterious meetings of the adepts of the Middle Ages, was a magic chain, which united all in the same wishes and in the same acts; they formed it by standing back to back and holding hands with the face outside the circle, in imitation of those antique sacred dances which are still to be seen represented on the basrelievos of old temples. The electric fur of the lynx, panther, and even the domestic cat were attached to their clothes in imitation of the ancient bacchantes. Thence came the tradition that the miscreants at the Sabbath each carried a cat hung from the girdle, and danced in this guise.

The trough of Mesmer was an imperfect magic chain; several great circles of illuminati, in different northern countries, possess more powerful ones. Even the society of certain Catholic priests, celebrated for their occult power and their unpopularity, is established after the plan, and in observance of the conditions, of the most powerful magic chains, and this is the secret of their strength, which they attribute solely to the grace or will of God, a commonplace and simple solution of all the problems of powerful influence and enthusiasm.

All enthusiasm propagated in a society by a series of communications and definitive practices produces a magnetic current, and is conserved or augmented by that current, whose tendency is to carry away, and often excite beyond measure, weak and impressionable people, nervous organisations, and temperaments disposed to hysteria or hallucinations. Such persons soon become powerful vehicles of magical force, and energetically project the Astral Light in the direction of the current itself; to oppose oneself under such circumstances to the manifestations of this force would be in some sense to struggle with fatality. When the young Pharisee Saül, or Schôl, threw himself, with all the fanaticism and obstinacy of a sectarian, across the stream of aggressive Christianity, he placed himself unconsciously at the mercy of the power he thought to combat, and so was overwhelmed by a formidable magnetic explosion, whose effect was doubtless rendered more instantaneous through the combined help of a cerebral congestion and a sunstroke. We know a certain sect of enthusiasts which people at a distance laugh at, but in which they enroll themselves when they come near it, even to assail it. We may go further: magic circles and magnetic currents are established of themselves, and affect those whom they subject to their action according to fatal laws. Each one of us is drawn into a circle of affinities which is his world, and by whose influence he is controlled. Great circles often make great men, and reciprocally. There are no misunderstood geniuses, there are *eccentric* men, and the word seems to have been coined by an adept. The man of eccentric genius is one who seeks to form for himself a circle by striving against the central force of attraction inherent in established chains and currents. His destiny is to be broken in the struggle, or to succeed. What is the two-fold condition of success in such a case? A fixed central standpoint and a persevering circular action of initiative. The man of genius is one who has discovered a real law, and who, consequently, possesses an invincible force of action and direction. He may die in his work, but that which he wishes will be accomplished in spite of his death, and frequently even on account of it, for death is a veritable assumption of genius. "When I shall be lifted above the earth," said the greatest of the Initiators, "I will draw all men unto me."

The law of magnetic currents is that of the movement of the Astral Light. This movement is always double, and reproduces itself in a contrary sense. A great action invariably produces an equal reaction, and the secret of gigantic success is always in the foreknowledge of such reactions. So Chateaubriand, inspired with disgust for the revolutionary saturnalia, foresaw and prepared the immense success of his "Genius of Christianity." To oppose one's self to a current whose revolution is beginning is to seek to be broken thereby, as was the great and unfortunate emperor Julian; to oppose one's self to a current which has described the circle of its action is to take the lead of a contrary current. The great man is he who comes at the right time and knows how to innovate seasonably. Voltaire, in the age of the Apostles, would have found no echo for his speech, and would perhaps have been nothing more

SCIENTIFIC AND MAGICAL THEOREMS.

than an ingenious parasite of the feasts of Trimalcyon. At the epoch we live in, all is ready for a fresh outburst of evangelical enthusiasm and Christian disinterestedness, precisely because of the universal disillusion, egotistic positivism, and public cynicism of the grossest interests. The success of certain books, and the mystical tendencies of minds are no unequivocal symptoms of this general disposition. We restore churches and build new ones, the more do we feel the want of faith, the more do we hope for faith; the entire world expects once again its Messiah, and he will not tarry in coming. Let there be found, for example, a man highly placed by rank or by fortune—a pope, a king, or even a Jewish millionaire, and let this man publicly and solemnly sacrifice all his material interests for the good of humanity, let him become the saviour of the poor, the propagator, and even the victim, of doctrines of self-devotion and charity, and he will draw round him a vast concourse, and a complete moral revolution will be produced in the world. But the high position of the person is before all things requisite, for in these times of meanness and charlatanism, every Logos coming from the lower ranks is suspected of ambition and interested trickery. Ye, then, who are nothing, and who own nothing, hope not to be apostles or messiahs. If ye have faith, and would act in accordance with your faith, find first the means of action, which are the influence of rank and the prestige of fortune. Formerly, gold was made by science; to-day, science must be reconstructed by gold. That which was volatile has been fixed, and now we must fix the volatile; in other words, we have materialised spirit, and now we must spiritualise matter. The sublimest utterance is unheeded now-a-days, unless it is produced under the guarantee of some name. What is the value of a manuscript? It is that of the author's signature at the publisher's. The firm of Alexandre Dumas et Cie, for example, represents one of the literary guarantees of our epoch; but it is of account only for its habitual productions, romances. Let Dumas invent a magnificent Utopia, or find an admirable solution of the religious problem, and his discoveries will only be considered the entertaining caprices of a novelist, and no one will take them seriously, despite the European celebrity of the Panurge of modern literature. We are in the age of acquired positions; everyone's worth is appraised in proportion to his social and commercial position. Unlimited liberty of speech has produced such a conflict of talk that no one asks any longer what is said, but who has said it. To those therefore who ask me: "If you possess the secret of great successes and of the force which can change the world, why do you not use it?" I reply: "This knowledge has come to me too late for myself, and I have spent in its acquisition the time and the resources which would, perhaps, have enabled me to make use of it. Illustrious men, rich men, great ones of this world, who are unsatisfied by what you possess, and who are conscious in your hearts of a nobler and larger aspiration, will you become the fathers of the new world, the kings of a renovated civilisation? A poor and obscure scholar has found the lever of Archimedes, and he offers it to you for the good of humanity alone, asking nothing whatever in return for it.

The printing press is an admirable instrument for the formation of the magic chain by the extension of speech. As a fact, no book is lost; writings find their way infallibly where they are meant to go, and the aspirations of thought attract speech. We have proved this a hundred times during the course of our initiation into magic; the rarest books have presented themselves to us without seeking as soon as they became indispensable to us. It is thus that we have discovered intact that universal science which numerous scholars have believed to be buried under several consecutive cataclysms; it is thus that we have entered into that great magic chain which began with Hermes or Enoch, and will only end with the world. So we have been able to evoke and bring before us the spirits of Apollonius, of Plotinus, of Synesius, of Paracelsus, of Cardan, of Cornelius Agrippa, and of many others more or less famous, but too religiously distinguished to be lightly named. We continue their sublime work, which others will take in hand after us, but to whom will it be given to complete it?

VI.—The Great Magical Arcanum.

THERE exists a principle and a rigorous formula which is the Great Arcanum. Let the wise man seek it not, for he has already found it; let the vulgar seek for ever, they will never attain it. This universal arcanum, the crowning and eternal secret of supreme initiation, is represented in the Tarot by a young and naked girl who only touches the earth with one foot, who holds a magnetic rod in each hand, and who appears to be running inside a crown which is supported by an angel, an eagle, a bull, and a lion. This figure is fundamentally analogous to the cherub of Ezekiel, and to the Indian symbol of Addhanari, corresponding to the Ado-naï of the prophet just mentioned. The comprehension of this figure is the key of all the occult sciences. The Great Magical Secret is represented by the lamp and poniard of Psyche, the apple of Eve, the fire stolen from heaven by Prometheus, the burning sceptre of Lucifer, but also by the Cross of the Redeemer. It is the ring of Gyges, the Golden Fleece, the allegorical picture of Cebes, which is its most audacious demonstration.* It is also represented by the lingam, for the Great Arcanum is connected with the mystery of universal generation, and by the serpent pierced with an arrow, which formed the seal of Cagliostro.

This secret is the kinghood of the sage, the crown of the initiate, whom it renders the master of gold and of light, which are fundamentally the same thing. By its means he solves the problem of the quadrature of the circle, directs the perpetual motion, and possesses the philosopher's stone. This great and indicible arcanum was never referred to even among adepts; it is essentially unexplainable in its nature, and is destruction both to those who divine it and those who reveal it. It is that terrible secret of life and death which is expressed in the Bible by those formidable and symbolical words of the serpent, which was itself symbolical, I. NEQUAQUAM MORIEMINI, II. SED ERITIS, III. SICUT DII, IV. SCIENTES BONUM ET MALUM. It is

* See Note 10.

the secret of Nature herself, of the generation of angels and worlds, and of God's omnipotence. It is the absolute knowledge of good and evil. "In the day that ye eat thereof, . . . ye shall be as gods," says the serpent. " Ye shall not eat of it, neither shall ye touch it, lest ye die," replies Divine Wisdom. Thus good and evil flourish on the same tree and issue from the same root. Good personified is God; evil personified is the Devil. To know the secret or science of God is to be God; to know the secret or science of the Devil is to be the devil. To seek to be at once Deity and Satan is to concentrate in ourselves the most absolute contradiction, the most unchangeably opposing forces; it is to strive to contain an infinite antagonism, it is to partake of poison which would quench suns and consume worlds, to assume the garment of Dejanira, and to doom ourselves to the swiftest and most terrible of deaths. Woe to him who wishes to know too much! If excessive and imprudent knowledge do not kill him, it will drive him mad. To eat of the fruit of the tree of knowledge of good and evil is to associate and assimilate good and evil one with another; it is to cover the radiant face of Osiris with the mask of Typhon, it is to raise the veil of Isis, and profane the sanctuary. The tree of knowledge has become the tree of death. For six thousand years the martyrs of Sinai have laboured and perished at the foot of this tree, that it might become once more the tree of life.

The Great Magical Secret is the secret of the direction of the Great Magical Agent; it depends on an incommunicable axiom, and on an instrument which is the supreme and unique Athanor of the Hermetists of the highest grade. When the adepts in alchemy speak of a great and unique Athanor which all can make use of, which is within the grasp of all, and which all men possess without knowing it, they allude to the philosophic and moral alchemy.* A strong and resolute will can arrive in a short time at absolute independence, and we all possess the Athanor, the chemical instrument, by which that which is ethereal is separated from that which is gross, and the fixed is divided from the volatile. This instrument, complete as the world, and precise as mathematics themselves, is designated by

* See Note 11.

the sages under the emblem of the Pentagram, the body of man and the absolute sign of human intelligence. The incommunicable axiom is kabbalistically enclosed in the four letters of the Tetragram, arranged in the following manner:

in the letters of the words AZOTH and INRI kabbalistically written, and in the monogram of Christ as it is embroidered on the labarum, and which Postel the Kabbalist interprets by the word Rota, from which the adepts have formed their Tarot.

To understand the alternative or simultaneous proportion of the forces which produce equilibrium is to possess the first principle of the Great Magic Arcanum, which constitutes true human divinity. It is the science of fire; everywhere we find the enchanter who pierces the lion and leads the serpents—the lion is the celestial fire, and the serpents are the electrical and magnetic currents of the earth. It is to this great secret of the Magi that we must refer all the marvels of Hermetic Magic, whose traditions still declare that the arcanum of the *magnum opus* consists in the government of fire.

It is forbidden to us to speak more plainly, but we complete our revelation by the following tables, whose union will reveal to the neophyte the Grand Secret of Secrets.

Theory of the G∴A∴ { To live in union with { The Providence of God. Light. Motion. Creation.

MYSTERIES OF MAGIC.

THEORY OF THE G∴ A∴

- **To know** — The truth of mystery, of life, in the spirit made visible by universal gravitation.
- **To will** — Justice by sacrifice to harmony and the progress of liberty.
- **To dare** — In the ratio of blind faith on the equilibrium of modifiable substance by balancing.
- **To be silent** — on the reality of dogma, action of the soul which is perfectible by antagonism.

God is
- Charity, which is above all Being.
- Mystery, which is beyond all Science.
- Sacrifice, which transcends all Justice.
- Providence, which is above all Reason.
- Perfection, which is beyond all Conception.

Satan is Hatred and
- The void in opposition to all being.
- Ignorance in opposition to all knowledge.
- Absurdity in opposition to all reason.
- Despotism in opposition to all justice.
- Falsehood in opposition to all truth.

The Divine Paraclete is — Genius — Enthusiasm — Harmony — Beauty — Rectitude.
- Intelligence, in its correspondence with Being.
- Progress, in its correspondence with knowledge.
- Love, in its correspondence with Justice.
- Wisdom, in its correspondence with Reason.
- Light, in its correspondence with Truth.

SCIENTIFIC AND MAGICAL THEOREMS. 93

The Four Characters of the Absolute.

The identity of the idea with existence is—Truth.
The identity of knowledge with existence is—Reality.
The identity of the Logos with existence is—Reason.
The identity of action with existence is—Justice.

THE DOCTRINE OF SPIRITUAL ESSENCES; OR, KABBALISTIC PNEUMATICS,

WITH THE MYSTERIES OF EVOCATION, NECROMANCY, AND BLACK MAGIC.

INTRODUCTION.

THE great and indispensable hypothesis of the destinies of futurity has been elaborated and directed from deduction to deduction by the seers of the ancient world. Kabbalistic pneumatics are a veritable science, which proceeds methodically and exactly, ascending from the known to the unknown by the way of the least questionable analogies, because facts make known laws to it, and on these laws it substantially lays the foundation of its ever-prudent hypotheses. It is, therefore, Kabbalistic Pneumatics which we are about to unveil to our readers, and we shall add an analysis of Isaac de Loria's profound treatise on the circular progression of the soul—*De Revolutionibus Animarum*—and that of the Sepher Druschim by the same doctor. We shall bring forth from the shadows of occultism these amazing books, whose key the modern world no longer possesses, and by so doing we believe ourselves to deserve well at the hands of science and reason.

By the help of these powerful lights we shall explain the strange phenomena which scientific smatterers find it so convenient to deny, but which overwhelm them, nevertheless, by their evidence. Yes, images tremble, statues weep, the consecrated bread is injected with blood, a hand may issue from the wall to alarm the impious festivities of Balthazar by a menacing inscription. The author of this book does not fear to acknowledge that he has himself had the most astounding and formidable visions; he has seen and touched angels and demons, as Maximus of Ephesus, and Schrœpfer of Leipsic, caused them to be seen and

THE DOCTRINE OF SPIRITUAL ESSENCES. 95

touched by their adepts. He has been enabled to compare the hallucinations of the waking state with the illusions of dreams, and from all this he has concluded that reason directing faith and faith supporting reason are the only true lights of our souls, and that all else is but a vain exertion of the mind, aberration of the senses, and delirium of thought. He is not, therefore, writing what is of mere conjecture, he boldly affirms what he knows.

It was after he had descended from gulf to gulf and from horror to horror to the bottom of the seventh circle of the abyss, it was after he had traversed in all its length the darkness of the dolorous city, that Dante returning, and taking the devil, so to speak, against the grain, rose consoled and victorious towards the light. We have performed the same voyage, and we present ourselves before the world with tranquillity on our countenance and peace in our heart. We come calmly to assure mankind that hell and the devil, the hopeless gulf, the chimæras, satyrs, ghouls, personified vices, three-headed dragons, and all the rest of the dismal phantasmagoria are a nightmare of madness, but that God only living, alone real, alone everywhere present, fills and leaves no void, fills, I repeat, the unlimited immensity with the splendours and eternal consolations of the sovereign reason.

The things which are above this life can be conjectured in two ways, either by the calculations of analogy, or by the intuitions of extasis, in other words, by reason or by folly. The sages of Judea chose reason, and have left us, in books which are generally ignored, their magnificent hypotheses. On reading them, it becomes evident at once that our creeds have come out of them like inexplicable fragments, and that the apparent absurdity of our dogmas disappears when they are completed by the splendid reasoning of these masters. One is astonished, moreover, to find all the most beautiful and grandiose aspirations of our modern poetry philosophically realised and completed therein. Goëthe studied the Kabbalah, and the epic of "Faust" has issued from the doctrines of the Sohar. Swedenborg, Saint Simon, and Fourier seem to have glimpsed the divine Kabbalistic synthesis through the darkness and hallucinations of a more or less extraordinary nightmare, according to the different characters of these dreamers. In reality, this synthesis is the most perfect and beautiful thing which can be attained to by human understanding.

The books which treat of spirits according to the Kabbalists are the *Pneumatica Kabbalistica*, found in the *Kabbala Denudata* of Baron de Rosenroth; the *Liber de Revolutionibus Animarum*, by Isaac de Loria; the *Sepher Druschim*, the book of Moscheh of Cordova, and some others less celebrated. We shall give here not merely their abridgement, but, in a certain way, their quintessence.

I.—IMMORTALITY.

ON matters which our science cannot in this life ascertain we can only reason by hypotheses. Humanity can know nothing of the superhuman, since the superhuman is that which exceeds the scope of humanity; the phenomena of decomposition which accompany death seem to protest in the name of science against this innate necessity of faith in another life which has brought forth so many dreams. Science, nevertheless, must take account of the want, for Nature, which does nothing without object, does not endow beings with desires that are not to be satisfied. Science, therefore, though necessarily ignorant of, must, at least, suppose the existence of things which are beyond her, and cannot put in question the continuity of life after the phenomenon called death, since no abrupt interruption is found in the *magnum opus* of Nature, which, according to the philosophy of Hermes, never proceeds by jumps.

The immortality of the soul is kabbalistically proved by analogy, which is the one doctrine of the universal religion, as it is the key of science and the inviolable law of Nature. Death, in fact, can no more be an absolute end than birth is a real beginning. What we call death is birth into a new life. Nature does not unmake what she has made in the order of the necessary progressions of existence, and she cannot belie her own fundamental laws. Birth proves the pre-existence of the human individual, since nothing is produced from nothing, and death proves immortality, as being can no more cease to be than nothing can cease to be nothing. Being and nonentity are two absolutely irreconcilable ideas, with this difference, that the wholly negative notion of nothingness is derived from the very conception of existence, whose antithesis cannot even be understood as an absolute negation, whilst the idea of being cannot even be compared with that of nonentity, to say nothing of being derived from it.

Pythagoras believed above all things in the immortality of the soul and the eternity of life. The perpetual succession of the seasons, of days and nights, of sleeping and waking, sufficiently explained to him the phenomenon of death. The individual immortality of the human soul consisted according to him in the persistence of memory. The Bible seems to give this idea a divine sanction when it says in the Book of Psalms—*In memoria æterna erit justus.*

According to Synesius, the dream state proves the individuality and immateriality of the soul, which, in this condition, creates itself a heaven, a landscape, palaces blazing with light, or darksome caverns, according to its affections or desires.

But the immortality of the soul, being one of the most consoling doctrines of religion, must be reserved for the aspirations of faith, and, consequently, never will be proved by facts accessible to the examination of science. Who indeed can be assured beforehand of his eternal destiny? Life here below appears to be a school in which we learn how to live. It is to be concluded from this that we shall live elsewhere. This is a dramatic farce which precedes the grand mystery.*

II.—The Astral Body.

WE have spoken at length of a substance diffused through infinity, the single substance which is heaven and earth, that is, volatilised or fixed, according to its different degrees of polarisation. This substance is what Hermes Trismegistus calls the Great Telesma. When it produces refulgence, it is called light. This is the substance which God created before all things, when He said, Let there be

* See Note 12.

light! It is at once matter and motion, a fluid and a perpetual vibration. The inherent force which puts it in motion is called magnetism. In the infinite this unique substance is ether or etherised light. In the stars, which it renders magnetic, it becomes astral light. In organised creatures, it is magnetic light or fluid. In man, it forms the astral body, or plastic mediator, which is a magnet that draws or repels the Astral Light under the pressure of the will.

The Astral Light transformed at the moment of conception into human light, is the first envelope of the soul, and it is by combining with the most subtil fluids that it forms this etherised body or sidereal phantom which Paracelsus speaks of in his philosophy of intuition—*Philosophia Sagax*—and which reproduces with the greatest facility the forms corresponding to ideas. It is the mirror of imagination, and is nourished by the Astral Light precisely as the physical body is nourished by the produce of the earth. During sleep it absorbs this light by immersion, and in the waking state by a kind of more or less slow respiration. When the phenomena of natural somnambulism occur, the plastic mediator is overcharged with ill-digested nourishment. The will then, though weighted by the torpor of sleep, instinctively drives the mediator towards the organs to disengage it, and a reaction occurs which is in some way mechanical, and which equilibriates the light of the mediator by the motion of the body. For this reason it is dangerous to awake somnambulists with a start, for the congested mediator may then suddenly retire towards the common reservoir and wholly abandon the organism, which thereby will be separated from the soul, and death will result. The somnambulistic state is, therefore, extremely dangerous, because, by blending the phenomena of the waking state with those of sleep, it constitutes a sort of great digression between the two worlds. The soul agitating the springs of individual life, while plunged in the universal life, experiences an inexpressible happiness, and would willingly loosen the nervous cords which keep it suspended above the current. The situation is identical in every species of extasis; if the will should plunge therein by an impassioned effort, or even abandon itself entirely therein, the subject may remain idiotic or paralysed, and may even die.

THE DOCTRINE OF SPIRITUAL ESSENCES. 99

Hallucinations and visions result from injuries inflicted on the plastic mediator, and from its local paralysis. Sometimes it ceases to radiate, and substitutes, as it were, condensed images for the realities revealed by light; sometimes its radiation is excessive, and it condenses without about some fortuitous and irregular centre, as the blood does in fleshly excrescences; then the chimeras of the brain take shape, and seemingly assume a soul, we appear to ourselves either radiant or deformed, according to the ideal of our desires or fears. Hallucinations, being dreams of waking persons, always suppose a state analogous to somnambulism, but, on the contrary, somnambulism is sleep borrowing phenomena from the waking state; hallucination is the waking state still subject in part to the astral intoxication of sleep.

Our fluidic bodies attract and repel one another, according to laws conformed to those of electricity. It is this which produces instinctive sympathies and antipathies. They are thus equilibriated by each other, and this is why hallucinations are frequently contagious; abnormal projections change the direction of luminous currents; the nervous excitement of a diseased person takes possession of the most sensitive natures about it, a circle of illusions is established, and a whole crowd is easily drawn away after it.

The fluidic body can be dissolved or coagulated by the volition of the soul acting on the Astral Light of which it is formed. It reacts on the nervous system, and thus produces the motions of the physical body. This light can indefinitely dilate and communicate its images to considerable distances; it magnetizes objects which are subject to the action of man, and by contracting can draw them towards him. It can assume all forms evoked by thought, and, in those fleeting coagulations of its radiating part which have been already referred to, can appear before the eyes and even offer a species of resistance to the touch. But these manifestations and exercises of the plastic mediator being abnormal, that luminous instrument of precision cannot produce them without being distorted, and they necessarily cause either permanent hallucination or madness.

The fluidic body, subject, like the mass of the Astral Light, to two opposite movements, attractive on the left and repulsive on the right, or reciprocally, in the two sexes, produces within us the struggle of opposite tendencies, and contributes to anxieties of conscience; frequently, it is influenced by the reflections of other spirits, and thus are produced either temptations or subtle and unexpected graces. This is the explanation of the traditional doctrine of two angels who aid and try us. The two forces of the Astral Light may be represented by a balance, wherein our good intentions for the triumph of justice and the emancipation of our liberty are poised.

The astral body is not invariably of the same sex as the physical, that is to say, that the proportions of the two forces often seem to contradict the visible organisation; it is this which produces the apparent errors of human passions, and which explains, without in any way justifying them from a moral point of view, the amorous eccentricities of Anacreon or Sappho.

The sidereal body, when disengaging itself at death, attracts and long preserves, by the sympathy of homogeneous things, the reflections of the past life. If a powerful sympathetic will can draw it into a particular current, it is manifested naturally, for nothing is more natural than prodigies. Thus apparitions are produced. But we shall develop this point more completely in the chapter devoted to necromancy.

III.—UNITY AND SOLIDARITY OF SPIRITS.

ACCORDING to the Kabbalists, God creates eternally the great Adam, the universal and perfect man, who contains in a single spirit all spirits and all souls. Intelligences therefore live two lives at once, one general, which is common to them all, and the other special and individual. Solidarity and reversibility among spirits depend therefore on their living really in one another, all being illuminated by the radiance of the one, all afflicted by the darkness of the one.

The great Adam was represented by the tree of life, which extends above and below the earth by roots and branches; the trunk is humanity at large, the various races are the branches, and the innumerable individuals are the leaves. Each leaf has its own form, its special life, and its share of the sap, but it lives by means of the branch alone, as the life of the branch itself depends on the trunk. The wicked are the dry leaves and dead bark of the tree. They fall, decay, and are transformed into manure, which returns to the tree through the roots.

The Kabbalists also compare the wicked, or reprobate, to the excrement of the great body of humanity. These excretions serve as manure to the earth, which brings forth fruits to nourish the body; thus death returns always to life, and evil itself serves for the renewal and nourishment of good. Death thus has no existence, and man never departs from the universal life. Those whom we call dead still survive in us, and we subsist in them; they are on the earth because we are here, and we are in heaven because they are located there.

The more we live in others, the less need we fear to die. Our life, after death, is prolonged on earth in those we love, and we draw on heaven to give them tranquillity and peace. The communion of spirits in heaven with earth, and on earth with heaven, is accomplished naturally, without disturbance and without prodigies; universal intelligence is like the sun's light, which falls at once on all the planets, and which the planets reflect to illuminate one another in the night.

The saints and angels have no need of words, nor of any sound, to make themselves understood; they think in our thoughts and they love in our hearts. The good which they have not had the opportunity to accomplish they suggest to us, and we perform it for them; they enjoy it in us, and we share its recompense with them, for spiritual rewards increase in proportion as they are shared, and what we give to another we double for ourselves.

The saints suffer and toil in us, and their perfect happiness will not be attained till the whole of humanity shall be happy, for they are a part of that indivisible humanity which in heaven, has a radiant and smiling face, on earth a toiling and suffering body, while in hell, which for sages is but a purgatory, it has fettered and burning feet. We are all members of one body, and the man who endeavours to supplant and destroy another man is like the right hand seeking to cut off the left through jealousy. He who kills another slays himself, he who steals from another defrauds himself, he who wounds another maims himself, for others exist in us and we in them.

The rich weary themselves, detest each other, and turn in disgust from life, their wealth itself tortures and burdens them, because there are poor in want of bread. The weariness of the rich is the distress of the poor, who suffer in their persons. God exercises His justice by the medium of Nature and His mercy by the mediation of His elect. If you thrust your hand into the fire, Nature will burn you without pity, but a charitable man can dress and soothe the burn. Law is inflexible, but charity is unlimited. Law damns, but charity pardons. The gulf of itself will never disgorge its prey, but a rope can be let down to him who has allowed himself to fall therein.

IV.—THE GREAT ARCANUM OF DEATH, OR SPIRITUAL TRANSITION.

WE are saddened, frequently, by remembering that the most beautiful life must end, and the approach of that terrible unknown called death embitters the joys of existence. Why are we born if existence must be so brief? Why bring up children, who must die, with so much care? This is what human ignorance asks in its most frequent and sorrowful doubts. This also is what the human embryo might vaguely demand at the approach of that birth which is about to usher it into an unknown world by despoiling it of its conserving envelope. In studying the mystery of birth, we shall find the key to the great secret of death.

Cast by the laws of Nature into the womb of a woman, the incarnated spirit slowly wakes therein, and laboriously creates for itself those organs which will be indispensable later on, but which in proportion to their growth increase its inconvenience in its present situation. The most blissful period in the embryo's life is that when, under the simple chrysalid form, it weaves about it the membrane which serves it as an asylum, and floats with it in a nourishing and preserving fluid. Then it is free and impassible, it shares in the universal life, and receives the impression of the memories of Nature which later on will determine the configuration of its body, and the individuality of its appearance. This happy age may be called the childhood of the embryo.

Its adolescence follows, the human form becomes distinct and the sex is determined; a motion takes place in the maternal egg, which is like the vague yearnings of the period which succeeds childhood. The placenta which is the exterior but real body of the fœtus, feels something unknown germinating within it and which tends already towards escape by breaking through it. The child at this time enters more distinctly into the dream life. Its brain, inverted as if it were a mirror of the mother's, reproduces the imaginations of the latter so forcibly, that it communicates their form to its own members. The mother is then for it what God is for us, an unknown, invisible Providence, towards which it aspires, even to the identification of itself with all that she desires. It depends on her, lives by her, but sees her not, it cannot even understand her, and could it philosophise it might possibly deny the personal existence and intelligence of that being, who for it is as yet only a necessary prison and a preserving environment. Little by little, however, this slavery troubles it, it grows restless, suffers, worries, and feels that its life is ending. An hour of anguish and convulsion comes, its bonds drop off, it feels itself sliding into the gulf of the unknown. This comes to pass, a painful sensation contracts it, it heaves a final sob, which changes into a first cry—it is dead to the embryonic life, it is born into human life!

In the embryonic period it seemed to it that the placenta was its body, and it was actually its special embryonic body, useless in another stage and rejected as refuse at the moment of birth. Our body in human life is like a second envelope which is useless to the third life, and for this reason we reject it at the moment of our second birth. Human life compared with the celestial is truly embryonic. When evil passions destroy us, Nature has a miscarriage, and we are born prematurely into eternity and are exposed to that terrible dissolution which St John calls the second death.

According to the constant traditions of ecstatics, the abortions of human life remain floating in the terrestrial atmosphere, above which they cannot rise, and which little by little absorbs and drowns them. They possess a human form, but it is always imperfect and mutilated; to one a hand is wanting, to another an arm, this one has already but the trunk remaining, that is only a ghastly revolving head. What prevents them from ascending heavenward is a wound received during earthly life, a moral injury which has resulted in a physical deformity, and by this wound little by little their whole nature ebbs away. The immortal soul will soon be left naked, and to conceal its shame, by manufacturing at all costs a new vestment, it will be obliged to wade through the exterior darkness and slowly traverse the dead sea, that is, the still and sleeping waters of the primeval chaos.

These wounded souls are the larvæ of the second embryotic state, they nourish their ærial bodies with the vapour of spilt blood and fear the points of swords. They frequently attach themselves to vicious men and share their life, as the embryo lives in the mother's womb; they can assume the most horrible forms, and it is these who appear in the guise of demons to the miserable performers of the nameless works of black magic. These larvæ fear the light, above all the light of spirits. A ray of intelligence is sufficient to overwhelm and precipitate them into that dead sea which must not be confounded with the asphaltite lake of Palestine.

All that we here unfold belongs to the hypothetical tradition of seers, and can only be affirmed before science in the name of that exceptional philosophy which Paracelsus terms the philosophy of sagacity—*philosophia sagax*. Those Kabbalists who speak of the world of spirits have simply narrated their intuitions in what they call *the Light of Glory*. Let us expose still further the teachings of these masters.

We read in the Hebrew book, *De Revolutionibus Animarum*, that there are souls of three kinds—the daughters of Adam, the daughters of angels, and the daughters of sin. There are also, according to the same work, three kinds of spirits—imprisoned spirits, wandering spirits, and free spirits. Souls are sent forth in couples; nevertheless there are some who are born widowed, and whose brides are held captive by Lilith and by Naêmah, the queens of the vampires: these are souls who have to expiate the temerity of celibate vows. Thus, when a man renounces from infancy the love of women, he enslaves the bride who was destined for him to the fiends of debauch. Souls grow and multiply their species in heaven as physical beings do on earth. Immaculate souls are the daughters of angels' kisses.

When the soul is separated from the body, it necessarily changes its environment, since it changes its envelope. The individual falls into his final sleep, and lapses into a species of dream before awaking on the other side of life. Each one then beholds, in a sweet vision or in an appalling nightmare, the paradise or perdition he believed in during his mortal existence. Those who are subject to nightmare can form some conception of the horror of the infernal visions which are the chastisement of an atrocious creed, and which take hold of the superstitiously credulous and the ascetically fanatical above all. Imagination has created its own tormentors, and in the delirium which follows death these monsters confront the soul with a frightful reality, surround, attack, and tear it to pieces, seeking to devour it in every way. The sage, on the contrary, is welcomed by pleasing visions; he imagines that he beholds his former friends approaching him and smiling. All this, however, is but a dream, as we have said, and the soul does not fail to awake from it. Then it has changed its environment. It has departed this life clothed only in its astral form, it ascends of itself above the atmosphere, as the air rises above the water when it escapes from a broken vial. The atmospheric air becomes solidified beneath the feet of its infinitely more ethereal envelope, the weight of which varies, however, in different persons, and while some cannot rise above their new earth-plane, others, on the contrary, ascend and soar at pleasure in space like the eagle.

But as nothing can enter Heaven save that which comes from Heaven, the divine spirit must ultimately return alone into the empyrean,* and thus two corpses are left by it in the earth and in the atmosphere, the one terrestrial and elementary, the other aerial and sidereal—the one already inert, the other still animated by the universal movement of the soul of the world, but destined to die gradually, being absorbed by the astral energies which produced it. The terrestrial body is visible, the other is unseen by earthly eyes in life, and can only be perceived by the application of the Astral Light to the Translucid, as we have explained elsewhere.

* See Note 13.

When a man has lived well, the astral body evaporates like a pure incense, ascending towards the superior regions; but if he have lived in sin, his astral body, which holds him captive, still seeks the objects of its earthly passions and endeavours to resume its life. It torments the dreams of young girls, bathes in the vapour of spilt blood, and hovers round places where the pleasures of its life elapsed; it still keeps watch over the treasures it possessed and concealed; it exhausts itself in grievous efforts to manufacture material organs and so live again. But the stars inhale and suck it up; it feels its understanding diminish, its memory is slowly lost, all its being dissolves. Its former vices appear to it, and pursue it under monstrous forms; they attack and devour it. The unhappy being thus loses in succession all the members which were subservient to its iniquities. Then it dies for the second and final time, for it forfeits self-consciousness and memory.

Souls which are destined to live, but which are not yet completely purified, remain imprisoned in their astral body for a longer or shorter period, and are burned therein by the odic light, which strives to assimilate and dissolve them. It is to liberate themselves from this body that such suffering souls occasionally obsess the living and abide within them in a state which the Kabbalists call *embryotic*. Those also who have neglected the cultivation of their minds during their mortal existence remain after death in a benumbed and torpid state, full of pains and disquietude; they recover their self-consciousness with difficulty, they dwell in darkness and the abyss, unable either to rise or to sink, and incapable of corresponding with heaven or earth. They are gradually drawn from this state by the elect, who instruct them, console them, and enlighten them; then they are allowed admission to new trials whose nature is unknown to us, for it is impossible that the same individual should be incarnated twice on the same earth.* The leaf once fallen from the branch can never be regrafted. The aurelia becomes a butterfly, but the butterfly never returns into the chrysalis state. Nature shuts the door on all that passes and impels life forward. The same morsel of bread cannot be twice eaten and digested. Forms pass, thought remains, and never does it reassume what it has once cast aside.

The Kabbalists compare the spirit to a substance which

* See Note 14.

remains fluidic in the divine environment, and under the influence of the essential light, but whose exterior hardens, like a cortex exposed to the air, in the colder regions of the rational or of visible forms. These cortices, or petrified envelopes, are the cause of errors or evil, which belong to the heaviness or hardness of their animal nature. In the Book of Sohar, and in that of the Revolution of Souls, perverse spirits or evil demons are invariably called *cortices*.

The cortices of the spirit world are transparent, those of the material are opaque; bodies are only temporary cortices from which souls must be liberated; but those who obey the flesh in this life create for themselves an interior body, or fluidic cortex, which becomes their prison and their torment after death, until the moment when they succeed in dissolving it in the heat of the divine light, whither their grossness long prevents them from ascending. They reach it only after infinite efforts and by the help of the just, who stretch forth their hands towards them, and during all this time they are devoured by the internal activity of the captive spirit as by a fiery furnace. Those who arrive at the pyre of expiation immolate themselves thereon, like Hercules on Mount Œta, and thus are delivered from their pains, but the courage of the majority fails before this supreme trial, which seems to them a second death more appalling than the first, and thus they remain in hell, which is everlasting by right and in fact, but into which souls are never precipitated, and in which they are never detained despite themselves.

The dead cannot return to earth any more than a child into its mother's womb. The human soul served, but also limited, by its organs, cannot place itself in communication with the objects of the visible world except by means of these organs. The body is an envelope which is proportional to the material environment in which the soul has to abide here below. By limiting the scope of the soul, it concentrates and makes its action possible. In effect, a soul devoid of body would be everywhere, but everywhere in so inappreciable a degree that it could act nowhere; it would be lost in infinity, absorbed, and as it were, annihilated in God. Imagine a drop of fresh water enclosed in a globule and thrown into the sea; so long as the globule remains unbroken the drop of water will preserve its own nature, but if the globule be destroyed, the drop of water must be sought in the vast sea. God in creating spirits could only endow them with individual self-consciousness by providing them with an envelope which centralises their action and prevents it from being dissipated by the very fact of its limitation.

After death the soul ascends because its envelope ascends, and its activity and consciousness are attached to its envelope, as we have said.

The Kabbalists formulate in a single axiom all the doctrine which we have been unfolding here. The spirit, they say, clothes itself to come down and unclothes itself to go up. The life of intelligences is wholly ascensional; the child in its mother's womb lives a vegetative life, receiving its nourishment by means of a cord which is attached to it, as the tree is attached to the earth and at the same time is nourished by its root. When the child passes from the vegetative to the instinctive and animal life, this cord is broken, and he can walk. When the child becomes a man he escapes from the bonds of instinct and can act as a reasonable being. When the man dies, he is freed from those laws of gravitation which pinned him in life to the earth. When the soul has expiated its faults, it becomes strong enough to leave the exterior darkness of the terrestrial atmosphere, and to rise up towards the sun. Then begins the eternal ascent of the holy ladder, for the eternity of the elect cannot be idle; they progress from virtue to virtue, from felicity to felicity, from triumph to triumph, from splendour to splendour. They see God as He is, that is, everywhere present in the infinite justice of natural law, in the rectitude which ever triumphs over all that may bechance, and in the infinite charity which is the communion of the elect. The chain of being, nevertheless, remains uninterrupted, and those of the highest grade can still exercise an influence on the lowest, but in accordance with hierarchic order, and in the same way that a king, by governing wisely, does good to the least of his subjects. Bonds of sympathy attach them always to the earth they have lived on, and on which they are more conscious than ever of being alive. From series to series prayers ascend and graces flow down without ever mistaking their path. But spirits once ascended can descend no more, for in the measure that they rise, degrees solidify beneath them. "The great chaos is closed," says Abraham in the parable of Dives, "and those who are here cannot go lower." Extasy may excite the energies of the sidereal body to such a pitch that it will bear up with it in its transport the material envelope, which proves that ascent is the soul's law. The facts of aërial suspension are possible, but for a man to live under earth or in water is unheard of. It would be equally impossible for a soul separated from its body to remain, even for a single instant, in the heaviness of our atmosphere. Therefore the souls of the dead are not around us, as the table-turners suppose. Those whom we love may still see and appear to us, but only by mirage and reflection in the common mirror of the light. Moreover, they can no longer interest themselves in mortal things, and are bound to us only by such of our sentiments as are sufficiently elevated to bear some conformity or analogy to their life in eternity.

IV.—HIERARCHY AND CLASSIFICATION OF SPIRITS.

THERE are spirits of exalted species, spirits of inferior degree, and spirits of a middle rank. Among the highest we may distinguish those most elevated, those least elevated, and those between the two; it is the same with the inferior and middle degrees. This division gives us three classes and nine categories of spirits. This natural hierarchy of men has created the hypothesis by analogy of the three ranks and nine choirs of angels, and also by inversion the three circles and nine degrees of hell. We read as follows in an ancient clavicle of Solomon, translated out of the Hebrew for the first time:—

"Now will I present to thee the key of the kingdom of spirits; it is the same as that of the mysterious numbers of Jezirah. Spirits are governed by the natural and universal hierarchy of things. Three command three by means of three. Know, however, that the principalities, virtues, and powers of Heaven are not persons but dignities. They are the degrees of the holy ladder on which spirits ascend and descend. Michael, Gabriel, Raphael, and others, are not names but titles. The first number is one; the first of the divine conceptions named Sephiroth is Keter or the Crown.

The first category of spirits is that of Hajoth Haccadosch, or the intelligences of the Tetragram whose letters are represented by the mysterious animals of Ezekiel's prophecy. Their empire is that of unity and synthesis, and they correspond to understanding. Their adversaries are Thamiel or the Two-headed, demons of revolt or anarchy, whose two chiefs, ever waging war with one another, are Satan and Moloch.

"The second number is two; the second Sephira is Chocmah, or Wisdom. The spirits of wisdom are the Ophanim, a name signifying wheels, because all discharge functions in heaven like vast wheels studded with stars. Their empire is that of harmony, and they correspond to reason. Their adversaries are the Chaigidel, or cortices which cleave to material and illusory appearances. Their chief, or rather guide, for evil spirits obey no one, is Beelzebub, whose name signifies the God of flies, because flies swarm round putrefying carcases.

"The third number is three; the third Sephira is Binah, or Understanding. The spirits of Binah are the Aralim, or strong ones. Their empire is the creation of ideas, and they correspond to activity and energy of thought. Their adversaries are the Satariel, or velatours, demons of absurdity, intellectual sloth, and mystery. The chief of the Satariel is Lucifuge, called falsely and antiphrastically Lucifer, as the Eumenides, who are the furies, are called the benevolent goddesses.

"The fourth number is four; the fourth Sephira is Gedulah or Chesed, magnificence or benignity. The spirits of Gedulah are the Haschmalim, or lucid ones. Their empire is that of beneficence, and they correspond to imagination. Their adversaries are Gamchicoth, or the disturbers of souls; the leader or guide of these demons is Astaroth or Astarte, the obscene Venus of the Assyrians, who is represented with the head of an ass or bull and the breasts of a woman.

"The fifth number is five; the fifth Sephira is Geburah, or Justice. The spirits of Geburah are the Seraphim, or fiery spirits of zeal. Their empire is that of the punishment of crimes. They correspond to the faculty of comparison and selection. Their adversaries are the Galab or incendiaries, genii of wrath and sedition, whose chief is Asmodeus, who is also called the black Samael.

THE DOCTRINE OF SPIRITUAL ESSENCES. 111

"The sixth number is six. The sixth Sephira is Tiphereth, Supreme Beauty. The spirits of Tiphereth are the Malachim or kings, and their empire is that of universal harmony; they correspond to judgment. Their adversaries are the Targaririm or disputatious, whose chief is Belphegor.

"The seventh number is seven; the seventh Sephira is Netsah, or Victory. The spirits of Netsah are the Elohim, or gods, that is, the representatives of God. Their empire is that of life and progress, and they correspond to the sensorium, or to sensibility. Their adversaries are the Harab-Serapel, or death-ravens, whose chief is Baal.

"The eighth number is eight; the eighth Sephira is Hod, or Eternal Order. The spirits of Hod are the Beni-Eloim, or sons of the gods. Their empire is that of order, and they correspond to deep feeling. Their adversaries are the Samael, or disputatious, whose chief is Adramelech.

"The ninth number is nine; the ninth Sephira is Jesod, or the fundamental basis. The spirits of Jesod are the Cherubim, or angels which fructify the earth, and who are represented in Hebrew symbolism under the figure of bulls. Their empire is that of productiveness, and they correspond to correct ideas. Their adversaries are the Gamaliel or obscene, whose queen, Lilith, is the demon of abortions.

"The tenth number is ten; the tenth Sephira is Malchuth, or the realm of forms. The spirits of Malchuth are the Ischim or virile, who are the souls of the saints, whose chief is Moses. Their adversaries are the wicked, who obey Nahema, the demon of impurity. The wicked are represented by the five accursed nations which Joshua had to exterminate. Johsua or Jehoshua the saviour is a type of the Messiah. His name is composed of the letters of the divine Tetragram changed into the Pentagram by the addition of the letter Schin—יהשוה. Each letter of this Pentagram represents a faculty of goodness assailed by one of the five accursed nations. For the actual history of God's people is the allegorical legend of humanity. The five accursed nations are the Amalekites or aggressors, the Geburim or violent, the Raphaïm or poltroons, the Nephilim or voluptuous, and the Anakim or anarchists. The Anakim are conquered by the god which is the paternal sceptre; the violent are conquered by the He, which is maternal mildness; the cowardly are conquered by the Vau which is the sword of Michael, and generation by labour and suffering; the voluptuous are vanished by the second He, which is the painful child-bearing of the mother. The aggressive, finally, are conquered by the Schin, which is the fire of the Saviour and the equilibriating law of justice.

"The princes of perverse spirits are the false gods which they adore. Hell has, therefore, no other government than the blind law which punishes perversity and corrects error, for false gods exist only in the false opinion of their worshippers. Baal, Belphegor, Moloch, Adramelek were idols of the Assyrians—soulless idols long since annihilated, and whose names alone remain. The true God has conquered all these demons, as truth triumphs over error. This has taken place in men's opinions, and the wars waged by Michael against Satan are emblems of the evolution and progress of minds. The devil is ever a refuse god. The idolatries of to-day were religions in the past; superannuated idolatries are superstitions and sacrileges. The pantheon of fashionable phantoms is the heaven of the ignorant. The sewer of phantoms with which even folly desires no further connection is hell. But all this exists only in the imagination of the crowd. Heaven for the wise is the Supreme Reason, as hell is foolishness. Here it will be seen that we make use of the word heaven in the mystical sense which is attributed to it by contrasting it with the word hell. To evoke phantoms we need only get drunk or go mad. Spectres are the families of intoxication and vertigo. The phosphorescence of the imagination, abandoned to all the vagaries of over-excited and diseased nerves, swarms with the monstrosities of absurd visions. Hallucination may also be attained by the confusion of sleeping and waking through the graduated use of stimulants and narcotics; but such works are crimes against nature. Wisdom dispels phantoms and enables us to communicate with superior intelligences by the contemplation of natural laws and the study of sacred numbers."

Here King Solomon addresses his son Roboam :—

"Remember, my son, that the fear of Adonai is only the beginning of wisdom. Maintain and preserve those who are devoid of understanding in the fear of Adonai which

THE DOCTRINE OF SPIRITUAL ESSENCES. 113

will give and ensure thee my crown. But learn thyself to triumph over fear by wisdom, and spirits will come down out of heaven to serve thee. I, Solomon, thy father, King of Israel and Palmyra, have sought and obtained for my portion the holy Chocmah, which is the wisdom of Adonai. And I have become the king of spirits both of heaven and earth, the master of the powers of the air and the living souls in the sea, because I possessed the key of the secret Gates of Light. I have accomplished sublime things by the power of the Schema Hamphorasch, and by the thirty-two paths of Jezirah. Number, weight, and measure determine all forms; the substance is single, and God eternally creates it. Blessed is he who comprehendeth letters and numbers. Letters are numbers, numbers notions, notions powers, and powers are the Elohim. The synthesis of the Elohim is the Schema. The Schema is one, its pillars are two, its power is three, its shape four, its reflection gives eight, which, multiplied by three, will produce the twenty-four thrones of wisdom. A three-gemmed crown is laid on each throne, each gem bears a name, each name represents an absolute idea. There are seventy-two names on the twenty-four crowns of the Schema.

"Thou shalt write these names on thirty-six talismans, two on each talisman, one on each side. Thou shalt divide these talismans into four series of nine each, according to the number of the letters of the Schema. On the first series thou shalt engrave the letter Jod represented by the Blossoming Rod of Aaron, on the second the letter He, represented by the cup of Joseph, on the third the Vau, represented by the sword of David my father; and on the fourth the final He, represented by the golden shekel. The thirty-six talismans shall be a book containing all natural secrets, and angels and demons shall speak to thee in its diverse combinations."

VI.—FLUIDIC PHANTOMS AND THEIR MYSTERIES.

PARACELSUS[*] tells us that the vital fluid emitted in dreams or regularly by the celibates of both sexes peoples the air with phantoms. We assume that we are here indicating

* See Note 15.

with sufficient perspicuity, after the manner of the masters, the supposititious origin of these larvæ and that additional details are unneeded. These larvæ possess an ærial body formed from the steam of blood. For this reason they seek out spilt blood, and were formerly nourished by the smoke of sacrifices. They are the monstrous offspring of impure nightmares once known as incubi and succubi. When sufficiently condensed to be visible, they are a mere vapour tinged by the reflection of an image; they have no individual life, but they imitate the life of those who evoke them, as the shadow imitates the body. They are not spirits, for they are mortal. They are a kind of animated mirage, imperfect emanations of human life. The traditions of black magic represent them as the offspring of the celibacy of Adam; all these notions are so ancient that we find traces of them in Hesiod, who expressly forbids linen stained by any defilement to be dried before fire.

Persons obsessed by phantoms are usually inflamed by an over-rigorous abstinence or weakened by the excesses of debauch. Such larvæ are above all produced round idiots and beings devoid of morality whose isolation abandons them to irregular habits. The ancients designated them under different names—larvæ, lemures, &c. They are the abortions of the vital light, plastic mediators devoid of body and soul, born of mental excesses and physical derangements. The cohesion of the parts of their fantastic organisms is so feeble that they fear a strong wind, large fires, and above all the points of swords. They become in a certain sense the vaporous appendices of the real bodies of their parents, for they live only by the life of those who have created or those who have appropriated them by evocation, so that if their semblance of bodies be wounded, the father may be really hurt, as the unborn child is actually disfigured by the imaginations of its mother. The whole world is full of phenomena which justify these extraordinary revelations and which cannot be otherwise explained.

These larvæ attract to themselves the vital heat of portly persons, and rapidly exhaust weak ones. Thence come the histories of vampires, which are terribly real and periodically established beyond doubt, as indeed is well known. It is for this reason that on the approach of mediums, that is, of persons obsessed by larvæ, a coldness is felt in the air.

THE DOCTRINE OF SPIRITUAL ESSENCES. 115

These roving mediators can be attracted by certain diseased persons who are in fatal sympathy with them, and who lend them a more or less durable existence. They then serve as supplementary instruments of the wills of these people, never however for their cure, but invariably to mislead and hallucinate them further.

If physical embryos have the faculty of assuming the forms impressed on them by the mother's imagination, still more are these wandering fluidic phantoms prodigiously variable, and transformable with astonishing facility. Their tendency to create themselves a body in order to attract a soul causes them to condense and naturally assimilate the corporeal molecules which float in the atmosphere. Thus, in coagulating the vapour of blood they reproduce blood, that blood which frenzied *hallucinés* behold flowing from pictures or statues. But it is not the hallucinated alone who see it. Vintras and Rose Tamisier are neither impostors nor people who are subject to vertigo; blood really flows, doctors examine and analyse it, it is true, human blood, and whence comes it? Can it form spontaneously in the atmosphere? Can it issue naturally from marble, from an oil painting, or from a Host? Certainly not; this blood has circulated in veins, then has been spilt, evaporated, and dried up; the serum has become vapour, the globules impalpable dust, the whole has floated and hovered in the air, and has then been drawn into the current of a specified electro-magnetism. The serum has again become liquid, it has reassumed and imbibed new globules, which have been coloured by the Astral Light, and blood has flown. Photography has abundantly proved that images are real modifications of light. Now, there exists an accidental and fortuitous photography which produces from the wandering mirages in the atmosphere, durable impressions on the leaves of trees, on their wood, and even in the heart of stones : it is thus those natural figures are found to which Gaffarel has consecrated several pages in his book on "Unheard of Curiosities," those stones to which secret virtue is attributed, and which are called *gamahés*; thus are traced those writings and drawings which so highly astonish the observers of fluidic phenomena. They are astral photographs, traced by the imagination of mediums with or without the concurrence of fluidic larvæ.

The existence of these larvæ has been demonstrated to us

in a decisive manner by an exceedingly curious experience. Several persons, in order to test the magic power of Home, the American, requested him to evoke relatives whom they pretended to have lost, but who really had never existed. The spectres did not fail to respond to the appeal, and the phenomena which commonly followed the evocation of the medium were fully manifested. This experience alone suffices to convict those who believe in the intervention of spirits in these strange phenomena of lamentable credulity and formal error. In order for the dead to return, it is before all things imperative that they should have existed, and demons would not be so easily made the dupes of our mystifications.

Like all Catholics, we believe in the existence of spirits of darkness, but we know also that Divine Power has made darkness their eternal prison, and that the Redeemer beheld Satan fall from Heaven like a thunderbolt. If demons tempt us, it is by the wilful complicity of our own bad passions; they are not permitted to insult God's empire and disturb the eternal order of Nature by useless and foolish manifestations.

Diabolical characters and signatures produced unconsciously by mediums are evidently no proof either of a tacit or formal compact between these diseased persons and the intelligences of the abyss. Such signs have served in all times to represent the astral vertigo, and have remained in the mirage state among the reflections of the misguided light. Nature has also her reminiscences and sends us the same signs *à propos* of the same ideas. In all this there is nothing supernatural or infernal.

"How can you expect me to admit," the Abbé Charvoz, the first convert of Vintras, said to us, "that Satan would dare impress his hideous stigmata on the consecrated species which have become the very body of Christ?" We declared at once that it would be equally impossible for us to pronounce in favour of so horrible a blasphemy, but, nevertheless, the signs printed in characters of blood on the Hosts of Vintras, consecrated regularly by Charvoz, were those which in black magic are absolutely recognized as the signatures of demons.

Astral writings are often ridiculous or obscene. The pretended spirits, questioned on the greatest mysteries of Nature, frequently reply by a coarse expression, once heroic in the military mouth of Cambronne. The designs traced by pencils left to themselves often reproduce those ill-formed priapuses which the *pâle voyou*, to borrow the picturesque expression of Auguste Barbier, sketches, as he whistles, along the great walls of Paris, fresh proof of what we have advanced, that is, that mind in no way presides over these manifestations, and that it would be above all a sovereign absurdity to recognise the intervention of disembodied souls.

The Jesuit, Paul Saufidius, who has written on the manners and customs of the Japanese, narrates a very remarkable anecdote. A troup of Japanese pilgrims, when crossing a desert, one day beheld a band of spectres whose number was equal to that of the pilgrims, and who walked at the same pace. These spectres, at first undefined and like larvæ, assumed as they approached all the semblance of the human form. They soon encountered the pilgrims, and mingled with them, gliding in silence between their ranks; then the Japanese saw themselves duplicated, each phantom having become the perfect image and, as it were, mirage of each pilgrim. The affrighted people cast themselves prostrate on the ground, and the bonze who conducted them fell to praying for them with great contortions and great cries. When the pilgrims ventured to rise, the apparitions had disappeared, and the pious band could continue its journey freely. This phenomenon, whose actuality we do not call in question, presents the two-fold character of a mirage and a sudden projection of astral larvæ, occasioned by the heat of the atmosphere and the exhaustion of the pilgrims.

Doctor Brierre de Boismont, in his curious work on "Hallucinations," narrates that a perfectly sensible man, who had never been subject to visions, was one morning tormented by a most insupportable nightmare. He beheld in his room a monstrous ape, horrible to see, who ground his teeth at him and made the most frightful contortions. He woke with a start, it was broad day, he sprang out of bed, and was terrified at finding the frightful object of his dream actually present before him, perfectly resembling that of the nightmare, equally grotesque, equally alarming, and making the same grimaces. The person in question could not credit his eyes; he remained motionless for half-an-hour, watching this singular phenomenon and wondering whether he was in a high fever or insane. He at length approached the fantastic animal to tcuch it, and the apparition vanished.

Cornelius Gemma, in his "Critical Universal History," tells us that in the year 454, in the Island of Candia, the phantom of Moses appeared to the Jews on the sea coast, and invited them to follow him, pointing with his finger towards the horizon in the direction of the Holy Land. He had his luminous horns on his forehead and his wand in his hand. The news of this prodigy spreads, and the Israelites in a crowd rush towards the coast. All saw or pretended to see the marvellous apparition; they numbered twenty thousand, says the chronicler, whom we suspect of a slight exaggeration in this respect. Their heads are turned at once, imaginations are excited, they expect a more glorious miracle than was formerly the passage of the Red Sea; they form in a serried column and direct their course towards the water; those behind push those in front with frenzied eagerness; they believe themselves to perceive the pretended Moses walking on the water. A terrible disaster resulted, for nearly all this multitude sank, and the hallucination was extinguished only with the life of the majority of the unhappy visionaries.

Human thought creates what it imagines; the phantoms of superstition project their real deformity in the Astral Light and live by the very terrors they produce. They owe their being to the delusions of imagination and to the aberration of the senses, and are never produced in the presence of any one who knows and can expose the mystery of their monstrous birth.

VII.—Elementary Spirits and the Ritual of their Conjuration.

THE material elements, analogous to the divine elements, are popularly classified as four, are explained as two, and really exist as three. The magical elements are in alchemy salt, mercury, sulphur, and azoth; in the Kabbalah, the Macroprosopus, the Microprosopus, and the two Mothers; in symbolism, the man, eagle, lion, and bull; in old physics, according to common notions and nomenclature, air, water, earth,

THE DOCTRINE OF SPIRITUAL ESSENCES. 119

and fire. But in magical science the water is no ordinary water, the fire is not merely fire, &c. These expressions conceal a more exalted meaning. The primitive substance is the only simple one; there is, therefore, but one material element, and this is invariably manifested in tetradic phases. Air and earth represent the male principle, fire and water are connected with the female. To these four elementary forms correspond the four following philosophical conceptions :—

> Mind,
> Matter,
> Motion,
> Rest.

All science consists actually in the comprehension of these four things which alchemy has reduced to three.

> The Absolute,
> The Fixed,
> The Volatile,

and which the Kabbalah connects with the essential idea of God, who is absolute reason, necessity, and liberty, a triadic notion expressed in the secret books of the Jews.

The Astral Light is the physical soul of the four elements, which are the four polar forces of the universal magnet, and are represented in symbolism by the Cross. They are the expression of two fundamental laws, resistance and motion. The beginning of the comprehension of the *magnum opus* is that of the four philosophic elements, which are primarily intellectual, for they are designated and realised by the Logos, the supreme formulation of reason. The water of the philosophers is the divisible substance, and the force also which divides and dissolves it ; it corresponds to the Kabbalistic woman. The philosophic earth is the quotient which coagulates on issuing from the divisor. Fire is movement; it is to water as one is to three, and it corresponds to the serpent. Air is the matrix of fire, it is to earth as a half is to eight.

The symbolic tetrad represented in the mysteries of Memphis and Thebes by the four-fold sphinx corresponded to the four elements. The chalice held by the man, or aquarius, corresponded to water; air was represented by the circle, or nimbus, which surrounds the head of the celestial eagle; fire by the wood which feeds it, by the tree which is fructified with the heat of the sun and earth, and by the royal sceptre symbolized in the lion; earth is represented by the sword of Mithra, who annually immolates the sacred bull, and mingles its blood with the sap which fills all earthly fruits.

The four elementary forms roughly divide and specialise the created spirits which the universal movement disengages from the central fire. In fact, created spirits, being called to emancipation through trials, are placed from their birth between these four forces, and it is in their power to declare for good or evil, to choose life or death. To find the fixed point, that is, the moral centre of the Cross, is the first problem they are set to solve, and their first conquest is that of their individual liberty. They begin, therefore, by being drawn some towards the north, others towards the south, some towards the right, others towards the left, and so long as they are not free agents, they cannot have the use of reason, nor can they be incarnated except in animal forms. These unemancipated spirits, the slaves of the four elements, are what the Kabbalists call elementary demons, or occult elements, and they people those elements which correspond to their condition of servitude. Sylphs, undines, gnomes, and salamanders, therefore, really exist, some wandering and seeking incarnation, others incarnate and living on the earth. These are vicious and imperfect men.*

The Astral Light is saturated with souls, which it releases, as we have said, in the incessant generation of existences, and whose imperfect wills can be dominated and employed by stronger ones, thus forming vast invisible chains which may occasion or determine great elementary commotions. The phenomena established in trials for sorcery have no other causes. The elementary spirits are like children, they torment those who concern themselves about them, unless at any rate they are governed by a lofty reason and excessive severity. It is these who frequently occasion our disturbing or fantastic dreams, who produce the movements of the divining rod, and the raps on our walls and furniture; but they can never manifest thoughts other than our own, and if we are not thinking at all, they address us with all the incoherence of dreams.

* See Note 16.

THE DOCTRINE OF SPIRITUAL ESSENCES.

They reproduce good and evil indifferently, because they are devoid of free will, and are consequently irresponsible agents; they appear to ecstatics and somnambulists under imperfect and fleeting forms, occasioning the nightmares of St Anthony, and probably the visions of Swedenborg; they are neither damned nor guilty, they are innocent and curious, and as they may be used or abused like children or animals, the magus who employs their services assumes a terrible responsibility, for he must expiate in his own person all the evil he has caused them to perform, and the magnitude of his torments will be proportioned to the extent of the power which he has exercised by their mediation.

To rule the elementary spirits, and become thus the king of the occult elements, the four trials of antique initiation must be undergone; and, as these initiations exist no longer, they must be supplied by analogous actions, as, for instance, by exposing oneself fearlessly in a burning house, by crossing a precipice on a plank or the trunk of a tree; by climbing a perpendicular mountain during a storm; by vigorously swimming out from a cascade or dangerous whirlpool. He who is afraid of the water will never reign over the undines; he who shrinks from the flames will never command salamanders; let him who is subject to giddiness leave the sylphs in peace, and forbear from irritating the gnomes, for inferior spirits will obey no power which has not been proved their master in their own individual element.

When courage and perseverance have acquired this incontestible power, the Logos of will-force must be imposed on the elements by particular consecrations of the air, fire, water, and earth, and this is the indispensable beginning of all magical operations. The air is exorcised by blowing towards the four cardinal points, and saying:—

Spiritus Dei ferebatur super aquas, et inspiravit in faciem hominis spiraculum vitæ. Sit Michael dux meus et Sabtabiel servus meus, in luce et per lucem. Fiat verbum halitus meus; et imperabo spiritibus æris hujus, et refrænabo equos solis voluntate cordis mei, et cogitatione mentis meæ, et nutu oculi dextri. Exorciso te, creatura æris, per Pentagrammaton et in nomine Tetragrammaton, in quibus sunt voluntas firma at fides recta. Amen. Sela, fiat.

The sylphide prayer must be then recited after tracing their sign in the air with an eagle's quill.

Prayer for the Sylphs.

Spirit of Light, Spirit of Wisdom, thou whose breath imparts and recalls the shape of every object; thou before whom the life of all creatures is a shadow which transforms, and a vapour which passes away; thou who sittest upon the clouds and fliest on the wings of the wind; thou whose outbreathing peoples the limitless immensity; thou whose inbreathing draws back within thee all that emanated from thee, unending movement in the everlasting stability, be thou blessed for ever! We praise thee and bless thee in the inconstant empire of the created light, of shadows, reflections, and images, and we aspire without ceasing towards thine immutable and imperishable splendour. May the beam of thine intelligence and the warmth of thy love come down on us; then shall the unsteady be established, the shadow be substance, the spirit of the air shall receive a soul, and dream be thought! No more shall we be swept away by the tempest, but shall bind with the bridle the winged steeds of the morning, and direct the course of the evening winds, that we may fly away and come into thy presence! O Spirit of spirits, O everlasting Soul of souls, O Imperishable Breath of Life, creative sigh, mouth which dost breathe forth and draw in the life of all beings in the ebb and flow of thine eternal speech, which is the divine sea of motion· and truth! Amen.

Water is exorcised by the laying on of hands, by breath, and by speech, mixing consecrated salt with a little of the ash which is left in the incense pan. The aspergillus is made of branches of vervain, periwinkle, sage, mint, ash, and basil, tied by a thread taken from a virgin's distaff, with a handle of hazelwood which has not yet borne fruit, and on which the characters of the seven spirits must be graved with the magic awl. The salt and ashes of the incense must be separately consecrated by saying—

Over the Salt.

In isto sale sit sapientia, et ab omni corruptione servet mentes nostras et corpora nostra, per Hochmaël et in virtute Ruach-Hochmaël, recedant ab isto fantasmata hylæ

THE DOCTRINE OF SPIRITUAL ESSENCES.

ut sit sal cœlestis, sal terræ, et terra salis, ut nutrietur bos triturans et addat spei nostrae cournua tauri volantis. Amen.

Over the Ash.

Revertatur cinis ad fontem aquarum viventium, et fiat terra fructificans, et germinet arborem vitæ per tria nomina, quæ sunt Netsah, Hod, et Jesod, in principio et in fine, per Alpha et Omega qui sunt in spiritu AZOTH. Amen.

In mingling the Water, Salt, and Ash.

In sale sapientiæ æternæ, et in aqua regenerationis, et in cinere germinante terram novam, omnia fiant per Eloim Gabriel, Raphael, et Uriel, in sæcula et æonas. Amen.

Exorcism of the Water.

Fiat firmamentum in medio aquarum et separet aquas ab aquis, quæ superius sicut quæ inferius, et quæ inferius sicut quæ superius, ad perpetranda miracula rei unius. Sol ejus pater est, luna mater, et ventus hanc gestavit in utero suo, ascendit a terra ad cœlum et rursus a cœlo in terram descendit. Exorciso te, creatura aquæ, ut sis mihi speculum Dei vivi in operibus ejus, et fons vitæ, et ablutio peccatorum. Amen.

Prayer of the Undines.

Terrible King of the Sea, thou who bearest the keys of the floodgates of heaven, and dost imprison the waters of the under world in their earthy caverns; King of the deluge and of the floods of the springtime; thou who unsealest the sources of the streams and fountains; thou who commandest the moisture, which is like the blood of earth, to become the sap of plants, we adore and invoke thee! Speak unto us in the great tumult of the sea, and we shall tremble before thee; speak also in the ripple of limpid waters, and we shall long for thy love! O Immensity, wherein all rivers of life are lost, and which are always reborn in thee! Ocean of infinite perfections, height which reflects itself in the depth, depth which projects itself on the height, lead us to true life by love and intelligence!

Lead us to immortality by renunciation, that we may be worthy one day to offer thee water, blood, and tears for the remission of sins. Amen.

Fire is exorcised by casting salt, incense, white resin, camphor, and sulphur therein, and pronouncing thrice the three names of the genii of fire—MICHAEL, king of the sun and lightning; SAMAEL, king of volcanoes; and ANAEL, king of the Astral Light; then by reciting the the Prayer of the Salamanders.

Prayer of the Salamanders.

Immortal, everlasting, ineffable, and uncreated Father of all things, who art borne on the ever-rolling chariot of worlds revolving unceasingly; ruler of the ethereal immensities, where the throne of thy power is established, from whose altitude thine insupportable eyes discern all things, and thy holy and beautiful ears do hear all things, listen to thy children, whom thou hast loved before the ages began; for thy golden, overwhelming, everlasting majesty shines over the world and over the starry Heaven; thou art exalted above them, O Glittering Fire, thence thou illuminest and dost commune with thyself by thine own splendour, and there issue from thine essence inexhaustible streams of life to nourish thine infinite spirit, which itself doth nourish all things, and is that unfailing storehouse of substance ever ready for generation, which adapts and appropriates the forms thou hast impressed on it from the beginning. From this spirit the three most holy kings who surround thy throne and form thy court, derive their immemorial origin, O universal Father! O sole and only father of beatified immortals and mortals!

Thou hast in particular created powers which are marvellously similar to Thine own eternal thought, and Thine adorable essence; Thou hast made them superior to the angels who proclaim Thy will to the world; finally, Thou hast created us third in the rank of our elementary empire. There our continual occupation is to praise Thee and adore Thy good pleasure; there we burn unceasingly in our aspiration to possess Thee. Father, mother, most tender of all mothers, admirable archetype of chaste love and maternity! Son, flower of sons! Form of all forms, soul, spirit, harmony, and number of all things. Amen!

The earth is exorcised by the sprinkling of water, by

THE DOCTRINE OF SPIRITUAL ESSENCES.

breathing, and by fire, with the perfumes proper to each day, and the prayer of the gnomes.

The Prayer of the Gnomes.

Invisible King, who hast taken the earth as a support and hast hollowed its depths to replenish them with Thine omnipotence! Thou, whose name shaketh the pillars of heaven, Thou, who causest the seven metals to circulate in the veins of the earth, monarch of the seven lights, recompenser of the subterranean workers, lead us into the desirable light, into the realm of splendour! We watch and we labour unceasingly, we seek and we hope, by the twelve stones of the Holy City, by the buried talismans, by the pole of loadstone which passes through the world's centre. Saviour, Saviour, Saviour, have pity on those who suffer, enlarge our hearts, detach our minds, elevate them, ennoble us. O stability and motion! O day clothed with night! Master, who never dost retain the wages of thy workers! O silvered whiteness! O golden splendour! O crown of living and melodious diamonds! Thou, who wearest the heavens on thy finger as a sapphire ring, Thou, who concealest beneath the earth, in the stone kingdom, the miraculous seed of stars, live, reign, be ever the dispenser of that wealth whereof Thou hast made us the custodians!

It must be borne in mind that the special kingdom of the gnomes is at the north, that of the salamanders at the south, that of the sylphs at the east, and that of the undines at the west. They influence the four temperaments of man, that is, the gnomes influence the melancholic, salamanders the sanguine, undines the phlegmatic, and sylphs the bilious. Their signs are—the hieroglyphic of the bull for the gnomes, who are commanded with the sword; of the lion for the salamanders, who are commanded with the cloven rod, or magical trident; of the eagle for the sylphs, who are ruled by holy pantacles; and finally, of the aquarius for the undines, who are evoked by the cup of libations. Their respective sovereigns are Gob for the gnomes, Djin for the salamanders, Paralda for the sylphs, and Nicksa for the undines.

When an elementary spirit torments, or, at any rate, troubles the inhabitants of this world, it must be adjured by air, water, fire, and earth, with breathing, sprinkling, burning of perfumes, and by tracing on the ground the star of Solomon and sacred Pentagram. These figures should be absolutely correct, and drawn either with the ash of consecrated fire, or with a reed soaked in various colours, mixed with pulverised loadstone. Then, holding the pantacle of Solomon in the hand, and taking up by turns the sword, rod, and cup, the conjuration of the four should be repeated in the following terms :—

Caput mortuum, imperet tibi Dominus per vivum et devotum serpentem. Cherub, imperet tibi Dominus per Adam Jotchavah! Aquila errans, imperet tibi Dominus per alas Tauri. Serpens, imperet tibi tetragrammaton per angelum et leonem! Michael, Gabriel, Raphael, Anael! FLUAT UDOR per spiritum ELOIM. MANEAT TERRA per Adam JOT-CHAVAH. FIAT FIRMAMENTUM per JAHUVEHU-ZEBAOTH. FIAT JUDICIUM per ignem in virtute MICHAEL.

Angel with the blind eyes, obey or pass away with this holy water. Work, winged bull, or return to earth if thou wouldst not be pricked with this sword. Fettered eagle, obey this sign, or retire before my breath. Writhing serpent, crawl at my feet, or be tortured by the sacred fire and evaporate with the perfumes I am burning. Water, return to water, fire burn, air circulate, earth return to earth by the power of the Pentagram, which is the morning star, and in the name of the Tetragram, which is written in the centre of the cross of light! Amen.

The sign of the Cross adopted by Christians does not exclusively belong to them. It is also Kabbalistic, and represents the oppositions and tetradic equilibrium of the elements. There were originally two methods of making it, the one reserved for priests and initiates, the other set apart for the neophytes and profane. Thus, for example, the initiate, raising his hand to his forehead, said: "Thine is," then brought down his hand to his breast, "the kingdom," then transferred it to the left shoulder, "justice," finally to the right shoulder, "and mercy;" then joining his hands, he added, "through the generating ages." Tibi sunt Malchut et Geburah et Chesed per aeonas—a sign of the Cross which is absolutely and splendidly Kabbalistic, and which the profanations of the Gnosis have entirely lost to the official and militant church. This sign made in this manner should precede and terminate the conjuration of the Four.

To conquer and subjugate the elementary spirits, we

THE DOCTRINE OF SPIRITUAL ESSENCES. 127

must never be guilty of the faults which are their characteristics. Never will a capricious and changeable mind be able to rule the sylphs. Never will a soft, cold, and fickle disposition be able to govern the undines; anger irritates the salamanders, and gross covetousness makes those whom it enslaves the sport and plaything of the gnomes. But we must be prompt and active, like the sylphs; pliant and observant as the undines; energetic and strong, like the salamanders; laborious and patient, like the gnomes; in a word, we must overcome them in their strength without ever being overcome by their weakness. When he is permanently established in this disposition, the whole world will be at the command of the enlightened thaumaturge. He will pass through the storm, and no rain will fall on his head; the wind will not displace a single fold of his garments; he will go through fire and not be burned, he will walk on the water and discern diamonds through the opacity of the earth. These promises, which may seem hyperbolic, are so only to the vulgar mind; for if the initiate do not materially and literally perform what is expressed by these words, he will accomplish things which are far greater and far more admirable.

Why, for example, if it be an established fact that persons in the ecstatic state temporarily lose their gravity, should it be impossible to walk or glide on the water? The convulsionaries of St Médard felt neither fire nor steel, and begged the most violent and incredible tortures as a relief. The extraordinary ascensions and amazing equilibrium of certain somnambulists are a revelation of Nature's secret forces. But we live in a century wherein no one has the boldness to acknowledge the miracles they have witnessed; and if any one should declare that he has beheld, or performed himself what he narrates, he will be told that he is joking at the expense of his hearers, or that he is ill. It is far better to be silent and to act.

The metals which correspond to the four elementary forms are gold and silver for air, mercury for water, iron and copper for fire, and lead for earth. Talismans are composed of these relatively to the forces they represent, and to the effects it is proposed to produce by their means. Divination by the four elementary forms, called aeromancy, hydromancy, pyromancy, and geomancy, is performed in various ways, all of which depend on the will and translucid, or imagination, of the operator. In fact, the four elements are merely instruments to assist second sight, which is the faculty of seeing into the Astral Light, and which is natural as the first, or sensible and ordinary sight, though it can operate only by means of the abstraction of the senses. Somnambulists and ecstatics are naturally gifted with second sight, but this vision is more lucid when the abstraction is more complete. Abstraction is produced by astral intoxication, that is, by a superabundance of light, which completely saturates and consequently deadens the nervous instrument. Sanguine temperaments are more disposed to aeromancy, the choleric to pyromancy, the phlegmatic to hydromancy, and the hypochondriac to geomancy. Aeromancy is confirmed by oneiromancy, or divination by dreams; pyromancy is supplemented by magnetism, hydromancy by crystallomancy, and geomancy by cartomancy. These are transpositions and improvements of methods. But divination, in whatsoever manner it be performed, is dangerous, or, at least, useless, for it weakens will-power, consequently impedes liberty, and fatigues the nervous system.

VIII.—NECROMANCY.

THE Abbè Trithemius, who in magic was the master of Agrippa, explains in his " Stenography " the secret of conjurations and evocations in an exceedingly natural and philosophical manner. To evoke a spirit, he says, is to enter into the ruling idea of that spirit, and if we rise morally higher in the same line, we shall draw that spirit after us and it will serve us. To conjure is to oppose to an isolated spirit the resistance of a current and of a chain —*cum jurare*, that is, to make a collective act of faith. The greater the power and enthusiasm of this faith, the more efficacious is the conjuration. We may be alone to evoke a spirit, but to conjure it we must speak in the name of a circle or association, and it is this which is represented by the hieroglyphic circle traced round the Magus while he is operating, and which he cannot leave without at the same moment losing all his power.

In virtue of the great magical dogma of the hierarchy

and of universal analogy, the possibility of real evocations may be Kabbalistically demonstrated; as to the phenomenal reality of the result of magical operations conscientiously accomplished, it is a question of experience; in our own case we have established it, and we place it in the power of our readers to renew and confirm our experiences.

There are evocations of intelligence, evocations of love, and evocations of hatred. There are two kinds of necromancy—the necromancy of light and the necromancy of darkness, evocation by prayer, pantacle, and perfumes, and evocation by blood, imprecations, and sacrileges. We have practised the first only, and we advise no one to devote themselves to the second. It is certain that the images of the departed appear to the magnetised persons who evoke them; it is equally certain that they never unveil to them any mysteries of the life beyond. They are beheld just as they would still be in the memory of persons who have known them. When the evoked spectres reply to those who address them, it is always by signs, or by an interior and imaginary impression, never with a voice which really strikes on the ears, and this is easily comprehensible—how should a shadow speak? With what instrument could it make the air vibrate by striking it in such a manner as to cause distinguishable sounds?

Electric touches on the part of the apparitions are nevertheless experienced, and these contacts sometimes seem to be produced by the hands of the phantom; this phenomenon however is wholly subjective, and the power of imagination, acting in concert with the occult force which we call the Astral Light, is its sole and only cause. This is proved by the fact that the spirits, or at least the spectres which pretend to be such, touch us certainly sometimes, but we never can touch them, which is one of the most alarming adjuncts of apparitions, for the visions seem occasionally so real that we cannot without agitation feel the hand pass through what appears to be a body and yet encounter no resistance.

There is no proof that spirits really leave the superior spheres to communicate with us, and the very contrary is probable. We evoke the reminiscences contained in the Astral Light, which is the common reservoir of universal magnetism. It is in this light that the Emperor Julian beheld the manifestation of his gods, but old, ill, and decrepit

—fresh proof of the influence of current and accredited opinions on the reflections of this same magic agent which causes tables to speak and answers by taps on the walls.

We read in ecclesiastical historians that Spiridion, bishop of Tremithante, subsequently invoked as a saint, called up the spirit of Irene, his daughter, to ascertain from her where a deposit of money, which she had received from a traveller, had been concealed. Swedenborg habitually communicated with the pretended dead whose forms appeared to him in the Astral Light. We have known several credible persons who have assured us that they beheld for years the dead who were dear to them. The well-known atheist, Sylvanus Maréchal, appeared to his widow and to a friend to inform them of a sum of 1500 francs in gold which he had hidden in a secret drawer of his desk. We have received the anecdote from an old friend of the family.

There should be always an adequate motive and lawful object in evocations, otherwise they are works of darkness and folly, most dangerous to health and reason. To evoke out of pure curiosity, and simply to know if we shall see anything, is to be disposed beforehand for fruitless fatigue. The supreme sciences tolerate neither doubt nor puerilities. The laudable motive in an evocation can be either love or intelligence. Evocations of love need less apparatus and are in every way more easy. The method of procedure is as follows :—

We must first carefully collect all the memories of him or her whom we seek to behold again, and the articles he or she made use of, and which preserve their impress ; then we must either furnish a room where the person dwelt in life, or a similar place, where their portrait must be hung with white and surrounded by the flowers which they loved, and which should be daily renewed. We must then fix on a definite day, either that of their birth, or the one which was most propitious for their and our affection, a day of which we suppose that the soul, however blessed it may be elsewhere, cannot lose the remembrance, and this must be selected for the evocation, for which we must prepare ourselves during a space of fourteen days. During this period we must be careful to give no one the same proof of affection which the defunct had a right to expect from us ; we must observe rigorous chastity, live in retirement, and make only a simple and slight collation daily. Every evening at the same hour we must shut ourselves in the chamber consecrated to the memory of the lamented person, with only a dim light such as a small funereal lamp or taper would afford, and placing this light behind us, we must unveil the portrait, before which we must remain an hour in silence, then perfume the chamber with a little good incense, and go out backwards.

On the day fixed for the evocation, we must array ourselves before morning as if for a festival, give no one the first greeting, take only one meal, consisting of bread, wine, and roots or fruits; the cloth should be white, two covers should be laid, and one portion of the bread, which should be served whole, must be broken; some drops of wine must also be placed in the person's glass whom we desire to evoke. This repast should be made in silence in the chamber of evocations, and in presence of the veiled portrait; all that was used at the meal must be then cleared away, except the glass of the dead person and his share of the bread, which must be left before the portrait. In the evening, at the time of the ordinary visit, we must repair to the chamber in silence, light a clear fire of cypress wood, and seven times cast incense therein, pronouncing the name of the person we desire to behold; the lamp must be afterwards extinguished and the fire suffered to go out. This day the portrait must not be uncovered. When the flame is extinguished, more incense must be placed on the ashes, and God must be invoked according to the formulæ of that religion which the deceased person professed, and according to the notion they entertained themselves of God. In reciting this prayer, we must identify ourselves with the evoked person, speak as they would speak, in a way, believe as they believed; then, after a silence of fifteen minutes, speak to them as if they were present, with faith and affection, praying them to manifest to us. Renew this prayer mentally, covering the face with both hands, then call on the individual thrice with a loud voice; wait, kneeling with closed or covered eyes, for some minutes, while mentally communing with them. Then call on them three times more in a gentle and affectionate tone, and slowly open the eyes. If we behold nothing, the experience must be renewed the year following, and up to the third time, on which, at least, it is certain that the desired apparition will be obtained, and the longer it has delayed the more will it be visible and startling in its reality.

Evocations of knowledge and intelligence are performed with more solemn ceremonies. Should a celebrated person be concerned, we must meditate on his life and writings for twenty-one days, form an idea of his appearance, countenance, and voice, mentally address him and imagine his replies, bear about us his portrait, or his name at least, submit to a vegetable diet for the twenty-one days, and observe a severe fast during the last seven, then construct the magical oratory as we shall describe it.* The oratory should be wholly shut up, but if we operate in the daytime, we may leave a small opening on the side where the sun will be found at the time of evocation, placing before this opening a triangular prism, and before the prism a crystal globe filled with water. If we operate at night, we must so arrange the magic lamp that its single ray shall fall on the smoke rising from the altar.

The object of these preparations is to endow the magical agent of the elements with a corporeal appearance, and to relieve the tension of imagination, which is not exalted without danger to the absolute illusion of dream. It will be readily understood, moreover, that a ray from the sun or from a lamp, variously coloured and falling on an unsteady smoke, cannot in any way create a perfect image. The brazier of sacred fire should be in the centre of the oratory, and the altar of perfumes at a little distance from it. The Magus should turn to the east for prayer and to the west for evocation; he should be alone or else assisted by two persons, who must observe rigorous silence; he must wear the magic vestments as described in the tenth chapter, and a crown of gold or vervain; he should take a bath before the operation, and all his under garments must be of unsullied and absolute cleanliness. He must then begin with a prayer suited to the disposition of the spirit to be evoked, and which would be approved by it were the person still living. Voltaire, for example, would never be evoked by reciting prayers in the style of St Bridget's. For the great men of old the hymns of Cleanthes or Orpheus should be repeated, with the oath which concludes the Golden Verses of Pytha-

* See "Thaumaturgical Experiences of Éliphas Lévi," c. i.

THE DOCTRINE OF SPIRITUAL ESSENCES. 133

goras. At our own evocation of Apollonius, we used the magical philosophy of Patricius, which contains the doctrines of Zoroaster and the works of Hermes Trismegistus, as a Ritual. We recited in a loud voice the Nuctemeron of Apollonius in Greek, and added the following conjuration :—

Βουλῆς δ' ὁ πατὴρ πάντων, καὶ καθηγητὴς ὁ τρισμέγιστος Ἑρμῆς. Ἰατριχῆς δ' ὁ Ἀσχληπιὸς ὁ Ἡφαίσθου. Ἰσχύος τε καὶ μωμῆς πάλιν Ὄσιρις με δ' ὦν ὦ τέκνον αὐτόσσυ. Φιλοσόφιας δὲ Ἀρνεϲάσκενις. Ποιητικῆς δὲ πάλιν ὁ Ἀσκλεπιος, ὁ Ἰμούθης.

Ὄυτοι τὰ κρύπτα, φῦσιν Ἕρμης, τῶν ἐμῶν ἐπίγνωσονται γραμμάτων πάντων, καὶ διακρινοῦσι, καὶ τῖνα υεναντοι κατεσχοσιν ἃ δὲ καὶ πρὸς εὐεργεσιὰς θνητῶν φθάνει, σήλαι χαὶ ὁϲελίσκοις χαραξῶσιν.

Μαγείαν, ὁ Ἀπολλώνιος, ὁ Ἀπολλώνιος, ὁ Ἀπολλώνιος διδάσκεις τοῦ Ζοροάστρου τοῦ Ωρομάζου, ἐστί δή τοῦτο, θεῶν θεραπεια.*

For the evocation of spirits belonging to religions which have emanated from Judaism, the Kabbalistic invocation of Solomon must be made use of, either in Hebrew or in any other language with which the spirit to be evoked was familiar.

Powers of the Kingdom, be under my left foot and in my right hand—Glory and Eternity, touch my two shoulders and direct me in the paths of Victory—Mercy and Justice, equilibrate and be the splendour of my life—Intelligence and Wisdom, bestow the crown on me—Spirits of MALCHUTH, lead me between the two pillars on which the whole edifice of the Temple depends—Angels of NETSAH and HOD, establish me on the Cubic Stone of JESOD! O GEDULAEL! O GEBURAEL! O TIPHERETH! BINAEL, be my desire—RUACH HOCHMAEL, be my light—be that which thou art and thou wilt be, O KETHERIEL! *Ischim*, assist me in the name of SADDAI! *Cherubim*, be my strength in the name of ADONAI! *Beni-Elohim*, be my brethren in the name of the Son, and by the virtues of ZEBAOTH. *Eloïm*, do battle for me in the name of TETRAGRAMMATON. *Malachim*, protect me in the name of יהוה. *Seraphim*, purify my affection in the name of ELVOH. *Hasmalim*, enlighten me with the splendours of

* This quotation, as it exists in the French text, is made almost unintelligible by innumerable typographical mistakes, which in the absence of any reference to the original are very difficult to correct in a satisfactory manner.

ELOI and Shechinah. *Aralim*, act—*Ophanim*, revolve and shine—*Hajoth a Kadosh*, cry, speak, shout—Kadosh, Kadosh, Kadosh—SADDAI, ADONAI, JOTCHAVAH, EIEAZEREIE! Hallelu-jah, hallelu-jah, hallelu-jah! Amen. אמן.

It must be remembered, above all, that the names Satan, Beelzebub, Adramelek, and others which occur in the conjurations, do not designate spiritual individuals, but legions of impure spirits. "Our name is legion," says the spirit of darkness in the Gospel, "because we are many." In hell, or the kingdom of anarchy, the majority is the law, and progression is accomplished in an inverted sense, that is, the most advanced in Satanic development, the most degraded consequently are the weakest and most unintelligent. Thus, a fatal law forces the demons downward when they wish and believe themselves to be rising, and those who call themselves chief are the most impotent and despised of all. As to the mob of the perverse it trembles before an unknown, invisible, capricious, implacable prince, who never explains his laws, and whose arm is always raised to strike those who cannot understand him. They give this phantom the names of Baal, Jupiter, and others far more venerable, and which cannot be uttered without profanation in hell, but this phantom is only the shadow and remembrance of God, disfigured by wilful perversity, and remaining in their imagination as a visitation of justice and a reproach of truth.

When the evoked spirit of light appears with a doleful or irritated countenance, we must offer it a moral sacrifice, that is, be interiorly willing to refrain from what offends it, then before leaving the oratory, we must dismiss it by saying:—"May peace be with thee! I have not wished to trouble thee, I shall endeavour to correct myself in whatever offends thee; I do and will pray both with thee and for thee: pray then for me and with me, and return to thy long sleep, awaiting that day when we shall wake together. Silence and farewell!"

We must not end this chapter without adding, for the benefit of the curious, some details of the ceremonies of black necromancy. We find in several ancient authors how it was practised by the sorcerers of Thessaly. A pit was dug, on the brink of which a black sheep was killed; then the psyllae and larvæ supposed to be present and hasten-

THE DOCTRINE OF SPIRITUAL ESSENCES. 135

ing to drink the blood were driven away by the Magic Sword. The triple Hecate and the infernal gods were called on, and thrice the shadow they desired to see was invoked.

In the middle ages, the necromancers profaned tombs and compounded philtres and ointments with the grease and blood of corpses; they mixed aconite, belladona, and poisonous fungi therewith; then they boiled and skimmed these frightful mixtures over fires composed of human remains and crucifixes stolen from churches; they added the dust of dried toads and the ashes of consecrated hosts; then they rubbed their foreheads, hands and stomachs with the infernal ointment, drew the Satanic pantacle, and evoked the dead beneath gibbets or in desecrated cemeteries. Their howlings were heard at great distances, and the belated traveller fancied that legions of phantoms were issuing from the earth; the very trees assumed in his eyes affrighting shapes, flaming orbs seemed glaring in the thickets, while the frogs of the marshes appeared to repeat hoarsely the words of the Sabbath. It was the mesmerism of hallucination and the contagion of madness.

The end of the proceedings of black magic is to disturb reason and produce all those feverish excitements which supply courage for the commission of great crimes. The grimoires, which were formerly seized by authority and burned whenever they were met with, are certainly anything but harmless books. Sacrilege, murder, and theft are indicated or hinted at as means to realisation in nearly all these operations. Thus in the Great Grimoire and in the Red Dragon, a later imitation of the Great Grimoire, we find necromantic proceedings which consist in tearing up the earth over tombs with one's nails, dragging out the bones beneath, and setting them crosswise on the breast, and thus arrayed assisting at the midnight mass on Christmas eve in a church, where at the moment of the elevation we must rise and rush out, shouting—"Let the dead rise from their tombs!" Then we must go back to the cemetery, take up a handful of the earth which lies nearest to the coffin, return at a run to the church which has been startled by the previous outcry, set down the two bones still crosswise and again shout—"Let the dead rise from their tombs!" When, if no one be found to arrest us and take us to the madhouse, we may retire at a slow pace, counting four thousand five hundred steps without turning aside, which supposes us to be either on a high road or capable of scaling walls. At the end of these paces we must lie down on the ground as if on a coffin, having previously strewn cross-wise the earth in our hand, after which we must once again repeat, this time in a lugubrious tone, the words, "Let the dead rise from their tombs!" and then call thrice on the person desired to appear. It is not to be disputed that anyone sufficiently idiotic and perverse as to abandon themselves to such practices must be disposed before-hand for all chimæras and phantoms. The receipt in the Great Grimoire is therefore certainly most efficacious, but we advise none of our readers to make use of it.

IX.—Mysteries of the Pentagram and other Pantacles.

The Pentagram expresses the mind's domination over the elements and it is by this sign that we bind the demons of the air, the spirits of fire, the spectres of water, and the ghosts of earth. It is the Star of the Magi, the burning star of the Gnostic schools, the sign of intellectual omnipotence and autocracy. It is the symbol of the Word made Flesh, and, according to the direction of its rays, it represents good or evil, order or disorder, the sacred lamb of Ormuz and St John, or the accursed goat of Mendes. It is initiation or profanation, Lucifer or Vesper, Mary or Lilith, victory or death, light or darkness.

The Pentagram, with two horns in the ascendant, represents Satan, or the goat of the Sabbath, and with the single horn in the ascendant it is the sign of the Saviour. It is the figure of the human body with the four members and a point representing the head; a human figure head downward naturally represents the demon, that is, intellectual subversion, disorder, and folly.

Now, if magic be a reality, if this secret science be the true law of the three worlds, this absolute sign, this sign as old as and older than history, should and must actually exercise an incalculable influence on souls disengaged from their material envelope. Armed therewith and suitably disposed, we can behold infinity through the medium of that faculty which is as the Soul's Eye, and can cause ourselves to be served by legions of angels and by demon hordes. The empire of the will over the Astral Light, which is the physical soul of the four elements, is represented in magic by the Pentagram. That which was used by the author in his evocation at London, scientifically perfected, is that which is engraved at the beginning of this chapter, and it is not to be found so complete either in the clavicles of Solomon or in the magic calendars of Tycho-Brahe and Duchenteau. If it be asked how a sign can exercise that immense power over spirits which is claimed for the Pentagram, we inquire in turn why the Christian world bows before the sign of the Cross. The sign by itself is nothing, it derives strength from the doctrine it resumes, and of which it is the Logos. Now, a sign which epitomizes by signification all the occult forces of Nature, and which has always manifested to elementary and other spirits a power superior to their own, naturally strikes them with fear and respect, and enforces their obedience by the empire of knowledge and will over ignorance and weakness.

The sign of the Pentagram is called also the sign of the Microcosm, and it represents what the Kabbalists of the Sohar term the Microprosopus. Its complete comprehension is the key of the two worlds—it is absolute natural philosophy and natural science. Its use, however, is most dangerous to operators who do not completely and perfectly understand it. It should be composed of seven metals, or at any rate be graved in pure gold on white marble, but it may be also designed in vermilion on a lambskin free from every defect and stain, this being the symbol of integrity and light. The marble should be virgin, that is, should never have been previously used; the lambskin should be prepared under the auspices of the sun. The lamb should have been killed in Paschal time with a new knife, and the skin must have been salted with salt consecrated by magical ceremonies. Negligence in even one of these difficult and, at first sight, arbitrary observances completely stultifies the great operations of science. The Pentagram is consecrated with the four elements; the magic figure is breathed on five times, it is sprinkled with consecrated water, and dried by the smoke of five perfumes, namely, incense, myrrh, aloes, sulphur, and camphor, with which a little white resin and ambergris may be mixed; then we must breathe five times, pronouncing the names of the five genii, who are Gabriel, Raphael, Anael, Samael, and Oriphiel; the pantacle must be subsequently laid on the earth and turned towards the north, south, east, and west, and to the centre of the astronomical cross, pronouncing the letters of the sacred Tetragram one after another. Finally, we must repeat softly the blessed names Aleph and the mysterious Thau, united in the kabbalistic name of Azoth.

The Pentagram must be placed on the altar of perfumes and on the tripod of evocations. The operator must also wear one about his person, with the figure of the Macrocosm, that is, the six-pointed star composed of two interlaced triangles. When a spirit of light is to be evoked, the head of the star, that is, one of its points, must be turned towards the tripod of evocation, and the two lower points towards the altar of perfumes. The reverse is to be done where a spirit of darkness is concerned, but, in this case, the operator must be careful to hold the end of the rod or the point of the sword towards the top of the Pentagram. We have said already that signs are the active voice of the will. Now the will must produce its voice perfectly in order to transform it into action; and a single negligence, representing a useless word or a doubt, stamps every operation with falsehood and inefficacy, and turns back all the vainly expended energies on the operator.

THE DOCTRINE OF SPIRITUAL ESSENCES. 139

Magical ceremonial must, therefore, be absolutely abstained from, or scrupulously and exactly accomplished in everything. The Pentagram graved in luminous lines on glass by means of the electrical machine also exercises a great influence on spirits and terrifies them. It was traced by the old magicians on the threshold of the door, to prevent evil spirits from entering and good ones from going out. This restraint resulted from the direction of the star's points. Two points on the outside repelled the evil, two on the inside detained them captive, one point only on the inner side captivated the good spirits. All these magical theorems, based on the unique dogma of Hermes, and on the analogical inductions of science, have been invariably confirmed by the visions of ecstatics and by the convulsions of cataleptics under the supposed possession of spirits. The G which Freemasons place in the centre of the Burning Star signifies GNOSIS and GENERATION, the two sacred words of the ancient Kabbalah. It also signifies GRAND ARCHITECT, for the Pentagram, from whatever side it may be looked at, always represents an A. By placing it in such a manner that two of its points are above and only one below, we may see the horns, ears, and beard of the hieratic goat of Mendes, when it becomes the sign of infernal evocations.

The allegorical star of the Magi is nothing else, as we have said, than the mysterious Pentagram ; and these three kings, children of Zoroaster, conducted by the Burning Star to the cradle of the microcosmic God, would. be sufficient to prove the wholly kabbalistic and truly magical origines of Christian doctrine. One of these kings is black, another white, the third brown ; the white king offers gold, symbol of life and light ; the black myrrh, image of death and darkness ; the brown presents incense, emblematic of the divinity of the conciliating dogma of the duadic cause; then they return into their own country by another road, to show that a new cultus is but a new path which leads humanity to the one and only religion, which is that of the sacred triad and the shining Pentagram, the sole eternal *Catholicism*. In the Apocalypse, St John beholds this same star fall from heaven to earth ; it is then called absynth or bitterness, and all the waters of the sea become bitter—striking image of the materialisation of dogma, which produces the fanaticism and arid sourness of controversy. It is to Christianity itself that the words of Isaiah may be then addressed—" How art thou fallen from heaven, bright star, which wert so splendid in the morning?" But the Pentagram, profaned though it be by men, shines unclouded for ever in the right hand of the Word of truth, and the inspired voice promises to whomsoever shall conquer, that he will give him the morning star—a solemn restitution held out to the star of Lucifer.

As will be seen, all mysteries of magic, all symbols of the gnosis, all figures of occultism, all kabbalistic keys of prophecy, are resumed in the sign of the Pentagram, which Paracelsus proclaims to be the greatest and most potent of all. Must we be astonished after this at the real influence exercised by this sign on the intelligences of every hierarchy? Those who brave the sign of the Cross shudder at the aspect of the Star of the Microcosm. The Magus, on the contrary, when he feels his will grow weak, casts his eyes on that symbol, takes it in his right hand, and feels himself to be armed with intellectual omnipotence, provided that he is truly a king worthy to be conducted by the star to the cradle of divine realisation; provided he knows, dares, wills, and can hold his peace; provided he understands the uses of the pantacle, cup, wand, and sword; provided, lastly, that the intrepid glances of his soul correspond to those two eyes which the upper ray of the Pentagram always presents to him open.

The intelligence of the wise man gives value to his pantacle, as his knowledge gives weight to his will, and spirits comprehending this power are at once subject to the sign when intelligently used. Let us briefly explain this marvel. All created spirits communicate with each other by means of signs, and all adhere to a certain number of truths expressed by certain determined forms, whose perfection increases in proportion to the detachment of the spirits, those who are not weighted by the chains of matter recognising by the first intuition whether a sign is the expression of a true power or of an imprudent will. Thus by the Pentagram spirits may be forced to appear in dream, either during the waking state or in sleep, *by bringing themselves before our Diaphane their own reflection which exists in the Astral Light, if they have lived, or a reflection analogous to their spiritual Logos if they have not lived on earth.* This explains all visions, and, more than all, shows why the dead invariably appear to seers either as they were on earth, or as they still are in the tomb, but never as they exist in the life which escapes the perceptions of our present envelope.

Women with child are more than others under the influence of the Astral Light, which concurs in the formation of the infant, and unceasingly presents to them the reminiscences of the forms with which it is replete. It is thus that the most virtuous women sometimes deceive the malice of observers by equivocal resemblances; they frequently impress on the fruit of their marriage an image which strikes them in a dream, and it is thus that the same physiognomies are perpetuated from generation to generation. The kabbalistic use of the Pentagram may then determine the appearance of the child to be born, and an initiated woman could give her son the features of Nero or Achilles, as much as those of Louis XIV. or of Napoleon.

Solomon's Seal.

The double triangle of Solomon, forming the six-pointed star, is the sign of the Macrocosmos, but it is less powerful than the Pentagram, the microcosmic sign. It is represented in the following manner :—

The double triangle of Solomon is explained by St John in a remarkable way. He says, " There are three who give testimony in Heaven, the Father, the Word, and the Holy Ghost . . . ; and there are three which give testimony on earth, the spirit, the water, and the blood." St John is thus in accordance with the masters of Hermetic philosophy, who give to their sulphur the name of ether, to their mercury the name of philosophic water, and to their salt the qualification of the dragon's blood, or menstruum of the earth. The blood or salt corresponds by opposition with the Father, the azotic or mercurial water with the Word or Logos, and the breath or spirit with the Holy Ghost—but the things of transcendental symbolism cannot be properly understood except by the true children of science.

Independently of these signs, the ancients made use, when evoking, of mystical combinations of the Divine names. The magic triangle of pagan theosophists is the celebrated ABRACADABRA, to which they attributed extraordinary virtues, and which they represented thus:—

```
A B R A C A D A B R A
 A B R A C A D A B R
  A B R A C A D A B
   A B R A C A D A
    A B R A C A D
     A B R A C A
      A B R A C
       A B R A
        A B R
         A B
          A
```

This combination of letters is a key of the Pentagram. The initial A is repeated five times and reproduced thirty times. The isolated A represents the unity of the first cause or of the intelligent, active agent. A united to B represents the fertilization of the duad by unity. R is the sign of the triad, because it hieroglyphically represents the effusion resulting from the union of the two principles. The number 11 of the letters of the word adds the unity of the initiate to the denary of Pythagoras, and the number 66, the total of the added letters, forms kabbalistically the number 12, which is the square of the triad,* and consequently the mystical quadrature of the circle. We may remark in passing that the author of the Apocalypse, that clavicle of the Christian Kabbala, has composed the num-

* Surely the square of the triad is 9! 12 is the triad multiplied by the tetrad.—TR.

THE DOCTRINE OF SPIRITUAL ESSENCES. 143

ber of the beast, that is, of idolatry, by adding a 6 to the double senary of the ABRACADABRA, which gives kabbalistically the number 18, assigned in the Tarot to the hieroglyphic symbol of the night of the uninitiated, the moon with the towers, the dog, wolf, and crab (the sceptic, the blind believer, and the enemy of progress),—a mysterious and obscure number, whose kabbalistic Key is 9, that of initiation. On this subject the sacred Kabbalist expressly says: " He that hath understanding (that is, the key of the kabbalistic numbers), let him calculate the number of the beast, for it is the number of a man, and the number of it is 666. It is, in fact, the decade of Pythagoras multiplied by itself and added to the sum of the triangular pantacle ABRACADABRA; it is therefore the epitome of all the magic of the ancient world, the entire programme of human genius, which the Divine Genius of the Gospel sought to absorb and supplant.

These hieroglyphical combinations of letters and numbers belong to the practical part of the Kabbalah. Such calculations, which now seem to us arbitrary or dry, belonged to oriental philosophical symbolism, and were of the greatest importance in the teaching of sacred things emanating from the secret sciences. The absolute kabbalistic alphabet, which connected primitive ideas with allegories, allegories with letters, letters with numbers, was what was then called the Keys of Solomon, preserved, though completely misunderstood, in the game of Tarot, whose antique symbols were noticed and appreciated for the first time, in our own days, by the erudite archæologist, Court de Gebelin.

X.—MAGICAL CEREMONIAL AND CONSECRATION OF TALISMANS.

CEREMONIES, vestments, perfumes, characters, and figures being necessary, as we have said, to employ the imagination in the education of the will, the success of magical operations depends on the faithful observance of every rite. These rites have nothing fantastic or arbitrary about them; they have been transmitted to us from antiquity, and subsist always by the essential laws of analogical realisation and the correspondence which necessarily exists between ideas and forms. After passing several years in consulting and comparing all the most authentic grimoires and magical rituals, we have been enabled, not without trouble, to reconstruct the ceremonial of universal and primitive magic. The only serious books that we have seen on this subject are manuscripts written in conventional characters, which we have deciphered by the help of the polygraphy of Trithemius. The value of others is wholly contained in hieroglyphics or in the symbols with which they are adorned, and they disguise the truth of their images by the superstitious fictions of a mystifying text. Such, for example, is the Enchiridion of Pope Leo III.,* which has never been printed with its true figures, and which we have recovered for our private use from an ancient manuscript.

The Rituals known under the name of the Claviculæ of Solomon are very numerous. Many have been printed, others remain in manuscript; a beautiful copy in extremely graceful caligraphy is preserved at the Bibliothèque Impériale; it is enriched with pantacles and characters which are, for the most part, to be found in the magical calendars of Tycho-Brahe and Duchentan. There are, lastly, printed Claviculæ and grimoires which are disgraceful speculations and mystifications of low publishing houses. The book so well known, and so much decried by our fathers, under the name of *Petit Albert*, belongs for the most part to this class; its only serious sections are some calculations borrowed from Paracelsus and some talismanic figures.

In questions of realisation and ritual, Paracelsus is an imposing authority on magic. No one has accomplished greater works than his, and for this very reason he has concealed the power of ceremonial, and teaches only in his occult philosophy the existence of the magnetic agent of the omnipotence of will-force; he epitomises the whole science of characters in two signs, which are the *macrocosmic* and *microcosmic* stars. This was sufficient for adepts, and it was of importance that the crowd should remain uninitiated. Paracelsus, therefore, did not teach the Ritual, but he practised, and his practice was a sequence of miracles.

The triad and tetrad are of great importance in magic.

* See Note 17.

THE DOCTRINE OF SPIRITUAL ESSENCES. 145

Their union composes the great religious and kabbalistic number which represents the universal synthesis. The world, in the belief of the ancients, was governed by seven secondary causes, called by Trithemius secundæi, and these universal forces are designated by Moses under the plural name of *Eloïm*, the gods. These forces, analogous yet contrary one to another, produce equilibrium by their contrasts, and regulate the revolution of the spheres. The Jews called them the seven great archangels, and gave them the names of Michael, Gabriel, Raphael, Anael, Samael, Zadkiel, and Oriphiel. The four last were called by the Gnostic Christians Uriel, Barachiel, Scaltiel, and Jehudiel. Other nations have attributed to these spirits the government of the seven chief planets, and have given them the names of their great divinities. All have believed in their relative influence, and astronomy has divided the ancient sky among them, and has attributed to them successively the government of the seven days of the week. This is the reason of the diverse ceremonies of the magic week and of the septuary cultus of the planets. We have said already that here the planets are signs and nothing more; they possess the influence which universal faith attributes to them because they are more truly the stars of the human mind than the stars of the sky.

The sun, which olden magic always regarded as fixed, is only a planet for the ignorant, so does it represent in the week the day of repose which we call, like the ancients, the day of the sun. The seven magical planets, that is, the seven strings of the human lyre, correspond to the seven colours of the prism and the seven notes of the musical octave; they also represent the seven virtues, and, by opposition, the seven vices of Christian morality. Thus faith, that aspiration towards the infinite, that noble self-confidence, sustained by the belief in all virtues, faith which in feeble natures can degenerate into pride, was represented by the Sun; hope, enemy to avarice, by the Moon; charity, opposed to luxury, by Venus, the brilliant star of the morning and evening; strength, superior to anger, by Mars; prudence, in opposition to idleness, by Mercury; temperance, opposed to gluttony, by Saturn, to whom a stone was given in place of his children; and, finally, justice, in opposition to envy, was represented by Jupiter, the conqueror of the Titans. Such are the symbols

K

borrowed by astrology from the Hellenic cultus. In the Jewish Kabbalah, the Sun represents the angel of light; the Moon, the angel of aspirations and dreams; Mars, the exterminating angel; Venus, the angel of love; Mercury, the angel of culture; Jupiter, the angel of power; Saturn, the angel of the solitudes. These governing powers of souls divide the human life into periods among themselves, and astrologers compute these periods on the revolutions of corresponding planets.

The spiritual sky has never changed, and astrology has been more invariable than astronomy. The seven planets are really nothing else but the hieroglyphic symbols of the keyboard of our affections. To compose talismans of the Sun, Moon, or Saturn is to attach one's will magnetically to signs which correspond to the principal energies of the soul; to consecrate anything to Mercury or Venus is to magnetise that thing with a direct intention either of pleasure or of knowledge or profit. Metals, animals, plants, and their analogous perfumes are here our auxiliaries. The seven magical animals are — among birds, corresponding to the divine world, the swan, the owl, the vulture, the stork, the eagle, and the pewit; among fishes, corresponding to the spiritual or scientific world, the seal, the œlurus, the lucius, the thimallus, the dolphin, and the cuttle-fish; among quadrupeds, corresponding to the natural world, the lion, the cat, the wolf, the goat, the ape, the stag, and the mole. The blood, fat, liver, and gall of these animals are used in enchantments; their brains combine with the perfumes of the planets, and it is recognised by the practice of the ancients that they possessed magnetic virtues corresponding to the seven planetary influences.

The seven sacraments are equally in correspondence with the great universal septenary. Baptism, which consecrates the element of water, corresponds to the moon; severe penitence is under the auspices of Samael, the angel of Mars; confirmation, which gives the spirit of understanding, and imparts to the true believer the gift of tongues, is under the providence of Raphael, the angel of Mercury; the Eucharist substitutes the sacramental realisation of God made man in place of the empire of Jupiter; matrimony is consecrated to the angel Anael, the purifying genius of Venus; Extreme Unction is the safeguard of the sick on the point of falling beneath the sickle of Saturn;

THE DOCTRINE OF SPIRITUAL ESSENCES. 147

and Holy Orders, which consecrate the priesthood of Light, is more specially marked by the characters of the Sun. Almost all these analogies were remarked by the erudite Dupuis, who thence concluded that every religion is false, instead of discovering the sanctity and perpetuity of a single dogma, ever reproduced in the universal symbolism of successive religious observances. He did not comprehend the permanent revelation transmitted to the mind of man by nature's harmonies, and has beheld only a succession of errors in the sequence of ingenious images and everlasting truths.

Magical works are also seven in number—1. Works of light and wealth, under the patronage of the Sun. 2. Works of divination and mysteries, under the invocation of the Moon. 3. Works of skill, science, and eloquence, under the protection of Mercury. 4. Works of wrath and chastisement, consecrated to Mars. 5. Works of love, favoured by Venus. 6. Works of ambition and policy, under the auspices of Jupiter. 7. Works of malediction and death, under the care of Saturn. In theological symbolism the Sun represents the Word of Truth; the Moon, religion itself; Mars, justice; Mercury, the interpretation and knowledge of mysteries; Venus, mercy and love; Jupiter, the risen and glorified Saviour; Saturn, God the Father, or the Jehovah of Moses. In the human body, the Sun is analogous to the heart, the Moon to the brain, Jupiter to the right hand, Saturn to the left, Mars to the left foot, Venus to the right, Mercury to the parts of generation, which has sometimes caused the genius of this planet to be represented by an androgynous figure. In the human face, the Sun rules the forehead, Jupiter the right eye, Saturn the left; the Moon reigns between the two eyes at the root of the nose, whose two wings are governed by Mars and Venus. Lastly, Mercury exercises his influence over mouth and chin. These notions of the ancients formed their occult science of physiognomy, since imperfectly recovered by Lavater.

The Magus who seeks to proceed to the operations of Light, should work on a Sunday from midnight to eight in the morning, or from three in the afternoon to ten in the evening. He must be vested in a purple robe, with a tiara and bracelets of gold. The altar of perfumes and the tripod of sacred fire must be surrounded by wreaths of laurel, heliotrope, and sunflowers; the perfumes must be cinnamon, strong incense, saffron, and red sandal-wood; the ring must be of gold, with a chrysolith or ruby, the carpets of lion-skin, the screens of hawk's feathers.

On Monday he should wear a white robe, embroidered with silver, with a triple necklace of pearls, crystals, and selenite; the tiara should be covered with yellow silk, and have silver characters forming in Hebrew the monogram of Gabriel, as it is found in the secret philosophy of Agrippa; the perfumes should be white sandal-wood, camphor, amber, aloes, and the ground seed of cucumber; the garlands should be of mugwort, moonwort, and yellow ranunculuses. Tapestries, garments, and objects of a black colour should be avoided, and no metal but silver should be worn.

On Tuesday, a day for the works of vengeance, the robe should be flame-coloured, or of the colour of rust, or blood, with belt and bracelets of steel; the rod should not be used, but merely the magic dagger and sword. The garlands should be of absynth and rue, and a steel ring with an amethyst for its stone should be worn on the finger.

On Wednesday, a day favourable to supreme science, the robe should be green, or of a stuff shot with various colours; the necklace should be of pearls in hollow glass beads, containing mercury; the perfumes should be benzoin, mace, and storax; the flowers, the narcissus, lily, the mercury, fumitory, and marjolane; the precious stone should be agate.

On Thursday, the day for great religious and political achievements, the robe must be scarlet, and on the forehead should be a brass tablet having the character of the spirit of Jupiter, and these words—GIARAR, BETHOR, SAMGABIEL; the perfumes must be incense, ambergris, balm, seed of paradise, macis, and saffron; the ring must be ornamented with an emerald or sapphire; the garlands and crowns must be of oak, poplar, fig, and pomegranate.

On Friday, the day for amorous operations, the vestment should be of azure blue, the hangings green and rose colour, the ornaments of polished copper, the crowns of violets, the garlands of roses, myrtle, and the olive leaf; the ring should be ornamented with a turquoise; lapis-lazuli and beryl will answer for tiara and bracelets; the screens must be of swan's feathers, and the operator must

THE DOCTRINE OF SPIRITUAL ESSENCES. 149

wear on his breast a copper talisman with the character of Anael and these words—AVEEVA VADELILITH.

On Saturday, a day of funereal operations, the vestment should be black or brown, with characters embroidered in orange-coloured silk; round the neck must be worn a leaden medal having the character of Saturn, and these words — ALMALEC, APHIEL, ZARAHIEL; the perfumes should be diagridium, scammony, alum, sulphur, and assafœtida; the ring should have an onyx; the garlands should be of ash, cypress, and black hellebore; on the onyx of the ring, during the hours of Saturn, should be engraved the double head of Janus by means of the consecrated awl.

Such are the antique magnificences of the secret cultus of the Magi. With similar ceremonies the great magicians of the middle ages proceeded to the daily consecration of pantacles and talismans relating to the seven genii. A pantacle is a synthetic character resuming the whole magical dogma in one of its special phases. It is thus the real expression of a completed thought and act of will; it is the signature of a mind. The ceremonial consecration of this sign attaches the intention of the operator still more strongly thereto, and establishes between himself and the pantacle a veritable magnetic chain. Pantacles may be indifferently traced on virgin parchment, paper, or metals. A talisman is a piece of metal which bears either pantacles or characters, and has received a special consecration for a defined intention. Gaffarel, in his learned work on the antiquities of magic, has scientifically demonstrated the real power of talismans, and the faith in their virtue is otherwise so great in nature that we gladly bear about us the keepsakes of those we love, persuaded that such relics will preserve us from danger and ensure our happiness. Talismans may be made either of the seven kabbalistic metals—gold, silver, iron, copper, fixed mercury, brass, and lead—or of precious stones, such as carbuncles, crystals, diamonds, emeralds, agates, sapphires, and onyxes. The Pentagram must be always engraved on one side of the talisman, with a circle for the Sun, a crescent for the Moon, a winged caduceus for Mercury, a sword for Mars, a G for Venus, a crown for Jupiter, and a scythe for Saturn. The other side of the talisman should bear the sign of Solomon, that is, the six-pointed star formed by two interlaced triangles; in the centre there should be placed a human figure for the Sun talismans, a cup for those of the Moon, a dog's head for those of Jupiter, a lion's for those of Mars, a dove's for those of Venus, a bull's or goat's for those of Saturn.* The names of the seven angels should be added either in Hebrew, Arabic, or magic characters similar to those of the alphabets of Trithemius. The two triangles of Solomon may be replaced by the double cross of Ezekiel's wheels, this being found on a great number of ancient pantacles. All objects of this nature, whether in metals or in precious stones, should be carefully wrapped in silk satchels of a colour analogous to the spirit of the planet, perfumed with the perfumes of the corresponding day, and preserved from all impure looks and touches. Pantacles and talismans of the Sun should not be seen or handled by deformed and ugly persons, or by immoral women; those of the Moon are profaned by the glances and touches of debauched men and menstruous women; those of Mercury lose their virtue if seen or fingered by paid priests; those of Mars should be concealed from cowards; those of Venus from depraved men, and from such as are under a vow of celibacy; those of Jupiter from the impious; and those of Saturn from virgins and children, not that the looks or contact of these can ever be impure, but because the talisman would bring them misfortune, and thus lose all its power.

Crosses of honour and similar decorations are veritable talismans which increase personal importance and worth. Their solemn distributions are consecrations. Public opinion may invest them with prodigious power. The reciprocal influence of signs on ideas and of ideas on signs has not been sufficiently noticed. It is equally true that the revolutionary achievement of modern times has been summed up symbolically in its entirety by the Napoleonic substitution of the Star of Honour in place of the Cross of St Louis. It is the Pentagram substituted for the labarum; it is the rehabilitation of the symbol of light; it is the typical resurrection of Adonhiram. They say that Napoleon believed in his star, and could he have been made to state what he understood by this star, it would have been found to be his genius. He did rightly, therefore, in adopting the Pentagram as his sign, for it is the symbol of human

* See Note 18.

THE DOCTRINE OF SPIRITUAL ESSENCES. 151

sovereignty by intelligent initiative. The mighty soldier of the Revolution knew little, but he divined almost everything; so was he the instinctive and practical magician of modern times. The world is still full of his wonders, and the country folk will never believe him to be dead.

Blessed and indulgenced objects, objects touched by holy images or by venerable persons, beads from Palestine, the *Agnus Dei* (composed of wax from the Paschal candle, and the annual remains of consecrated chrism) scapulars, and medals, are real talismans.

The greater the importance and solemnity brought to bear in the confection of talismans and pantacles, the greater is the virtue they acquire. Their consecration should be performed on the special days we have enumerated, with the apparatus described. They are consecrated by the four exorcised elements, after conjuring the spirits of darkness by the Conjuration of the Four. When taking up the pantacle, and sprinkling some drops of magic water thereon, we must say:—

In nomine Eloïm et per spiritum aquarum viventium, sis mihi in signum lucis et sacramentum voluntatis.

Presenting it to the smoke of the perfumes,

Per serpentem aneum sub quo cadunt serpentes ignei, sis mihi, &c.

Breathing seven times on the pantacle or talisman,

Per fermamentum et spiritum vocis, sis, mihi, &c.

Lastly, placing thereupon some grains of purified earth or salt,

In sale terra et per virtutem vitæ æternæ, sis mihi, &c.

Then the conjuration of the Seven must be made in the following manner:—Throwing alternately on the sacred fire one pastile of the seven perfumes, we must say:—

In the name of Michael, let Jehovah command thee and drive thee hence, Chavajoth!

In the name of Gabriel, let Adonaï command thee and drive thee thence, Belial!

In the name of Raphael, vanish before Elchim, Sachabiel!

By Samael Zebaoth and in the name of Eloïm Gibor, depart Adramelek!

By Zachariel and Sachiel-Meleck, be subject to Elvah, Samgabiel!

In the divine and human name of Schaddaï and by the

sign of the Pentagram which I hold in my right hand, in the name of the angel Anaël, by the power of Adam and of Heva, who are Jotchavah, begone, Lilith! Let us rest in peace, Nahemah! By the holy Eloïm and the names of the genii Cashiel, Sehaltiel, Aphiel, and Zarahiel, at the mandate of Orifiel, withdraw from us, Moloch! We refuse thee our children to devour.

The chief magic instruments are—the rod, the sword, the lamp, the cup, the altar, and the tripod. In the operations of supreme and divine magic, the lamp, rod, and cup are used; in black magic, the rod is replaced by the sword, and the lamp by the candle of Cardan. The magic rod, which must not be confused with the simple divining rod, nor with the fork of the necromancers, nor with the trident of Paracelsus, the true and absolute magic rod, must be a single and perfectly straight beam of the almond or hazel tree, cut by a single blow with the magic pruning-knife, or golden sickle, before the sun rises, and at the moment when the tree is about to blossom. It must be longitudinally perforated without splitting or breaking it, and a needle of magnetized iron, occupying its whole extent, must be introduced; then a polyhedral prism triangularly cut must be fitted to one of its ends, and to the other a similar figure of black resin. In the middle of the rod must be placed two rings, one of red copper, the other of zinc; the rod must be gilt on the side of the resin, and silvered on the side of the prism up to the central rings, and it must be wrapped in silk to the extremities exclusively. On the copper ring must be engraved these characters ידרשלימסחקפשה, and on the zinc one המלך שלמה. The consecration of the rod should last seven days, beginning at the new moon, and should be made by an initiate, possessing the Great Arcanum, and himself having a consecrated rod. This is the transmission of the magical priesthood, which has never ceased since the misty origin of the transcendant science. The rod and other instruments, but the rod above all, must be carefully hidden, and under no pretext should the magus permit it to be seen or touched by the profane; otherwise it will lose all its virtue. The manner of transmitting the rod is one of the secrets of science which it is never permitted to reveal. The length of the magic rod should not exceed that of the operator's arm; the magician should

THE DOCTRINE OF SPIRITUAL ESSENCES. 153

never use it except when alone, and should not even handle it unnecessarily. Many ancient magi made it only the length of the fore arm, and concealed it beneath their long mantles, shewing the simple divining rod only in public, or some allegorical sceptre made of ivory and ebony, according to the nature of their operations. The magic rod is the *Verendum* of the magus; he should not so much as refer to it in any clear and precise way; no one should boast of having it, and the secret of its consecration should be transmitted on condition of absolute confidence and discretion alone.

The sword is less occult, and must be made in the following manner :—It must be of pure steel with a copper handle made in the form of a cross with three pommels, as it is represented in the Enchiridion of Leo III., or else with two crescents for guard. On the middle knot of the guard, which should be covered with a gold plate, the sign of the Macrocosm must be engraved on one side, and that of the Microcosm on the other. On the pommel must be inscribed the Hebrew monogram of Michael, as it is seen in Agrippa, and on the blade these characters באל יהוה מי מבה on one side, and on the other the monogram of Constantine's labarum with the following words *Vince in hoc, Deo duce, ferro comite*. The consecration of the sword must take place on Sunday, in the hours of sunlight, under the invocation of Michael. The sword blade must be thrust into a fire of laurel and cypress wood; it must then be dried and polished with ashes of the sacred fire, moistened with the blood of the mole or serpent, these words being said :— *Sis mihi gladius Michaelis, in virtute Eloīm Sabaoth fugiant a te spiritus tenebrarum et reptilia terræ;* it must then be perfumed with the perfumes of the Sun, and wrapped up in silk with branches of vervain, which must be burned on the seventh day.

The magic lamp should be made of four metals—gold, silver, brass, and iron. The pedestal should be of iron, the joint of brass, the reservoir of silver, and the central triangle of gold. It should have two arms, composed of three metals intertwisted, but in such a manner as to leave a triple conduit for the oil. It should have nine wicks, three in the middle and three in each arm. On the pedestal must be engraved the Hermetic Seal, with the two-headed Androgyne of Khunrath above. The lower rim of the pedestal should represent a serpent biting its own tail.

On the reservoir for the oil the seal of Solomon must be engraved. Two globes must be adapted to this lamp, one ornamented with transparent pictures representing the seven genii, the other larger and double, arranged to hold water tinctured with various colouring in four compartments between the two glasses. The whole must be enclosed in a revolving pillar of wood, which shall permit at will the escape of one of the lamp's rays, which may be turned on the altar of perfumes at the moment of invocation. This lamp is of great use in assisting the intuitive operations of slow imaginations, and in instantaneously creating for magnetised persons shapes of terrible reality, which, multiplied by mirrors, will at once enlarge and change the operator's cabinet into one vast hall filled with visible souls. The intoxication of perfumes, and the exaltation of invocations, soon transform this phantasmagoria into a real dream; we recognise those whom we have known, and ghosts speak; then if we close the pillar of the lamp, an extraordinary and unexpected phenomenon will be produced by redoubling the perfumes.

XI.—BLACK MAGIC.

WE approach the domain of black magic. We are about to assail, even in his sanctuary, the darksome deity of the Sabbath, the formidable goat of Mendes, the phantom full of horrors, the dragon of every theogony, the Ahriman of the Persians, the Typhon of the Egyptians, the Python of the Greeks, the old serpent of the Jews, the bearded idol of mediæval alchemists, the Baphomet of the Templars. Let us declare, for the edification of the uninitiated, for the satisfaction of M. le Comte de Mirville, for the justification of Bodin the demonologist, and for the greater glory of the Church, which has persecuted the Templars, burned the magicians, and excommunicated the Freemasons, let us say boldly and loudly, that all initiates of the occult sciences—I speak of the inferior initiates and the betrayers of the Great Arcanum—have adored, do, and will always adore that which is signified by the frightful figure of the sabbatic goat.

THE DOCTRINE OF SPIRITUAL ESSENCES. 155

Yes, in our profound conviction, the grand masters of the order of the Templars adored Baphomet, and caused him to be adored by their initiates; yes, there have existed, and there may still be, assemblies presided over by this figure, seated on a throne and with a flaming torch between its horns; only the worshippers of this sign do not think it the representation of the devil as we do, but rather that of the god Pan, the god of our modern philosophical schools, the god of the Alexandrian theurgists, and of our present neoplatonic mystics, the god of Lamartine and Cousin, of Spinoza, Plato, and the early Gnostics; even the Christ of dissident sacerdotalism; and this last designation should not astonish students of religious antiquities who have followed through their various transformations the phases of doctrine and symbolism in India, Egypt, and Judea. The bull, dog, and goat, are the three symbolical animals of Hermetic magic, wherein all the traditions of Egypt and India are summed up. The bull represents the earth or salt of the philosophers; the dog, that is, Hermanubis, the Mercury of the sages, fluid air and water; the goat represents fire, and is at the same time the symbol of generation. In Judea, two goats, one pure and one unclean, were consecrated; the clean one was sacrificed in expiation of sins, the other, loaded by imprecation with the same sins, was turned adrift into the desert—a strange observance, but one profound in its symbolism—reconciliation by self-sacrifice, and expiation by liberty! Now, all the fathers who have concerned themselves with Jewish types, have recognised in the immolated goat the figure of Him who took on Himself the very form of sin. Thus the Gnostics were not beside symbolic traditions when they gave to the Christ deliverer the mystical figure of the goat. All the Kabbalah and all magic is, in fact, divided between the cultus of the sacrificed goat and that of the emissary goat. There is, therefore, a magic of the sanctuary and one of the wilderness, a white church and a black church, a priesthood of public assemblies, and the Sanhedrim of the Sabbath.

The Baphomets of the Templars, whose names should be spelt kabbalistically backward, is composed of three abbreviations—TEM OHP AB, *Templi omnium hominum pacis abbas*, the father of the temple, universal peace of men. According to some, it was a monstrous head, according to others, a goat-shaped demon. A sculptured casket, unearthed in the ruins of an ancient commandry of the Templars, was observed by antiquaries to be a baphometic figure, conformable in its attributes to our goat of Mendes and the androgyne of Khunrath. It is bearded, but with the entire body of a woman; in one hand it holds the sun, in the other the moon, joined to it by chains. This virile head is a beautiful allegory which attributes to thought alone the first and creative cause. The head here represents mind, and the female body matter. The stars, bound to the human form and directed by that nature of which intelligence is the head, have also a sublime significance. The terrible Baphomet is, in fact, like all monstrous enigmas of ancient science, nothing more than an innocent and even pious hieroglyph. Let us declare emphatically to combat the remnants of manichæanism that Satan, as a superior personality and power, has no existence. THE DEVIL, IN BLACK MAGIC, IS THE GREAT MAGIC AGENT EMPLOYED FOR EVIL PURPOSES BY A PERVERSE WILL.

We have spoken of Manichæanism, and it is by this monstrous heresy that we shall account for the aberrations of black magic. The doctrine of Zoroaster misunderstood, the magical law of two forces producing universal equilibrium, has created in illogical minds a negative divinity, subordinate but hostile to the active divinity, and thus has caused the madness of dividing God. The evil divinity, born in the imagination of sectarians, became the prompter of all follies and crimes. Sanguinary sacrifices were offered him, monstrous idolatry usurped the place of the true religion, black magic caused the supreme and luminous magic of veritable adepts to be calumniated, and atrocious gatherings of sorcerers, ghouls, and vampires took place in caverns and abandoned places; for imbecility soon changes into frenzy, and it is only a step from human sacrifices to cannibalism.

The mysteries of the Sabbath have been variously described; all the revelations made on this subject may be divided into three series: 1, Those which are connected with a fantastic and imaginary Sabbath; 2, Those which betray the secrets of the occult assemblies of real adepts; 3, Revelations of lunatic and criminal assemblies, whose object was the practice of black magic. For a great number of pitiable wretches abandoned to these stupid and

THE DOCTRINE OF SPIRITUAL ESSENCES. 157

abominable pursuits, the Sabbath was only a long nightmare, whose dreams appeared to be realities, and which they obtained by means of beverages, fumigations, and narcotic frictions. Baptista Porta gives us, in his Natural Magic, the pretended receipt for the sorcerer's unguent, by means of which they were carried to the Sabbath. It was composed of children's fat, of aconite boiled with poplar leaves, and some other drugs; soot must be mixed with these, which would render the nakedness of sorceresses, who go to the Sabbath rubbed over with this pomade, the very reverse of attractive. A more serious receipt is given by the same mystificator, and which we leave in its original Latin to retain its grimoire character:—
Recipe—suim, acorum vulgare, pentaphyllon, verspertillionis sanguinem solanum somniferum et oleum, the whole to be well boiled and stirred to the consistence of an ointment.

We imagine that opiates like the pith of green hemp, *datura stramonium*, and the laurel-almond, would enter with no less success into similar compounds. The fat or blood of night-birds joined to such narcotics, with the ceremonies of black magic, would impress the imagination and determine the direction of dreams. It is to Sabbaths dreamed in this manner that we must refer the tales of goats issuing from pitchers and returning therein at the conclusion of the ceremony, of infernal powders collected behind the same creature, known as Maître Leonard; of banquets where abortions were eaten without salt and along with toads and serpents; of dances where monstrous animals or human beings with impossible shapes took part, &c. Nightmare alone could produce and alone explain such horrors. But the Sabbath was not always a dream, it was a real fact; secret nocturnal assemblies exist even at this day, and the rites of the ancient world are practised there; some of these assemblies have a religious character and a social object, others are conspiracies and orgies. When Christianity proscribed the public exercise of the ancient forms of worship, it reduced their partisans to the necessity of meeting in secret to celebrate their mysteries. Initiates presided at these assemblies and soon established among the different shades of such persecuted beliefs a sort of orthodoxy which true magic enabled them to do with the greater facility, because proscription unites wills and strengthens the bonds of brotherhood between men.

In this manner, the mysteries of Isis, of the Eleusinian Ceres, and of Bacchus, were blended with those of the benevolent goddess and primeval druidism. The assemblies were commonly held between the days of Mercury and Jupiter, or between those of Venus and Saturn; the rites of initiation were celebrated; mysterious signs exchanged, symbolic hymns sung, banquets partaken of, and the magic chain was successively formed at the table and in the dance; then the assembly broke up after renewing their pledges in the presence of the chiefs, and receiving their instructions in return. The neophite of the Sabbath was led, or rather carried, to the meeting with his eyes covered by the magic mantle, in which he was indeed wholly enveloped; he was made to pass between great fires, and alarming noises were caused round him. When his face was uncovered he found himself surrounded by infernal monsters and in front of a colossal and monstrous goat, which he was required to adore. All these ceremonies were trials of his strength of character and his belief in his initiators. The final trial was decisive above all, because it presented, at first sight, something ridiculous and humiliating to the mind of the neophyte; it was a question of respectfully kissing the goat's posterior, and the order was given without circumlocution. If he refused, his head was again covered, and he was borne away with such rapidity that he believed himself transported on a cloud; if he consented, he was taken behind the symbolic idol, and there found not a repulsive and obscene object, but the youthful and gracious face of a priestess of Isis or Maia, who gave him a maternal salute, and he was then admitted to the banquet. As for the orgies which, in many assemblies of this nature, were said to follow the feast, we must beware of supposing that they were generally allowed at these secret *agapæ*, but it is known that various Gnostic sects did practise them at their gatherings from the earliest Christian centuries. That the flesh had its protestants in the ages of asceticism and compression of the senses is no cause for surprise, but we should not accuse transcendant magic of the irregularities which it never has authorised. Isis is chaste in her widowhood, Diana Panthea is a virgin, Hermanubis having both sexes can satisfy neither, the Hermetic Hermaphrodite is pure, Apollonius Tyaneus never yielded to the seductions of pleasure, the Emperor

Julian was a man of repellant austerity, Plotinus was rigorous as an ascetic in his morals, Paracelsus was such a stranger to the extravagances of love that even his sex was doubtful, Raymond Lully was initiated into the final mysteries of science only after a hopeless love which made him chaste for ever. It is also a tradition of supreme magic that pantacles and talismans lose all their virtue when he who wears them enters a house of ill-fame or commits an adultery. The Sabbath of debauchery should not, therefore, be considered as that of the veritable adepts. As to the appellation Sabbath, some derive it from the name of Sabasius, and other etymologies have been conjectured. The simplest, in our opinion, is that which makes it come from the Jewish Sabbath, for it is certain that the Jews, the most faithful trustees of the secrets of the Kabbalah, were almost always the great masters of magic in the middle ages. The Sabbath was the Sunday of the Kabbalists, the day of their religious assembly, or rather the night of their habitual meeting. This festival, surrounded with mysteries as it was, found its safeguard in the very fright of the vulgar, and escaped persecution through the terror it occasioned. As for the diabolic Sabbath of the necromancers, it was a spurious imitation of that held by the magi. Horrible rites were practised at it and abominable potions composed. Here sorcerers and sorceresses made their plans and instructed one another how to sustain mutually their repute for prophecy and divination, for diviners were generally consulted at that epoch, and exercised a lucrative calling while possessing a veritable power. These assemblies of sorcerers and sorceresses neither had nor could have regular rites; all depended on the caprice of the chiefs and the whims of the assembly. What was recounted by those who assisted thereat served as a type to the nightmares of all such dreamers, and it is from the medley of these impossible realities and demoniacal hallucinations that the revolting and stupid histories figuring in magic trials and in the works of Spranger, Delancre, Delrio, and Bodin, have undoubtedly issued.

After attributing a positive existence to the absolute negation of good, after enthroning the absurd and creating a god of lies, it remained for human imbecility to invoke this impossible idol. We were lately informed that the most venerable father Ventura, formerly superior of the

Theatines, on reading one of our books, declared that the Kabbalah was, in his opinion, an invention of the devil, and that the star of Solomon was another artifice of the same personage to persuade the world that he, the devil, was the same as God. Such is the serious teaching of those who are rulers in Israel! The ideal of darkness and nothingness inventing a sublime philosophy which is the universal basis of faith and the keystone of every temple! The demon setting his signature by the side of God's! My venerable masters in theology, you are more sorcerers than you suppose or is imagined; and He who said—The devil is a liar like his father—would also have something to remark on the decisions of your reverences.

The evokers of the devil must before all things belong to a religion which believes in a devil who is the rival of God. To have recourse to a power we must believe in it. A firm faith being therefore granted in the religion of Satan, here is the method of communicating with this pseudo-God :—

Magical Axiom.

Within the circle of its action, every Logos creates what it affirms.

Direct Consequence.

He who affirms the devil creates the devil.

Conditions of Success in Infernal Evocations.

1. Invincible obstinacy. 2. A conscience at once hardened by crime and most subject to remorse and terror. 3. Affected or natural ignorance. 4. Blind faith in everything incredible. 5. A completely false notion of God.

It is requisite afterwards :—Firstly, to profane the ceremonies of the religion one belongs to and trample its holiest symbols under foot; secondly, to make a bloody sacrifice; thirdly, to procure the magic fork. This is a branch of a single beam of hazel or almond, which must be cut at a single stroke with the new knife used in the sacrifice; the rod must terminate in a fork which must be bound with iron or with steel made from the same knife that it has been cut with. A fifteen days fast must be observed, taking only one meal without salt after sundown; this repast must be made off black bread and blood seasoned with unsalted spices, or off black beans, and milky, narcotic herbs; every five days, after sunset, one must get

THE DOCTRINE OF SPIRITUAL ESSENCES.

drunk on wine in which five heads of black poppies and five ounces of bruised hemp have been steeped, the whole being contained in a cloth woven by a prostitute, or, strictly, the first cloth at hand may be used, if woven by a woman. The evocation may be performed either during the night between Monday and Tuesday or that between Friday and Saturday. A solitary and prohibited place must be chosen, such as a cemetery haunted by evil spirits, an avoided ruin in the country, the vault of an abandoned convent, the spot where an assassination has been perpetrated, a druidic altar, or a former temple of idols. A black robe without seams or sleeves must be provided, a leaden cap blazoned with the signs of the Moon, Venus, and Saturn, two candles of human fat set in crescent-shaped candlesticks of black wood, a magic sword with a black handle, the magic fork, a copper vase holding the blood of the victim, a censer containing incense, camphor, aloes, ambergris, and storax, mixed and moistened with the blood of a goat, a mole, and a bat; four nails torn from the coffin of an executed criminal, the head of a black cat which has been fed on human flesh for five days, a bat drowned in blood, the horns of a goat *cum quo puella concubuerit*, and the skull of a parricide, are also indispensable. All these horrible and with difficulty collected objects being obtained, they must be arranged as follows:—

A perfect circle must be traced with the sword, an opening or way out being, however, left; in the circle a triangle must be inscribed, and the pantacle thus traced by the sword must be dyed with blood; then, at one of the angles of the triangle the three-footed chafing-dish must be placed, which should also have been mentioned among the indispensable objects; at the opposite base of the triangle three small circles must be made for the operator and his assistants, and behind the circle of the former, not with the blood of the victim but with the operator's own blood, there must be traced the sign of the labarum or the monogram of Constantine. The operator or his acolytes should have naked feet and covered heads. The skin of the immolated victim must have also been brought, and, cut up into strips, must be placed within the circle forming an inner circle fastened at four corners with the four nails already spoken of. Near these nails, but without the circle, must be placed the cat's head, the human, or rather

L

the inhuman skull, the goat's horns, and the bat; they must be aspersed with a branch of birch dipped in the victim's blood, then a fire of cypress and alder wood must be lighted, and the two magic candles placed on the right and left of the operator circled with vervain wreaths.

The formulæ of evocation found in the magical elements of Peter d'Apono or in the Grimoires, whether printed or in manuscript, may then be recited. Those in the Great Grimoire, repeated in the common Red Dragon, have been wilfully altered in printing, and should read as follows:—

"Per Adonaï Eloïm, Adonaï Jehova, Adonaï Sabaoth, Metraton On Agla Adonaï Mathon, verbum pythonicum, mysterium salamandræ, conventus sylvorum, antra gnomorum, dæmonia Cœli Gad, Almousin, Gibor, Jehosua, Evam, Zariatnatmik, veni, veni, veni."

The great invocation of Agrippa consists only in these words:—"DIES MIES JESCHET BOENEDOESEF DOUVEMA ENITEMAUS." We do not pretend to understand what they mean, they have possibly no meaning, and can certainly have none which is rational, since they are of efficacy in conjuring up the devil, who is supreme senselessness. Doubtless in the same opinion, Mirandola affirms that the most barbarous and absolutely unintelligible words are the best and most powerful in black magic. Ridiculous practices and imbecile evocations induce hallucination better than rites which are calculated to keep the understanding vigilant. Dupotet affirms that he has tried the power of certain signs over ecstatics, and those in his "Magic Unveiled" are analogous if not absolutely identical with the diabolical signatures found in old editions of the "Great Grimoire." The same causes will always produce the same effects, and there is nothing new under the moon of the sorcerers any more than beneath the sun of the sages.

The conjurations should be repeated in a raised tone, accompanied by imprecations and menaces till the spirit responds. The spirit is usually preceded by a violent wind which seems to howl through the whole country. Domestic animals tremble at it, and seek a hiding place; the assistants feel a breath upon their faces, and their hair, damp with cold sweat, stands up on their heads. The great and supreme charge is, according to Peter d' Apono:—

"*Hemen-Etan! Hemen-Etan! Hemen-Etan!* EL *

ATI* TITEIP* AZIA* HYN* TEU* MINOSEL* ACHA-
DON* VAY* VAA* EYE* AAA* EIE* EXE* A EL
EL EL A* HY! HAU! HAU! HAU! VA! VA!
VA! VA! CHAVAJOTH.
"Aie Saraye, aie Saraye, aie Saraye! per Eloym, Archima, Rabur, BATHAS super ABRAC ruens supervenius ABEOR SUPER ARBERER *Chavajoth! Chavajoth! Chavajoth!* impero tibi per clavem SALOMONIS et nomen magnum SEMHAMPHORAS."

Evocations were frequently followed by pacts, which were written on parchment of goat skin with an iron pen and blood drawn from the left arm of the victim. The memorandum was double, the demon took away one and the voluntary reprobate swallowed the other. The mutual engagement was that the devil should serve the sorcerer for a certain number of years, and that the sorcerer should belong to the devil after a definite time. The Church by her exorcisms has consecrated the belief in all these things, and it may be said that black magic with its prince of darkness is a realistic, living, and terrible creation of Roman Catholicism; that it is even its special and characteristic work, for the priests do not invent God.*
So true Catholics cling from the bottom of their hearts to the preservation and even regeneration of this *magnum opus* which is the philosophic stone of the official and positive cultus. In thieves' slang the devil is called the *boulanger;* all our desire, and we speak no longer as a magus but as a devoted child of Christianity, and of that Church to which we owe our first education and our earliest enthusiasms, all our desire, we say, is that the phantom of Satan may be no longer called the pot-boiler of the ministers of morality and the representants of the highest virtue. Will they understand our sentiment? Will they pardon the boldness of our aspirations in view of our unselfish intentions and of the sincerity of our faith? The devil-creating magic which dictated the Grimoire of Honorius, † the Enchiridion of Leo III., the exorcisms of the Ritual, and the sentences of the Inquisition, the black magic of sorcerers, and of pious people who are not sorcerers, is something truly detestable in the one and infinitely deplorable in the others. It is above all to combat, by exposing them,

* See Critical Essay.   † See Note 19.

these unhappy aberrations of the human mind, that we have published this book. May it help in the cause of the holy work!

XII.—WITCHCRAFT AND SPELLS.

"WHOSOEVER looketh on a woman to lust after her hath already committed adultery with her in his heart," said the Great Master. What we desire persistently we perform. Every true will is confirmed by acts; every will confirmed by an act is an action. Every action is subject to a judgment, and this judgment is eternal. The good or evil which you desire, whether for yourself or others, within the scope of your will and the sphere of your activity, follows infallibly, if your will be confirmed and your determination fixed by deeds. Actions should be analogous to the desire. The wish to do harm or to be loved should be confirmed by works of hatred or love if it is to be efficacious. Whatever bears the impress of the human soul belongs to that soul; whatever man appropriates, in whatever manner, becomes his body in the wider sense of the term, and whatever is done to the body of a man is experienced mediately or immediately by his soul. For this reason every species of hostile action towards our neighbour is looked on by moral theology as a beginning of homicide. A bewitchment is a homicide, and the baser because it eludes the victim's right of self-defence and the punishment of the laws. This principle established, for the acquittal of our conscience and the warning of the weak, let us make bold to assert that bewitchment is possible, and not only possible, but, in a certain sense, necessary and fatal. It is continually taking place in the world, unknown both to agents and victims. Involuntary witchcraft is one of the most terrible dangers of human life.

Sensual sympathy necessarily subjects the most ardent desire to the most powerful will. Moral diseases are more contagious than physical ones, and we can die of an evil acquaintance even as of a contagious contact. The horrible plague which for some centuries only has avenged on Europe the profanation of the mysteries of love is a revelation of the analogical laws of nature, and, hideous as it is, presents only a feeble image of the moral corruptions daily consequent on an illicit sympathy. A story is told of a jealous and infamous man who, to avenge himself on a rival, voluntarily contracted an incurable complaint, and made it at once the common scourge and curse of a divided couch. This appalling history is that of every sorcerer who practises witchcraft. He poisons himself that he may poison, he condemns himself to hell that he may torture others, he inhales perdition that he may breathe it forth, he wounds himself to death that he may inflict death; but possessed of so much unhappy courage, it is positive and certain that he will empoison and destroy by the mere projection of his perverse will.

There are then two kinds of bewitchment—involuntary and voluntary bewitchment; we may also distinguish physical from moral witchcraft. Power attracts power, life attracts life, and health attracts health—this is a law of nature. If two children live, and above all sleep together, and if one of them be strong and the other weakly, the strong one will absorb the sickly one, who will waste gradually away. In boarding-schools certain pupils absorb the intelligence of others, and in every circle of men an individual will soon be found who avails himself of the wills of the rest. Bewitchment by means of currents is a very common thing; one is carried away by the crowd both morally and physically. But we have to establish specially in this chapter the almost absolute power of the human will over the determination of its acts, and the influence of every exterior demonstration of a will on things themselves exterior.

Voluntary bewitchments are still frequent in rural districts, because among ignorant and isolated people the forces of nature have full play, not being weakened by any doubt or deflection. An open, absolute hatred, unmixed with disappointed passion or personal cupidity, is a death-sentence for its object, under certain given conditions. I say, unmixed with amorous passion or self-interest, because a desire, being an attraction, counterbalances and annuls the power of projection. A jealous man will never efficaciously bewitch his rival, nor will a covetous heir shorten, by the mere fact of his will, the lifetime of an avaricious uncle. Bewitchments attempted under such conditions fall back on their performers, and are rather favourable than hurtful to their object, as they deliver them from a hostile action which destroys itself through unmeasured over-excitement.

The instrument of witchcraft is nothing else than the Great Magic Agent itself, which under the influence of an evil will becomes really and positively the demon. Witchcraft properly so called, that is, ceremonial operation with a view to bewitching, acts only on the performer, and serves to fix and confirm his will by laboriously and perseveringly formulating it, the two conditions necessary to render the will efficacious. The more difficult and horrible the operation, the more potent it is, because it acts better on the imagination, and confirms the effort in direct ratio of resistance. This explains the fantasticalness and even the atrocity of the operations of black magic among the ancients and in the Middle Ages—the devil's masses, the administration of the sacraments to reptiles, the effusions of blood, the human sacrifices, and other monstrosities, which are the very essence and reality of witchcraft and necromancy. These and similar practices have in all ages brought down on sorcerers the just repression of the laws. Black magic is really but a combination of sacrileges and murders graduated with a view to the permanent perversion of the human will and the realisation in a living man of the monstrous phantom of the fiend. It is, therefore, properly speaking, the religion of the devil, the worship of darkness, the hatred of goodness exaggerated to the point of paroxysm; it is the incarnation of death and the permanent creation of hell.

What sorcerers and necromancers sought above all in their evocations of the impure spirit was that magnetic power which is the possession of the true adept, and which they sought to usurp that they might abuse it shamefully. The true magus, without ceremonial, and by his simple reprobation, casts spells on those whom he condemns and whom he deems it necessary to punish; he even does so by his pardon of those who do him evil, and never do the enemies of the initiates carry far the impunity of their injustice. The executioners of martyrs always perish miserably, and the adepts are the martyrs of intelligence; Providence seems to contemn those who contemn them and to inflict death on those who would deprive them of life. The legend of the Wandering Jew is the popular version of this arcanum. A nation drove a wise man to his execution; it cried to him, "Go forward!" when he wished to rest a moment; and lo, this nation undergoes the same doom! It is proscribed wholly and for centuries, it is told to get onward, finding neither rest nor compassion. . . . The magi condemn after the fashion of skilful physicians, and for this reason there is no appeal from their sentences when they have passed judgment on a guilty person. They use neither ceremonies nor invocations; they have only to forbear from eating at the same table with the doomed individual, and if they be forced to do so, they must neither accept from nor offer him salt.

Far different are the bewitchments of sorcerers, which may be compared to a real poisoning of the Astral Light. They exalt their will with ceremonies till it becomes venomous at a distance, but they expose themselves most frequently to the danger of being the first to be destroyed by their infernal machinations. Let us reveal here a few of their infamous proceedings.

They procure either some of the hair or garments of the person whom they wish to curse; then they choose an animal which they consider the symbol of that person; by means of the hair or garments, they place this animal in magnetic rapport with the individual; they give it his name, then they slay it with one blow of the magic knife, open its breast, tear out the heart, which they envelop while still palpitating in the magnetised objects, and for three days they hourly pierce this heart with nails, red-hot pins, or long thorns, pronouncing maledictions at the same time on the name of the bewitched person. They are then convinced (and often rightly) that the victim of their infamous manœuvres experiences as many torments as if he had himself been probed to the heart with every one of the points. He begins to waste away, and at the end of a certain time dies of an unknown complaint.

Another spell used in the country consists in consecrating certain nails for works of vengeance with the fœtid fumigations of Saturn, and invocations of evil genii, then in following the footsteps of the person whom it is desired to torment, and pricking in the form of a cross every step which can be traced on the earth or in the sand.

One still more abominable is practised as follows:—A large toad is taken, baptism is administered to it, and it is given the name and surname of the person whom it is desired to curse; it is made to swallow a consecrated host whereon the formulæ of execration have been pronounced; then it is enveloped in the magnetised objects, bound with the hair of the victim, on which the operator has previously spat, and the whole is buried either beneath the threshold of the bewitched person's door, or in a place which he is bound to pass daily. The elementary spirit of the toad becomes a nightmare and vampire for the victim's dreams, unless, at anyrate, he knows how to send it back to the malefactor.

Let us come now to bewitchment with waxen images. The necromancers of the Middle Ages, anxious to please by means of sacrileges him whom they looked on as their master, mixed baptismal oil, and the ashes of burnt hosts, with wax. Apostate priests were always found to surrender to them the treasures of the Church. With this accursed wax they formed an image resembling as closely as possible the person they desired to bewitch; they clothed the image with garments similar to his, gave it the sacraments which he himself received, called down on its head all the maledictions which could give expression to the hate of the sorcerer, and inflicted daily on this anathematised figure imaginary tortures, so that the person whom the figure represented might be sympathetically reached and tormented.

Witchcraft is more infallible if the hair, blood, or, better than either, a tooth of the person to be bewitched can be obtained. Bewitchment is also accomplished by the glance, which is called in Italy the *jettatura*, or the evil eye.

The method of *Ceremonial Witchcraft* varies with times and with persons. All crafty and domineering people find its secrets and practice in themselves, without even actually computing them or reasoning on their sequence. They follow the instinctive inspirations of the great agent, which marvellously assimilates itself to our vices and virtues; but it may be generally said that we are subjected to the will of others by the analogies of our attractions, and above all by our failings. To flatter the weaknesses of an individuality is to avail one's self of it and make it an instrument in the order of the same errors or depravities. Now, when two natures with analogical defects are brought to bear on one another, there occurs a sort of substitution of the stronger for the weaker, and a veritable obsession of one mind by the other. Frequently the weaker struggles and seeks to revolt, then he falls deeper than ever into servitude. Thus, Louis XIII. conspired against Richelieu, and afterwards bought his forgiveness, so to speak, by abandoning his accomplices. We have all a dominant weakness, which is for our soul like the umbilical cord of its birth in sin, and it is by this that the enemy can always seize us—vanity for some, idleness for others, egotism for the greater number. You become, thereupon, not mad, not idiotic, but positively deranged, in all the force of the expression, that is, subjected to foreign impetus. In this state you have an instinctive horror of everything that may restore you to reason, and will not even hear representations which are contrary to your lunacy. This is one of the most dangerous maladies which can attack the moral nature of man. The sole remedy for such witchcraft is to make use of madness for the cure of madness, and to find for the sufferer imaginary satisfactions in a contrary order to that in which he has lost himself. Thus, for example, we may cure an ambitious person by making him desire the glories of Heaven—mystical remedy; we may cure a debauched person by an innocent affection—natural remedy; we may obtain honourable successes for a vain person, give an example of disinterestedness to an avaricious one, and procure him a just profit by an honourable participation in generous enterprises, &c. Acting thus on the moral nature, we shall heal a large number of physical diseases, for the moral nature influences the physical in virtue of the magical axiom—" That which is above is like that which is below," for which reason the Master said, speaking of a paralytic woman—" Satan hath bound her!" A disease comes always from defect or excess, and you will invariably find a moral disorder at the root of a physical evil.[*] This is an unvarying law of Nature.

A threat is a real spell, because it acts vividly on the imagination, above all, if this imagination easily receive belief in occult and illimitable power. The frightful menace of hell, that bewitchment of humanity during so many centuries, has created more nightmares, more violent madness than all vices and excesses put together. It is this which the mediæval Hermetic artists represented in the incredible and unheard of monsters which they carved

[*] See Note 20.

over the doorways of their basilicas. But bewitchment by threat produces an absolutely contrary effect to that which the operator desired when the menace is evidently vain, when it revolts the legitimate pride of the threatened individual, and consequently provokes his resistance, finally, when it is ridiculous in its atrocity. The sectaries of the hell-dogma have discredited heaven. Inform a reasonable man that equilibrium is a law of life and motion, and that moral equilibrium, or liberty, rests on an eternal and immutable distinction between truth and falsehood, good and evil; tell him that, endowed as he is with free-will, he must place himself by his works in the empire of truth and goodness, or fall back eternally, like the rock of Sysiphus, into the chaos of falsehood and wickedness, then he will understand your dogma; and if you call truth and goodness heaven, falsehood and evil hell, he will believe in your heaven and hell, above which the divine ideal rests calm, perfect, and equally inaccessible to anger and offence, because he will comprehend that if perdition as a principle be eternal, like liberty, it cannot be as a fact more than a passing purgation for souls, since it is an expiation, and the idea of expiation necessarily supposes that of reparation and the destruction of evil.

The first method—moral and rational—of counteracting witchcraft is to be reasonable and just, and never to give a handle or argument to anger. Legitimate anger is a thing to be feared, for which reason we should hasten to acknowledge and expiate our wrongdoings. Should anger persist after this, it certainly proceeds from vice; seek to know what vice, and unite yourself firmly to the magnetic currents of the opposite virtue. No spell will then have further power over you. Cause all linen and garments which you have worn to be carefully washed before giving them away, or else burn them; never use a garment worn by a stranger without purifying it with water, sulphur, and such aromatics as camphor, incense, or amber.

Paracelsus, the greatest of the Christian magi, opposed to bewitchment a spell of an opposite character. He compounded sympathetic remedies, and applied them not to the suffering parts but to representations of the same, formed and consecrated according to ceremonial magic. His success was prodigious, and never has any physician approached the phenomenal cures of Paracelsus, who, however, had discovered magnetism long before Mesmer, and had carried to its final consequences this brilliant discovery, or rather, this initiation into the magic of the ancients, who understood better than we do the Great Magic Agent, and did not make the Astral Light, the universal magnesia of the sages, an animal and special fluid emanating only from some particular individuals.

Bewitchment is also cured by substitution, when possible, and by the rupture or turning aside of the astral current. Rural traditions on this subject are admirable, and undoubtedly come from remote antiquity—they are remnants of the teaching of the Druids, who were initiated into the mysteries of Egypt and India by wandering hierophants. Now, in vulgar magic, a bewitchment, that is, a will determined and confirmed in ill-doing, invariably produces its effect, and cannot retract without danger of death. The sorcerer who frees some one from a spell must have another object for his malevolence, or it is certain that he himself will be assailed, and perish by his own witchcraft. The astral movement being circular, every azotic or magnetic projection which does not encounter its *medium* returns with increased force to its starting-point; this explains one of the strangest histories in any sacred book, that of the demons sent into the swine, who precipitated themselves into the sea. Demoniacal possessions are nothing but bewitchment, and an incredible number of possessed persons still exist in our own day. Antipathy itself is the presentiment of a possible bewitchment, which may be one of love or hate, for affection is frequently known to succeed antipathy. The Astral Light warns us of coming influences by a more or less sensible and lively action on the nervous system. Instantaneous sympathies, electrifying loves are explosions of the Astral Light as exactly produced, and as mathematically explicable and demonstrable as the discharges of powerful electric batteries. The nervous apparatuses destined for attraction or projection are particularly the eyes and hands. The polarity of the hands is situated in the thumbs, for which reason, according to the magical tradition still preserved in country places, we must, when we find ourselves in suspicious company, keep the thumb doubled up and concealed in the hand, taking care not to attract the notice of any one, but for all that endeavouring to be the first to look at those from whom we have anything to fear, so as to avoid unexpected fluidic projections and fascinating glances. There are also certain animals who have the property of breaking the currents of Astral Light by an absorption peculiar to them. These animals are violently antipathetic to us, and have something fascinating in their glance. Among such are the toad, the basilisk, and the tard. These animals when tamed and carried alive about the person, or kept in the rooms that we live in, guarantee us from the hallucinations of ASTRAL INTOXICATION, a term which explains all phenomena of insane passions, mental exaltations, and madness.

A great means of resisting bewitchment is not to fear it; bewitchment acts like contagious diseases. In times of pest, those who are afraid are the first to be attacked. The way not to fear an evil is not to think about it, and I strongly counsel nervous people, the weak, credulous, hysterical, and superstitious, devotees and foolish persons, devoid of energy and will, never to open a work on magic, never to listen to those who speak of the occult sciences, even to scout them, and to drink water only, as the great pantagruelist magician, the excellent curé of Meudon, maître François Rabelais, recommends. As for the wise, they have few witcheries to fear save those of fortune, but, as they are priests and physicians, they may be called on to cure the bewitched, and should then proceed as follows: They must cause the victim to perform some good action towards the sorcerer, to render him some service which he cannot refuse, and to seek, directly or indirectly, to lead him to the communion of salt. A person who believes himself bewitched by execration and the interment of a toad should carry about him a living toad in a box of horn. For the bewitchment of the pierced heart, the sufferer must be made to eat a lamb's heart, seasoned with sage and vervain, as also to wear a talisman of Venus or of the moon in a purse filled with camphor and salt. For bewitchment by the waxen figure, a more perfect figure must be fashioned, everything possible belonging to the person must be put on it, seven talismans must be placed round the neck with a large central pantacle representing the Pentagram, and it must be every day rubbed lightly with a mixture of oil and balsam, after pronouncing the Conjuration of the Four to turn aside the influence of elementary spirits. At the end of seven days the image must be consumed in consecrated fire, and we may rest assured that the statue fabricated by the sorcerer will at the same time lose all its virtue.

There are certain loves which destroy as much as ever hatred does; there are absorbing passions under which we feel ourselves wasting away like the brides of vampires. The bewitchments of benevolence are a torment to the wicked. The prayers we address to God for the conversion of a man do him harm if he will not be converted. The vows of parents pledging the future of their children are bewitchments which cannot be sufficiently condemned; children dedicated in white, for example, scarcely ever prosper; those formerly vowed to celibacy commonly fell into debauchery, or ended in despair and insanity. It is not permitted to man to do violence to destiny, still less to impose restrictions on the lawful use of liberty.

We come now to the most criminal abuse of Magic, the fabrication of philtres and sorcery in its application to poisoning. Here it must be understood that we write not to instruct others in this diabolical art, but to forewarn. Had human justice, when punishing the adepts, arraigned only the sorcerers, it is certain that its penalties would have been just, and that the severest intimidations could never be excessive for these and similar wretches. Alexandre Dumas, in his romance of "Monte Cristo," has exposed some practices of this deadly science. We shall not reproduce after him its miserable criminal experiments, how the sorcerers poisoned plants, how animals nourished on such plants became unwholesome flesh, and when they were made, in their turn, the food of men, caused death, yet left no trace of poison; we shall not relate by what venomous unguents they poisoned the walls of houses, and the air by fumigations which required for the operator the glass mask of St Croix; we leave the ancient Canidia, her abominable mysteries, and will not inquire how far the infernal rites of Sagane have perfected the art of Locusta. It is enough to say that these malefactors of the worst kind distilled together the virus of contagious diseases, the venom of reptiles, and the noxious sap of plants; that they extracted the poisonous and narcotic humour from fungi, from the datura stramonium its asphyxiating properties, from the peach and the laurel-almond that liquid one drop of which, placed on the tongue or in the ear, destroys, like a flash of lightning, the strongest and best constituted living being. They stewed milk, in which vipers and asps had been drowned, with the white juice of the milk-thistle; they collected carefully and brought with them from their long voyages, or else caused to be imported at great expense, the essence of the upas, or the deadly fruit of Java, the juice of the manioc, and other poisons; they pulverised silex, mixed up the dried saliva of reptiles with polluted ashes, composed hideous philtres with the virus of mares or secretions of bitches on heat, mingled human blood with vile drugs, and thence fabricated oil whose mere odour was fatal; they even disguised recipes for poisoning in the technical terms of alchemy, and in more than one pseudo-hermetic book the secret of the powder of projection is nothing more than the powder of consecution. In the Great Grimoire one of these recipes is still to be found, less disguised than others, but entitled "Method of Making Gold;" it is a frightful decoction of verdegris, vitriol, arsenic, and sawdust, which, when in condition, should immediately consume a twig dipped therein, and eat through a nail. Baptista Porta, in his "Natural Magic," gives a recipe for the poison of the Borgias; but, as may be well imagined, he is deceiving his readers, and does not divulge the truth, which would have been too dangerous in such a matter. We may therefore give his recipe to gratify the curiosity of our readers.

The toad by itself is not venomous, but it is like a sponge for poisons; it is the fungus of the animal race. "Take, therefore, a large toad," says Porta, "and shut it up in a glass bowl with asps and vipers, feed them for several days on poisonous fungi, foxglove, and hemlock exclusively, then irritate them by beating, burning, and torturing them in every conceivable way till they expire of rage and hunger, sprinkle their bodies with the dust of pulverised crystal and spurge, place them in a well-corked retort, and gradually evaporate all their moisture by heat; allow the whole to grow cool, and separate the ashes of the dead reptiles from the incombustible dust which will be found at the bottom of the retort; you will then have two poisons, a liquid one and one in powder. The first will be as powerful as the terrible *Aqua Toffana*, the second will, in a few days, dry up, age, and finally cause death amidst horrible sufferings, or in a universal debility, to any one who has swallowed a single pinch with his drink. It must be confessed that this recipe has the most hideous and blackest magical complexion, and revoltingly recalls the abominable concoctions of Canidia and Medea.

Similar powders the sorcerers pretended to receive at the Sabbath, and sold them at great prices to the ignorant and malicious. By the tradition of such mysteries they spread terror in country places, and succeeded in casting their spells. The imagination once impressed, the nervous system once attacked, the victim rapidly wasted away, the very fear of his relatives and friends completing his destruction. The sorcerer was almost always a species of human toad swollen with long-cherished spite; they were poor, rebuffed by all, and consequently full of hatred. The fear they inspired was their consolation and revenge. Poisoned themselves by a society whose vices and refuse only were known to them, they in turn poisoned all who were weak enough to dread them, and avenged on youth and beauty their accursed old age and unendurable hideousness.

The mere operation of these evil works and the accomplishment of these hideous mysteries constituted and confirmed what was then called the compact with the evil spirit. It is certain that the performer was dedicated body and soul to evil, and justly merited the universal and irrevocable reprobation expressed by the allegory of hell.

To preserve oneself from bad influences, the first condition is to forbid any over-excitement to the imagination. All excitable people are more or less foolish, and a fool is always governed by his folly. Set yourself, therefore, above puerile fears and vague desires; believe in the supreme wisdom, and be assured that this wisdom, having given you intelligence as the one means of attaining the knowledge of itself, can never seek to lay snares for your reason or understanding. You behold everywhere about you effects which are in proportion to causes, causes directed and modified by intelligence in the domain of humanity; in a word, you find goodness stronger and more esteemed than evil; why should you assume an immense irrationality in infinity, when there is reason in the finite? God is visible in His works, and asks nothing from His creatures which contradicts the laws of their nature; have confidence, not in men who slander reason, for such are impostors or fools, but in the eternal reason which is the divine Logos, that veritable light offered like the sun to the intuition of every human being coming into this world. If you believe in the absolute reason, and if you desire truth and justice above all things, you need fear no one, and will love only the loveable. Your natural light will instinctively repel that of the wicked, because it will be governed by your will. Thus, even venomous substances which may be administered you will not affect your understanding; they will indeed make you sick but never criminal.

The beverages which enfeeble the mind and disturb reason may assure the ascendancy already acquired by a perverse will. Prussic acid is the most terrible agent of such mental poisoning, for which reason we should avoid all distillations which savour of almonds, remove from our bedrooms all almond plants, the *datura stramonium*, almond soaps, essence of almonds, and in general all compositions with a predominating almond scent, above all, when their action on the brain is seconded by that of amber. To diminish the activity of the intelligence is to proportionately augment the strength of an insensate passion, and the love which is inspired by the philtres of sorcerers is a veritable stupefaction and the most shameful of all moral slaveries. The more we debilitate a slave the less is he able to free himself, and this is actually the secret of the sorceress of Apuleius and the beverages of Circe. The use of tobacco is a dangerous auxiliary of stupefying philtres and the poisoning of the rational faculties. The absorption of one will by another frequently changes a whole series of destinies, and it is not for ourselves only that we should watch over our relations and learn to distinguish between pure and impure atmospheres, for the most dangerous philtres are invisible —those currents of radiating vital light which, mingling and interchanging, produce attractions and sympathies, as magnetic experiences leave no room to doubt. But the most terrible of all philtres are the mystical exaltations of misdirected devotion. What impurities will ever equal the nightmares of St Anthony, or the torments of St Theresa and St Angèle de Foligny? The last mentioned applied a red-hot iron to her rebellious flesh, and found the material fire a refreshment to her concealed ardours. With what violence does nature demand what we refuse her, but what

THE DOCTRINE OF SPIRITUAL ESSENCES. 177

we are continually thinking of in order to detest it more strongly! The excessive fear of a thing renders it almost invariably inevitable.

What contributes to rendering women hysterical is their soft and hypocritical education. If they took more exercise, if they were instructed frankly and freely in worldly matters, they would be less capricious, less vain, less frivolous, and consequently less accessible to sinful seductions. Weakness is always in sympathy with vice, because vice itself is weakness under the mask of strength. Folly holds reason in horror, and in every way delights in the exaggerations of falsehoods. Cure, therefore, first, your diseased intelligence. The cause of all bewitchments, the poison of all philtres, the power of all sorcerers, are there.

XIII.—THE KEY OF MESMERISM.

MESMER recovered the secret science of Nature, he was not its inventor. The primeval, one, and elementary substance whose existence he proclaims in his Aphorisms, was known to Hermes and Pythagoras. Synesius, who celebrates it in his hymns, discovered its revelation among the Platonic reminiscences of the Alexandrian School. "A single source, a single root of light springs up and spreads out into three branches of splendour. An air circulates round the earth and vivifies, under innumerable forms, every portion of animated substance." *

Animal magnetism is nothing else than an artificial sleep produced by the voluntary or enforced union of two souls, one of which is awake while the other is sleeping, that is, one of which directs the other in the choice of reflections so as to change dreams into visions and ascertain truth by means of images. The Astral Light has an immediate action on the nerves, which are conductors in the animal economy, and convey it to the brain; so, in the somnambulistic state, it is possible to see by the nerves, without the need of radiating light, the astral fluid being a latent light, as physics have recognised the existence of latent caloric. Magnetism between two persons is undoubtedly a marvellous discovery, but the magnetizing of one person, whose

* Hymns of Synesius, Hymn 2.

will makes himself lucid, and the direction of one's own clairvoyance, is the perfection of magical art; the secret of this *magnum opus* does not need seeking, it was known and made use of by a large number of initiates, and above all by the famous Apollonius of Tyana, who has left us a theory concerning it. The secret of magnetic lucidity, and the direction of the phenomena of magnetism, depend on two things—on the harmony of minds and the perfect union of wills in a possible direction and in a direction determined by science; this is for magnetism operated between several. Solitary magnetism demands the preparations we have detailed at the beginning when we enumerated and described in all their arduousness the requisite qualities for a veritable adept.

If it have been up to the present almost impossible to direct the phenomena of magnetism, it is because no initiated and truly emancipated mesmerist has yet been found. Who, in fact, can flatter himself that he is such? Have we not always to make new efforts at self-control? It is certain all the same that Nature obeys the sign and command of one who feels strong enough not to doubt it. I say she will obey, I do not say that she will belie herself or that she will disturb the order of her possibilities. The cure of nervous disorders by a word, a breath, or a touch; resurrection in certain cases; resistance of evil wills sufficient to disarm and overthrow murderers; even the faculty of rendering one's self invisible, by influencing the sight of those whom it is important to escape from—all these are natural effects of the projection or retention of the Astral Light. The magus magnetist should command the natural medium, and, consequently, the astral body which establishes communication between the soul and the organs; he can therefore say to the material body—"Sleep!" and to the astral mediator—"Dream!" Then visible objects change their appearance, as in opium visions. The Astral Light is projected by the glance, by the voice, by the thumbs and palms of the hands. Music is a powerful auxiliary of the voice, and hence comes the word enchantment. No musical instrument is more of an enchanter than the human voice, but the distant sounds of the violin or harmonica increase its efficacy. The subject whom it is desired to influence is thus prepared; then when he is half asleep, and as it were is enveloped in the charm, the hand

THE DOCTRINE OF SPIRITUAL ESSENCES. 179

must be extended towards him, he must be commanded to slumber or to see, and he will obey despite himself. If he resist, looking fixedly at him, a thumb should be placed on the forehead between the eyes, and the other thumb on his breast, touching him lightly with an even and rapid contact, then slowly inhale or draw in the breath, softly exhale it, and repeat in a low voice—" Sleep!" or " Behold!"

The human body is subject, like the earth, to a double law—it attracts and it radiates; it is magnetized by an androgyne magnetism, and reacts on the two powers of the soul, the intellectual and sensitive, in inverse reason, but in proportion to the alternated preponderances of the two sexes in the physical organism. The art of the magnetist is wholly in the knowledge and use of this law. To polarise the action, and give the agent a bi-sexual and alternated force, is the means still unknown and vainly sought of directing at will the phenomena of magnetism; but a tact well exercised, and great precision in the interior movements so as not to confound the signs of magnetic inbreathing with those of outbreathing, are of palmary importance; while the occult anatomy and individual temperament of persons under control must also be perfectly known. What causes the greatest obstacle to the direction of magnetism is the bad faith or ill-will of subjects, of women above all, who are essentially and invariably attitudinising, who love to impress themselves by the impression of others, and who are the first to be deceived when they act their nervous melodramas—this is the true black magic of magnetism. So is it impossible for operators uninitiated into the supreme arcana, and unassisted by the illumination of the Kabbalah, to ever govern this refractory and fugitive element. To be master of the woman we must divert and deceive her skilfully by permitting her to imagine that it is she who is deceiving us.

There are two methods of magnetizing—firstly, in acting on the will of the subject either by intimidation or by persuasion in such a manner that the impressed will shall modify, according to our desire, the plastic mediator and the actions of that person. Secondly, in acting by the will on the plastic mediator of another, whose will and acts are consequently subordinated to such action.

There is magnetizing by radiation, by contact, by glance,

and by speech. The vibrations of the voice modify the motions of the Astral Light and are a powerful instrument of magnetism. Warm breathing magnetizes positively and cold breathing negatively. By placing the right-hand on the head and the left on the feet of a person wrapped in wool or silk, a magnetic spark passes through them, and a complete nervous revolution in the organism may be occasioned with the rapidity of lightning. Magnetic passes are useful only in directing the will of the mesmerist and confirming it by acts. They are signs and nothing more.* The act of will is expressed and not operated by such signs. Pulverized coal absorbs and retains the Astral Light, which explains the magic mirror of Du Potet. Figures drawn with charcoal appear luminous to a magnetized person, and assume for such, according to the direction determined by the will of the operator, the most attractive or terrifying forms. The astral or rather vital light of the plastic mediator absorbed by the charcoal becomes wholly negative, and this is why animals whom electricity tortures, as cats for example, like to roll among the ashes. Medicine will one day utilize this peculiarity, and nervous persons will find great benefit therefrom.

In his "Magic Unveiled" the Baron Du Potet states, with some hesitation, that it is possible, by a powerful projection of the magnetic fluid, to kill a living being as if he were struck with lightning. Magic power extends further; but it is not only the pretended magnetic fluid, it is the whole Astral Light, it is the element of electricity and of thunder, which can be placed at the disposal of the human will. What must be done to acquire this formidable power? Zoroaster tells us: we must be acquainted with those mysterious laws of equilibrium which subject to the empire of good even the powers of evil themselves; we must have purified our body by holy trials, wrestled with the phantoms of hallucination, and grappled bodily with the light, as Jacob strove with the angel; we must have overcome those fantastic dogs which bark in dreams, and in a word, according to the oracle's energetic expression, have heard the light speak. Then shall we be master thereof, then shall we be able to turn it, like Numa, against the enemies of the sublime mysteries; but if we are not perfectly pure, if the ascendancy of some animal passion

* See Note 21.

THE DOCTRINE OF SPIRITUAL ESSENCES. 181

still subject us to the fatalities of the tempests of life, we shall be burned by the fire that we kindle and perish like Tullus Hostilius.

It was the glory of Mesmer to have recovered, without an initiator and without occult knowledge, this universal agent of life and its prodigies; his "Aphorisms," which the scientists of his time could only look on as paradoxes, will become one day the basis of the physical synthesis. He recognised the existence of a primitive, fluidic, universal matter, capable of stability and motion, which, by becoming fixed, determines the constitution of substances, and which by continual motion modifies and renews its forms. Only one step remained for him to make; it was to declare that the effects attributed in physics to the four imponderable fluids are the manifestations of a single force diversified in its applications, and that this force, inseparable from the first and universal matter whose motion it causes, now radiant, now ablaze, now electrical, and now magnetic, has but one name indicated by Moses in Genesis, when he makes it appear, at the summons of the Almighty, before all substances, and all forms—LIGHT!

XIV.—MODERN SPIRITISM.

THE existence of the universal magnet specialised in metals, plants, animals, and men, was known to the ancient hierophants. To that mysterious force the names of Od, Ob, and Aour, were given among the Jews. It is the double vibration of the universal and vital light—astral light in the stars, magnetic light in stones and minerals, animal magnetism in animals and men. Everything in Nature reveals its existence. The experiments of Mesmer and his successors have proved that animal magnetism can communicate to inert objects the life and will of man. There is, therefore, small room for astonishment at the phenomenon, so frequent in our own days, of speaking and moving tables; but ignorance loves to be surprised, because surprise makes it wonder, and wonder enchants it; then it has no wish to be disillusioned, and will not hear the simple truth-speakers. Nearly the whole truth on the phenomena of table-turning is most simply and clearly expressed in the letter of an anonymous savant which is cited by M. Morin.

"Be sure," says this savant, "that there are neither spirits, nor the souls of the dead, nor angels, nor demons, in the tables, but all these may be there if you wish it, when you wish it, and how you wish it, since it depends on your imaginativeness, your temperament, and your private opinions old or new. *Mensambulance* is only a phenomenon ill observed by the ancients, misunderstood by the moderns, yet perfectly natural, and which concerns physics on the one part and psychology on the other, but it was inexplicable before the discovery of electricity and heliography, because, in order to explain a fact in the psychical order, we are forced to lean on the corresponding fact in the material order, as the ancient poets did in their comparisons and the prophets in their parables.

"Now, it is well known that the daguerreotype has not only the faculty of receiving impressions from objects, but also from the images of objects, and the phenomenon under consideration, which could well be called *mental photography*, does not only produce realities but also the dreams of our imagination, with such fidelity that we are occasionally deceived, being unable to distinguish between a copy from life and a proof taken from the image. It will be said that this mental photography is a very extraordinary thing, and as much was declared of ordinary photography, but we have since become familiar with it. It will be the same with the last discovery ; we shall become accustomed to it and each of us will be able to try his hand at the tables as others at the daguerreotype, some successfully, some badly, for a number of indispensable precautions and conditions are required to ensure success. The first hairbrained and clumsy person who comes to it is no more qualified to obtain a 'good test' on one side than on the other.

"The magnetizing of a card-table and of a person is absolutely identical ; it is the invasion of a foreign body by the intelligent vital electricity, or by the thoughts of the magnetist and his assistants. Nothing can afford a more just and easily grasped idea of it than the electric machine collecting the fluid on its conductor, to obtain therefrom a third force, which is manifested in outbursts of light, &c.

THE DOCTRINE OF SPIRITUAL ESSENCES.

Thus electricity accumulated on an isolated body acquires an energy of reaction equal to the action, whether for magnetism, decomposition, inflammation, or the despatch of its vibration to a distance. These are the sensible effects of blind as distinguished from intelligent electricity, which corresponds to the former, and is produced by the cerebral pile of man. This electricity of the soul, this spiritual and universal ether, which is *the ambient medium* of the metaphysical or incorporeal world, needs to be investigated before admitted by science, which knows nothing of the great phenomenon of life beyond.

"Cerebral electricity, which, for myself and my co-workers, is no longer a matter of hypothesis, seems to require, before it can be manifested to the senses, the help of ordinary statical electricity, so that when this is wanting in the atmosphere, as when the air is full of moisture, no motion can be obtained in the tables, which will clearly tell you on the morrow what they lacked the previous day.

"The intelligence of the table is the sum, or, if it be preferred, the reflection of the intelligence of those who magnetize it, it may be even said of a whole assembly which is attentive and united in sentiments and opinions. At other times it is only the repercussion of the ideas of a single person, whose will is stronger, who can arrest or quicken the table at a distance, and can impose on it any sequence of ideas which may please him. There is no need that the ideas should be consciously in the brain of the sitters; the table discovers and formulates them of itself, and always in suitable terms; it frequently requires time to accomplish certain crambos; it begins a verse, erases it, corrects or inverts it after our own fashion. If the sitters are sympathetic and on good terms with one another, it trifles, jokes, and laughs with us like an educated talker, it joins in the general tone of the conversation, it is a social spirit, but if we ask it for an epigram on an absent person it offers us a plagiarism; and as for things of the other world, it is as full of conjectures as we are; it makes up its little philosophical systems, discusses and sustains them with the most crafty eloquence. In a word, it contrives for itself a reason and a conscience out of materials found in ourselves.

"All this may appear fantastic and incredible in the extreme, but after investigation others besides ourselves will come to the same conclusion. The Americans are convinced that the dead return, others that angels and demons do so, and to each group comes the reflection of his own preconceived belief; so the initiates of the temples of Serapis, Delphos, and other theurgico-medical establishments of the same kind, were convinced beforehand that they entered into communication with the deities adored in each sanctuary, which never failed to take place. To us who know the value of the phenomenon, nothing ever occurs which we are unable to explain without difficulty in accordance with our principles; we are absolutely certain that after charging a table with our magnetic influx, we have created an intelligence analogous to our own, which possesses free-will like ourselves, can converse and dispute with us with a superior degree of lucidity, because the mass is stronger than the individual, as the whole is greater than the part.

"The most favourable condition is to have children almost without mental influence as our only collaborateurs; then it is almost as if one stood alone in the presence of his conscience and in private conversation with himself, save that the ephemeral reasoner formulates what exists in our own conscience in a merely chaotic or nebulous state. There is no response in all the ancient oracles that does not find its natural explanation in the theory whose key we give here. Christianity, which undertook to deliver the world from superstitious beliefs, whose dangers and inanities it discerned, but did not discover their cause, had great battles to fight for the extinction of oracles and sybillism, and had to employ something more than persuasion, the Inquisition itself having no other end in view. Read Ammianus Marcellinus, the persecution of the consulters of tables, instituted by early Christian emperors, and the sermons of Tertullian on those who interrogated *Capellas et Mensas*. No less than seventeen centuries and a half were required to exterminate the sorcerers by fire and sword; the last survivors were Urbain, Grandier, and Cagliostro, but the phenomenon being natural, reappeared now under the form of the convulsionaries of St Médard, now under the *hallucinés* of St Paris, whose reality was borne witness to by Talleyrand in his youth, he himself having crucified a sybil with the help of the Abbé de Lavauguillon without doing any injury to her. Mesmer

THE DOCTRINE OF SPIRITUAL ESSENCES. 185

resuscitated the same thing. The phenomenon is, indeed, as old as man. The Indian and Chinese priests practised it before the Egyptians and Greeks; it is known to the Esquimaux; it is the *phenomenon of Faith*, that source of all prodigies; when faith grows weak, miracles disappear. He who said, 'By faith ye may move mountains,' would not be surprised at a table being lifted. By faith the mesmerist charms away rheumatism, and rural shepherds obtained from the end of their cranes, as we from the feet of our tables, responses analogous to the personal beliefs of the questioners, and were as much astounded at finding their thoughts, instincts, and feelings thus formulated, as the savage is amazed at beholding his likeness reflected in a looking-glass. The worst off are those who think they are having commerce with the devil, who re-echoes their fancies, and sometimes the state of their conscience.

' Glassed in the table, man so monstrous seems
At times, that he himself the demon deems.'

"The greater the number of believers joined in any single faith about a table, the more the pile is charged, and the more powerful and wonderful are the results. The primitive Christians gathered round the holy table to communicate with God and they beheld God, as those who believe in magic and sorcery see sorcery and enchantments everywhere. The guests at Balthazar's feast beheld the menace which originated in their consciences against the author of such orgies reproduced on the walls and nothing more. Those who believe in apparitions, in phosphorescent lights, in mysterious noises, are equally provided for according to their notions, for it is rendered to every man according to his faith.

"Man is a microcosm or little world; he bears within him a portion of the great whole in a chaotic state. The task of our *semidei* is to disentangle that part which is due to them by incessant mental and physical labour. They must fulfil their service by the continual invention of new products, new moralities, and set in order the coarse and formless materials distributed by the Creator, who made them in his own image that they in turn may create and may complete the work of creation—a vast labour which will only be accomplished when the whole shall have attained such a height of perfection that it will be like to God and worthy to survive to itself. We are far from this final moment, for it may be said that everything has still to be made, remade, and finished here below, institutions, systems, and products.

Mens non solum agitat sed creat molem.

We exist in life, that ambient intellectual medium which nourishes a necessary and perpetual solidarity in man and things; each brain is a ganglion, a station of the universal neuralgic telegraph constantly *en rapport* with the central station and with all others by means of thought-vibrations. The spiritual sun enlightens souls as the material sun illumines bodies, for the universe is double and follows the law of couples. The ignorant station-holder misinterprets the divine despatches and often renders them in a false and ridiculous sense. Therefore, education and true science can alone destroy superstitions, and the nonsense sown broadcast by ignoramus interpreters placed in the *stations of instruction* among all the peoples of the earth. These blind interpreters of the Logos have always sought to impose on their disciples the obligation of judging without examination *in verba magistri.* We would ask no more, alas! if they would interpret exactly the interior voices which deceive false minds alone. 'It is for us,' they declare, 'to disentangle the oracles, that mission is exclusively ours, *spiritus flat ubi vult,* and it breathes only on us.' No, it breathes everywhere, and the beams of spiritual light enlighten every conscience, but as there are owls that fly the day, there are also refracting bodies and many which are destitute of the reflecting power. These are indeed the majority; O when all souls and bodies shall equally reflect the two-fold light how far clearer shall we see then than to-day!"

We believe with the savant of M. A. Morin that present phenomena open to us the way to the greatest and most important discoveries. This mental photography of current ideas is of immense importance in revealing the great communion of life. One soul does in fact sustain life throughout the whole of Nature. It is active in intelligent creatures and passive in others. Now, the active acts on the passive and borrows its strength; man can appropriate the strength of the lion, the agility and cunning of the ape; he can also impose his own thought on both and make use of them as instruments—all this is a question of magnetism.

Do you think the great painter, for example, finds the colours which glow on his canvas in the wares of the artists' colourman? No, his genius commands the sun which yields its reflections to him. Intellectual omnipotence is a magic, and matter placed at the disposal of mind becomes itself intelligence. Day stands in need of night in order to shew itself, and

> "Apollo's time of abdication comes,
> We know what genius now to call on most;
> Its virtue ALL THE WORLD, 'tis NO ONE named;
> They best dispense it who possess it not,
> Just as the magnet's positive effect
> Its constant agent finds in pole opposed.
> Dumb Nature speech inspires, wide ignorance
> Creates the symbol, in a single word,
> The man of genius is perchance that man
> Who most attracts the mind of all the fools."

We do not yet know the powers which human magneticalness can dispose of, and when the prodigies of faith become the conquests of science, man, enthroned above all superstitions, will have taken his place in the universe, will know that he is born to command Nature, and is the plenipotentiary of God here below.

But, returning to Spiritism, something strange and unheard of seems now taking place in the world. Christianity by setting all our hopes in death disgusted men with life, and here a new belief seems trying to reconcile us to existence by annihilating death. For spiritists, in fact, there is no death. Life present and life to come, barely divided by a thin partition which spirits can pass through, are henceforth one and the same life. We are surrounded by those we loved, they touch us, make signals to us, write to us, walk with us, and bear half our burdens. At times even their hands become visible and palpable to clasp our own. No more tears shed over tombs, no more wailing, no more funereal wreaths in memory of those who are no more, for so far from having ceased to exist they are living more truly than we are. The old broken-down wall which once separated definitely the two existences of man, is like the partition which divided the dwellings of Pyramus and Thisbe; it permits speech to pass between, it does not even prevent kisses. All this is so specious, so astounding, so beautiful, that we easily allow ourselves to be possessed by a flattering credulity, and do not sufficiently reflect to perceive that the pretended new religion destroys the cultus and the hierarchy, renders the priesthood useless, overturns the temple for the tomb's profit, and substitutes for the sacraments of the living the doubtful and problematic contact of the dead. In these multiplied evocations reason is fatigued, faith materialised, the severe grandeurs of theology are transformed into romantic and sentimental trivialities, a Christ as ridiculous as Rénan's is talked of, and a Virgin Mary who comes every evening to kiss the withered and toothless mouth of the old man Girard de Caudemberg. In the same way that solar photography reproduces with infuriating fidelity the blemishes and scars on a face, this astral photography reproduces the nothingness of silly conversations, the temerity of conjecture, and the follies of idiotic thoughts. The medium Rose evokes Madame Lafarge and makes her acknowledge her guilt—an impious outrage on the grave of an unfortunate woman, whose memory, protected by a doubt, concerns the honour of an honourable family, some of whose members still live and believe in her innocence. By the side of enormities like this, we find from the pencil of mediums pages which may not have been actually written before, but which we seem to have already read, so much do these verbiages resemble one another. Sometimes the pretended spirit naively copies from an author whom, doubtless, he thinks little known. The writer of this book was one day astonished at finding in a number of *La Vérité*, a spiritualistic journal published at Lyons, a page from the introduction to his " History of Magic," under the signature of Plato. The pencil writes dull and vapid songs which it attributes to Béranger, and ridiculous discourses which it fathers on Lacenaire; it is a tohu-bohu of pretentious stupidities and mutilated reminiscences, it is the Sabbath of the most drivelling devils imaginable, it is a chaos of extravagances. Then by the side of all this are observations full of keenness, bold hypotheses, and real fragments of science sewn up with the old pack thread of Tabarin or Jocrisse. Apollonius Tyaneus writes St-Simonian tirades and signs them St Augustine; St Augustine declaims against the Church Catholic; St Louis talks like Jean Journet; St Vincent de Paul speechifies; it is altogether the anarchic noise of mobs, the madness of crowds, the confusion of multitudes photographed while in motion; it is the impersonal and multiple spirit which idiotically drowns the animals it seeks refuge in, that spirit whose name is legion and which is everywhere driven out by the gentle influence of the Word of Truth.

In the opposite camp, M. de Mirville blows the infernal trumpet and proclaims the reign of Satan. M. Gougenot Desmousseaux, his double, offers him the aspergillus to exorcise the Prince of Darkness. Insults rain down in place of holy water : the voltairian strong-minded absurdly deny facts to avoid investigating causes. The respectable M. Velpeau explains by a slight cracking of the muscles of the calf, those blows which break tables and almost demolish walls. For many people still, Home, the American, is only a skilful conjuror, a greater number shrug their shoulders and will hear nothing on the subject, while true science in the midst of all this chaos, grave, silent, and dejected, is studying, observing, and waiting.

Luther one day had a visit from a spirit, whether white or black the reformer does not tell us ; but he believed it, nevertheless, to be the devil. And behold the devil arguing with the monk, and the monk convinced by his arguments, and so came the Reformation into the world ! Spiritists and table-turners, this is your whole history. A voice addresses you, you know not whose it is ; often your pretended revelations swarm with falsehoods and contradictions, yet you think yourselves free of the hierarchy, and that you know more than your curé and the Pope. The world beyond is revealed to you directly or by the mediation of beings beneath yourselves, diseased and ignorant, or insane creatures, who are entranced and know not what they write, yet behold you are, like Israel, strong against God ! You arrange eternal dogma as you please, you deny this, admit that, you invent fantastic paradises and an endurable perdition; you retail cheap morality along with all this, for it certainly looks well, and carries no obligation along with it.

Thus, after the thunders of the prophets, after the glories of the apostles, after the splendours of the fathers, after the patient, laborious, but incomplete reasoning of the scholastic philosophers, after the despairing courage of reformers and philosophy, God, at the end of His resources, sends talking-tables to spell out in jumps the indecent saying of Cambronne, a complaisant seasoning of idiotic doctrines and an encouragement to intellectual onanism. Is it God ? No, it is the God you have made yourselves who is reduced to such paltry expedients! Yet you pass before Bedlam without taking your hat off and repeating that passage in Scott—

"This is my own, my native land!"

Faith in God is the firm adhesion of the soul to the necessary hypotheses of the understanding. Faith in Jesus Christ and in His Church is the soul's firm adherence to the necessary hypotheses of the heart. If God be, He is good; if good, He loves us; if He love us, He must efficaciously cure our evils. He must come to us since we cannot go to Him. The Incarnation, redemption, the sacraments, the unchangeable dogma, the indefectible hierarchy, become necessary, and all these are proved by the real existence and perpetual presence in the Church of an evidently divine power which changes the ignorant into sages, the weak into heroes, the simplest women, and even the poorest children, into veritable angels on earth. Woe to him who misunderstands, shame to him who resists and denies this power, for it is the Spirit of Charity! By the side of this reasonable faith, a fond and fanciful faith, anarchic as madness and capricious as dreams, has always endeavoured to establish itself—it is the faith of visionaries who take the phantoms of their imaginations to be divine revelations, of those who seek knowledge from ecstacy, intoxication, sleep, catalepsy, in fine, from all states which by suspending free will in man, render him more or less insane. And they see not that alienation is forfeiture of manhood, that the spirit of vertigo is the spirit of lies and wickedness, and that by abandoning themselves to automatic trances, they leave the direction of their thought to the dark unknown, and become voluntarily deranged, which is horrible and wholly contrary to Nature. They develop thereupon into prophets of the vortex, seers of vertigo, oracles of the great chaos, interpreters of fatality. They gaze into a broken glass, and fancy they behold the multitude of celestial spirits which have already served as nourishment to their minds, while their doctrinal reveries resemble the nightmares of painful digestion. Where is the essential difference between our modern hypnotists and those ancient Indian gnostics who with eyes fixed on their navel awaited the manifestation of the uncreated light? Necromancy replacing Christianity, death-lights substituted

THE DOCTRINE OF SPIRITUAL ESSENCES. 191

for the speech of the living God, spectral fluid descending on us instead of grace, the eucharistic communion neglected for I know not what banquets where the soul is asphyxiated by breathing the phosphorus emanating from corpses—this, pitiable beings, is what you take for a religious renovation, this is your faith and your cultus, this the darksome God whom you adore!

Read the Fathers of the first centuries, scan the great epochs of Christianity, listen to St Augustine aspiring towards the infinite, and St Jerome meditating on heaven, amidst the noise of the falling Roman Empire, hearken to the peal of the eloquence of Chrysostom and St Ambrose, then come down to the spiritualistic vagaries of Home, or the pantheistic lucubrations of Allan Kardec, and you will smile in pity and disgust. Is death but a bitter deception? Are the realities of the life beyond to be the derision of our aspirations in this? Is the true Paradise less radiant than Dante's, and perdition less terrible than his hell? What, do disembodied spirits, like those of Swedenborg, promenade with hats on their heads? Do they obsess the living to make them write puerilities? Don't you see that the hell of the Middle Ages with its grandiose terrors would be preferable to this ridiculous degradation of souls? Let God torture me if there be a God who is capable of torturing me, but do not let Him make me a fool!

Spiritism is a photography of current notions. The books of Allan Kardec swarm with Saint-Simonism, Swedenborgianism, and Mormonism, but they are less learned than Saint-Simon, less elevated than Swedenborg, less logical than Joe Smith. Must we believe that we continue growing old after death and that we reject on earth the dotage of the life beyond? What a sad prospect for great men! What a melancholy advantage for the living!

Magical doctrine is not that of mediums. Dogmatising mediums can only teach anarchy since their inspiration is the result of disorderly excitation. They are ever predicting disasters, ever denying hierarchic authority, ever posing as sovereign pontiffs. The initiate, on the contrary, respects the hierarchy above all, loves and preserves order, is deferential to sincere belief, rejoices at every sign of immortality in faith, and of redemption by charity, which wholly consists in discipline and obedience.

The study of the strange phenomena which take place in the presence of men like Home is no less of the highest importance. It is a question of seriously recanting the too premature denials of the eighteenth century, of unfolding before science and reason less narrow horizons than those of a bourgeois criticism which denies everything it is unable to explain. Mr Home is a person afflicted with contagious somnambulism and contagious hallucination. The facts which take place in his presence prove that the forms of an over-excited imagination are as real as the impressions of photography. We cannot see that which has no existence; the phantoms of dreams and the reveries of the waking state are real images existing in the Astral Light. But if the images attracted by diseased brains have any reality about them, can they not be really projected outside the brain or entire nervous organism of the medium, and thus influence the organism of those who voluntarily or otherwise enter into nervous sympathy with the medium?

And now let us answer those who see manifestations of the other world, and facts of necromancy in these phenomena. Our teaching on this point is that of the rabbins who compiled the Sohar.

Axiom.

The spirit clothes itself to come down, and strips itself to go up.

Created spirits are clothed with bodies because they must be limited, in order that their existence may be possible. Denuded of all body, and consequently unlimited, created spirits would lose themselves in the infinite, and for want of the ability of self-concentration somewhere they would be dead and impotent everywhere, plunged, as they would be, in the immensity of God. All created spirits, therefore, have bodies, some more subtle, some grosser, according to their environment. The soul of a dead person cannot live in our atmosphere any more than we could exist in the earth or water. It dwells above the air, which is an earth for it,[*] as the Saviour declares in the Gospel—"The great gulf is fixed, and those who are above can no longer go down to those below." The hands which Mr Home causes to appear are, therefore, air coloured

[*] See Note 22.

by the reflections which his diseased imagination attracts and projects. They may be touched as they are seen; they are part illusion, part nervous and magnetic force. Such phenomena of the Astral Light are always produced at critical epochs for humanity. They are phantoms of the world's fever, the hysterics of an out-wearied society. In the days of the Cæsars Rome was full of spectres; the doors of the Temple opened of themselves in Vespasian's time, and the cry of "The gods depart!" was heard. Now, when the gods depart, the devils return; religious sentiment is transformed into superstition when faith is lost; for souls have need of faith, because they are athirst for hope.

Sacred and beautiful kingdom of the sky, Jesus the Man-God, and Mary the mother of God! Angels of Fra Angelico, saints of the Golden Legend, Virgins of the paradise of Dante, how far more sublime and poetic, how far more fair are ye than the ghosts of Cahagnet or the wandering larvae of Allan Kardec! Severe and incorruptible dogma, which distributes the elect on the golden ladder of the hierarchy, profound teaching, full of light for docility of mind, and of darkness for pride; sun of glory and of justice, men see you not, because their eyes are blinded! Let them return to reason, and they will return to faith, for faith and true reason are sisters, and both are God's cherished daughters. Woe be to him who discerns them not, but threefold woe to him who would divide them!

THE GREAT PRACTICAL SECRETS;

OR,

REALISATIONS OF MAGICAL SCIENCE.

INTRODUCTION.

THE transcendant sciences of the Kabbalah and of magic guarantee to man an exceptional, true, efficient, practical power, and we must condemn them as vain and untruthful if they do not impart it. Judge the doctors of the law by their works, said the Great Master, and the rule is infallible. If you wish me to believe in what you know, shew me what you do!

In order to upraise man to moral emancipation, God hides Himself from him, and, in a certain sense, surrenders to him the government of the world. He leaves His existence to be divined by the grandeurs and harmonies of Nature, so that man may progressively perfect himself by continually enlarging the idea he conceives of his Maker. Man knows God only by the names which he gives to this Being of beings, and distinguishes Him only by the representations of Him which he attempts to trace. He is thus in a certain sense the creator of Him by whom he was created. He believes himself to be the image of God, and by indefinitely enlarging his own reflection he believes that he is outlining in infinite space the shadow of One who is bodiless, shadowless, and unconfined.

TO CREATE GOD, TO ACCOMPLISH OUR OWN CREATION, TO MAKE OURSELVES INDEPENDENT, IMPASSIBLE, AND IMMORTAL—here certainly is a programme more rash than the dream of Prometheus. Its foundation is bold even to impiety, the thought ambitious even to madness. Nevertheless, it is a programme which is only paradoxical in the form, which lends itself to a false and sacrilegious interpretation. In one sense it is perfectly reasonable, and its realisation and complete fulfilment is promised by the science of the adepts. Man, in fact, makes himself a God conformed to his own intelligence and goodness; the God he adores is always his own magnified likeness. To conceive the Absolute in goodness and justice is to be one's self most just and good. Intellectual and moral qualities are riches and the greatest of all riches. They must be acquired by toil and struggle. The inequality of aptitudes and the case of children born with a more perfect organisation than others will be objected, but we must believe such organisms to be the result of a more advanced labour of Nature, and that the children so endowed have acquired them, if not by their individual efforts, at least by the joint efforts of the human beings with whom their existence is bound up. It is a secret of Nature who does nothing by chance. The possession of more developed intellectual faculties, as also that of money and lands, constitutes an imprescriptable right of transmission and inheritance.

Yes, man is called to finish the work of his Creator, and each of the moments he employs to improve or spoil himself is decisive for eternity. It is by the acquisition of an invariably upright mind, and an invariably just will, that he makes himself alive for life eternal, since nothing survives to injustice and error but the wretchedness of their disorder. To understand what is good is to desire it, and, in the order of justice, to desire is to perform. For this reason the Gospel tells us that men will be judged according to their works. Our works constitute us what we are to such an extent that our bodies receive from our habits a modification and sometimes a complete change of appearance. A shape acquired or imposed becomes a providence or fatality for our entire existence. Those bizarre figures with which the Egyptians endowed their human symbols of divinity represent the fatal forms. Typhon, by his crocodile mouth, is doomed to devour unceasingly to fill his hippopotamous belly. So is he devoted by his voracity and ugliness to eternal destruction.

Man can destroy his faculties by negligence or abuse. He can create for himself new faculties by the good use of those which he has received from Nature. It is said frequently that the affections are not to be commanded, that faith is not possible for all, that character cannot be transformed, but all these assertions are only true for the perverse or the indolent. We can make ourselves confiding, pious, loving, self-sacrificing, when we sincerely wish to be so. We can enrich the mind with the serenity of justice, and the will with the omnipotence of justice. We can reign in heaven by faith and on earth by knowledge. The man who can govern himself is the king of all Nature.

We are now about to show by what means the true initiates became masters of life by subduing suffering and death, how they operated on themselves and others the transformations of Proteus, how they exercised the divination of Apollonius, how they manufactured the gold of Raymond Lully and of Flamel, how to renew their youth they possessed the secret of Postel the Resuscitated, and the fabulous Cagliostro. We shall reveal, in fine, the ultimate secrets of magic.

I.—THE MAGNUM OPUS.

THE *magnum opus* is pre-eminently the creation of man, by himself, that is, the full and complete conquest which he can make of his faculties and his future; it is pre-eminently the perfect emancipation of his will, which assures his universal dominion over Azoth and the domain of Magnesia, that is, a full power over the Great Magical Agent. This Magic Agent, which the old Hermetic philosophers disguised under the name of the *first matter* of the *magnum opus*, determines the species of modifiable substance, and metallic transmutation, as well as the universal medicine, can be really attained by its means. This is no hypothesis, it is a fact already tested and rigorously demonstrable.

Nicolas Flamel and Raymond Lully, both poor, have evidently distributed immense riches. Agrippa never progressed beyond the first part of the *magnum opus*, and he died in the attempt, struggling towards complete self-possession and to establish his independence.

Like all magical mysteries, the Hermetic operations, and

THE GREAT PRACTICAL SECRETS. 197

the secrets of the *magnum opus*, are triple; they are religious, philosophical, and natural, or material, all interdependent. The gold of the philosophers is, in religion, the absolute and supreme reason; in philosophy it is truth; in visible nature it is the sun, which is the emblem of the sun of truth, as that is itself the shadow of the First Source whence all splendours spring; in the subterranean and mineral world it is the purest and most perfect gold. For this reason the search after the *magnum opus* is called the search after the Absolute, and the great work is itself called the work of the sun.

All Hermetic science is contained in the doctrine of Hermes Trismegistus, sculptured primitively, it is said, on an emerald table. We have explained already its first articles; those which refer to the operation of the *magnum opus* are as follows :—

" Thou shalt separate the earth from the fire, the ethereal from the gross, gently, and with great industry.

" It ascends from earth to heaven, and again it comes down from heaven to earth, and it is invested with the potency of superior and inferior things.

" Thou wilt possess by this means the glory of the whole world, and all darkness will depart from thee.

" It is the strong power of every power, for it will overcome all things subtle and penetrate all things solid.

" It is thus that the world was created."

To separate that which is ethereal from that which is gross, in the first operation, which is wholly interior, is to emancipate the soul from every vice and prejudice, which is accomplished by the use of the philosophic salt, namely, wisdom ; of mercury which is personal skill and toil ; finally, of sulphur which represents vital energy and the warmth of will. By this means is achieved the transmutation of the least precious things, even the refuse of the earth, into spiritual gold. It is in this sense that we must understand the parables of the *turba philosophorum* of Bernard Trevisan, Basilius Valentininus, Marius the Egyptian, and other alchemical prophets ; but in their works, as in the *magnum opus*, we must skilfully separate the ethereal from the gross, the mystical from the positive, allegory from theory. If we wish to read them with pleasure and profit, we must first interpret them allegorically in their entirety, then descend from allegories to realities by the way of the correspondences or analogies indicated in the one dogma—that which is above is as that which is below, and conversely. All the masters in knowledge have recognised that it is impossible to arrive at material results if the analogies of the universal medicine and the philosophers' stone have not been found in the two superior degrees of the religious and philosophical worlds. Then they say the work is easy, simple, and inexpensive; otherwise, it dissipates unprofitably the fortune and life of the seekers.

The first matter of the *magnum opus* is, in the superior world, enthusiasm and activity; in the intermediate world, it is intelligence and industry; in the inferior world, it is toil; in science, it is sulphur, mercury, and salt, which condensed and volatilized by turns composes the azoth of the sages.

The Hermetic art is, therefore, at once a religion, a philosophy, and a natural science. As a religion it is that of the ancient Magi and the initiates of all the ages; as a philosophy, its principles may be found in the Alexandrian School, and in the theories of Pythagoras; as a science, its methods must be ascertained from Paracelsus, Nicholas Flamel, and Raymond Lully. The science is real for those alone who admit and understand both the philosophy and the religion, and its processes will succeed only for the adept who has attained to sovereign power of will, and thus has become the monarch of the elementary world.

The disciples of Hermes before promising to their adepts the elixir of perpetual youth and the powder of projection recommend them to seek the philosophical stone. What is this stone, and why is it thus named? The great Initiator of the Christians invites His believers to build upon the rock or stone if they do not wish their edifices to be destroyed. He is Himself called the corner stone, and He tells His most faithful disciple, " *Tu es* PETRUS *et super hanc* PETRAM *ædificabo ecclesiam meam.*" This stone, say the masters in alchemy, is the true salt of the philosophers, which is the third ingredient in the composition of azoth. Now AZOTH, as we know, is the name of the great Hermetic and true philosophical agent, so their salt is represented under the form of a cubic stone, as may be seen in the twelve Keys of Basilius Valentinus, or in the allegories of Trevisan. This

THE GREAT PRACTICAL SECRETS. 199

stone is the foundation of absolute philosophy; it is the supreme and immoveable reason, and the doctrine of universal harmonies by the sympathy of contrary things. Before thinking of the metallic work we must be for ever established on the absolute principles of wisdom; we must possess that reason which is the touchstone of truth. Never will a prejudiced man be the king of Nature and the master of transmutations. The philosophical stone is, then, before all things, needful. To find the absolute in the infinite, the indefinite, and the finite, such is the *magnum opus* of the sages; such is the whole secret of Hermes; such is the stone of the philosophers. This stone is one and multiple; it is decomposed by analysis and recomposed by synthesis. In the analysis it is a powder, the alchemical powder of projection; before the analysis, and in the synthesis, it is a stone. This stone, say the masters, must not be exposed to the air, nor to the glances of the profane; it must be kept concealed and preserved with care in the most secret place of the owner's laboratory, and the key of that place must be always carried about the person.

He who possesses the Great Arcanum is a true king, and more than a king, for he is inaccessible to all fears and to all vain hopes. In any malady of soul or body, a single morsel detached from the precious stone, a single grain of the divine powder, are more than sufficient to cure him. He that hath ears to hear let him hear, as the Master sayeth.

To find the philosopher's stone, we must then, as Hermes tells us, separate the volatile from the fixed with great care and minute attention. Thus, we must separate our certitudes from our beliefs, and clearly distinguish the respective domains of science and faith; clearly understand that we do not know what we only believe in, and that we no longer believe anything which we have attained to the knowledge of; and that thus the essence of the things of faith is the unknown and indefinite, whilst it is entirely the reverse in the things of science. It will thence be concluded that knowledge rests on reason and experience, whilst the basis of faith is in sentiment. In other words, the philosophical stone is the true certitude which human prudence assures to conscientious researches and to modest doubt, whilst religious enthusiasm gives it exclusively to faith. Now, it belongs neither to reason devoid of aspirations, nor to aspirations devoid of reason. True certitude is the reciprocal acquiescence of the reason which knows in the sentiment which believes, and of the sentiment which believes in the reason which knows. The definitive alliance of faith and reason will result not from their absolute distinction and separation, but from their mutual control and fraternal concurrence. Such is the meaning of the two pillars of Solomon's porch, one of which is called Jakin, and the other Bohas, one being white and the other black. They are distinct and separate, they are even contrary in appearance, but if blind force should seek to unite them, the arch of the Temple would fall in. In their separation they are one sustaining force, but joined they are two forces which mutually destroy each other. In the same way the spiritual power diminishes so soon as it attempts to usurp the temporal, and the temporal power is the victim of its encroachment on the spiritual. Gregory VII. lost the papacy, and the schismatic kings have lost and forfeited the monarchy. Human equilibrium has need of two bases, the world gravitates by means of two forces, generation requires two sexes. Such is the meaning of the Arcanum of Solomon represented by the two pillars of the Temple, Jakin and Bohas.

The sun and moon of alchemists correspond to the same symbol, and concur in the perfection of the philosopher's stone. The sun is the hieroglyphic sign of truth, because it is the visible source of light, and the brute stone is the symbol of stability. For this reason the ancients adored the sun under the figure of a black stone, which they called Heliogabalus, and the alchemists of the Middle Ages also indicated the philosophic stone as the first means of manufacturing the gold of the philosophers, that is, of transforming all vital powers, represented by the six metals, into the sun, that is, into truth and light, the first and indispensable operation of the *magnum opus*, and one which leads to the secondary adaptations, and makes known by the analogies of nature the natural and unregenerate gold to the creators of the spiritual and living gold, to the possessors of the true salt, the true mercury, and the true sulphur of the philosophers.

To find the philosophic stone is then to have discovered the Absolute, as it is otherwise called by the masters. Now, the Absolute is that which tolerates no errors, it is

THE GREAT PRACTICAL SECRETS.

the separation of the fixed from the volatile, it is the rule of the imagination, it is the very necessity of being, it is the immutable law of truth and reason; the Absolute is that which is. God Himself cannot exist save in virtue of a supreme and inevitable reason. It is therefore this reason which is the Absolute; it is in this we must believe if we desire our faith to possess a reasonable and solid basis.

He who would attain to the comprehension of the Grand Word,* and to the possession of the Grand Secret, must, after studying the principles here laid down, read the Hermetic philosophers attentively, and he will attain initiation as others have attained it, but the unique dogma of Hermes must be taken as the key of their allegories, and the order indicated in the kabbalistic alphabet of the Tarot must be followed to classify the subjects and direct the operation. All the alchemical masters who have written on the *magnum opus* have employed symbolical and figurative expressions, and they have rightly done so, as much to repel the profane from a work which for them would be dangerous as to make themselves understood by the adepts by revealing to them the entire world of analogies ruled by the one and sovereign dogma of Hermes. Thus for them gold and silver are the king and queen, or the moon and sun; sulphur is the flying eagle; mercury the winged and bearded goat, seated on the cube and crowned with flames; matter, or salt, is the winged dragon; the metals in ebullition are lions of various colours; finally, the whole work has the pelican and phœnix for its symbols.

The transformations of Hermetic chemistry are the artificial development of natural germs. No one makes gold, but we can assist nature to make it, and all the science of Hermes consists in the sagacity which selects and arranges nature's own materials in order that she may perform her work, which she never fails to do when the instruments she makes use of are found naturally or artificially disposed as she herself disposes them. The whole secret of Hermetic philosophy is contained in this single indication. We have discovered pisciculture and Hermeticism is metalliculture. But who will reap carps by sowing herring-roe? How then can gold be produced

* See Note 23.

from salt, sulphur, and mercury?* M. Louis Lucas, the learned inventor of the biometer, has already demonstrated that, according to the notions of the ancients, substance is single, and owes its special forms to the diversity of its modes of molecular polarisation and to the varied angularity of its magnetic radiation. All beings are thus individual magnets, and the problem to be resolved by the magic of Hermes is this:—How to accumulate and fix the latent caloric in an artificial body in such a manner as to change the molecular polarisation of natural bodies by their amalgamation with the artificial body.

The creation of gold in the *magnum opus* is performed by transmutation and multiplication. Raymond Lully, one of the grand and sublime masters of the science, says that to make gold we must have gold, *ex nihilo nihil fit;* we cannot actually create wealth, we augment and multiply it. Let the aspirants to knowledge, therefore, thoroughly understand that neither miracles nor conjuring tricks are to be expected of the adept. Hermetic science, like all true sciences, is mathematically demonstrable; even its material results are as rigorous as those of a well-done equation. Hermetic gold is not only a true doctrine, a light wherein there is no shadow, a truth devoid of all alloy of falsehood, it is also a real, material, pure gold, the most precious which can be found in the mines of earth. But the vivific gold, the vivific sulphur, or the true fire of the philosophers, must be sought in the house of mercury. This fire is alimented by air; to describe its attractive and expansive power, we cannot suggest a better comparison than that of the thunderbolt which is at first only a dry, terrestrial exhalation joined to a humid vapour, but which, by dint of excitation, assuming a fiery nature, acts on the humidity inherent in it, which it attracts to itself and changes into its own nature, after which it precipitates itself with rapidity towards the earth, whereto it is attracted by a fixed nature similar to its own. The salt and sulphur serve only to prepare the mercury.

These words, enigmatic in their form but fundamentally clear, express briefly what the philosophers understand by their mercury fecundated with sulphur which becomes the lord and regenerator of the salt: it is AZOTH the universal *magnesia*, the Great Magic Agent, the Astral Light,

* See Note 24.

fecundated by animal energy, by intellectual power, which they compare to sulphur because of its affinities with divine fire. As for salt, it is absolute matter. Every material thing contains salt, and all salt can be converted into pure gold by the combined action of sulphur and mercury, which sometimes act so rapidly that transmutation can be instantaneously accomplished without fatigue to the operator and almost without expense; at other times, and according to the more contrary disposition of the atmospheric media, the operation requires several days, months, and sometimes even years. All depends on the interior *magnes* of Paracelsus. The work wholly consists in *projection*, and the projection is perfectly accomplished by the effective and realisable comprehension of a single word. There is indeed but one important operation in the work; it consists in sublimation, which is nothing else, according to Geber, than the elevation of the dry substance by means of fire, with adherence to its proper vase.

As we have already said, there exist two palmary natural laws, two essential laws which produce by counterpoise the universal equilibrium of things; these are stability and motion, analogous, in philosophy, to truth and invention, and, in absolute conception, to necessity and liberty, which are the very essence of God. The Hermetic philosophers give the name of fixed to all that is ponderable, to all that by its nature tends to central rest and immobility; they call everything which more naturally and readily obeys the law of motion volatile, and they form their stone of the analysis, that is, of the volatilisation of the fixed, then of the synthesis, that is, of the fixation of the volatile, which they accomplish by the application to the fixed, called their salt, of sulphurated mercury or the light of life directed and rendered all-powerful by a secret operation. They avail themselves also of all nature and their stone is found wherever salt exists, which causes it to be said that no substance is foreign to the *magnum opus*, and that even the most seemingly contemptible and vile materials may be changed into gold, which is true in this sense that, as we have said, they all contain the productive salt, represented in our emblems by the cubic stone itself. To know how to extract from all matter the pure salt concealed therein is to possess the secret of the stone, which is therefore a saline stone, decomposed and reconstituted by the Od or universal Astral Light; it is one and multiple, for, like common salt, it can be dissolved and incorporated with other substances. Obtained by analysis, it might be called the *universal quicksilver;* recovered by the synthetic method, it is the true *panacea* of the ancients, for it cures every disease, whether of soul or body, and has been called pre-eminently the medicine of all nature. When by absolute initiation we dispose of the forces of the Universal Agent, we have always this stone at our disposal, for its extraction is a simple and easy operation quite distinct from projection or metallic realisation. This stone in its sublimated state must not, as we have said, come in contact with atmospheric air, which may partly dissolve it and destroy its virtue; it would not be safe, moreover, to inhale its emanations. The wise man more readily preserves it in its natural envelopes, which the Kabbalists call skins. To express hieroglyphically this law of prudence, they gave to their mercury, which was personified in Egypt by Hermanubis, a dog's head, and to their sulphur, represented by the Baphomet of the Templars, or the prince of the Sabbath, that goat's head which has caused the secret associations of the middle ages to be so much decried.*

The *magnum opus* of Hermes is an essentially magical operation, and the most supreme of all, for it supposes the absolute in knowledge and in will. There is light in gold, gold in light, and light in all things. The intelligent will, which assimilates light, thus directs the operations of substantial form, and only employs chemistry as a very secondary instrument. The influence of human will and intelligence on the operations of nature, partly dependent on its Logos, is besides a fact so certain that all serious alchemists have succeeded in proportion to their attainments and faith, reproducing their thought in the phenomenon of the fusion, salification, and recomposition of metals.

The Great Agent of the sun's operation is that force described in the symbol of Hermes on the Emerald Table, it is universal magic power, it is the igneous spiritual motor, the Jewish Od, and the Astral Light according to the expression adopted in this work. It is the secret, living, philosophical fire of which no Hermetic philosopher speaks, save with the most mysterious reserves; it is the

* See Note 25.

universal sperm whose secret they guarded, and which they only represented under the figure of the caduceus of Hermes. An immense physical secret was thus concealed under the kabbalistic parables of the ancients. We have succeeded in unravelling it, and we present it literally to the investigations of gold-makers :—

1. The four imponderable fluids are only diverse manifestations of one universal agent, which is light.
2. Light is the fire which is used in the *magnum opus* under the form of electricity.
3. Human will directs the vital light by means of the nervous organisation; this is now called magnetizing.
4. The secret agent of the *magnum opus*, the Azoth of the sages, the living and vivifying gold of the philosophers, the universal productive metallic agent, is MAGNETIZED ELECTRICITY, the first matter of the *magnum opus*.

The great Hermetic Arcanum, revealed for the first time clearly and without mystic figures, is this :—What the adepts call dead substances are bodies as they exist in nature ; living substances are those assimilated and *magnetized* by the will of the adept. So that the *magnum opus* is more than a chemical operation; it is a veritable creation of the human Logos initiated into the power of the Logos of God Himself. This secret is contained in the thirty-first Semita of the Sepher Jezirah, commented on by the alchemist Rabbi Abraham. (Ed. Amsterdam, 1642, p. 144.)

Semita XXXI.

Vocatur intelligentia perpetua; et quare vocatur ita ? Eo quod ducit motum solis et lunæ juxta constitutionem eorum ; utrumque in orbe sibi conveniente.

Rabbi Abraham F ... D ...
dicit :

Semita trigesima prima vocatur intelligentia perpetua : et illa ducit solem et lunam et reliquas stellas et figuras, unum quodque in orbe suo, et impertit omnibus creatis juxta dispositionem ad signa et figuras.

"The thirty-first path is called perpetual intelligence, and it rules the sun and moon with the other stars and objects, each in its respective orb. And it distributes what is fitting to all created things according to these."

This text, it will be seen, is still completely obscure for those who do not know the value of each of the thirty-two paths. These are the ten numbers and twenty-two hieroglyphical letters of the Kabbalah. The thirty-first is connected with ש, which represents the magic lamp or light between the horns of Baphomet. It is the kabbalistic sign of Od or the Astral Light, with its two poles and equilibriated centre. As we have said, in alchemical language the sun signifies gold, the moon silver, and the other stars or planets correspond to the other metals. The secret fire of the alchemical masters was therefore electricity and this is half of their Great Arcanum, but they knew how to equilibriate its force by a magnetic influence which they concentrated in their Athanor.

II.—THE UNIVERSAL MEDICINE.

MOST of our physical maladies are derived from our moral diseases, following the universal and magical dogma, and by reason of the law of analogies. Any great passion to which we abandon ourselves is always a great disease in preparation. Mortal sins are so named because positively and physically they cause death. So soon as the will is irrevocably confirmed in the path of absurdity, the man is dead, and the rock which he will break on is at hand. It is, therefore, true that wisdom preserves and prolongs life. Every one knows that a sober, moderately industrious, and perfectly regulated life usually lengthens existence. The Great Master has said :—" My flesh is meat indeed, and my blood is drink indeed. He that eateth my flesh and drinketh my blood hath everlasting life." And when the crowd murmured, He added :—" Here the flesh profiteth nothing; the words which I speak to you are spirit and life." Therefore He meant to say :—" Drink of my spirit and live by my life." And when He was about to die, He attached the memory of His life to the sign of bread, and that of His spirit to the sign of wine, and instituted thus the communion of faith, hope, and charity. In the same sense, the Hermetic masters say :—Make gold potable, and you will have the universal medicine; that is, appropriate truth to your use, let it be the spring which you daily drink of, and then you will have within you the immortality of the sages. Temperance, tranquillity of soul, simplicity of character, calmness and reasonableness of will, not only make us happy but strong and healthy. It is by becoming good and rational that man makes himself immortal; we are all the authors of our destinies, and God does not save us without our own concurrence.

Death has no existence for the wise man, it is a phantom made hideous by the ignorance and weakness of the crowd. Change is the evidence of movement and movement is life. The very corpse would not decompose were it dead; all the molecules which form it remain alive and are in motion to disintegrate. And you think that mind is the first to be dissipated and lives no more! You believe that thought and love can cease when the grossest matter never perishes. If change must be called death, we are daily dying and daily being born anew, for our bodies are always changing. Fear, therefore, to soil and tear our garments but fear not to leave them when the hour of rest has come. The embalming and preservation of bodies are a superstition against Nature. It is an attempt to create death, it is the enforced immobility of a substance which life has need of. But we must not destroy or make away with corpses, for nothing is abruptly performed by Nature, and we must not run the risk of violently breaking the bonds of a soul that is releasing itself. Death is never instantaneous, it is accomplished by degrees. So long as the blood is not absolutely cold, so long as the nerves can be galvanised, the man is not wholly dead, and if none of the essential organs of life be destroyed the spirit may be recalled, either accidentally or by a powerful will. A philosopher has said that he would reject universal testimony rather than believe in a resurrection from the dead, and therein he has spoken rashly, for it is on the faith of universal evidence that he believed in the impossibility of resurrection.

Let us now be bold enough to assert that resurrection is possible, and even occurs more often than is imagined. How many persons whose dissolutions have been judicially and scientifically established have been subsequently discovered in their coffins dead, it is true, but who have come back to life and have bitten through their hands to open the arteries and escape by a new death from unendurable agonies? A doctor will tell us that such persons were in a lethargy. What is lethargy, however? The etherisation or stupor produced by chloroform is a real lethargy which sometimes ends in actual death, when the soul, rejoiced at its temporary liberation, makes an effort of the will to depart finally, which is possible with those who have conquered hell, that is, with those whose moral strength is greater than that of astral attraction. Thus resurrection is possible only for elementary souls, and these above all are exposed to awake unwillingly in the tomb. Great men and true sages are never buried alive.

The body is a garment of the soul, to which the latter is joined by sensibility, and when sensibility ceases it is a sure sign that the soul is departing. When the garment is completely worn out or seriously and irreparably torn, it quits it and never reassumes it. But when, by some accident, it loses this garment without it being worn or destroyed, the soul, in certain cases, can take it up again, either by its own effort or by the help of another will stronger and more active than its own.

Death is neither the end of life nor the beginning of immortality, it is the continuation and transformation of life. Now, a transformation being always a progress, few dead persons consent to return to this life, and reassume the garment they have just rejected. This makes resurrection one of the most difficult achievements of supreme initiation, and its success is never certain but should be regarded as accidental or unexpected. To resuscitate a dead person, the most powerful chains of attraction which can bind it to the form it has quitted must be suddenly and energetically brought together. It is necessary, therefore, to be beforehand acquainted with this chain, then to seize it, then to produce a will-effort strong enough to rejoin it instantaneously and with irresistible power. The method of procedure is indicated in Scripture. The prophet Elias and St Paul employed it with success. The dead person must be magnetized by placing our feet upon their feet, our mouth against their mouth, then concentrating the whole will, and calling the soul which has escaped for a long time towards us with all the mental caresses and affection of which we are capable. If the operator can inspire the soul of the defunct with great love or respect, if in the thought which he magnetically transmits to it, the thaumaturge can persuade it that life is still necessary to it, and that happy days are still in store for it here below, it will certainly return.

It suffices sometimes to take the person by the hand and raise them quickly, calling them in a loud voice. This method, which commonly succeeds in swoons, may be also efficacious in death, when the magnetist who exercises it is endowed with a powerfully sympathetic speech and possesses what may be called the eloquence of voice. He must also perform the work by a great outburst of faith.

In the same way, it is the faith as well as the knowledge of the doctor which is the real virtue of remedies, and the only true efficacious medicine is thaumaturgy. So occult therapeutics are exclusive of all common medication. They chiefly employ words, insufflations, and communicate by the will a varied virtue to such simple substances as water, oil, wine, camphor, and salt. The water of the homœopathists is a veritably magnetized and enchanted water which works by means of faith. The tonic substances added in almost infinitesimal quantities are consecrations and as it were signs of the doctor's will.

What is vulgarly called charlatanism is a great means of real success in medicine, if such charlatanry be skilful enough to inspire great confidence and to form a circle of belief. In medicine more than all it is faith which saves. There is scarcely a village without its compounder of occult medicines, and such persons have almost everywhere and always achieved an incomparably greater success than the doctors approved by the faculty. The remedies they prescribe are often bizarre or ridiculous, and succeed better on account of it, because they exact and obtain more faith on the part of subjects and operators.

Insufflation is one of the most important practices of occult medicine, because it is a perfect sign of life-transfer. To inspire, in fact, means to breathe on some one or something, and we already know, by the one dogma of Hermes, that it is the virtue of things which has created words, and that an exact proportion exists between ideas and words, which are the first forms and verbal realisations of ideas. Accordingly as the breathing is warm or cold, it is attractive or repulsive. The warm breathing corresponds to positive electricity, and the cold to negative electricity. Electrical and nervous animals fear the cold breathing, as we may ascertain by breathing on a cat whose familiarities are importunate. By fixedly regarding a lion or tiger, and breathing in their face, we should so stupify them that we should force them to recoil before us. Warm and prolonged insufflation restores circulation, cures rheumatic pains, re-establishes equilibrium in the humours of the body, and dissipates weariness. Coming from a good and sympathetic person, it is a universal composer. Cold insufflation appeases those pains which are caused by congestions and fluidic accumulations. These two breathings must therefore be alternated, by observing the polarity of the human organism, and by acting in an opposite manner on the poles, subjected, one after another, to a contrary magnetism. Thus, to cure an inflamed eye, the healthy one should be gently and warmly insufflated, then cold insufflations must be practised at a distance on the irritated organ in exact proportion with the warm ones. Magnetic passes themselves act like a breathing by the transpiration and radiation of the interior air, which is all phosphorescent with vital light; slow passes are a warm breathing which collects and raises the spirits, rapid ones are a cold breathing which disperses the energies and neutralises tendencies to congestion. The warm insufflation should be made either transversely or from beneath upwards; the cold insufflation is more efficacious when directed from above downwards.

All the power of the occultist doctor is in the consciousness of his will, and all his art consists in producing faith in his patient. Everything is possible to him who believes, as the Master has told us. He must dominate his subject by his presence, tone, and gestures, must inspire confidence by something of paternal manner, and divert him by some pleasant and cheerful talk. Rabelais, who was more magician than he seemed, chose pantagruelism as his special panacea. He made his patients laugh, and all the remedies they subsequently used succeeded the better in consequence; he established between himself and them a magnetic current, by means of which he transmitted to them his assurance and good temper; he flattered them in his prefaces by calling them his most illustrious and cherished patients, and he dedicated his works to them. So we are convinced that Gargantua and Pantagruel have cured more ill-humours, more dispositions to folly, more ultra-bilious manias in that epoch of religious animosities and civil wars, than all the medical faculty could then ascertain and study.

Occult medicine is essentially sympathetic. A reciprocal affection, or at least good-will, must be established between doctor and patient. Syrups and juleps have little inherent virtue, they are what the opinion common to agent and patient makes them, so homœopathy suppresses them without grave inconvenience. Oil and wine combined either with salt or camphor would be sufficient for the healing of all wounds, and for all exterior frictions or soothing applications. Oil and wine are the pre-eminent medicaments of evangelical tradition. It is the balm of the Samaritan, and in the Apocalypse the prophet, describing the great exterminations, prays the avenging powers to spare the oil and wine, that is, to leave a hope and a cure for so many wounds. Extreme unction among the primitive Christians, and in the mind of the apostle St James, who has transmitted the precept in his epistle to the faithful of the whole world, was the pure and simple practice of the Master's traditional medicine. "Is any man sick among you? Let him call in the priests of the church and let them pray over him, anointing him with oil in the name of the Lord." This divine therapeutic was progressively lost, and Extreme Unction has come to be regarded as a religious formality necessary in the hour of death.* Nevertheless, the thaumaturgic virtue of Holy Oils cannot be wholly consigned to oblivion by the traditional dogma, and its memory is retained in that passage of the Catechism which refers to Extreme Unction.

III.—RENEWED YOUTH.

THE universal principle of life is a substantial movement, or a substance eternally moved and motive, invisible and impalpable, in a volatile state, and which is materially manifested when fixed by the phenomena of polarisation. This substance is indefectible, incorruptible, and immortal, but its form manifestations are continually changed by the perpetuity of motion. Thus, all dies because all lives, and if we could immortalise a form, we should arrest motion

---

* And yet the forgiveness of sin was in some way attached to the ceremony or to the prayer of faith which accompanied it, and which evidently was the life of the ceremony.—TR.

and create the only true death. To imprison a soul for ever in a mummified human body, such would be the horrible solution of the paradox of pretended immortality in the same body and on the same earth. Everything is regenerated by the universal solvent, whose power is consecrated in the quintessence, that is, in the equilibrating centre of the two-fold polarity. The four elements of the ancients are the four polar forces of the universal magnet, and it is in their exact proportion that we must seek the universal medicine of the body, as that of the soul is offered us by religion in Him who eternally sacrifices Himself on the Cross for the salvation of the world.

The great magical means of preserving the youth of the body is to prevent the soul from growing old, by carefully preserving its primeval freshness of sentiments and thoughts, which the corrupt world calls illusions, and which we name the primitive reflections of eternal truth. To believe in bliss on earth, to believe in friendship and love, to believe in a maternal Providence which takes account of all our steps and recompenses all our tears, is to be completely duped, says the corrupted world, and it fails to perceive that the dupe is he who thinks himself to be strong when depriving himself of all the delights of the soul. To believe in good, in the moral order, is to possess good, and this is why the Saviour of the world promised the Kingdom of Heaven to those who become as little children. Infancy is the age of faith; the child as yet knows nothing of life, so is he glowing with confiding immortality. Can he doubt of self-devotion, tenderness, friendship, love, when he is in the arms of his mother? Become children in heart and you will keep young in body!

The realities of God and Nature infinitely surpass all the dreams of men both in goodness and beauty. Thus the *blasés* are those who have never known how to be happy, and the disillusioned prove, by their disgust, that they have only drunk at muddy springs. To enjoy even the sensual pleasures of life, we must possess moral sense, and those who calumniate existence have certainly abused it. Supreme magic directs man to the purest moral code. *Vel sanctum invenit, vel sanctum facit,* an adept has said, for it shews us that to be happy even in this world we must be holy. To be holy! something said with ease, but how shall we obtain faith when we believe no longer?

THE GREAT PRACTICAL SECRETS. 213

How recover the taste for virtue in a heart depraved by vice? . . . It is a question of recurrence to the four maxims of science—to know, to dare, to will, and to keep silent. Silence must be imposed on our disgusts, we must study duty and begin practising it as if we loved it. You are a sceptic, for example, and you wish to be a Christian. Perform the exercises of a Christian, pray regularly, using Christian formulæ, approach the sacraments assuming faith, and faith will come. By analogous exercises, a fool, if he willed it persistently, might become a man of understanding.

By changing the habits of the soul we assuredly change those of the body. What contributes above all to make us old by deforming us are rancorous and bitter thoughts, unfavourable judgments on others, the fury of wounded pride and of ill-satisfied passions. A benevolent and mild philosophy would save us from all these evils. If we closed our eyes on our neighbour's faults, taking account of his good qualities only, we should find goodness and kindness everywhere. The most perverse man has his good points, and softens when we know how to take him. Had we nothing in common with human vices we should not even perceive them. Friendship and the self-abnegation which it inspires, are found even in the prisons and galleys. The abominable Lacenaire faithfully returned money when it was lent to him and many times performed acts of generosity and benevolence. No one is absolutely bad or absolutely good. "No one is good but God," said the best of masters.

What we mistake for the zeal of virtue in ourselves is often only a secret self-love, dissimulated jealousy, and a haughty instinct of contradiction. "When we see manifest disorders and scandalous sinners," say the authors of mystical theology, "believe they are subjected by God to greater trials than we are, that certainly, or at least very probably, we are not of such worth as they, and that we should do far worse in their place."

Peace, peace! This is the supreme soul-good, to give us which Christ came into the world. "Glory to God in the highest and peace on earth to men of goodwill!" The early Christian fathers reckoned sadness as an eighth deadly sin. In fact, the very repentance of the Christian is not a sadness but a consolation, joy, and triumph. "I desired evil and I desire it no longer, I was dead and am alive." The father of the prodigal son has killed the fatted calf for his son has returned, and what can the prodigal do? Weep, feel a little confused, but above all be joyful. Folly and wickedness are the only sad things in the world. As soon as we are delivered from them, let us laugh and utter cries of joy, for we are saved and all the dead who love us rejoice in Heaven.

We all bear within us a principle of death and a principle of immortality. Death is the animal, and the animal ever produces folly.* God loves not fools, for his Divine Spirit is named the Spirit of Intelligence. Folly is atoned for by suffering and enslavement. The rod is made for beasts.

IV.—TRANSFORMATIONS.

ST AUGUSTINE seriously doubts whether Apuleius could really have been changed into an ass by a Thessalian sorcerer, and theologians have debated long on the transmutation of Nabuchodonosar into a wild beast. This merely proves that the eloquent doctor of Hippo was ignorant of magical secrets, and that the theologians in question had not advanced far in exegesis. In the opinion of the vulgar, transformations and metamorphoses have ever been the very essence of magic. Now, the crowd, which is the echo of opinion, is never entirely right and never wholly wrong. Magic really changes the nature of things, or, rather, modifies their appearances at pleasure, according to the strength of the operator's will and the fascination of aspiring adepts. Speech creates forms, and when a person reputed infallible gives anything a name, he really transforms the object into the substance which is signified by the name that he gives it. The masterpiece of speech and of faith, in this order, is the real metamorphosis of a substance whose outward semblance does not alter. Had Apollonius presented to his disciples a cup of wine, and had he said to them, "This is my blood which ye shall drink for ever to perpetuate my life within you," and had his disciples for centuries believed this transformation continued by the repetition of the same words, had they taken the wine, notwithstanding its scent

* " *La mort c'est la bête et la bête produit toujours la bêtise.*" The play on words in the original cannot be rendered into English.—TR.

and its savour, for the true, human, living blood of Apollonius, this master in theurgy would have to be acknowledged the most skilful of fascinators and the most powerful of magi; it would remain for us to adore him.

It is well known that mesmerists can, in the imagination of their somnambulists, endow water with any taste they may choose, and if we suppose a magus with sufficient power over the Astral Light to mesmerise at the same time a whole assembly, otherwise prepared for mesmerism by a sufficient over-excitement, we could easily explain, not indeed the gospel miracle of Cana, but others of the same kind.

The fascinations of love, resulting from the universal magic of nature, really transform persons and objects. Love is a dream of enchantments which transfigures the world, all becomes music and fragrance, all is intoxication and bliss. The being beloved is beautiful, is good, is splendid, sublime, infallible, radiant with health and happiness . . . then when the dream is dispelled, we appear to have fallen from the clouds, we look with disgust on the shameless sorcerer who has taken the place of the fair Mélusine, on the Thersites whom we took for Achilles or Nereus. Love begins as magician and ends a sorcerer. After creating the illusions of heaven on earth, it realises those of hell; its hatred is as outrageous as its enthusiasm, because it is passional, that is, subjected to influences which are fatal for it. For this reason, the sages proscribe love, which they proclaim the enemy of reason.

The life of creatures is a progressive transformation whose forms may be determined, renewed, and preserved longer, or else destroyed sooner. If the notion of metempsychosis were true, might we not say that debauch, represented by Circe, changes men really and materially into swine, for the chastisement of vices would, on this hypothesis, be a lapse into those animal forms which correspond to them? Now, metempsychosis, which has been frequently misunderstood, has a perfectly true side—animal forms communicate their sympathetic imprints to the astral body of man and are soon reflected on his features, according to the force of his habits. A man of intelligent and passive mildness assumes the ways and inert physiognomy of a sheep, but in somnambulism it is no longer a person of sheep-like appearance but a sheep itself which is seen, as the ecstatic and learned Swedenborg experienced times out of number. Thus we can really change men into animals and animals into men, we can metamorphose plants and alter their virtues, we can give minerals ideal properties—it is all a question of will-power. We can equally become visible or invisible, and in this is the explanation of the ring of Gyges and its mysteries.

Let us first remove from the minds of our readers all absurd suppositions of effects destitute of causes or which contradict their causes. To become invisible one of three things is necessary—either to interpose an opaque medium between the light and our body, or between our body and the eyes of the spectators; or we must fascinate the eyes of those present in such a manner that they cannot make use of their faculty of seeing. Now of these three methods of becoming invisible, the last alone is magical. Have we not noticed that, under the influence of a strong preoccupation, we may look without beholding and knock up against an object which was actually before our eyes?* "Seeing, let them see not," said the Great Initiator, whose history, moreover, tells us that one day when on the point of being stoned in the Temple, he made himself invisible and went out.

It is unnecessary to reproduce the mystifications of common grimoires on the ring of invisibility. Jamblichus and Peter d'Apono are the only authors who have treated the subject seriously. What they say is plainly allegorical, and those representations which they give of it, or which can be reproduced after their descriptions, prove that they are indicating nothing else but the great magic Arcanum. One of these figures represents the cycle of universal harmonical movement equilibrated in imperishable being; another, which should be made from an amalgamation of the seven metals, deserves a detailed description. It should have a double collet and two precious stones, a topaz constellated at the sign of the sun, and an emerald at the sign of the moon. On the inner side it should bear the occult characters of the planets and on the outer their known signs, twice repeated and in kabbalistic opposition to one another, that is, five on the right and five on the left, the signs of the sun and moon resuming the four diverse intelligences of the seven planets. This configura-

* See note 26.

THE GREAT PRACTICAL SECRETS. 217

tion is nothing less than a pantacle expressing all the mysteries of magical dogma, and the symbolic sense of the ring is that, to exercise omnipotence, of which ocular fascination is one of the most difficult proofs that can be afforded, we must possess the whole science and know how to make use of it.

Fascination is performed by magnetism. The Magus commands interiorly a whole assembly not to see him, and it does not see him. Thus he enters guarded doors and issues from prisons in the face of his stupified jailers, who experience a kind of strange numbness and recollect having beheld him as in a dream, but only after he has passed. Thus the secret of invisibility consists wholly in a definable power, that of averting or paralysing the attention, so that the light reaches the visual organ without exciting the seeing faculty of the soul. To exercise this faculty we must have a will habituated to sudden and energetic action, great presence of mind, and no less great skill in producing distractions among a crowd. For example, let a man who is hunted by assassins, after dashing into a cross street return at once, and come with collected mien before his pursuers, or let him mix with them and seem occupied in the same chase, and he will undoubtedly make himself invisible. He who wishes to be seen always makes himself conspicuous, and he who would remain unperceived obliterates himself and disappears. The true ring of Gyges is the will; it is also the rod of transmutations, and by a clear and strong formulation it creates the magical Logos. The all-powerful words of enchantments are those which express this creative power over forms. The Tetragram, which is the supreme word of magic, means—It is what it will be, and applied with a plenitude of intelligence to any transformation whatsoever, it will renew and modify all things, in the face of evidence and common-sense. The *hoc est* of the Christian sacrifice is a translation and application of the Tetragram, and thus this simple phrase operates the most complete, invisible, incredible, and clearly-stated of all transformations. A still stronger word than *transformation* has been judged necessary by the councils to express the miracle, that of *transubstantiation*.

The Hebrew words, יהוה, אנלא, אתיה, אמן, have been regarded by all Kabbalists as the keys of magical transformation. The Latin words, *est, sit, esto, fiat*, have the same virtue when pronounced with a complete comprehension. The Comte de Montalembert narrates seriously, in his legend of St Elizabeth of Hungary, that one day this pious lady, surprised by her princely husband, from whom she wished to conceal her good works, at the moment when she was carrying some food to the poor in her apron, declared to him that she was carrying roses, and on examination she was not found to have spoken falsely, for the loaves had changed into roses. This story is a graceful magical apologue, and means that the truly wise man cannot lie; that the Logos of wisdom determines the form of objects, or even their substance, independently of their forms. Why, for example, should not the noble spouse of St Elizabeth, a good and solid Christian like herself, and who believed firmly in the real presence of the Saviour in true human body on an altar where he saw only a host of flour, why should he not believe in the real presence of roses under the form of loaves?* Doubtless, she showed him bread, but as she had said, "They are roses," and he believed her incapable of the smallest untruth, he beheld, and wished only to behold, roses. This is the secret of the miracle.

We must speak here of lycanthropy, or the nocturnal transformation of men into wolves, histories so well substantiated that sceptical science has had recourse to furious manias, and to masquerading as animals, for explanations. But such hypotheses are puerile, and explain nothing. Let us seek elsewhere the solution of the mystery, and establish—First, That no person has been killed by a were-wolf except by suffocation, without effusion of blood and without wounds. Second, That were-wolves, though tracked, hunted, and even maimed, have never been killed on the spot. Third, That persons suspected of these transformations have always been found at home, after the pursuit of the were-wolf, more or less wounded, sometimes dying, but invariably in their natural form. And now let us establish phenomena of another order. Nothing in the world is better attested, and more incontestably proved, than the real and visible presence of St Alphonsus de Ligouri by the bedside of the dying pope, whilst the same personage was seen at his own home, a great distance from Rome, transported in prayer and ecstasy. The simultaneous presence of the missionary Francis Xavier in

* See note 27.

several places at once has been no less rigorously proved. These may be said to be miracles, but real miracles are still objects for scientific investigation. The apparitions of those who are dear to us, coincident with the moment of their death, are phenomena of the same order, and referable to the same cause.

We have spoken of the sidereal body, which is the mediator between the soul and the material organisn. This body remains awake very often while the other is asleep, and by thought transports itself through all space which universal magnetism opens to it. It thus lengthens, without breaking, the sympathetic chain which attaches it to the heart and brain, and this is why there is danger in waking up dreaming persons with a start, for a shock may sever the chain at a blow, and cause instantaneous death. The form of our sidereal body is conformable to the habitual condition of our thoughts; and, in the long run, it is bound to modify the features of the material organism. Let us now be bold enough to assert that the were-wolf is nothing more than the sidereal body of a man whose savage and sanguinary instincts are represented by the wolf, and who, whilst his phantom is wandering abroad, sleeps painfully in his bed, and dreams that he is a veritable wolf. What renders the were-wolf visible is the almost somnambulistic over-excitement caused by the fear of those who see it, or their disposition, more particularly among simple country-folk, to place themselves in direct communication with the Astral Light, which is the common medium of dreams and visions. The blows inflicted on the were-wolf really wound the sleeper by the odic and sympathetic congestion of the Astral Light, and by the correspondence of the immaterial with the material body.* Many persons will believe themselves to be dreaming when they read of such things, and will ask us if we are really ourselves awake; but we only beg scientific men to reflect on the phenomena of gestation, and the effects of the imagination of women on the form of their offspring. A woman who had been present at the execution of a man who was broken on the wheel gave birth to a child, every one of whose limbs was broken. Let them explain how the impression produced on the soul of the mother could reach and break the infant's members, and we will explain

* Note 28.

how blows dealt and received in dream can really bruise, and even grievously wound, the body of the person who receives them in imagination, above all when his body is in pain and subject to nervous and magnetic influences.

We act by the imagination on the imagination of others, by our sidereal body on theirs, and by our organs on their organs. So that by sympathy, whether of inclination or of obsession, we possess one another, and are identified with those whom we would influence. Reactions against this empire make the most pronounced antipathy succeed the liveliest sympathy. The identification of existences is the aim of love, but in identifying them, it frequently makes them rivals and consequently enemies, if at the bottom of the two natures there be an unsociable disposition like pride; to saturate two united souls with an equal degree of pride is to disjoin them by making them rivals.

The *fatal ascendancy* of one person over another is the true rod of Circe. Almost every human countenance bears some resemblance to an animal, that is, it has the *signature* of a specialised instinct. Now, instincts are balanced by contrary instincts, and dominated by stronger ones. To govern sheep, the dog evokes the fear of the wolf. If you are a dog and would be loved by a pretty little cat, be metamorphosed into a cat and you will win her. But how is this change to be accomplished? By observation, imitation, and imagination. We think that our figurative language will be understood here, and we commend this revelation to all magnetists as the most profound secret of their art. It may be formulated technically as follows: *To polarise one's own animal light in equilibrated antagonism with an opposite pole.* Or better still: To concentrate in one's self absorbing specialities in order to direct radiations towards an absorbent reservoir, and *vice versa*. This regulation of our magnetic polarisation may be performed by help of the animal forms we have spoken of, and which will serve to fix imagination. For example, you seek to act magnetically on a person polarised like yourself, which you will know at first contact if you be a magnetist; they are merely a trifle less strong than yourself—they are a mouse, you a rat. Turn into a cat and you will catch them.

When we dream of a living person, their sidereal body is either present to ours in the Astral Light, or at any rate the reflection of this body, and the way in which we are impressed by meeting it, frequently reveal to us the secret dispositions of that person in our respect. Love, for example, fashions the sidereal body of the one to the image and resemblance of the other, so that the sensuous medium of the woman is like a man and that of the man is like a woman. It is this change which the kabbalists sought to express in a hidden way when they remark in explaining an obscure passage of Genesis: "God created love by placing a rib of Adam in the breast of Eve, and a portion of the flesh of Eve in the breast of Adam, so that the depth of the female heart is the bone of man, and the basis of the male heart is feminine flesh"—an allegory which is certainly not devoid of profundity and beauty.

The wand of Circe is the fascinating power of woman, and the companions of Ulysses transformed into swine are no mere history of the past. But no metamorphose is accomplished without destruction. To change a hawk into a dove, it must first be killed, then cut in pieces, so as to annihilate the least vestige of its original form, and then boiled in the magic bath of Medea. Remark how the modern hierophants proceed to accomplish human regeneration; for example, what is done to transform a more or less weak and passionate man into a stoical Jesuit missionary, which is the great secret of this order, ever misconstrued, often calumniated, but invariably victorious. Read the "Exercises of St Ignatius" attentively, and mark with what magic power this man of genius operates the realisation of faith. He counsels his disciples to see, touch, smell, and taste things invisible; he desires the senses to be exalted in prayer up to the point of voluntary hallucination. If you are meditating on an article of faith, St Ignatius would have you, in the first place, construct the locality, dream of it, see it, touch it. If it be hell, he gives you burning rocks to handle, he makes you float in darkness as thick as pitch; he places liquid sulphur on your tongue, he fills your nostrils with an abominable stench, he shows you frightful torments, and makes you hear superhuman groans; he bids your will create all this by constant exercises. Each one does it after his own fashion, but always in the way most likely to impress him. It is no longer the intoxication of opium; it is a dream without sleep, a hallucination devoid of madness, a rational and voluntary vision, a veritable creation of intelligence and faith. Henceforth, in his preaching, the Jesuit may truly say: "What we have seen with our eyes, what we have heard with our ears, what our hands have handled, that we declare unto you." The Jesuit thus formed is in communication with a circle of wills exercised like his own; each of the fathers is as strong as the whole society, and the society is stronger than the world.

V.—DIVINATION.

ONE of the privileges of the initiate of the Great Arcanum, and that which resumes them all, is Divination. According to the vulgar meaning of this word, to divine is to conjecture what we do not know, but its true significance is ineffable in its sublimity. To divine (*divinare*) is to exercise divinity. The Latin word *divinus* has another and higher meaning than *divus*, which is equivalent to the man-god. *Devin* (diviner), in French, contains the four letters of the word DIEU (God), plus the letter N, whose shape corresponds to the Hebrew א aleph, and which kabbalistically and hieroglyphically expresses the Great Arcanum, whose symbol in the Tarot is the figure of the juggler. He who perfectly understands the absolute numerical value of א multiplied by N with the grammatical force of the N final in words expressing *science, art,* or *power,* who then adds the five letters of the word DEVIN in such a manner as to make five go into four, four into three, three into two, and two into one, by translating the resulting number into primitive Hebrew characters, will write the occult name of the Great Arcanum, and will be in possession of a word of which the sacred Tetragram itself is only the equivalent and image.

To be a diviner in all the force of the term is, therefore, to be divine, and something still more mysterious. The two signs of human divinity or of divine humanity are prophecies and miracles. To be a prophet is to perceive beforehand the effects which exist in causes, it is to read in the Astral Light; to perform miracles is to act on the universal agent and subject it to our will. The essence of divination, that is, of the Great Magic Arcanum, is represented by all the symbols of silence, and is closely bound up with the single and primitive dogma of Hermes. It gives absolute certitude in philosophy, the secret of universal faith in religion ; in physics, the compositon, decomposition, recomposition, realisation, and adaptation of the philosophical mercury, named Azoth by the alchemists ; in dynamics, it multiplies our powers by those of the perpetual motion ; it is at once mystical, metaphysical, and material, with correspondences of effects in the three worlds ; it procures charity in God, truth in science, and gold in riches ; for metallic transmutation is at once an allegory and reality, which is well known to all the adepts in the true knowledge.

Divination is intuition, and the key of intuition is the universal and magical dogma of analogies. By analogies the Magus interprets dreams, for the analogies in the reflections of the Astral Light are as rigorous as the shades of colours in the solar light, and can be calculated and explained with consummate exactitude. The one indispensable condition is a knowledge of the dreamer's degree of intellectual life, which he will reveal of himself by his own dreams in a way that will profoundly amaze him.

Somnambulism, presentiments, and second sight are only an accidental or habitual disposition to dream in a voluntary or waking sleep, that is, to perceive the analogical reflections of the Astral Light, which is the great book of divination. There are two classes of seers, the instinctive and the initiated. This is why children, ignorant persons, shepherds, and even idiots, have more tendency to natural divination than scholars and thinkers. The simple herd-boy, David, was a prophet even as Solomon, the King of the Kabbalists and Magi. The perceptions of instinct are frequently as exact as those of knowledge. Those least clairvoyant in the Astral Light are those who reason most. Somnambulism is a purely instinctive state, and therefore somnambulists require to be guided by a seer of science ; sceptics and reasoners only lead them astray. Divinatory vision occurs only in ecstatic trance, and to attain this state doubt and illusion must be rendered impossible by enchaining or lulling thought.

Divinatory instruments are merely means to self-magnetisation and diversion from the exterior light in order to fix the attention on the inner light exclusively; they are a means of communication between diviner and consultant, and often serve alone to concentrate the two wills on one sign. Vague, complicated, variable figures assist in collecting the reflections of the Astral Light, and it is thus that we see visions in coffee-grouts, clouds, the white of eggs, &c., those fatidic forms which only exist in the Translucid, or imagination of the operators. Vision in water is occasioned by dazzling and fatiguing the optic nerve, which transfers its natural functions to the Translucid and produces a cerebral hallucination which mistakes the reflections of the Astral Light for real images; thus nervous persons, with weak sight and lively imagination, are best fitted for this kind of divination, which is more successful still when performed by children. But let us not misapprehend the function that we attribute to imagination in the divinatory arts. Doubtless we see by means of imagination, which is the natural side of the miraculous; but what we behold is true, and the marvellous side of this natural operation consists in this. We appeal to the experience of all veritable adepts. The author of this book has performed all kinds of divination, and the results he has obtained have been invariably in proportion to the exactitude of his scientific operations and the good faith of those who consulted him.

The magic mirror of Dupotet, like the mantle of Apollonius, is a method of concentrating the attention on the interior light. Vision in the thumb-nail, when very smooth and blackened, is a variety of the magic mirror; the colour, black, like water, absorbs the visual rays, dazzlement and vertigo ensue, followed by lucidity in subjects naturally apt to it, or suitably disposed. Geomancy and cartomancy are other means of reaching the same ends; combinations of symbols and numbers, being at once fortuitous and necessary, present a sufficiently true likeness of the chances of destiny to enable imagination to behold the realities called up by such symbols. The more the interest is excited, the greater is the desire to see, the more complete is the confidence in intuition, and the clearer also is the vision. To cast the geomantic points by chance, or to tell fortunes by cards in a trifling manner, is to play like children. Chances are oracles only when magnetised by intelligence and directed by faith.

THE GREAT PRACTICAL SECRETS. 225

Of all oracles the Tarot is the most astonishing in its results, because every possible combination of this universal key of the Kabbalah gives as solutions the oracles of science and truth, on account of the analogical precision of its numbers and figures. This miraculous and unique book of the ancient Magi is an instrument of divination which may be employed with complete confidence; its information is always correct, at least in a certain sense, and when it predicts nothing it reveals hidden things, and gives the most sage advice to those who consult it.

The more ceremonies we employ in the exercise of divination, the more we excite the imagination of ourselves and our consultants. The conjuration of the four, the prayer of Solomon, the magic sword to drive away phantoms, may, therefore, be successfully used. The genius of the day and hour should be also invoked, and a special perfume offered to him; then we must place ourselves in magnetic and intuitive *rapport* with the consultant, by asking him what animal is sympathetic with him and which in antipathy, what is his favourite flower, and which colour he prefers. Flowers, colours, and animals are connected in analogical classification with the seven genii of the Kabbalah. Those who love blue are idealists and dreamers; those who like red are materialistic and passionate; those who like yellow are fantastical and capricious; the lovers of green have frequently a mercantile or crafty character; those who give the preference to black are ruled by Saturn. Those fond of horses are industrious and of noble character; the friends of dogs are affectionate and faithful, those of the cat independent and libertine. Frank persons have a horror of spiders; proud minds are antipathetic to the serpent. Upright and fastidious souls cannot tolerate rats and mice; the voluptuous hold toads in horror, because they are cold, solitary, hideous, and dreary. Flowers have analogous sympathies to those of animals and colours, and magic being the science of universal analogies, by one taste, one only tendency in any person, all others may be divined. It is an application of the analogical anatomy of Cuvier to facts in the moral order.

The physiognomy of the face and body, the lines on the forehead, the lines on the hand, also furnish invaluable indices to the Magus. Metoposcopy and chiromancy have become sciences in themselves, and the Chevalier d'Arpentigny has given the latter a new degree of certitude by his remarks on the analogies which really exist between the characters of individuals and the general or detailed peculiarities of their hands. The consultant should be also interrogated on his habitual dreams, for these are the reflections of both the outer and inner life. Great attention was paid to them by the ancients; they were looked on as certain revelations by the patriarchs, and most religious revelations have been given in dreams. The monsters of hell are Christianity's nightmares; never could brush or chisel have produced such deformities if they had not been beheld in dream.

Temperament also is made known by dreams, and as the temperament exercises a continual influence on life, it is requisite to understand it well in order to conjecture the destiny of an individual with certitude. We should mistrust those whose imagination habitually reflects monstrosities. Dreams of blood, of enjoyment, and of light, are indices of a sanguine temperament; dreams of water, mud, rain, and tears, result from a more phlegmatic disposition; nocturnal sweats, darkness, terrors, phantoms, belong to the choleric and hypochondriac.

VI.—ASTROLOGY.

OF all the arts derived from ancient Magian wisdom, astrology is in these days the most misunderstood. The universal harmony of Nature and the necessary connection between all effects and all causes are no longer believed in. True astrology, moreover, that which refers to the one and universal dogma of the Kabbalah, was profaned by the Greeks and Romans of the Decline; the doctrine of the seven firmaments and three mobilities issued of old from the decade of the ten Sephiroths, the character of the planets governed by angels, whose names have been changed into those of pagan divinities, the influence of the spheres on each other, the destiny inherent in numbers, the scale of proportion between the celestial hierarchies corresponding to those of humanity, all have been materialised and reduced to superstition by the calculators of nativities and the casters of horoscopes in the Decadence and Middle

Ages. To restore astrology to its primitive purity would be, in a certain sense, to create a new science; let us only attempt to indicate its first principles, with their more immediate and approximate consequences.

We have said that the Astral Light receives and preserves the imprints of things visible; it follows that the daily aspect of the heavens is reflected in this light, which, being the chief life-agent, operates, by a series of apparatus naturally adapted to this end, the conception, gestation, and birth of children. Now, if this light be sufficiently prodigal of images to endow the fruit of pregnancy with the visible marks of the mother's fancy or craving, much more should it transmit to the still mobile and unformed temperament of the newly-born child the atmospheric impressions and various influences which result at a given moment in the whole planetary system from such and such particular disposition of the stars.

Nothing is indifferent in Nature; a pebble more or less on a road may crush or profoundly alter the fortunes of the greatest men, or even of the greatest empires; much more then the position of a particular star cannot be indifferent to the destinies of the child who is being born, and who enters by the fact of his birth into the universal harmony of the sidereal world. The stars are bound together by attractions which balance them and cause them to perform their revolutions with regularity in space, the network of light extends from sphere to sphere, and there is no point on any planet to which one of these indestructible threads is not attached. The precise place and moment of birth should therefore be calculated by the true astrological adept, then, after an exact computation of the starry influences, it remains for him to reckon the chances of condition, that is, the opportunities or obstacles which the child must one day meet with in his state of life, in his relatives, in the disposition he inherits, and, consequently, in his natural aptitude for the fulfilment of his destinies. Human liberty and enterprise must also be taken into account, should the child come to be truly a man and to extricate himself by a bold will from blind influences and the chain of fatality. It will be seen that we do not allow too much to astrology, but what we leave it is incontestable, it is the scientific and magical calculus of probabilities.

Kabbalistic astrology must not be confounded with

judicial astrology. We will explain this distinction. Infancy is dedicated to the Sun, childhood to the Moon, youth to Mars and Venus, the age of puberty to Mercury, mature age to Jupiter, old age to Saturn. Now, the whole of humanity lives under laws of development which are analogous to those of the individual. It is on this basis that Trithemius establishes his prophetic clavicula of the seven spirits, and by means of which it is possible, following the analogical proportion of successive occurrences, to predict great future events with certainty, and fix beforehand, from age to age, the destinies of nations and the world.

Astrology is as ancient as, and even more ancient than, astronomy, and all seers of clairvoyant antiquity have accorded to it the most complete confidence; now, what comes to us surrounded and supported by such imposing authorities should not be lightly condemned and rejected. Long and patient observations, decisive comparisons, experiments continually repeated, led the ancient sages to their conclusions, and those who pretend to refute them should begin the same labour in an inverse sense. Paracelsus was perhaps the last of the great practical astrologers; he healed the sick by talismans formed under astral influences, and recognised in all bodies the mark of their ruling star; this was according to him the true universal medicine, the absolute natural science, lost by men through their own fault, and recovered by a small number of initiates only. To recognise the sign of each star on men, animals, and plants is the true natural science of Solomon, that science said to be lost and whose principles are preserved notwithstanding, like all such secrets, in the symbolism of the Kabbalah. It will be understood that to read the writing of the stars, we must be acquainted with the stars themselves, a knowledge which must be obtained by the Kabbalistic domification of the Heavens, and by the comprehension of the Kabbalistic planisphere, recovered and explained by Gaffarel. In this planisphere, the constellations form Hebrew characters, and the mythological figures may be replaced by the Tarot figures. To this same planisphere Gaffarel refers the origin of patriarchal writing, and the first outlines of primitive alphabets might be discovered in the concatenations of starry attractions; the celestial book would thus have served as the model for that of Enoch, and the Kabbalistic alphabet would be the synthesis of heaven. This is not wanting in poetry, nor above all in probability, and the study of the Tarot, which is evidently the primitive and hieroglyphic book of Enoch, as was divined by the erudite William Postel, will be sufficient to convince us of this.

The signs impressed in the Astral Light by the reflections and attractions of the stars are then reproduced, as the ancient sages discovered, on all bodies by the conjunction of this light. Men bear the seals of their planets on their foreheads, and especially on their hands; animals in their entire shapes and special peculiarities; plants reveal them on their leaves and in their seed; minerals in their veins, and in the peculiarities of their fractures. The study of these characters was the occupation of the whole life of Paracelsus, and the figures on his talismans are the fruit of his researches; but he has given no key to them, and the astro-Kabbalistic alphabet, with its correspondences, still remains to be accomplished; the science of unconventional magical writing is confined, as regards publicity, to the planisphere of Gaffarel. The serious art of divination consists wholly in the knowledge of these signs. Chiromancy is the art of discerning in the lines of the hand the writing of the stars, and metoposcopy seeks the same or analogous characters in the countenances of its consultants. In reality the lines formed on the human face by nervous contractions are determined by necessary laws, and the radiation of the nervous tissue is absolutely analogous to the network formed between the spheres by the chains of stellar attractions. The fatalities of life are, therefore, necessarily written in our wrinkles, and one or more mystic letters of the Kabbalistic planisphere may often be recognised at first sight on the face of a stranger. If the letter be fretted and indented, there is an internal struggle between destiny and will, and already in his strongest emotions and tendencies his whole past is laid bare to the Magus; the future may then be easily conjectured, and if events deceive at times the sagacity of the diviner, the consultant remains none the less astonished at the superhuman knowledge of the adept.

The head of man is shaped on the model of the starry spheres; it attracts and repels, and it is this which first is formed and appears in the gestation of the infant. It is, therefore, affected in an absolute manner by the astral influence, and its diverse protuberances bear witness to the variety of its attractions. Phrenology, therefore, should find its final message in scientific and purified astrology, whose problems we indicate as objects of the patience and good faith of students.

According to Ptolemæus, the sun dessicates, the moon moistens; according to the Kabbalists, the sun represents rigorous justice, and the moon is in sympathy with mercy. It is the sun which causes storms, and the moon who, by a kind of gentle atmospheric pressure, induces the sea to ebb, flow, and, as it were, to breathe.

We read in the Sohar, one of the great sacred books of the Kabbalah, that "the magic serpent, son of the Sun, sought to devour the world, when the Sea, daughter of the Moon, set her foot on his head and subdued him." For this reason, among the ancients, Venus was the daughter of the sea, as Diana was identified with the moon, and for this also the name of Mary signifies Star or Salt of the sea. To consecrate this Kabbalistic doctrine in the faith of the uninitiated, it is said in prophetic language, "The woman shall crush the serpent's head."

Jerôme Cardan, one of the boldest speculators, and indisputably the most accomplished astrologer of his day—Jerôme Cardan, who, if the legend of his death may be believed, was a martyr to his faith in astrology—has left a calculation by means of which every one can forecast the good or evil fortune of every year in his life. He grounds his theory on his own experiences, and declares that this calculation has never deceived him. To know then what will be the destiny of any year, he collects the events of those which preceded it by four, eight, twelve, nineteen, and thirty: the number four is that of realisation; the number eight that of Venus, or natural things; the number twelve, which is that of the cycle of Jupiter, corresponds to successes; the cycles of the moon and Mars correspond to the number nineteen; thirty is that of Fatality, or Saturn. Thus, for example, I seek to ascertain what will befall me in this year 1855, and I pass over in my mind what really decisive events took place, in the order of life and progress, four years back; what I experienced of either natural happiness or misfortune eight years ago, what I can recall in the way of success or failure twelve years back, the vicissitudes and misfortunes, or sicknesses, of nineteen years since, and what

sad or calamitous occurrences I experienced at a distance
of thirty years. Then, taking into account irrevocably
accomplished facts and the progress of age, I calculate the
chances analogous to those which I already owe to the
influence of the same planets, and find that in 1851 I had
moderately but sufficiently remunerative occupations, with
some embarrassment in my position; that in 1847 I was
violently separated from my family, and from this separation ensued great sufferings for mine and me; that in 1843
I travelled as a pioneer, addressing crowds, and persecuted
by ill-intentioned persons, in a word, I was at once honoured
and proscribed; and that, finally, in 1825 the family life
ceased to exist for me, and I was definitely devoted to
a fateful path, which led me to knowledge and misfortune.
I may, therefore, expect that I shall this year undergo toil,
poverty, weariness, banishment of the heart, change of
place, notoriety, and contradictions, with some event which
will be decisive for the rest of my days, and I already find
in the present every reason to put faith in this future. I
conclude that, for myself and for this year, experience
completely confirms the accuracy of Cardan's astrological
prediction.

This calculation, moreover, is connected with that of the
climacteric years of old astrologers. *Climacteric* means
arranged in gradations, or calculated on the degrees of a
scale. Johannes Trithemius, in his work on Secondary
Causes, has very curiously computed the return of fortunate
or disastrous years for all the empires of the world.

According to the great masters of astrology, comets are
the stars of exceptional heroes, and only visit the earth to
herald great changes therein; planets preside over collective existences, and modify the destinies of men in the
aggregate; the fixed stars, the furthest and feeblest in their
action, attract individuals and decide their tastes; sometimes a group of stars influences, all together, the destinies
of a single man, and often a large number of souls are
drawn by the distant rays of the same sun. When we
die, our interior light follows on the attraction of its star,
and thus we live in other universes, wherein the soul
creates for itself a new envelope analogous to the progress
or decadence of its beauty, for our souls separated from
our bodies resemble shooting stars; they are globules of
animated light which always seek their centre to recover

equilibrium and motion, but they must first of all disengage themselves from the serpent's folds, that is, from the unpurified Astral Light which surrounds and imprisons them, so long as their will-power cannot elevate them above it. The immersion of the living star in the dead light is a frightful torture; the soul at once freezes and burns therein, and has no other means of escaping than by entering the current of exterior forms and taking a fleshly envelope, then energetically struggling against blind instincts to strengthen that moral liberty which will allow it, at the moment of death, to burst the chains of earth and take flight triumphantly towards its consoling star, whose light has smiled upon it.

Following this hint, the nature of hell-fire will be understood (it is identical with the demon or old serpent), also in what the salvation or reprobation of men consists, all called and all in turn elected, but in a small number, after having been liable by their own act to fall into the eternal fire. Such is the grand and sublime revelation of the Magi, a revelation which is the mother of all symbolism, all doctrines, and all forms of worship. It will be understood already how far Dupuis was mistaken in believing religions to be issued from astronomy only. On the contrary, it is astronomy which is born of astrology, and primitive astrology is one of the branches of the holy Kabbalah, the scicnce of sciences and the religion of religions.

The ancients, comparing the calm and peaceful immensity of heaven, all peopled by immutable lights, with the agitations and darkness of this world, believed themselves to have found in this beautiful gold-lettered book, the final message on the destinies of men; they traced in imagination lines of correspondence between those brilliant points of the divine writing, and the first constellations sketched by Chaldean shepherds are also said to have been the first characters of Kabbalistic writing. These characters, expressed originally by signs, then comprised in hieroglyphical figures, would, according to M. Moreau de Dammartin, author of a very singular treatise on the origin of alphabetical characters, determine the ancient Magi in the selection of the Tarot figures, which this scholar, like ourselves, recognises as essentially a hieratic and primitive book. Thus, in his opinion, the Chinese *tseu*, the Hebrew

Aleph, and the Greek *Alpha*, expressed hieroglyphically by the figure of the Juggler, were borrowed from the constellation of the Crane, near the astral Fish of the eastern hemisphere. The Chinese *tcheou*, the Hebrew Beth, and the Latin B, represented by the Empress, are taken from the constellation of the Great Bear, &c. The Kabbalist Gaffarel erected a planisphere where all the constellations form Hebrew letters; but it is to be confessed that the configuration appears often more than arbitrary, and one is at a loss to understand why, on the indication of a single star, Gaffarel traces, for example, a *Daleth* rather than a *Dzain;* four stars again give *Thau* as well as a *He* or an *Aleph*.

Scholars, moreover, are not agreed on the shape of the letters of the primitive alphabet. The Italian Tarots, the recovery of whose Gothic originals is much to be desired, corresponds in the arrangement of its figures to the Hebrew alphabet used since the Captivity, and called the Assyrian; but fragments of anterior Tarots exist whose disposition is not the same. As nothing should be conjectured in matters of research, we must wait for new and more convincing discoveries to determine our conclusions.

As regards the alphabet of the stars, we consider it as variable as the configuration of clouds, which seem to assume all the shapes that imagination can give them. It is the same with star groups as with points in geomancy, and with the card-medleys of modern fortune-telling. They are all pretexts for self-magnetisation and instruments to fix and determine natural intuition. Thus, a Kabbalist used to mystical hieroglyphics, will perceive signs in the stars which a shepherd will not find there; but, on his side, the shepherd will discern combinations which will escape the Kabbalist. Country folk recognise a rake in the belt and sword of Orion; a Jewish Kabbalist would see in the same constellation, taken as a whole, all the mysteries of Ezekiel, the ten Sephiroths arranged triadwise, a central triangle composed of four stars, then a line of three stars, forming the *jod*, and the two figures united expressing all the mysteries of Bereschit; then four stars, making the wheels of Mercavah, and completing the divine chariot. Looking at it in another way, he would see a well formed *ghimel* placed above a *jod* within a large *daleth* upside down, a figure representing the conflict between good and evil, with the final triumph of good. In reality, *ghimel* superposed on *jod* is the triad emanating from unity, the divine manifestation of the Word, whilst the inverted *daleth* is the triad composed of the maleficent duad multiplied by itself. The constellation of Orion thus considered would be identical with the figure of St Michael doing battle with the dragon, and the appearance of this sign under this form would be for the Kabbalist an omen of victory and happiness.

The imagination is exalted by a long contemplation of the sky, and then the stars respond to our thoughts. Lines traced mentally from one to the other by the first observers must have supplied men with the earliest notions of geometry. Accordingly as the soul is disturbed or placid, the stars seem scintillating with menaces or sparkling with hope. Heaven is thus the mirror of the human soul, and when we think that we are reading the stars it is in ourselves we read.

Gaffarel, applying the presages of celestial writing to the destinies of empires, declares that the ancients did not vainly represent all signs of evil augury as situated in the northern division of the sky, for in every time calamities have been looked on as coming from the north to spread abroad over the earth by the invasion of the south. For this reason, he says, "the ancients have pictured in the boreal sky a serpent or dragon, near two bears, since those animals are the true symbols of tyranny, pillage, and oppression of all kinds. And, as a fact, go over the annals, and you will see that all the great desolations which have ever taken place came from the north. The Assyrians or Chaldeans, incited by Nabuchodonosor and Salmanasar, sufficiently proved this truth by the conflagration of the most sumptuous and sacred town and Temple in the universe, and by the entire destruction of a people whom God Himself had taken under His particular protection, and of whom He called Himself specially the father. And that other Jerusalem, Rome the blessed, has it not often experienced the fury of the evil northern race, when, by the cruelty of Alaric, Genseric, Attila, and other princes of the Goths, Huns, Vandals, &c., she has beheld her altars overthrown, and the towers of her superb buildings made level with the railings? . . . . Most fittingly, therefore, in the secrets of this celestial writing do we read

THE GREAT PRACTICAL SECRETS. 235

miseries and misfortunes on the northern side, since *à septentrione pandetur omne malum*. Now, the word which we translate *pandetur* means equally *depingetur* and *scribetur*, and the prophecy equally signifies—All the miseries of the world are written in the northern side of the sky."

We have transcribed the whole of this passage because it is not without significance for our own time, when the north is again menacing Europe, but it is also the fate of Boreal frosts to be overcome by the sun, and darkness dissipates itself before the light. Such is our final prophetic message and the secret of the future.

The following is the table of the magical characters traced by the old astrologers on the model of the zodiacal constellations; each of these characters represents the name of a good or evil genius. It is well known that the signs of the Zodiac are connected with various celestial influences, and consequently express an annual alternative of good or evil.

The names of the genii signified by the above characters are:—

For Aries, SATAARAN and *Sarahiel.*
For Taurus, BAGDAL and *Araziel.*
For Gemini, SAGRAS and *Saraiel.*
For Cancer, RAHDAR and *Phakiel.*
For Leo, SAGHAM and *Seratiel.*
For Virgo, IADARA and *Schaltiel.*
For Libra, GRASGARBEN and *Hadakiel.*
For Scorpio, RIEHOL and *Saissaiel.*
For Sagittarius, VHNORI and *Saritaiel.*
For Capricornus, SAGDALON and *Semakiel.*
For Aquarius, ARCHER and *Ssakmakiel.*
For Pisces, RASAMASA and *Vacabiel.*

The sage who seeks to read the heavens must observe also the doings of the moon, whose influence is very strong in astrology. The moon successively attracts and repels the magnetic fluid of the earth, and thus the ebb and flow of the sea is produced; we must, therefore, well understand its phases and be able to discern its days and hours. The new moon is favourable to the commencement of all magical works; from the first quarter to the full moon its influence is warm; from the full moon to the last quarter it is dry; from the last quarter to the end it is cold.

We give as follows the special characteristics of each of the moon's days, with the twenty-two keys of the Tarot and the seven planetary signs:—

1. *The Juggler or Magus.*

The first day of the moon is that of the creation of the moon itself. This day is consecrated to mental enterprises, and should be propitious to well-timed innovations.

2. *The Female Pope, or Occult Science.*

The second day, whose genius is Enediel, was the fifth of creation, for the moon was made on the fourth day. The birds and fishes are living hieroglyphics of magical analogies and of the universal dogma of Hermes. The water and the air, which were then filled with the forms of the Word, are the elementary figures of the Mercury of the sages, that is, of intelligence and speech. This day is favourable to revelations, initiations, and the great discoveries of science.

3. *The Celestial Mother, or Empress.*

The third day was that of man's creation. So the moon in the Kabbalah is called the MOTHER when it is represented as accompanied by the number three. This day is favourable to generation, and generally to all productions, whether physical or mental.

4. *The Emperor, or Ruler.*

The fourth day is unlucky; it was that of the birth of Cain; but it is favourable to unjust and tyrannical undertakings.

5. *The Pope, or Hierophant.*

The fifth day is fortunate; it was that of the birth of Abel.

6. *The Lover, or Liberty.*

The sixth day is one of pride; it was that of the birth of Lamech, who said to his wives: "I have slain a man to my own hurt, and a stripling to my own bruising. Sevenfold vengeance shall be taken for Cain, but for Lamech seventy times sevenfold." This day is propitious to conspiracies and revolts.

7. *The Chariot.*

The seventh day was that of the birth of Hebron, who gave his name to the first of the holy cities of Israel. A day of religion, prayers, and success.

8. *Justice.*

Murder of Abel. A day of expiation.

9. *The Ancient, or Hermit.*

Birth of Methusaleh. Day of blessing for children.

10. *Ezekiel's Wheel of Fortune.*

Birth of Nabuchodonosor. Dominion of the animal. Fatal day.

11. *Strength.*

Birth of Noah. Visions on this day are deceiving, but it is one of health and longevity to children born on it.

12. *The Sacrifice.*

Birth of Samuel. Prophetic and Kabbalistic day, favourable to the accomplishment of the *magnum opus*.

13. *Death.*

Day of Chanaan's birth. An unlucky day and fatal number.

14. *Angel of Temperance.*

Benediction of Noah. The angel Cassiel of the hierarchy of Uriel governs this day.

15. *Typhon, or the Devil.*

Birth of Ishmael. Day of exile and reprobation.

16. *The Blasted Tower.*

Day of the birth of Jacob and of Esau, and of the predestination of Jacob to Esau's ruin.

17. *The Shooting Star.*

Fire from heaven burns Sodom and Gomorrah. Day of salvation for the good and destruction to the wicked; dangerous if it fall on a Saturday. It is under the dominion of Scorpion.

18. *The Moon.*

Birth of Isaac; wife's triumph. Day of conjugal affection and virtuous hope.

19. *The Sun.*

Birth of Pharaoh. A beneficent or unfortunate day for the great ones of the world, according to the different merits of the great.

20. *The Judgment.*

Birth of Jonas, the instrument of God's judgments. A day propitious to divine revelations.

21. *The World.*

Birth of Saul, earthly royalty. Danger to mind and reason.

22. *Influence of Saturn.*

Birth of Job. A day of trial and sorrow.

23. *Influence of Venus.*

Birth of Benjamin. A day of preference and tenderness.

24. *Influence of Jupiter.*

Birth of Japhet.

25. *Influence of Mercury.*

Tenth Plague of Egypt.

26. *Influence of Mars.*

Deliverance of the Israelites and passage of the Red Sea.

27. *Influence of Diana, or Hecate.*

Splendid victory gained by Judas Machabeus.

28. *Influence of the Sun.*

Samson carries away the gates of Gaza. Day of strength and rescue.

29. *The Fool of the Tarot.*

Day of miscarriage and failure in all things.

By means of this rabbinical table, which Jean Belot and others have borrowed from the Hebrew Kabbalists, it will be seen that the old masters concluded *à posteriori* from facts to presumable influences, which is completely within the logic of the secret sciences. It will be seen also how many various meanings are included in the twenty-two Keys which form the universal alphabet of the Tarot, and the truth of our assertions when we claim that all the secrets of the Kabbalah and magic, all the mysteries of the ancient world, all the science of the patriarchs, all historical traditions of primeval times, are comprised in this hieroglyphical book of Thoth, Enoch, or Cadmus.

A very simple method of finding celestial horoscopes by onomancy is that which we are about to describe; it reconciles Gaffarel with ourselves, and gives results which are most astonishing in their accuracy and depth. Take a black card, wherein you must cut the name of the person you are consulting for; place this card at the end of a tube, which diminishes on the side of the observer's eye and increases towards that of the card; then look through it at the four cardinal points alternately, beginning at the east and ending at the north. Take note of all the stars you see through the letters, then convert the letters into numbers, and with the sum of the addition similarly written down, renew the operation; count how many stars you have, then, adding this number to that of the name, you again cast up, and write the total of the two numbers in Hebrew characters. Renew the operation, and set down separately the stars you have met with; seek next in the celestial planisphere the names of all the stars; classify them according to size and brilliancy, choosing the largest and most brilliant as the polar-star of your astrological operation. Find, lastly, on the Egyptian planisphere (a sufficiently complete copy may be seen in the atlas to Dupuis' larger work) the names and figures of the genii to whom the stars belong, and you will then know what fortunate or unfortunate signs enter into the name of the person, what their influence will be, whether in infancy (which is the name traced at the east), in youth (the name traced at the south), in maturity (the name traced at the west), or in old age (for which the name is traced at the north), or, finally, in the whole life (to which belong the stars entering into the entire number formed by the addition of the letters and stars). This operation is plain, easy, and requires few calculations; it carries us back to the furthest antiquity, and evidently belongs to the primeval magic of the patriarchs, of which we may be convinced by studying the works of Gaffarel and his master, Rabbi Chomer.

This onomantic astrology was that of all the ancient Hebrew Kabbalists, as is proved by the observations pre-

THE GREAT PRACTICAL SECRETS. 241

served by Rabbi Chomer, Rabbi Kapol, Rabbi Abjudan, and other masters. The menaces of the prophets to various empires of the world were based on the characters of the stars found vertically above them in the uniform correspondence between the celestial and terrestrial spheres. Thus, by inscribing in the sky of Greece its Hebrew name, and rendering that into numbers, they found the word Charab, whose sum is twelve, and which signifies destroyed, desolated. They concluded that after a cycle of twelve periods Greece would be desolated and destroyed.

Shortly before the conflagration and overthrow of Jerusalem by Nabuzardan, the Kabbalists noticed eleven stars arranged vertically above the Temple after this fashion—

```
* * * * * * * *
      *
  *       *
```

and which all entered into the word *Hibschich*, written from north to south, and which signifies reprobation and abandonment without mercy. The sum of the numbers of the letters is 423, precisely that of the duration of the Temple.

The empires of Persia and Assyria were threatened with destruction by four vertical stars which entered into the letters of the word *Rob*, and the fatal number indicated by these letters was 208 years. Four stars also foretold to the Kabbalistic rabbins of that time the fall and dismemberment of the empire of Alexandria, by their entering into the word *parad*, to divide, whose number, 284, indicates the entire period of that kingdom both in its root and branches.

According to Rabbi Chomer, the destinies of the Ottoman power at Constantinople were fixed and announced beforehand by four stars, which, arranged in the word *caah*, signify to be feeble, sick, and drawing to its end. The stars which were most brilliant in the letter *aleph* give that letter the value of one thousand. The three letters united make 1025, which must be reckoned from the taking of Constantinople by Mahomet II., a computation which promises still some centuries of existence to the enfeebled empire of the Sultans.

The MANE THECEL PHARES, which Balthasar, in his intoxication, beheld written on the wall of his palace by the flicker of the torches, was an onomantic intuition of the same kind as the rabbins. Balthasar, doubtless initiated by his Hebrew diviners into the reading of the heavens, mechanically and instinctively operated on the lamps of his festival, as he might have done on the stars of the sky. The three words which he formed in his imagination became soon ineffaceable in his eyes, and eclipsed all the glare of his banquet. It was not difficult to predict to a king who surrendered himself to orgies in a besieged town an end like that of Sardanapalus. We have said, and we repeat, in concluding this chapter, that magnetic intuitions alone give value and reality to all Kabbalistical and astrological calculations, puerile possibly, and completely arbitrary, if made without inspiration, by cold curiosity, and without a powerful will.

VII.—THE BOOK OF HERMES OR OF THOTH.

WE approach the conclusion of our work, and it is here that we must provide its universal key and impart its final secret. The universal key of magical arts is the key of all ancient religious dogmas, the key of the Kabbalah and the Bible, the clavicula of Solomon. Now, this clavicula or little key, looked on as lost for centuries, has been recovered by us, and we have been enabled to open the sepulchres of the elder world, to make the dead speak, to behold the monuments of the past in all their splendour, to understand all the enigmas of the past, and penetrate into every sanctuary. The use of this key was, among the ancients, permitted only to the high priests, and its secret was confided to the flower of the initiates alone. This key consisted of a hieroglyphical and numeral alphabet, giving expression to a series of universal and absolute ideas by means of characters and numbers; then a scale of ten numbers multiplied by four symbols and bound together by twelve figures, representing the twelve signs of the zodiac, plus four genii, those of the four cardinal points.

The symbolic tetrad, represented in the mysteries of Memphis and Thebes by the four forms of the sphinx, the man, the eagle, the bull, and the lion, corresponded with

the four elements of the old world—water being signified
by the chalice which the man or aquarius holds ; air by the
circle or nimbus which surrounds the head of the celestial
eagle ; fire by the wood which feeds it, by the tree which
the heat of the sun and earth fructifies, and lastly by the
sceptre of royalty, of which the lion is the emblem ; earth
by the sword of Mithra, who annually immolates the
sacred bull and pours out with its blood the sap which
swells in all the fruits of the earth.

Now, these four signs, with their analogies, are the explanation of the one word hidden in every sanctuary, of
that word which the bacchantes seemed to divine, when,
during the celebration of the feasts of Iacchos, they were
exalted into delirium for the glory of IO EVOHE! What
then was meant by this mysterious word? It was the
name of the four primitive letters of the mother tongue:
the JOD, symbol of the vine-stock or paternal sceptre of
Noah; the HE, symbol of the chalice of libations; the
VAU, which joins the preceding signs, and was represented
in India by the great and mysterious lingam. Such, in the
divine word, was the three-fold sign of the triad ; then the
maternal letter appeared a second time to express the
fecundity of nature and woman, to formulate also the
dogma of universal and progressive analogies, descending
from causes to effects and remounting from effects to
causes. The sacred word, moreover, was not pronounced ;
it was spelt and read off in four words, which are the four
sacred words : JOD HE VAU HE.

In the sixteenth century, a man of exalted faith and
wide erudition had discovered the key of all religious
mysteries, and published a small work: *Clavis Absconditorum à Constitutione Mundi*, " The Key of Things kept
Secret from the Foundation of the World." This man
was an illuminated Hebraist and Kabbalist, named
William Postel.* He believed that he had found the
true signification of the Tetragram in a hieroglyphic book
anterior to the Bible, and which he called the Genesis
of Enoch, doubtless to conceal its real name from the uninitiated; for on the ring of his symbolic key, whose

* He was born in the Diocese of Avranches and was so precocious that he was made *maître d'école* at the age of fourteen. He visited the far East, and died in 1581, being ninety-six years old. He was persuaded that the King of France was destined to universal monarchy as the lineal descendant of Noah's eldest son.

representation he gives as an occult explanation of his singular work, he thus traces his mysterious tetrad:—

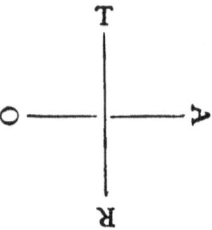

forming in this manner a word which, read from left to right, beginning below, makes ROTA, by beginning at the top, makes TARO, and even TAROT, if the initial letter be repeated to mark the circle more distinctly, and which, read from right to left, as Hebrew should be read, makes TORA, the sacramental name which the Jews give to their sacred book.

Let us compare with this enigma of Postel the erudite observations made by Court de Gebelin, in the sixth volume of his *Monde Primitif*, on a book of the ancient Egyptians, which has come down to our own times under the futile pretext of a game of cards: let us examine the mysterious figures of these cards, of which the first twenty-two are evidently a hieroglyphic alphabet, where symbols are explained by numbers, while the entire game is divided into four tens, each accompanied by four figures with four colours and four different symbols, and we shall have the right to ask if the Tarot of the Bohemians be not the Genesis of Enoch, the Taro, Rota, or Tora of William Postel, and his initiates the true Hebrew Kabbalists! If in this state of doubt we penetrate the learned obscurities of the Sohar, the great sacred book of the supreme Kabbalah, our conjectures will soon change into certitude when we learn that the Jod, the tenth and principal letter of the Hebrew alphabet, has been always regarded by initiated Kabbalists as the sign of the First Cause, represented by the Egyptian phallus and by the rod of Moses; that the He, the second letter of the name of יהוה and the fifth of the alphabet, signifies the passive and demonstrative form of the active principle, and corresponds to the cteïs of ancient sacred hieroglyphs; that the Vau, the third letter of the Tetragram, and the sixth of the alphabet, signifies

THE GREAT PRACTICAL SECRETS. 245

crook, entanglement, attraction, and corresponds to the hieroglyphic signs of the cross, the sword, and the lingam, as we have before said; finally, that the He, repeated at the end of the Tetragram, possibly represented the circle which would result from the superposition of two cups, one upright, the other inverted. We have then the key of the denary symbols of the Tarot, the first of which represents a blossoming rod, the second a royal chalice, the third a sword piercing a crown, and the fourth a circle enclosing a lotos flower.

It remains for us, in order to be fully initiated into the mysteries of the Genesis of Postel, to thoroughly understand the series of absolute theological and philosophical ideas which the ancients attached to the ten first numbers. Here Pythagoras is in agreement with the depositaries of the secret of Moses, for they all have drawn from the same fountain; and we have seen that in the tetrad the secret signs of the supreme Kabbalah express precisely the same doctrine as the hieroglyphs of Egypt and the sacred symbols of India. The phallus, the cteïs, the lingam of life, the sceptre of Osiris, the cup or flower of Isis, the lingam of Horus and the cycle of Hermes, Aaron's blossoming rod, the patera which contains the manna, the sacrificial sword and the dish for offerings, the pontifical staff, the eucharistic chalice, the Cross and the Divine Host, all religious signs, correspond to the four hieroglyphic signs of the Tarot, which are the hieratic explanation of the four letters of the great and divine Tetragram.

What most attracted the attention of Court de Gebelin when he discovered the Tarot, were the hieroglyphs of the twenty-first card, entitled the World. This card, which is no other than the identical key of William Postel, represents naked and victorious Truth in the centre of a crown which is divided into four parts by four lotos flowers. At the four corners of the card are seen the four emblematic animals which are the analysis of the sphinx, and which St John borrowed from the prophet Ezekiel, as Ezekiel himself had borrowed them from the bucephalous or other sphinxes of Egypt and Assyria. These four figures, which a tradition, incomprehensible to the Church herself, still gives as the attributes of our four evangelists, represent the four elementary forms of the Kabbalah, the four seasons, the four metals, and lastly the four mysterious letters of the Jewish TORA of Ezekiel's wheel, ROTA, and of the TAROT which, according to Postel, is the key of things hidden from the beginning of the world. It must be also remarked that the word Tarot is composed of the sacred letters of the monogram of Constantine—a Greek P crossed by a T between the Alpha and Omega, which signify the beginning and the end. Disposed in this manner, it is a word analogous to the INRI of the Freemasons, whose two I's express equally the beginning and the end, since in the Kabbalah the Iod and all its derivations are symbolic of the phallus and of creation; the beginning and the end, expressed thus by the same letter, gives the notion of the eternal evolution of the divine cycle, and therein the INRI is more profound, and belongs to a higher grade of initiation than the Tarot.

If we compare the hieroglyphic form of the Cross in the primitive Church with these discoveries, we shall be struck by many additional analogies. The first Christians usually composed the Cross from the four segments of the circle. I have seen one with ten branches issuing from one another, and four rivers at its root; a copy may be found in the Latin work of Bosius on the triumph of the Cross. The first crosses were without Christ, and sometimes bore a dove with the inscription, INRI, to suggest that there is a concealed sense in this inscription, and that it is the province of the Holy Spirit to make us understand it. The four Kabbalistic animals are also frequently at the four arms of the Cross, which thus becomes a philosophical emblem of the Tetrad.

Those who doubt what we advance here may consult the Gnostic yet orthodox writings attributed to St Dionysius, the Areopagite, and those of St Irenæus, Synesius, and Clement of Alexandria. But without leaving the canon of the New Testament, they will find in the Apocalypse an ample magical and kabbalistical clavicula, which appears to have been devised according to the numbers, symbols, and hieroglyphic figures of the Tarot. There, in fact, we find the sceptres, chalices, swords, and crowns, disposed by determined numbers and corresponding to each other by means of the denary and sacred septenary; there we find the four kings of the four quarters of the world, and the four horsemen which figure in our ordinary cards; we find the winged woman, and the Logos in kingly garments, afterwards in pontifical costume with several diadems on His tiara. Finally, the Apocalyptic key, which is the vision of Heaven, is identical with the number twenty-one of the Tarot, and reveals to us a throne surrounded by a double rainbow, and at the four corners of this crown the four sacramental animals of the Kabbalah. These coincidences are, at least, very curious, and afford much food for thought.

Enraptured by his discovery, Postel naïvely imagined that he possessed the bond of universal religious concord, and the future tranquillity of the world. It was at this period that he wrote his *Traité de la Concorde Universelle*, his book on the *Raisons d'être du Saint Esprit*, and that he dedicated to the fathers of the Council of Trent, then assembled, the *Clavis absconditorum à constitutione Mundi*. The epistle he addresses them is curious:—he poses frankly as a prophet, and declares to the bishops and doctors that their anathemas are unseasonable, since all men must ultimately be saved, this being the consequence he draws from the unity and perpetuity of analogical and rational revelation in the world.

The fathers of the council did not even do him the honour of chastising him. His book and letter were looked on as the productions of a madman and remained unanswered; but a little later on, having advanced some propositions on the redemption of the human race which appeared to be heterodox, he was shut up in a monastery, wherein he died in the conviction that he should rise again to explain to men his great discovery of the keys of the occult world and the mysteries of the Tetragram; for it seemed to him impossible that such a revelation could be wholly lost to posterity.

The erudite Gaffarel does not doubt that the Theraphim of the Hebrews, by means of which they consulted the Urim and Thumim, were the figures of the four Kabbalistic animals, whose symbols were summarised, as we shall presently show, by the sphinxes or cherubim of the Ark. But he cites in connection with the usurped Theraphim of Michas, a curious passage of Philo, which is an entire revelation on the ancient and sacerdotal origin of our Tarots. Gaffarel expresses himself as follows: " He (Philo the Jew) says, speaking of the history concealed in the before-mentioned chapter of Judges, that Michas made of fine gold and silver three figures of young boys and three young calves, in addition to a lion, an eagle, a dragon, and a dove, in such a manner that if any one sought him to learn a secret concerning his wife, he interrogated by the dove ; if touching his children, by the young boy ; if for wealth, by the eagle ; if for power or authority, by the lion ; if for fecundity, by the cherub or calf ; if for length of days, by the dragon." This revelation of Philo, though treated lightly by Gaffarel, is of palmary importance to us. Here, in fact, we have the key of the tetrad, the figures of the four symbolic animals in the twenty-first key of the Tarot, or the third septenary, thus repeating and epitomising all the symbolism expressed by the three superposed septenaries ; next the antagonism of colours signified by the dove and the dragon ; then the circle or ROTA, formed by the dragon or serpent to express longevity ; finally, the Kabbalistic divination of the complete Tarot, as it was afterwards practised by the Egyptian Bohemians, whose secrets were imperfectly divined and recovered by Etteilla.

We find in the Bible that the high priests consulted the Lord on the golden table of the holy Ark, between the cherubim, or bull-headed and eagle-winged sphinxes, and that they consulted by means of the Theraphim, by the Urim, the Thumim, and the Ephod. The Ephod, as we know, was a magic square of twelve numbers and twelve words graven on precious stones. The word *Theraphim* in Hebrew means hieroglyphs or symbolical signs ; the Urim and Thumim were the above and below, the east and west, the yea and nay, and these signs corresponded to the two columns of the Temple, Jakin and Bohas. When, therefore, the high priest wished to elicit an oracle, he drew by lot the Theraphim, or golden plates which bore the images of the four sacred words, and placed them in threes round the breastplate or Ephod, between the Urim and Thumim, that is, between the two onyxes which served as the clasps to the chains of the Ephod. The right onyx signified Gedulah, or mercy and magnificence, the left corresponded to Geburah, and signified justice and wrath ; and if, for example, the sign of the lion was found near the stone where the name of the tribe of Judah was engraved, on the left side, the high priest would interpret the oracle thus : " The rod of the Lord is provoked against Judah." If the Theraphim represented the man, or the chalice, and was also found on the left, near the stone of Benjamin, the high priest would read: " The mercy of the Lord is wearied by the offences of Benjamin, which outrage him in his love. For this reason will He pour forth on him the chalice of his indignation, &c." When the sovereign priesthood ceased in Israel, when all the oracles of the world were silenced in the presence of the Word made flesh, and speaking by the mouth of the most popular and the mildest of sages, when the ark was lost, the sanctuary profaned, and the Temple destroyed, the mysteries of the Ephod and the Theraphim, no longer traced on gold and precious stones, were written, or rather drawn, by some erudite Kabbalists on ivory, on parchment, on silvered or gilt copper, then, lastly, on simple cards, which were always suspected by the official Church as containing a dangerous key to her mysteries. Thence have come those Tarots whose antiquity, revealed to the learned Court de Gebelin by the science of numbers and hieroglyphics itself, so much exercised at a later period the questionable perspicacity and persevering investigation of Etteilla.

Etteilla or Alliette, an *illuminé* hair-dresser, exclusively engrossed by his divinatory system, and the emolument he could derive from it, neither proficient in his own language nor in orthography, pretended to reform, and thus attribute to himself the Book of Thoth. On the Tarot which he published, and which has become very scarce, we find the following naïve advertisement: " Ettiella, professor of Algebra, reformer of Cartomancy, and correctors (*sic*) of the modern *inaccuracies* of the ancient Book of Thoth, lives in the Rue de l'Oseille, No. 48 à Paris." Etteilla would have certainly done wisely not to have corrected the *inaccuracies* which he speaks of; his works have caused the ancient book discovered by Court de Gebelin to descend into the region of common magic and fortune-telling. He proves nothing who tries to prove too much, says an axiom of logic ; of this Etteilla is another example, but his efforts, nevertheless, led him to a certain acquaintance with the Kabbalah, as may be seen in some rare passages of his unreadable works.

The true initiates, contemporaries of Etteilla, the Rosicrucians, for example, and the Martinists, who were in possession of the real Tarot, as is proved by a book of

St Martin, where the divisions are those of the Tarot, and this passage of an enemy of the Rosicrucians: "They claim to possess a volume wherein they can learn all that is to be found in other books which now are or which can ever come into existence. This volume is their own reason, in which they find the prototype of all that subsists by their facility in analysing, summarising, and creating a kind of intellectual world and of all possible beings. See the philosophical, theosophical, and microsmic cards"—("Conspiracy against the Catholic Religion and against Crowned Heads," by the author of "The Veil raised for the Curious." Paris, Crapard, 1792)—the true initiates, we repeat, who included the secret of the Tarot among their greatest mysteries, were far from protesting against the errors of Etteilla, and left him to re-veil, not reveal, the arcanum of the veritable claviculæ of Solomon. So is it not without profound astonishment that we have recovered intact and unknown this key of all the doctrines and all the philosophies of the elder world. I speak of it as a key, and such it truly is, having the circle of four decades for its ring, and for its trunk or body the scale of twenty-two characters, then the three degrees of the triad for its wards, as Postel understood and represented it in his "Key of things kept Secret from the Foundation of the World."

Without the Tarot, the magic of the ancients is a sealed book to us, and it is impossible to penetrate any of the great mysteries of the Kabbalah. It only provides the interpretation of the magic squares of Agrippa and Paracelsus, as we may prove by forming these same squares with the keys of the Tarot, and in reading the hieroglyphs which will thus be found collected.

The seven magical squares of the planetary genii are, according to Paracelsus, as follows:—

Saturn.

2	9	4
7	5	3
6	1	8

Jupiter.

6	12	12	10
5	10	11	11
9	6	7	12
14	6	4	1

Mars.

14	10	22	22	18
20	12	7	20	2
8	17	9	9	8
12	3	9	5	26
11	23	8	6	11

The Sun.

9	22	1	32	25	19
7	11	27	18	8	3
19	14	16	15	23	24
18	20	22	21	17	13
22	29	10	19	26	12
36	5	35	6	12	13

Venus.

22	47	18	41	0	35	8
25	23	47	17	42	11	29
10	6	14	9	18	36	12
3	31	16	25	43	19	37
38	14	32	31	26	44	20
21	39	8	33	22	27	45
46	15	40	19	24	03	27

Mercury.

8	52	39	5	24	61	66	11
49	15	14	52	52	12	10	56
41	43	22	14	45	19	18	48
33	34	35	29	20	38	39	25
40	6	27	59	31	30	31	33
17	47	55	28	25	43	42	24
9	51	53	12	13	51	∞	16
64	12	15	61	61	6	7	47

The Moon.

37	70	29	70	21	62	12	14	41
16	28	70	30	71	12	53	14	46
47	20	11	7	31	72	22	35	15
16	48	68	40	81	32	62	25	56
57	17	49	29	7	66	33	65	25
26	58	40	56	31	42	74	34	66
53	27	59	10	51	2	41	75	35
36	68	19	60	11	65	43	44	76
77	28	20	69	61	12	25	60	5

By adding up each column of these squares, the characteristic number of the planet is invariably obtained, and by finding the explanation of this number among the hieroglyphs of the Tarot, the significance of all those figures, whether triangular, square, or transverse, which are formed by the numbers, may be obtained. The result will be a complete and profound knowledge of all the allegories and all the mysteries concealed by the ancients under the symbol of each planet, or rather of each personification of their influences, whether celestial or human, on all the events of life.

The religious and Kabbalistical key of the Tarot will be now given in technical verses after the fashion of the ancient lawgivers.

1. א. All things announce a conscious, active cause,
2. ב. Vivific Oneness based on number's laws;
3. ג. Who all containing is by nought confined,
4. ד. And all preceding hath no bound assign'd.

5. ה This only Lord should man adore alone,
6. ו. Who doth true doctrine to pure hearts make known.
7. ז. But acts of faith require a single chief,
8. ח. Whence we proclaim one altar, law, belief;
9. ט. The changeless God will never change their base.
10. י. He rules our days and dooms through every phase.
11. כ. His mercy's wealth, which vice to nought will bring.
12. ל. His people promises a future King.
13. מ. The tomb's a path which to new worlds ascends,
And life through all subsists, death only ends.

Pure, sacred, steadfast truths we here repeat
The venerated numbers thus complete!

14. נ. The angel blest doth calm and moderate,
15. ס. The evil is the fiend of pride and hate.
16. ע. God doth the lightning and the fire subdue ;
17. פ. He rules the dewy eve and evening dew ;
18. צ. The watchful moon He sets to guard our heights,
19. ק. His sun's the source of life's renewed delights.
20. His breath revivifies the dust of graves,

o
or } ש. Where crowds descend who are of lust the slaves ;
21.

21
or } ת. The mercy-seat He covers with His crown,
22.   And on the cherubs pours His glory down.

By means of this purely dogmatic explanation the figures of the Kabbalistic alphabet of the Tarot will be already understood, but a table of its variations, according to divers Kabbalistic Jews, may also be added.

1. *Alpha. Being, spirit, man or god ; the intelligible object ; unity the mother of numbers, the primitive substance.*

All these ideas are hieroglyphically expressed by the figure of the JUGGLER, who, in other words, represents the active principle in the oneness of divine and human autocracy. His body and arms form the letter א; he wears a nimbus about his head in the form of ∞, the symbol of life and the universal spirit ; in front of him there are swords, cups, and pantacles, and he lifts the miraculous rod towards heaven. He has a juvenile aspect and curly hair, like Apollo or Mercury; he has a smile of assurance on his lips, and the glance of intelligence in his eyes.

2. *Beth. The house of God and of man, the sanctuary, the law, the gnosis, the Kabbalah, the occult church, the duad, woman, the mother.*

Hieroglyph of the Tarot, vulgarly called the Female Pope, POPE JOAN; a woman crowned with a tiara, with the horns of the moon or Isis, the head surrounded by a veil, the solar cross on her breast, and supporting on her knees an open book, which she partly conceals beneath her mantle.

The author of a pretended history of Pope Joan has discovered and adapted to his thesis for good or for bad, two curious and ancient figures of the female pope or sovereign priestess of the Tarot, who is endowed in them with all the attributes of Isis; in the one she holds and caresses her son Horus, in the other she has long and flowing hair. She is seated between the two columns of the duad, wears a sun with four rays on her breast, sets one hand on a book, and makes with the other the sign of sacerdotal esoterism, *i.e.*, she opens only three fingers, keeping the rest clasped to signify mystery; the veil is behind her head, and on either side of her seat there is a sea whereon the flowers of the lotus are blooming. I deeply commiserate the unfortunate scholar who declines to see anything in this time-honoured symbol but a monumental portrait of his so-called Pope Joan.

In other Tarots the duad is symbolised by the Greek Juno, with one hand elevated towards heaven and one pointing to the earth, as if formulating by this gesture the unique and dualistic dogma which is the base of magic, and which begins the marvellous symbols of the Hermetic Emerald Table.

3. *Ghimel. The Word, the triad, plenitude, fruitfulness nature, generation in the three worlds.*

Symbol, THE EMPRESS, a winged woman, crowned, seated, and bearing on the top of her sceptre the globe of the world; she has the eagle, image of life and the soul, as her sign. This figure is the Greek Venus Urania, and was represented by St John in his Apocalypse as the woman clothed with the sun, crowned with twelve stars, and with the moon beneath her feet. It is the mystical quintessence of the triad, spirituality, immortality, the Queen of Heaven.

4. *Daleth. The door or government among the Easterns, initiation, the Tetragram, the tetrad, the cubic stone, or the base thereof.*

Hieroglyph, THE EMPEROR, a sovereign whose body represents a right-angled triangle, and the legs a cross, the image of the Athanor of the philosophers.

5. *He. Indication, demonstration, instruction, law, symbolism, philosophy, religion.*

Hieroglyph, THE POPE, or supreme hierophant. In the more modern Tarots this sign is replaced by the image of Jupiter. The grand hierophant seated between the two columns of Hermes and Solomon makes the sign of esoterism, and supports himself on a cross with three horizontals of triangular form. Before him are two inferior ministers on their knees, so that having above him the capitols of the two columns, and below him the two heads of his ministers, he is the centre of the quinary, and represents the divine Pentagram, of which he affords the complete significance. In effect, the pillars are necessity or law, the heads, liberty or action. From each pillar to each head a line may be drawn, and two lines from each pillar to each of the two heads. Thus will be obtained a square divided into four triangles by a cross, and in the centre of this cross will be the supreme hierophant, we had almost said like the garden spider in the centre of its web, if such a comparison were appropriate to the things of truth, glory, and light.

6. *Vau. Concatenation, interlacement, lingam, entanglement, union, embrace, strife, antagonism, combination, equilibrium.*

Hieroglyph, man between vice and virtue. Above him beams the Sun of Truth, and in this sun is Love bending his bow and threatening vice with the shaft. In the order of the ten Sephiroth, this symbol corresponds to Tiphereth, that is, to idealism and beauty. The number six represents the antagonism of the two triads, that is, of absolute negation and absolute affirmation; it is, consequently, the number of labour and liberty; and for this reason it corresponds to moral beauty and glory.

7. *Dzain.* *Weapon, sword, cherub's sword of fire, sacred septenary, triumph, royalty, priesthood.*

Hieroglyph, a cubic chariot with four pillars, and an azure and starry drapery. Within the chariot, and between the four pillars, a victor crowned with a circle, from which rise and radiate three golden pentagrams. The victor has three superposed squares on his cuirass; he has the Urim and Thumim of the sovereign sacrificer on his shoulders, represented by the two crescents of the moon in Gedulah and Geburah; he holds in his hand a sceptre surmounted by a globe, a square, and a triangle; his attitude is proud and calm. To the chariot is harnessed a double sphinx or two sphinxes joined at the buttocks, but one of them turns his head, so that they look in the same direction. The one turning his head is black, the other is white. On the square which forms the front of the chariot there is the winged disc of the Egyptians surmounting the lingam of India. This symbol is perhaps the most beautiful and complete of all those which compose the clavicula of the Tarot.

8. *Cheth.* *Balance, attraction and repulsion, life, terror, promise, and menace.*

Hieroglyph, JUSTICE, with sword and balance.

9. *Teth.* *Good, hatred of evil, morality, wisdom.*

Hieroglyph, a sage supported on his staff and holding a lamp in front of him; he is wholly enveloped in his mantle. His inscription is THE HERMIT OR CAPUCHIN, because of his oriental hood; but his real name is PRU-DENCE, and he completes thus the four cardinal virtues which appeared imperfect to Court de Gebelin and Etteilla.

10. *Jod.* *Cause, manifestation, praise, manly honour, phallus, virile fecundity, the paternal sceptre.*

Hieroglyph, THE WHEEL OF FORTUNE, that is, the cosmic wheel of Ezekiel, with a Hermanubis ascending on the right, a Typhon descending on the left, and a Sphinx equilibrating both, and holding a sword in its lion-like claws—admirable symbol, disfigured by Etteilla, who replaced Typhon by a man, Hermanubis by a mouse, and the Sphinx by an ape, an allegory in all respects worthy of the Kabbalah of Etteilla.

11. *Caph.* *The hand in the act of grasping and holding.*

Hieroglyph, STRENGTH, a woman crowned with the vital ∞, and closing calmly and without effort the jaws of a raging lion.

12. *Lamed.* *Example, teaching, public lesson.*

A man hanging by one foot with his hands tied behind his back, so that his body forms a triangle with inverted point, and his legs a cross above the triangle. The gibbet has the shape of a Hebrew Tau; the two trees which support it have six lopped branches each. The cross, superposed on an inverted triangle, is an alchemical symbol known to all adepts, and represents the accomplishment of the *magnum opus.* This personage who is thus hanging is therefore the adept, bound by his engagements, and with his feet turned towards heaven, signifying spiritualization; it is also the antique Prometheus, expiating by an immortal agony the penalty of his glorious theft. It is vulgarly the traitor Judas, and his execution menaces those who reveal the Great Arcanum.

13. *Mem.* *The firmament of Jupiter and Mars, domination and power, new birth, creation, and destruction.*

Hieroglyph, DEATH reaping crowned heads in a pasture where men are growing.

14. *Nun.* *The firmament of the sun, temperatures, seasons, motion, revolutions of life, which is ever new and ever the same.*

Hieroglyph, TEMPERANCE, an angel, bearing the sign of the sun on her forehead, and the square and triangle on her bosom, pours from one ewer into another the two essences which compose the elixir of life.

15. *Samech. The firmament of Mercury, occult science, magic, commerce, eloquence, mystery, moral strength.*

Hieroglyph, THE DEVIL, the goat of Mendes, or the Baphomet of the Templars, with all his pantheistic attributes. This is the only hieroglyph which Etteilla perfectly understood and properly interpreted.

16. *Gnain. The firmament of the Moon, deteriorations, subversions, changes, weaknesses.*

Hieroglyph, a tower struck by lightning, probably that of Babel. Two individuals, doubtless Nimrod and his false prophet, or minister, are precipitated from top to bottom of the ruins. One of them in his fall represents perfectly the letter *y*, gnain.

17. *Phe. The firmament of the Soul, outpouring of thought, moral influence of the idea on forms, immortality.*

Hieroglyph, THE BURNING STAR and eternal youth, an admirable allegory:—A naked woman, who represents at once Truth, Nature, and Wisdom unveiled, inclines two urns towards the earth, and pours out fire and water on it; above her head glitters the Septenary, circling round an eight-pointed star, that of Venus—symbol of peace and love; the plants of earth flourish round the woman, and on one has alighted the butterfly of Pysche, emblem of the soul, replaced in some copies of the sacred book by a bird, a more Egyptian and probably more ancient symbol. This figure is analogous to many Hermetic symbols, and is not without analogy with the Burning Star of Masonic initiates, which gives expression to most of the mysteries of the secret Rosicrucian doctrine.

18. *Tsade. The elements, the visible world, reflected light, material forms, symbolism.*

Hieroglyph, THE MOON, dew falling, a crab in the water, rising towards the earth, a dog and a wolf tied to the foot of two towers and barking at the moon, a path lost in the distance, and sprinkled with drops of blood.

19. *Coph. Compounds, the head, the Apex, the Prince of Heaven.*

Hieroglyph, a radiant SUN, and two naked children joining hands in a fortified enclosure. In other Tarots, it is a spinner unwinding destinies; in others, again, a naked child mounted on a white horse, and displaying a scarlet standard.

20. *Resch.* *The vegetative, the generative power of the earth, eternal life.*

Hieroglyph, THE JUDGMENT. A genius sounds a trumpet, and the dead rise from their graves. These dead people revivified are a man, a woman, and a child—the triad of human life.

21. *Schin.* *The sensitive, flesh, eternal life.*

Hieroglyph, THE FOOL. A man in fool's dress wandering aimlessly, burdened with a wallet which he carries behind him, and which is doubtless full of his follies and vices. His disordered clothes reveal what should be concealed, and a pursuing tiger is biting him, while he does not know how to avoid it or defend himself.

22. *Thau.* *The microcosmos, the universal synthesis.*

Hieroglyph, Kether, or the Kabbalistic CROWN, between the four mysterious animals; in the midst of the Crown is Truth, holding a magic wand in each hand.

Such are the twenty-two keys of the Tarot which explain all its numbers. Thus, the juggler, or key of the unities, explains the four aces with their quadruple progressive signification in the three worlds and in the First Cause. Thus, the ace of deniers or of the circle, is the soul of the world; the ace of swords is militant intelligence: the ace of cups is loving intelligence; the ace of clubs is creative intelligence. They are also the principles of motion, progress, productiveness, and virility. Each number multiplied by a key gives another number, which, explained in its turn by the keys, completes the philosophical and religious revelation contained in every sign. As each of the fifty-six cards can be multiplied by the twenty-two keys in turn, a series of combinations results which gives all the most astonishing consequences of revelation and of light. It is a truly philosophical machine which prevents the mind from going astray, even while leaving it its own initiative and freedom; it is mathematics in their application to the absolute, the alliance of the real and the ideal, a lottery of thoughts, all of which are as rigorously exact as numbers; in fine, it is perhaps at once the simplest and grandest thing ever conceived by human genius.

If we now take a Tarot and join by fours all the pages comprising the Wheel or ROTA of William Postel, if we place the four aces, the four duads, &c., together, we shall have ten packets of cards giving the hieroglyphical explanation of the triangle of the Divine Names on the scale of the denary which we give on page 286. They may be then read off as follows, comparing each number with its corresponding Sephiroth.

יהוה

Four letters of the name all names combining—

1. Keter. The four aces.
See on God's crown four mystic gems are shining!

2. Chocmah. The four twos.
His wisdom's fount a four-fold stream diffuses.

3. Binah. The four threes.
His intellect its four-fold proof produces.

4. Chesed. The four fours.
Four bounties ever from His mercy rise.

5. Geburah. The four fives.
Four times His rigour will four faults chastise.

6. Tiphereth. The four sixes.
His beauty is revealed by four pure rays.

7. Netsah. The four sevens.
As oft His conquest in our songs we praise.

8. Hod. The four eights.
Four times He triumphs in His life eternal.

9. Jesod. The four nines.
Foundations four support His throne supernal.

10. Malchut. The four tens.
Four times the same His single realm declare,
Like to the gems that star His crown of glory rare!

By this simple arrangement the Kabbalistic sense of each plate may be seen. Thus, for example, the five of clubs signifies rigorously the Geburah of Jod, that is, the justice of the Creator and the wrath of man; the seven of cups the victory of mercy, or the triumph of woman; the eight of swords signifies conflict or eternal equilibrium; and so on for the rest. We may thus understand how the ancient pontiffs made use of it to elicit oracles; the plates drawn by lot, always gave a new Kabbalistic sense rigorously exact in its combination, which alone was fortuitous; and as the faith of the ancients attributed nothing to chance, they read the responses of Providence in the Tarot, which were called by the Hebrews Theraph or Theraphim, as was perceived first of all by the erudite Gaffarel, one of the accredited magicians of the Cardinal de Richelieu.

As to the trump cards they may be explained by a final couplet:—

King, Queen, Knight, Knave.
The bridegroom, youth, and child, then all the human race—
Thy path by these degrees back to the One retrace.

The ten Sephiroths and twenty-two Tarots form what the Kabbalists call the thirty-two paths of the absolute science. The method of reading the hieroglyphs of the Tarot is to arrange them either in a square or triangle, placing the even numbers in opposition and conciliating them with the uneven. Four signs always express the absolute in any order whatsoever, and are explained by a fifth. Thus the solution of all magical questions is that of the Pentagram, and all antinomies are explained by harmonious unity.

So disposed, the Tarot is a veritable oracle, and answers all possible questions with more clearness and accuracy than the Android of Albertus Magnus; so that a prisoner devoid of books, had he only a Tarot which he knew how to make use of, could, in a few years, acquire a universal science, and could converse with an unequalled doctrine and inexhaustible eloquence. This wheel, in fact, is the true key of the oratorical art, and of the great art of Raymond Lully; it is the true secret of the transmutation of darkness into light; it is the first and most important of all the arcana of the *magnum opus*. By means of this universal key of symbolism all the allegories of India, Egypt, and Judea are made intelligible; the Apocalypse of St John is a Kabbalistic

THE GREAT PRACTICAL SECRETS. 263

book, whose sense is exactly indicated by the figures and numbers of the Urim, Thumim, Theraphim, and Ephod, all summarised and completed by the Tarot; the sanctuaries of eld are no longer full of mysteries, and the signification of the objects of the Hebrew cultus may for the first time be understood. As a fact, who does not recognise in the golden table, crowned and supported by cherubim, which covered the ark of the covenant and served as the propitiatory, the same symbols as in the twenty-first key of the Tarot? The ark was a hieroglyphical synthesis of the whole Kabbalistic doctrine; it contained the Jod, or blossoming staff, of Aaron; the He, or cup; the gomor, which held the manna; the two tables of the law, a symbol analogous to that of the sword of justice; and the manna contained in the gomar, four objects which wonderfully interpret the letters of the divine Tetragram.

We have ourselves discovered, in a sufficiently extraordinary manner, a sixteenth-century medal, which is a key to the Tarot. We scarcely know whether we should confess that this medal, and the place where it was to be found, were shown to us in a dream by the divine Paracelsus; however this may be, the medal is in our possession. On one side it represents the juggler, in a German costume of the period, holding his girdle in one hand, and the Pentagram in the other. On the table in front of him, between an open book and a clasped purse, he has ten deniers or talismans arranged in two lines of three each, and in a square of four; the legs of the table form two ה, and those of the juggler two inverted ו. The back of the medal contains the letters of the alphabet disposed within a magic square, after the following manner:—

A	B	C	D	E
F	G	H	I	K
L	N	M	O	P
Q	R	S	T	V
X	V	Z	N	

It will be seen that this alphabet has only twenty-two letters, the V and N being repeated, and that they are arranged in four quinaries, with a tetrad for basis and key. The four final letters are two combinations of the duad and triad, and read Kabbalistically they form the word Azoth, by ascribing to the configuration of the letters their value in primitive Hebrew, and in reckoning N as א, Z as it is in Roman characters, V as the Hebrew ו Vau, which between two vowels, or letters of the value of vowels, is pronounced O, and X as the primitive Tau, which was precisely of this shape. The whole Tarot is therefore explained in this wonderful medal, truly worthy of Paracelsus, and which we offer for the examination of antiquaries. The letters disposed by four times five are summarised by the word אZהמ, analogous to those of the Tetragram and INRI, and containing all the mysteries of the Kabbalah.

Vestiges of the Tarot are found among all nations of the world. The Italian version is the most faithful and the best preserved, but it may be still farther improved by precious indications borrowed from the Spanish game; the two of cups, for example, in the *Naïbi*, is completely Egyptian, and we there see two antique vases whose handles are formed by two ibises superposed on a cow; in the same cards a unicorn is seen in the centre of the four of deniers; the three of cups shows us the figure of Isis issuing from a vase; while from two other vases two ibises come forth, one bearing a crown for the goddess, the other a lotus, which he appears to be offering to her. The four aces bear the image of the sacred hieratic serpent, and, in certain games, the double triangle of Solomon is found instead of the symbolic unicorn.

The German Tarots are more mutilated, and little beyond the numbers of the keys can be found in them, these being crowded with pantagruelian figures. The Chinese Tarot preserves several emblems; the deniers and swords may be easily recognised, but it would be more difficult to identify the cups and clubs.

It was at the epoch of the Gnostic and Manichæan heresies that the Tarot was lost to the Church, and it was at the same period that the meaning of the divine Apocalypse was also lost. It was no longer known that the seven seals of this Kabbalistic book are seven pantacles to be explained by the analogies of the numbers, characters, and symbols of the Tarot. Thus the universal tradition of the one religion was for an instant broken, the darkness of doubt spread over the whole earth, and to the uninitiated it appeared that true catholicism, universal revelation, had for a moment vanished. The explanation of the work of St John by the signs of the Kabbalah will be a perfectly new revelation.

ETERNAL LIFE, OR THE PEACE OF GOD.

THE end of all occult philosophy is to assure us that unalterable serenity of soul which is the life of Heaven and the surpassing peace of the elect. To attain such peace it is necessary:—

I.

To believe in the wisdom of God and the harmony of natural laws. This faith will prevent us from anticipating evil, and being vexed by disorders which we cannot prevent, for what appears irregular to us is often the result of a law which escapes us. We shall find in this consideration the great secret of resignation.

II.

Never to disturb ourselves by the apprehension of evil, for the evil which may overtake us will never be stronger than ourselves. There is but one real evil, injustice, and it is in our power to be just. Calamities which are foreign to our conscience are either trials or favours of Providence.

III.

To labour unceasingly in the reformation of our characters. By our characteristic vices we torment ourselves and others. A vicious character is therefore a habitual injustice, which deserves, and entails unfailingly, both trouble and reprobation.

IV.

Never to surrender ourselves wholly to pleasure. Pleasure exists for us, but we are not made for it.

V.

To believe sincerely in the indestructibility of all that is good, all that is true, all that is beautiful, and all that is pure.

VI.

To believe that suffering is production, production a struggle, struggle progress, and progress true life.

VII.

Never to permit the cynicism of incredulity to parade itself before us.

VIII.

To believe in the reality of all that is good, even in the most fleeting forms of life. A glass of water given in my name shall deserve eternal life, said the great Initiator. It is then of an infinite value like all that comes from God.

IX.

To be humble, and never imagine that we are great because we possess a great knowledge or profound thoughts. One dewdrop reflects all the glories of a beautiful day, yet nothing thereof belongs to it; it is thus with our souls. The sun drinks the dew, and God can draw to Himself all our intelligence and genius. We are but trembling and fugitive mirrors, like the drop of water, and should nature break us, there would be no void in immensity. Heaven has no need of us, it is we who have need of Heaven.

X.

To preserve ourselves from puerile beliefs which trouble the conscience, and to hold one idea more than all in detestation—that God desires to confound human reason and is honoured by prejudice and folly, that, like the Sphinx, He proposes enigmas for solution, and kills cr tortures everlastingly those who solve them, and those who, unable to do so, do not harass themselves about them; whereas the Supreme Reason which exists in God seeks the elevation of man's reason to itself by faith in His rectitude and justice, the God of the sages being the light of generous souls, and not the murky agitation of the slothful and servile mind.

XI.

To raise the independence of the conscience above all human influences and all fears, since nothing worse than death can befall us, and death we have no cause to dread, for it is a natural and necessary thing, which independence and mental greatness will survive, when the mind irrevocably joins itself to truth and justice, which are eternal.

XII.

Never to be overcome by love. Love because we ought, and because we wish to. Love becomes a glory when it is in no sense shameful. Its joys wait on those who never purchase them at the price of infamy. To prefer one's pleasure before one's honour is to be base. Now, by baseness we become unworthy even of a courtesan's love. A woman despises the man she degrades, and when she feels herself contemptible, she esteems the man who contemns her.

XIII.

Not to leave the performance of our own duties to Providence. Never to complain of the evil we can prevent. To look upon the struggle against evil as our first duty, assured that we should be fools and impious if we imputed to God the inconveniences which result from our own folly and idleness.

XIV.

To seek the infinite in the intellectual and moral order only. The whole world is not large enough to satisfy our soul; it thirsts for an infinite perfection, which sufficiently proves that it is immortal. The treasures of earth when immense are only an immense embarrassment, and never satisfy their owner. The dignities of this world are often great calamities; all that can end is as if it were already ended, and the vulture of Prometheus returns unceasingly to enlarge the void in the heart of man who is chained to the rock of power, for the more he is elevated above others the more is he lonely, and God weighs with an infinite weight on the isolation of pride.

XV.

Not to believe in delusions; God's realities being a thousand times more admirable than man's dreams, we must never be content to imagine what we can estimate and know. Youth, friendship, love, poetry, glory—all these are true, all these are eternally true, notwithstanding that everything changes its zone like spring. Spring is no illusion for the swallows, they have the boldness to follow and overtake it always.

XVI.

To do one's duty in the present and fear nothing for the future. To be happy when happiness offers itself as if we had but one day to live, provided that we find happiness in the satisfaction of legitimate desires. Resignation to God, confiding joy in the midst of nature's festivals, gaiety which intoxicates itself in the sunlight, enthusiasm for the beautiful, devotion to the good, all these do not calculate, do not reason with, the anxiety of the morrow. Happy is he, says Horace, who each day can say to himself—This day I have lived; let the tempest come to-morrow, it cannot deprive me of the serenity of the day that is closing. You have enough of daily trial, said the Christus; do not store up disquietude for the morrow; sufficient to each day is the evil thereof. . . . Do you wish to have no apprehension for the morrow? Do good to-day; good actions are the seed of happiness.

XVII.

To obey the law; forestall duty, but never endure slavery. The deaths of the martyrs were sublime because the outrage of their conscience was attempted. We cannot renounce our convictions, affections, or national habits, at the command of an imperious master. We may be silent in the face of oppression, we may abstain from armed resistance, but let us die, if need be, embracing the altar of the fatherland.

XVIII.

Never to dispute about the essential nature of God. Faith in God should make men better, not lead their reason astray; and how should we define the Infinite? How explain what we cannot understand? The more we dispute, the less we adore. Let us reason as we please on the necessity of adoration, but when we pronounce the name of the Indefinable, let us preserve supreme silence.

THE GREAT PRACTICAL SECRETS.

Let us bow and adore! It is not the elephant of the Brahmans, nor the three-headed Ancient of the Gnostics, nor anything which the idolatry of the nations has consecrated; it is nothing that we can see, handle, hear, taste, or describe. It is that which we should worship in the profound peace of the spirit and in the heart's enthusiasm.

XIX.

To respect the conscience of others and never impose on them even truth. Break not forcibly the yoke of slaves who love their yoke! Be devoted always, never too zealous! If souls rejoice in their folly, it is cruel to deprive them of it without restoring their reason. We must have patience; we must leave the faquir to his chain and the old world to its idols, waiting till all this shall end of itself. Lose not the time in denouncing the darkness with vain discourses; make the light shine, but let it not be the light of a consuming torch. Overthrow henceforth neither the statues of Jupiter, nor of St Nicholas, even when an imbecile people attempt to adore St Nicholas. Philosophers, respect relics if you wish not your books to be burned. The light shines for all men coming into the world, but all have the right to open or shut their eyes as may please them.

XX.

To allow no real existence to evil. God, in fact, does not will it; Nature rejects it; suffering protests against it. Reasonable beings cannot desire it; universal harmony leaves no place for it. Life triumphs continually over it, as over death. Satan cannot therefore be a king; he is the most abject slave of the fatality he has evoked. The eternal reprobation of evil consists in the eternal triumph of good. Order cures disorder by punishment, and punishment itself is a good, since it is a cure. Evil, moreover, condemns and destroys itself. Pride is a diadem of humiliation, lust an abortion of pleasure, avarice the cultus of wretchedness. The ways of evil are broad at the beginning, but they contract in proportion to our advance, and end by the prolonged crushing and suffocation of their victim. They are blind alleys where we must perish if we lack the boldness and strength to turn back. In order to prove the existence of another world, it is sometimes asserted that the wicked can be happy in this life. This is untrue; the wicked are the last and most miserable of men.

XXI.

Not to seek the glory which comes from the premature esteem of men, but that derived from honour, that consciousness of justice and self-devotion which soon or late will produce its effect. Men finish by submitting to the ascendency of genius and talent, but they detest it because envy is the vice and torment of the weak. For them glory is but a triumph of egotism, because, egoists as they are, they cannot understand it otherwise. They invariably deny the existence of voluntary sacrifice, and seek for some slavish and infamous motive in the renunciation of the heroes of humanity. Let them rail; they speak without knowledge, and with no wish to listen. They crown willingly the inanity which does not give them umbrage. Having no need of their crowns, it may well be that they may bear them one day to our tombs. And should they even despoil our tombs, what harm could that do to our remains? What would that matter above all to our souls, if these, as we doubt not, survive our earthly errors? Love good for good's sake, knowledge for the sake of knowledge, the beautiful for beauty's sake, truth for the sake of truth. Think you that Homer composed his admirable poems in view of those alms which he nevertheless stood in need of? The cities of Greece, wherein he begged his bread, dispute his name and birthplace, and it is uncertain which performed for him the final honours and deserved to possess his remains. " Let the dead bury their dead," says the Christus. " Seek first the kingdom of God and His justice, and all other things shall be added unto you."

EPILOGUE,

EMBODYING THE SPIRIT OF THE AUTHOR'S PHILOSOPHY.

I.—THE VISION OF THE WANDERING JEW.

"Go onward!" cried the Jew Ahasuerus to Christ as He staggered beneath His Cross. "Do thou go onward," replied the Saviour of the world, "till I return hither and bid thee rest."

From that time Ahasuerus has traversed the world unceasingly, and every year, about Easter, he returns to the home of his accursed race, to see if he shall meet Jesus. He approaches, he arrives, broken-down, breathless, ready to expire with fatigue—he arrives and finds no one. He raises his eyes and beholds in the ever implacable sky a hand which points westward! "Go onward!" cries a voice to him which seems to be an eternal echo of his own on the day of his crime, and the old Ahasuerus bows his head; the sigh of deliverance which swelled already in his heart sinks silently and without tears; he recommences his age-long journey.

In the days when the Crusaders took Jerusalem, the Wandering Jew was told that Christ had returned to the Holy Mount; but he found only a priest encircled by military. "A Jew! a Jew!" cried some whose hands were blood-stained. "Get on! get on!" shouted the soldiers, as they smote the old man with their truncheons and goaded him with the points of their lances. Ahasuerus bowed his head and took his departure amidst the maledictions of the crowd.

"Alas!" he murmured, "not yet can the Cross absolve me, since it has not taught forgiveness to its defenders. Men venerate it only as an instrument of torture and a recollection of revenge! Madmen, they would avenge Him who saved them by pardoning them, and they do not see that they condemn themselves by annulling the forgiveness of the man-god! They see not that persecution practised by the Christians is an abjuration of the martyrs and a restoration of their executioners!"

Therefore, when Ahasuerus found the Jews oppressed by the Christians, he pledged them to die rather than renounce the faith of their fathers, and he himself, with his world-old staff in his hand, his beard and hair blown by the wind, led them forward from exile to exile. Better than anyone, nevertheless, did he know that Jesus was the only Son of God!

At a later period he saw the Cross cast down and the scaffolds rise up; he heard the holy guillotine spoken of, and was in no way surprised—had not the Inquisition already inaugurated its festivals of death in the name of the Holy Cross? The cultus was the same, the altar alone was changed. There was talk also of humanity and progress, and justly, for the axe is more speedy and less cruel than the bloody pillory of Golgotha.

Once more he beheld the solemnities of the Golden Calf established; he knew how such orgies end, and when they asked him, "What is the carpenter's son making now?" he answered, shaking his head, "A coffin!" For he felt that the time was short and his pace seemed to slacken; he surveyed in turn the expiring century and the whirl of events.

On the day when the successor of St Peter fell, to be supported henceforth by a sceptre, when he departed from the Eternal City exiled and cursed in his turn, Ahasuerus entered the deserted Vatican, and, with his elbow resting on the empty chair of the popes, he let his head fall on his hand, and for a moment seemed to sleep. He saw in a dream the country about Jerusalem clothed once more with its primeval fertility; the vine of the Promised Land with its giant grapes, and the olive trees loaded with fruit, clad the hills, while the valleys were rich in bay trees and roses in full bloom. The mountain of Moria was covered with an innumerable multitude, formed by deputations from every nation of the earth, and on the summit of the Holy Mount rose a vast altar. In the centre of the altar was a gigantic golden candlestick reaching to the clouds, surmounted by a golden monstrance, in whose centre there appeared, white and transparent, the Divine Host of the

EPILOGUE. 273

Sacrifice of Love, the wheaten synthesis, the symbol of divine and human unity, the bread of social union and universal communion.

An old man was standing erect before the altar, holding in one hand a white and thin cake, like that in the monstrance, and in the other a chalice. Celestial music was heard, and from the front row of every phalanx rose clouds of incense. Several men in splendid vestments brought forward a table which they covered with white linen. One of these men wore the dress of the sovereign pontiff of the Christian Law, the second that of the chief of the Imans, the third was habited like the high priest of the Jewish Law, a fourth wore the ornaments of the Grand Lama, and all acted and prayed in concert, seeming as united as brethren.

It was the day on which Christ rose from the dead, and already more than two thousand times the world had celebrated the anniversary, but none had been so splendidly impressive as this one. The music ended; silence fell on the throng, and every eye turned towards the West. Then another old man· was seen to appear, whose beard and hair covered his breast and shoulders; he cast down his staff of travel, straightened himself with a long sigh, and, raising his tear-filled eyes to Heaven, allowed himself to be clothed in a white garment. He looked at the Host, and exclaimed, weeping, "'Tis He!" He looked at the priest, who, elected by universal suffrage, performed on this day the office of supreme pontiff, and repeated, "'Tis He!" He looked at the silent and recollected crowd, and extended his hands in an attitude of thanks, still saying, "It is He! It is He, living in all; He only everywhere and for ever!"

Then the priest of the people came down from the altar; a chair was set before the Holy Table, on which was placed the Host and chalice, and the pastor, addressing the ancient man, said, "Rest thyself, Ahasuerus!"

Then the pontiffs of every past religion came after the priest of the universal association to imprint the kiss of peace on the white beard of the reconciled outcast, after which all gathering about the table communicated with him. Then Ahasuerus felt himself informed with new life; it seemed to him as if he were himself the Christ, and that breaking the bread which multiplied on the Holy Table, he distributed it to the multitude.

S

So finished the dream of the Wandering Jew; a clatter of arms and anguished cries awoke him, as the brigands of the nations pillaged the Holy City. He issued from the palace of the popes, which tottered over tombs torn open, and again set out to continue his circuit of the world, which soon, perchance, he will recommence no more. Pity him not, all ye who encounter him bent, breathless, and travel-stained. He is more fortunate than all the great politicians of our century or the last monarchs of the world; he knows whither he is going.

II.—The Farewell to Calvary.

JESUS crossed the desolate meadows of Judea, and paused on the arid summit of the ancient Calvary. There an angel with frowning brow and darkened eye was seated enveloped in his two vast wings. It was Satan, the King of the old world.

The rebel angel was sad and fatigued, and he turned away his eyes in disgust from a world where the sin was without genius, and where the satiety of a cowardly corruption had succeeded the titanic combats of the giant passions of eld. He felt that in tempting mankind he had instructed the strong and had deceived only the weak; he therefore deigned no longer to tempt any one, and gloomy beneath his golden diadem, he heard vaguely the fall of souls into eternity, like the monotonous drops of an unceasing rain.

Prompted by a power which was unknown to him, he had taken his seat on Calvary, and pondering over the death of the Man-God, he felt jealous of it. He was a powerful and beautiful angel, but he was jealous of the Christus, and this jealousy was typified by a serpent plunging its fangs into his breast and devouring his heart. Jesus stood before him, with Mary His mother, and gazed at him in silence with profound compassion. Satan in his turn beheld the Redeemer, and bitterly smiled.

"Comest thou," he asked, "to endeavour to die once more for a world which thy first passion could not save? Hast thou tried vainly to change stones into bread for the nourishment of thy people, and dost thou come to confess thy defeat? Hast thou fallen from the summit of the Temple, and has thy divinity been broken in the descent? Dost thou come to adore me that thou may'st possess the world? Go, it is now too late, and I would not deceive thee! The empire of the world has passed over to those who adored me in thy name, and I myself am weary of dominion devoid of glory. If thou be discouraged as I am, sit down beside me, and think no longer of either God or men."

"I come not to sit down beside thee," replied Christ; "I come to raise thee up, to forgive, and to console thee, that thou mayest cease being wicked."

"I desire not thy pardon," the evil angel answered, "and it is not I who am wicked. The wicked one is he who implants the thirst for knowledge in minds and then shrouds truth in an impenetrable mystery. It is he who reveals to their desire an ideal virgin, whose intoxicating beauty is able to make them delirious, and who gives her to them only to tear her immediately from their embraces, and load her with eternal chains. It is he, in fine, who endows angels with liberty, and has prepared infinite torments for those who would not be his slaves—he who has slain his innocent son with the pretext of visiting the crimes of the guilty upon him, and who yet has not pardoned the guilty, but has laid the death of his son as a new crime at their doors!"

"Why do you remind me so bitterly of the ignorance and errors of men?" said Jesus. "Better than thou do I know how they have distorted the image of God, but well dost thou also know that God is not like the image they have made of Him. God has not endowed thee with the thirst of knowledge except to slake it for ever in the waters of eternal truth, but why close thine eyes and seek the day within thee instead of looking up to the sun? If thou seek the light where it is, thou shalt find the light, for in God there are neither shadows nor mysteries; the shadows are in thee alone, and mysteries are the limitations of thine own mind. God has not given liberty to his creatures to take it back again, but He has given it as a bride and not as an illegitimate love; He desires us to possess it, not to outrage it, for this chaste daughter of Heaven never survives violence, and when its virginal dignity is wounded, liberty is dead for him who has misused it. God does not wish for slaves, revolted pride has created servitude. God's law is the royal rule of His creatures and the title-deeds of their eternal liberty. God has not killed His Son, but the Son of God laid down His life freely that He might destroy death, and for this reason He now lives in the whole of humanity, and will save all generations, for from trial to trial he leads the human family into the Promised Land, whose first fruits have been already tasted. I come therefore to announce to thee, O Satan, that thy last hour has arrived, unless, at least, thou art willing to be free and reign over the world with me, by love and intelligence. But thou shalt be called Satan no longer, thou shalt reassume the glorious name of Lucifer, and I will set a star upon thy forehead and a torch in thy hand. Thou shalt be the genius of toil and industry, because thou hast much struggled, much suffered, and dolorously thought. Thou shalt spread thy wings from pole to pole, and brood over the world. Instead of the haughtiness of isolation, thou shalt be the sublime pride of self-devotion, and I will give thee the sceptre of earth and the key of heaven."

"I understand thee not, I shall never understand thee; well dost thou know that I can love no longer," and with a sorrowful gesture the fallen angel showed Christ the wound which furrowed his breast, and the serpent devouring his heart.

Jesus turned towards his mother and looked at her; Mary understood the glance of her son, she drew near to the unhappy angel, and did not disdain to stretch forth her hand towards him and touch his wounded breast. The serpent thereupon dropped of itself and expired at the feet of Mary, who crushed its head; the wound in the angel's heart was healed, and a tear, the first he had shed, coursed slowly down the face of the repentant Lucifer; this tear was as precious as the blood of a god, and all the blasphemies of hell were atoned for by it. The regenerated angel prostrated himself on Calvary, and, weeping, kissed the place where the Cross was once driven in. Then he rose triumphant in hope and radiant with love, to cast himself into the arms of Christ. Calvary trembled thereat; its arid summit was suddenly clothed with fresh and brilliant verdure, and blossomed out in flowers, while, in the place where the Cross had stood, a young vine rose loaded with ripe and fragrant grapes.

Then said the Saviour: "This is the vine which shall provide the wine of universal communion, and it shall grow till all its branches encircle the earth." Then taking his mother by one hand he extended the other to the angel, and said to him: "Let our symbolic forms now return into heaven, I shall never more come down to die on this mountain. Here shall Mary weep her son no more, nor Lucifer bring remorse for his now obliterated crime. We are one spirit henceforth—the spirit of intelligence and love, the spirit of liberty and courage, the spirit of life victorious over death."

All three then took their flight through space, and rising to an immense height, they beheld the earth and all its kingdoms extending roads towards each other, like interlacing arms; they saw the country green already with the first fraternal harvests, and from East to West they heard the mysterious prelude of the canticle of union, while northward on the crest of a bluish mountain they saw, in dim outline, the gigantic form of a man raising his arms to heaven. On his limbs were still the recent traces of the fetters he had broken, and his breast was scarred like Lucifer's. Beneath his right foot, on the sharpest peak of the mountain, there still palpitated the dead body of a vulture whose wings and head hung down. This mountain was Caucasus, and the liberated giant was the antique Prometheus. Thus the great divine and human symbols met and acknowledged each other under the same sky; then they vanished to make place for God Himself, who came to dwell for ever among men.

III.—The Reign of Messiah.

WHEN the spirit of understanding shall have spread over the whole earth, a time will come when the Gospel spirit shall be the light of nations. The basis of power will be understood to be absolute reason, as it is declared in the long misconstrued proem of the Gospel according to St John. Then will Christ be daily born no longer symbolically on our altars, but really and corporeally in every part of the earth. Has He not declared that the least among us is Himself? So the birth of every child shall be a Christmas, and all shall venerate the Saviour in one another. Christ will be no longer poor, hungry, proscribed, destitute of bride and of children, hunted and crucified. He will be rich like Job when his trials were over, in universal abundance; He will be bridegroom and father, He will reign and pardon all His persecutors. For one day all nations shall be one nation, all thrones be subject to one throne, and on this will be seated a just man filled with the spirit of Jesus Christ, and who thus will be Jesus Christ Himself, as we all may be if He be within us. This King shall reconcile the East with the West and the North with the South; he will endow the peoples with true liberty, for he will immoveably establish the pillars of justice. By repressing license, he will abolish misery. All will have the right and opportunities to do well, none to degrade themselves and do viciously. Punishment will be succeeded by moral hygiene, criminals will be looked on as diseased, and will be subjected to the treatment of the deranged. The great expiation of the Cross is sufficient for all human offences, and will eventually abolish the gibbet, which will be execrable from the moment that it is useless.

Error will thenceforth be accorded no real existence; truth only exists, falsehood is as perishable as a dream. There will be then only one religion in the world, and the universal pontiff will declare from the pinnacle of supreme authority that Jews, Mohammedans, Buddhists, &c., are Christians ill-instructed, of whom he is none the less father and head. He will bless them and convene them to the great council of the nations; he will throw open to them the inexhaustible wealth of prayers and indulgences, and will really and truly bestow his benediction ON THE CITY AND ON THE WORLD.

This will be the period of the return of the Prodigal Son, who no longer possesses anything, but his brother will lend to him, and he will work that he may regain his portion. It will be the hour when the five foolish virgins, having at length procured oil for their lamps, will come back knocking at the gate, AND SHOULD THE BRIDEGROOM REFUSE TO OPEN TO THEM, THE PRUDENT VIRGINS WILL STRETCH OUT THEIR HANDS AND HELP THEM TO COME IN BY THE WIN-

DOW, for the final message of Christianity is reciprocity, restoration, universal love; and I assure you, in all truth, that there is not a saint in heaven who is not willing to descend into hell to deliver poor souls therefrom, even were it necessary to take their place with the doors shut against them for ever. Can you even conceive a heaven poised over hell? an eternal feast in face of an eternal pyre, a house of peace and prayer with a vault full of groans and torments beneath? One only dream can fill the everlasting repose of each of the beatified, the deliverance of some reprobate; and if this were a hopeless dream, it would become a nightmare more terrible than even the torments of hell.

It was in this manner that the Gnostics—that is, *those who knew*, in other words, the initiates of primitive Christianity—interpreted the oracles uttered by the spirit of Jesus Christ; they were followed by the disciples of Origen, but the Church condemned them, and rightly, for they divulged the secret doctrines, and profaned the mysteries of the Master. In extending the hopes of the multitude, the law must not be deprived of its awful penalty, and the dogma of eternal perdition only signifies after all the eternal divorce between good and evil.

IV.—THE FINAL VISION.

ABOVE material forms and the terrestrial atmosphere, there is a realm where souls break from the chains which bind them. The ethereal aromas, obedient to fancy, clothe it successively with all the splendours of ideal grace, and populate the spiritual world of poetry and vision with creatures of marvellous beauty. Into this region our fairest dreams transport us while we sleep; there in laborious watches inspiration carried those great poets, who, in all ages, were enabled to foresee, by the perceptions of harmony, the great destinies of humanity. There images exist and analogies reign, for poetry is in imagery, and the harmony of images is essentially analogical. In this ideal region Æschylus beheld the torments of Prometheus, and Moses heard Jehovah speak. There the greatest of the Oriental poets, the Eagle of Patmos, the singer of the

Apocalypse, saw the Christian Church, under the figure of a woman in labour who brings forth painfully the Man of the Future. In this wondrous world of poetry and revelation, God appeared to him veiled in light and holding the everlasting Gospel in His hand, which opened slowly, while plagues tormented the world and angels of destruction furrowed the earth to make place for the city of harmony and holy unity, the New Jerusalem which comes down ready built out of heaven, because the conception of harmony exists in God, and will be realised of itself on earth when men understand it.

The glorious vision of Christ, after traversing the earth, ascended into this ethereal region, and there the Redeemer disclosed to the once rebellious and henceforth regenerate angel the great army of martyrs. All the victims of human despotism might be seen there, all who had chosen to die rather than be false to their consciences, the victims of Antiochus, the martyrs of ancient Rome, and those tortured by the second Rome—some for their legitimate beliefs, others for dreams and delusions, had faced human tyranny bravely, and all were pure in God's sight, for they had suffered in the preservation of the noblest and most beautiful of gifts—liberty.

Long had their white-robed souls sighed beneath the altar and cried out for justice. At length the hour was come, and all, with their palms in their hands, came before the Redeemer, as He stood between His mother and the restored angel to ask what revenge they desired on their persecutors.

"Lord, let their souls be delivered to us, that we may dispose of them for eternity as they disposed of us in time!"

Christ thereupon committed to their keeping the keys of heaven and hell, saying, "The souls of your oppressors are in your power."

A cry of joy and triumph pealed from the heights of heaven to the depths of the abyss, the martyr-spirits threw open the gates of hell, and stretched forth their hands to their murderers. Each of the reprobates found an elect for his protector, heaven enlarged its boundary, and the virgin mother wept with joy when she beheld so many children whom she thought she had lost for ever crowding around her. While all heaven was smiling on this magnificent spectacle, a new sun rose over the earth, and night folded its wings in the west. The darksome clouds of the past fled, crowded with phantoms, which were the shades of the grand extinct monarchies and the ancient vanished religions. Between the night and coming morning, the light whitened the head of an aged man, as he sat with his face turning eastward. This was the wanderer of the Christian centuries, the outlaw of a savage civilisation, the type of the Parias, the old Ahasuerus at length resting. The people had found a fatherland, the Wandering Jew had received his pardon.

The earth now was the Temple of God; universal reciprocity had realised Christian charity; all laboured and lived for each, as each for all. All rejoiced peaceably in the fruit of their toil; none of God's children perished through want beside the table of their father, for the fair division of labour made life easy to the whole race; confederacy had increased the wealth of the earth, and the union of every interest had given human toil a direction so divine, and an energy so marvellous, that the very seasons had altered; there was a new heaven and a new earth, according to the promise of the apostle; and Jesus said to the angel of light and genius,—" Behold the work thou must accomplish! Behold the new city of intelligence and love!

"The earth is ready, it thrills with expectation. Men now see it, as once it was seen by the prophet, covered with bones and ashes; but fresh life stirs already in the dust, and a divine tremor passes through the dry bones. Soon will they rise, and a new people will cover the countries of the world. Then shall humanity issue as from a long sleep, and will seem to behold the day for the first time!"

Having spoken these words, Christ prostrated Himself before the throne of His Father, saying, "Lord, Thy will be done on earth, as it is in heaven."

And the Virgin, who is the type of the regenerated woman, and the angel of liberty transformed into the genius of order and harmony, with all the compensated martyrs, and all repentant reprobates delivered from their agonies, responded together by that mysterious word which joins the will of creatures to that of their Creator, and all human energes to divine power—Amen!

THANKS be unto Thee, oh my God, that Thou hast led me to this admirable Light! Thou art the supreme intelligence and absolute life of those numbers and those forces which obey Thee to populate the infinite with an inexhaustible creation. Thou art proved by mathematics, Thou art celebrated by the harmonies of existence, Thou art adored by all perishable forms!

Thou wast known to Abraham, Thou wast divined by Hermes, Pythagoras calculated Thy movements, Plato aspired unto Thee in all the dreams of his genius, but one only initiator, one sage alone, hath revealed Thee to the little ones of earth, one alone has been able to say of Thee —I and my Father are one; to Him be glory, therefore, since all His glory is thine!

Father, Thou knowest that he who writes these lines has much struggled and much suffered; he has endured poverty, calumny, revengeful proscription, imprisonment, the desertion of those he loved, and never, notwithstanding, has he considered himself unfortunate, since truth and justice remained for his consolation.

Thou only art holy, oh, God of truthful hearts and upright souls, and Thou knowest if ever I have thought myself pure in Thy sight! Like all men I have been the sport of human passions; at length I have conquered them, or Thou, rather, hast overcome them in me, and hast given me to repose in the profound peace of those who seek and who covet Thee only.

I love mankind, because men, unless they are beside themselves, are only wicked through error or infirmity. They naturally love what is good, and it is by this love, which Thou hast given them as a support in the midst of their trials, that they must be, sooner or later, led back to the religion of justice by the love of truth.

Let my book now go wherever Thy Providence may send it. If it contain the words of Thy wisdom, it will be stronger than oblivion; if, on the contrary, it abound but in errors, I know that my love of justice and of truth will, at least, survive it, and thus immortality cannot fail to engarner the aspirations and desires of my soul which Thou has created immortal!

SUPPLEMENT.

THE KABBALAH.

ALL religions have preserved the remembrance of a primeval book, written in emblems by the sages of the first centuries of the world, and whose symbols, afterwards simplified and made common, furnished letters to the art of writing, characters to speech, and to occult philosophy its mysterious signs and pantacles. This book, attributed to Enoch, seventh lord of the earth after Adam, by the Hebrews; to Hermes Trismegistus by the Egyptians; to Cadmus, the mysterious founder of the sacred city, by the Greeks, was the symbolical synthesis of primeval tradition, since called Kabbalah, or Cabala, from a Hebrew word which is the equivalent of tradition.

This tradition wholly reposes on the single dogma of magic—that the visible is for us the proportional measure of the invisible. Now, the ancients having observed that equilibrium is the universal law of physics, and one which results from the apparent opposition of two forces, argued from physical to metaphysical equilibrium, and asserted that in God, that is, in the first living and active cause, two properties necessary to one another must be recognised—stability and movement, necessity and liberty, rational order and volitional autonomy, justice and love; consequently also, severity and mercy; and it is these two attributes which, in a certain sense, the Kabbalistic Jews personified under the names of *Geburah* and *Chesed*. Above *Geburah* and *Chesed* dwells the supreme Crown, the equilibrating power, designated under the name of Malchut in the occult and Kabbalistic verse of the *Paternoster*, which is found in the Greek text of the Gospel according to St Matthew, and in several Hebrew copies—'Ὅτι σὴ ἐστὶν ἡ βασίλεια καὶ ἡ δύναμις, καὶ ἡ δόξα, εἰς τοὺς αἰῶνας. Ἀμην.

"For thine is the kingdom, the power, and the glory, world without end. Amen."*

Malchut based on Geburah and Chesed is the Temple of Solomon, having Jakin and Bohas, unity and the duad, for its pillars; it is the Adamic doctrine founded on the resignation of Abel for the one part, and on the labours and remorse of Cain for the other part; it is the demonstration of the universal lever sought in vain by Archimedes. But Geburah and Chesed, maintained in equilibrium by the Crown above and the Kingdom beneath, are two principles which may be viewed in their abstract nature or in their realisation. As abstract or idealised, they take the superior names of *Chocmah*, wisdom, and *Binah*, intelligence. In their realisation they are called stability and progress, that is, eternity and victory, *Hod* and *Netsah*.

Such, according to the Kabbalah, is the basis of all religions and all sciences, the primal and immutable conception of things, a threefold triangle and a circle, the idea of the triad explained by the balance multiplied by itself in the domains of the ideal, then the realisation of this idea in forms. Now, the ancients attached the first principles of this simple and sublime theology to the essential conception of numbers, and thus qualified all the figures of the primitive decade:—

1. *Keter.* The Crown, the equilibrating power.
2. *Chocmah.* Wisdom, equilibrated in its immutable order by the impulse of intelligence.
3. *Binah.* Active Intelligence, equilibrated by Wisdom.
4. *Chesed.* Mercy, Wisdom in its second conception, ever benevolent because it is strong.
5. *Geburah.* Severity, necessitated by Wisdom itself and by Goodness. To permit evil is to prevent good.
6. *Tiphereth.* Beauty, luminous conception of equilibrium in forms, intermediate between the Crown and the Kingdom, mediating principle between the

* The sacred word *Malchut*, employed for *Keter*, which is its Kabbalistic correspondent, and the balance of *Geburah* and *Chesed* repeated in the circles or firmaments, which the Gnostics called Æons, provide in this occult verse the keystone of the whole Christian temple. The Protestants have translated and preserved it in their New Testament, without discovering its supreme and wonderful significance, which would have unveiled to them all the mysteries of the Apocalypse; but it is a tradition of the Church that the revelation of these mysteries is reserved for the last days.

Creator and creation. (What a sublime conception is to be found here of poetry and its sovereign priesthood!)
7. *Netsah.* Victory, that is, the eternal triumph of intelligence and justice.
8. *Hod.* Eternity of the mind's conquests over matter, of the active over the passive, of life over death.
9. *Jesod.* The Foundation, that is, the base of every creed and truth, what in philosophy we call the ABSOLUTE.
10. *Malchut.* The Kingdom, that is, the universe, entire creation, the work and mirror of Deity, proof of the Supreme Reason, formal consequence which obliges us to go back to virtual premises, the enigma whose answer is God, that is, the Supreme and Absolute Reason.

These ten palmary notions attached to the ten first characters of the primeval alphabet, signifying at once numbers and principles, are what the masters in Kabbalah call the ten Sephiroth. The sacred Tetragram, traced in the following manner, indicates the number, source, and cor-

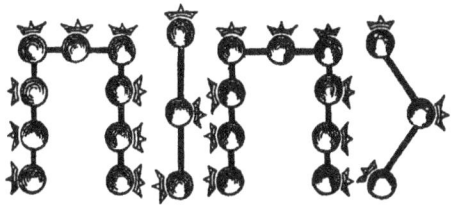

respondence of the Divine names. It is to the name of Iotchavah, written with these twenty-four signs, crowned with a triple flower of light, that the twenty-four thrones in heaven and the twenty-four crowned ancients of the Apocalypse must be referred. In Kabbalah the occult principle is called the Ancient, and this principle multiplied and, as it were, reflected in secondary causes, creates its own images, that is, as many Ancients as there are diverse conceptions of his single essence. These images, less perfect as they recede from their source, cast in the darkness a final reflection or glimmer, which represents a horrible and disfigured Ancient, who is vulgarly called the devil. Thus an initiate has dared to say that "the devil is God as

He is understood by the wicked," and another, in still stranger terms, that "the devil is formed from the shreds of Deity." We may resume and elucidate these exceedingly novel assertions, by remarking that in symbolism itself the demon is an angel cast out of heaven for desiring to usurp divinity. This belongs to the allegorical language of prophets and legendaries. Philosophically speaking, the devil is a human idea of divinity which has been surpassed and dispossessed of heaven by the progress of science and reason. Moloch, Adramelek, Baal, were, among primitive Eastern peoples, personifications of the one God, but dishonoured by barbarous attributes. The God of the Jansenists, creating the majority of human beings for hell, and delighting in the eternal tortures of those He will not save, is a conception still more barbarous than that of Moloch; thus the God of the Jansenists is already, for all wise and enlightened Christians, a true Satan fallen from heaven.

The Kabbalists, when multiplying the Divine Names, have joined them all either to the unity of the Tetragram or to the figure of the triad, or to the sephiric scale of the decade; they trace the scale of these Divine Names and Numbers in a triangle, which may be rendered as follows into Roman letters :—

```
         J
        J A
       S D I
      J E H V
     E L O I M
     S A B A O T
    A R A R I T A
   E L V E D A A T
   E L I M   G I B O R
   E L I M   S A B A O T
```

The total of these Divine Names, formed from the single Tetragram, but outside of the Tetragram itself, is one of the bases of the Hebrew Ritual, and composes the occult force which Kabbalistic rabbins invoke under the name of Semhamphoras. The Jews, the depositaries of the tradition of Seth, the first tradition of the one only revelation, brought from Chaldea by Abraham, taught by Joseph to the Egyptian priesthood, garnered and purified by Moses, and concealed beneath the symbolism of the Bible, did not preserve it in all its purity, and allowed themselves to be carried away by the unjust ambitions of the posterity of Cain. They believed that they were a chosen people, and thought that God had given them truth as a patrimony, rather than confided it as a deposit which belonged to humanity at large. We find, in fact, in the Talmudists, beside the sublime traditions of the Sepher Jezirah, sufficiently strange disclosures. Thus, they do not hesitate to attribute the idolatry of the nations to the patriarch Abraham himself, when they say that he transmitted his heritage to the Israelites, that is, he gave them the knowledge of the true Divine Names—the Kabbalah, in a word, was to be the legitimate and hereditary possession of Isaac—but they tell us that the patriarch gave presents to the children of his concubines, and by these presents they understand veiled dogmas and obscure names which soon became materialised and transformed into idols. False religions and their absurd mysteries, eastern superstitions and their detestable sacrifices, what a gift from a father to his despised family! Was it not sufficient to drive Agar with her son into the desert? Was it necessary, with their one loaf and pitcher, to give them a burden of falsehood to aggravate and empoison their exile?

The glory of Christianity is that it called all men to the truth, without distinction of peoples or castes, but not, however, without distinction of intellect and virtue. "Cast not your pearls before swine," said the Divine Founder of Christianity, "lest, trampling them under their feet, they turn and rend you."

The Apocalypse, or Revelation of St John, which contains all the Kabbalistic secrets of the doctrine of Jesus Christ, is a book no less obscure than the Sohar. It is hieroglyphically written with numbers and images, and the apostle appeals frequently to the intelligence of initiates. St John, the beloved disciple, and the depository of the secrets of the Saviour, did not, therefore, write to be understood by the multitude.

The Sepher Jezirah and the Apocalypse are the masterpieces of occultism; they contain more meanings than words, their expression is as figurative as poetry and as exact as mathematics. The Apocalypse epitomises, completes, and surpasses all the science of Abraham and

Solomon, as we shall prove in explaining the keys of the transcendent Kabbalah. The beginning of the Sohar is astonishing in the comprehensiveness of its outlines and the grand simplicity of its images. This is what we read:—

"The intelligence of occultism is the science of equilibrium. Forces which are produced without being balanced perish in the void. Thus perished the kings of the old world, the princes of the giants. They have fallen like trees without roots, and their place is no more found. It was through the conflict of unequilibrated forces that the devastated earth was bare and unformed when the breath of God made itself a place in the heaven and spread out the mass of waters. All the aspirations of Nature were then directed towards unity in form, towards the living synthesis of equilibrated forces, and the forehead of God, crowned with light, rose over the vast sea, and was reflected in the inferior waters. His radiant eyes appeared, darting two shafts of light which intersected the rays of the reflection. The forehead of God and His two eyes formed a triangle in heaven, and the reflection formed a triangle in the waters. Thus was the number six revealed, which was that of universal creation."

The text, which would not be intelligible in a literal version, we here translate by interpretation. Moreover, the author of the work takes care to intimate that the human form, which he attributes to God, is merely an image of his concept, and that God cannot be expressed by any thought, nor by any form. Pascal has said that the Deity is a circle whose centre is everywhere and whose circumference is nowhere.* But how can a circle be conceived without a circumference? The Sohar inverts this paradoxical figure, and would say freely of Pascal's circle that the circumference is everywhere and the centre nowhere. It is not, however, to a circle, but to a balance, that he compares the universal equilibrium of things. "Equilibrium is everywhere," he says, "and the central point where the balance is suspended may, therefore, be found everywhere." We here find the author of the Sohar stronger and more profound than Pascal.

The author of the Sohar continues his sublime dream. The synthesis of the Logos formulated by the human figure ascends slowly and issues from the water like the rising sun. When the eyes appeared, Light was created;

* See Note 29.

when the mouth was revealed, spirit was created and speech was heard. The shoulders, arms, and breast come forth, then labour begins. The Divine Image with one hand puts back the waters of the sea, and with the other raises continents and islands. Ever it grows taller and taller; the generative organs appear, and all creatures begin to multiply. At length it stands erect, it sets one foot on the land and one on the sea, it is mirrored wholly in the ocean of creation, it breathes on its reflection, it calls its image into life. "Let us make man," its says, and man is created! We know nothing so splendid in any poet as this vision of creation accomplished by the ideal type of humanity. Man is thus the shadow of a shadow, but he is the representation of divine power. He also can extend his hands from east to west, earth is given to him for a domain. Behold the Adam Kadmon, the primitive Adam of the Kabbalists! Behold in what sense he is represented as a giant! Behold wherefore Swedenborg, pursued in his dreams by reminiscences of the Kabbalah, affirms that all creation is but a gigantic man, and that we are made in the likeness of the universe!

The Sohar is a Genesis of light, the Sepher Jezirah is a scale of truths. Therein are explained the thirty-two absolute signs of speech, numbers, and letters; each letter reproduces a number, an idea, and a form, so that mathematics are applied to ideas and forms no less rigorously than to numbers in an exact proportion and by a perfect correspondence. By the science of the Sepher Jezirah the human mind is grounded in truth and reason, and can take account of all possible progress of intelligence by the evolutions of numbers. The Sohar represents, therefore, absolute truth, and the Sepher Jezirah provides the means of attaining, appropriating, and using it.

The Kabbalists held all that resembled idolatry in detestation; they gave, nevertheless, a human figure to God, as we have seen, but it was purely hieroglyphic. They held God to be the intelligent, loving, and living Infinite. He was for them neither the collection of existences, nor abstract existence, nor a philosophically definable Being. He is in all, distinct from, and greater than all; His very name is ineffable, and yet this name expresses only the human Ideal of His Divinity. What God is in Himself it is not given to man to understand.

God is the absolute of faith; but the absolute of reason is Being. Being is of itself, and because it is, its *raison d'être* is in itself. It may be asked, "Why does something exist? That is, why does such or such a thing exist?" But it cannot be asked without absurdity, "Why does Being exist?" This is supposing existence before existence. Reason and science prove to us that the modes of Being are equilibrated according to harmonious and hierarchic laws. Now, the hierarchy is synthetised by ascending and becoming more and more monarchic. Reason, nevertheless, cannot pause at the conception of a single universal chief without being overwhelmed by the heights which she seems to leave above this supreme King; she is silent, therefore, and makes place for adoring faith. What is certain, even for reason and science, is that the idea of God is the greatest, holiest, and most serviceable of all human aspirations, and that on it morality reposes with its eternal sanction. In humanity this belief is, therefore, the most real of all the phenomena of Being, and, were it false, Nature would be asserting what is absurd, the void would give expression to life, God would at once be and not be. It is to this philosophical and incontestible reality, called the idea of God, that the Kabbalists gave a name. All the characters of this name produce numbers, the hieroglyphs of its letters express all the laws and all the actualities of Nature.

The Kabbalists write the Divine Tetragram in four chief ways—J H V H, which they do not pronounce but spell, *Jod, he, vau, he,* and which we pronounce Jehovah, contrary to all analogy, for the Tetragram thus disfigured is composed of six letters—ADNI, which we pronounce *Adonaï*, and which means Saviour—AHIH, which we pronounce *Eieie*, and which signifies Being—finally, AGLA, which is pronounced as it is written, and which hieroglyphically encloses all the mysteries of the Kabbalah. In fact, the letter *Aleph* is the first of the Hebrew Alphabet; it expresses unity and represents the dogma of Hermes hieroglyphically. "That which is above is as that which is below." This letter has, in fact, two arms, one of which points to earth and the other to heaven with a similar gesture. The letter *Ghimel* is the third of the alphabet; it expresses numerically the triad and hieroglyphically child-birth, fecundity. The letter *Lamed* is the twelfth; it is the expression of the perfect cycle. As a hieroglyphical sign, it represents the circulation of the perpetual movement and the relation of the radius to the circumference. The letter *Aleph* repeated is the expression of the synthesis. Thus, the name AGLA signifies unity, which by the triad accomplishes the cycle of numbers to return into unity; the fruitful principle of Nature which is one with unity; the primal truth which fertilises science and directs it back to unity; syllepsis, analysis, science, and synthesis; the three Divine Persons, who are one God; the secret of the *magnum opus*, that is, the fixation of the Astral Light by a supreme projection of will-power, which the adepts represented by a serpent transfixed by a dart, and forming therewith the letter *Aleph;* then the three operations—to dissolve, to evaporate, and to condense, corresponding to the three indispensable substances—salt, sulphur, and mercury, all expressed by the letter *Ghimel;* then the twelve keys of Basilius Valentinus expressed by Lamed; finally, the work accomplished conformably to its principle, and reproducing the principle itself.

Such is the origin of that Kabbalistic tradition which comprises all magic in a word. To know how to read and pronounce this word, that is, to understand the mysteries of and translate into practice these absolute branches of knowledge, is to have the key of prodigies. To pronounce the word AGLA we must turn to the East, that is, unite ourselves in intention and knowledge with Eastern tradition. We must not forget that, according to the Kabbalah, the perfect word is speech realised by acts, whence comes that expression frequently found in the Vulgate, *facere verbum*, in the sense of accomplishing an action. To pronounce the word AGLA Kabbalistically, is therefore to undergo all the trials of initiation and fulfil all its works.

The name of Jehovah is subdivided into seventy-two explanatory names which are called *Schemhamphoras*. The art of employing these names and finding therein the keys of universal science, is what Kabbalists have called the *claviculæ* of Solomon. As a fact, at the end of the collection of evocations and prayers which bear this title, there are usually found seventy-two magic circles forming thirty-six talismans. This is four times nine, that is, the absolute number multiplied by the tetrad. Each of these talismans bears two of the seventy-two names with the emblematic sign of the number, and of that one of the four letters of Jehovah's name to which they correspond. It is this which gave rise to the four emblematic decades of the Tarot—the club represents the *Jod;* the cup, the *He;* the sword, the *Vau;* and the denier the final *He.* In the Tarot the complement of the ten is added, which synthetically repeats the character of unity.

The popular traditions of magic declare that the possessor of the Clavicles of Solomon can converse with all orders of spirits and compel all natural forces into his service. Now, these Keys, several times lost and again re-discovered, are nothing more than the talismans of the seventy-two names, and the mysteries of the thirty-two paths symbolically reproduced in the Tarot. By help of these signs, and by means of their combinations, which are as infinite as those of numbers or letters, we may, in effect, attain to the mathematical and natural revelation of all Nature's secrets, and, consequently, enter into communication with the whole hierarchy of intelligences and genii.

It is certain that the secrets of the supreme Kabbalah were lost to the Synagogue when Jesus Christ recovered them, as the Jewish author of the Sepher Toldos Jeschu avows. Catholic doctrine is wholly derived from it, but under how many veils and with what strange modifications! The plurality of persons in the unity of God has issued from the three first letters of the Tetragram, the *He* having merely been taken for the Son to avoid the deification of the mother, who must continue human, and who, in accordance with Postel's prevision, has later on seemed to absorb all the honour of the other persons. In the Sohar we find the Divine Mother, the second conception of the Elohim, co-operating in the creation, which would have been impossible without her. It is she who softens and moderates the severities of the paternal *Jod*, and who opposes water to fire, mercy to anger. "Fire," say the authors of the Sohar, "sprang forth from the Divine *Jod* like a serpent, and would have consumed the earth in its embraces, when the Divine Mother (blessed be her name!) led forth the waters and poured the liberating waves upon the serpent's burning head." Here, recollecting that Mary in Hebrew means "the Sea," or "the Salt of the Sea," we understand why she is represented with the new moon beneath her feet, for the rabbins say that the moon is the image of the divine ctels of the tetradic *He*, or maternal power of the Elohim, and we are no longer astonished at the immense influence imputed to a simple mortal, who by her immaculate conception goes back beyond the beginning of time. Her Son has given the honour of His birth to His mother, and the mother of the Eternal Son should be eternal as He is. Everything in the Catholic cultus recalls the numbers of Pythagoras, the triad of Divine Persons, the tetrad of the Gospels, the septenary of the seven gifts of the Holy Spirit and of the Sacraments, the sacred decade of the Decalogue, and the duodenary of the patriarchs and apostles. The frightful and Manichæan creation of hell counterpoising heaven, is only an exaggerated realisation of the equilibrating duad of Zoroaster, equilibrated in the tradition of the Sohar, by the two ancients, one of whom is the shadow of the other, the *Macroprosopus* and the *Microprosopus*, the shadow of humanity veiling God, and the light of God illuminating humanity, so that God seems to be for us the celestial man, while man is as the god of earth. Thus, all apparent doctrinal absurdities conceal the lofty and primeval revelations of the wisdom of the ages, and this is the reason that Christianity, enriched by so many opulent inheritances, prevailed over dessicated and impoverished Judaism, which had even ceased to understand the allegories of its Ark and Golden Candlestick. But by just so much as the internal riches of the universal and Kabbalistic doctrine are beautiful and precious, so are the materialised interpretations, given in our own days to these mysteries, deplorable. To deny the ancient doctrine is easy, but it refutes denial by the very fact of its existence. What must be done, then, to overcome the Sphinx of modern times? Its enigma must be explained and revealed to itself; all minds must be directed to that science which accounts even for the aberrations of faith, and a return must be made to the consciousness of a single revelation, permanent and universal in humanity. This revelation is analogy explained by the Logos, it is Nature unceasingly addressing herself to reason, it is the mathematical harmony of existences proving that the part is in proportion to the whole, and that the whole, necessarily indefinite in the absolute, necessitates without explaining it, the hypotheses of infinity.

It is in the vast field of this hypothesis that humanity unceasingly enlarges the circle of the sciences, and puts

back, by the conquests of knowledge, the limits of the
kingdom of faith. Now, what becomes of faith in presence of this ever aggressive boldness? Faith is that
confidence which impelled Columbus forward when America receded before him; it is belief in the unknown portions of the grand totality, whose existence is demonstrated
by its known parts; it will be plainly seen that it can be
no negation of reason, and that the object of faith being
necessarily hypothetical in form, since knowledge alone
can define, all definitions of it are a confusion of faith and
science. The true act of faith consists, therefore, solely in
the adhesion of our intelligence to the immoveable and
universal reason, which excludes all monstrosity and falsehood from the domain of first causes. The reasonable
being supposes necessarily the *raison d'être*, it is the absolute, it is the law; it is, because it is. God himself, in
whatever manner He be conceived, cannot exist without
raison d'être, only insanity will provide a personal, arbitrary, and unexplainable authority as the cause of immutable law. The impassible, unmerited, and irresponsible
supremacy of God would be the highest of injustices, and
the most revolting of absurdities. What, then, is Deity
for us? It is the undefined conception of a supreme personality. With dogmatic religions it is otherwise; for
them God is the first and final definition of the hypothetical world; but so often as God is defined He is limited,
and beyond His altars and cultus there dawn always on the
unwearied aspirations of humanity, the formless altar of the
coming worship, and the nameless inscription which the
Athenians placed on the most divine and philosophical of
their temples—IGNOTO DEO.

RELIGION FROM THE KABBALISTIC STANDPOINT.

The religious sentiment exists in man. Nature creates
nothing without an end in view. Religion is therefore
a real thing. What is, is! The religion of the Kabbalists
is at once all hypothesis and certitude, for it proceeds by
analogy from the known to the unknown. They recognise
religion as a need of humanity, as an evident and necessary
fact, and there alone for them is the divine, permanent,

and universal revelation. They contest nothing which exists, but account for everything. So their doctrine, by clearly marking the line of eternal separation between science and faith, gives the highest reason as a basis of faith, which guarantees it a lasting and incontestable duration. The popular forms of dogma, which alone can vary and be destroyed by one another, follow afterwards; the Kabbalist is not shaken by so small a thing, and provides at once a reason for the most astonishing formulæ of mysteries.

The word God expresses an ideal unknown in its essence, but well known by the various notions which men conceive of it. Above all these more or less intelligent conceptions rules that of a supreme intelligence and primal power. The abstract notion of the mathematical laws which govern universal motion, saddens the greater number of minds, who, seeing human liberty involved, in a certain sense, in the immense machine of the universe, find this machine, however grand it be, inferior to man, if it have no self-consciousness. There the universal sentiment is stayed, and phantasy does the rest. Some make God uni-personal, others multi-personal; it is no less certain that, for science, God is the most probably inevitable hypothesis of a supreme conscience in the eternal mathematics. We say most probably inevitable, out of respect to the liberty of conscience of sincere atheists, but the Kabbalah, which is the mother of the exact sciences, admits of no doubt when it authorises a hypothesis; and starting from the very existence of the religious sentiment, and from the name which signifies in all nations and for all men this invisible and infinite Being, the Kabbalah, we say, would conclude out of hand His necessary existence, because the Word attests the thing, as the shadow the body.

Man can only conceive of God as an infinite, or, rather, indefinite man, for whence would he obtain the terms of comparison for a different image of Divinity? It follows that whatsoever tends to define and personify God falls necessarily into anthropomorphism, and, consequently, into idolatry. For this reason the Kabbalists have distinguished the essence of Deity from the conception of Him in man, and to the human idea alone do they give a name, that of Jehovah or Adonai. As to the supreme reality, it is for them the *non ens*, the inappreciable, the unspeakable, the undefined. Estimating, moreover, as we have said, the Divine actualities by their mirage or shadow in the human mind, they consider that this shadow or mirage presents to us all the divine notions in an inverted way, and that science should reverse them to reach the harmony which results from the analogy of contrary things. This judgment by antithesis on vulgar notions is one of the greatest secrets of the Kabbalah, and one of the occult keys of exegesis. This key is represented by the two triangles, one upright and the other inverted, which form the six-pointed star of the mysterious seal of Solomon. Each of these two triangles, taken separately, represents an incomplete, and therefore radically false, conception of the Absolute; truth is in the union of the two.

Let us apply this to the interpretation of the Bible. Open it at the first chapter of Genesis, for example. We there find the history of the creation of the world in six days. Invert the sense, take the antithesis, and we shall have the creation of God in six nights. This requires explanation. God, says Genesis, made man in His own image, and philosophy proves that man also makes God after his own likeness. Well, the philosophical fact serves as basis to the theurgic affirmation, by virtue of the analogy of contrary things. The observed progress of the human mind, seeking to define God, revealed to Moses, by antithesis and by the analogy of contraries, the successive periods of creation. In two words, being unable to judge of Deity except by its reflection in the human mind, Moses followed all the outlines of that reflection and mentally reproduced them. Thus he obtained his cosmogony by the study of universal theology.

The first chapter of Genesis Kabbalistically inverted gives a luminous summary of universal theogony and its progressive growth in the human mind. Isolated, this summary would seem irreligious, and would represent divinity as a fiction of man, while the isolated text of Moses resembles a fable and distorts reason. But the two united, the star formed with the double triangle, we shall be astonished at the truth and light we shall discover. The text in the Bible can be read by all, the inversion we give as follows, so far as the first chapter is concerned.

The Occult Genesis.— Chapter I.

From the beginning the vastness of heaven and the extent of earth have created in man the idea of God.

But this conception was unformed and vague; it was a veil of darkness over an immense apparition, and the spirit of man brooded upon his conceptions as over the face of the waters.

And man said: Let there be a supreme intelligence. And there was a supreme intelligence. And man saw that this idea was good, and he distinguished the spirit of light from the spirit of darkness; and he called the spirit of light, God, and the spirit of darkness, the devil; and there was a realm of good, and a realm of evil. This was the first night.

Man also said: Let there be an impassable boundary between the dreams of heaven and the realities of earth. And man made a division, and he separated the things which were above from the things which are below, and so it was arranged. And man called his imaginary separation, heaven, and the evening and the morning were the second night.

And man said: Let us divide in our worship the mass of vapours from the dry vault of heaven. He gave to the heaven which was without water, the name of father; to the mass of vapours, the name of mother. And man saw that this was good. And he said: Let us make all the vegetation of symbols, where doctrines issue from one another, as the seed from the herb, and the herb from the seed, to germinate in heaven.

Let us plant the Edenic apple, with its mysterious and ever-renewing fruits. And the sky brought forth symbols like grass, and mystic trees flourished. And man saw that this was good. And the evening and the morning were the third night.

Man also said: Let there be mystical stars in my sky, and let them divide knowledge and ignorance, day and night! And it was so done; and man made two splendid divinities; a greater for the initiated, and a lesser for the common people, and small gods numerous as the stars. And he placed them in the asylum of his sky, to rule the earth and to divide knowledge and ignorance. And man saw that this was good, and the evening and the morning were the fourth night.

Man also said: Let the clouds bring forth flying dragons and fantastic animals. And the clouds brought forth monsters to terrify children, and winged devils. And man blessed them, saying: Increase and multiply, and fill heaven and earth; and man set in turn upon his altars all the animals of earth. And the evening and the morning were the fifth night.

Man then adored animals and reptiles of every kind; and having seen that this throve with him, he said: Let us make a god to our own image and likeness, and let Him be King of the mythological leviathans, of the celestial monstrosities, and the colossi of hell. And man created God to his own image and likeness, and said to Him: Grow and multiply Thy images: I give thee the empire of heaven and the domain of earth. And it was so done; and man saw all that he had created, and it was very good. And there was an evening, and there was a morning, which were the sixth night.

This occult Genesis was what Moses thought out before writing his own, and here is how he must have reasoned. Matter is the external form of mind, and it reacts on intelligences. Harmony results from the analogy of these two contraries. In the mind of man, which wars against matter, the laws of progress are analogous to those of progress and motion in matter itself. Therefore, the creation of the world outside of God must be parallel to that of the conception of God in man. And it is thus that, taking for numerical basis the sacred triad and its duplication, which signifies its reflection, Moses wrote his cosmogony of six days, analogous to the six great nights of human initiation into all religious mysteries. This key of revelation is also that of all religious practices, and of their influence on the civilisations and destinies of men. We will explain our meaning. The action of thought on form and the reaction of form on thought being given, it must be concluded that exterior objects act on man, or react on him as much as he can act on them. Man, following his divine ideal, builds a temple, then he is influenced by the temple he has made, and cannot enter it without remembering his God. The vague ideal has taken a shape, a body, and it becomes a visible and palpable reality. Must it be said that man deceives himself? Yes, doubtless, in all defects that the form attributes to his ideal, but not in all that it realises of perfection and truth. Thus, religion has made forms of worship which create that piety which is the strength of religion. Religious ceremonies are transcendental Kabbalistic practices, and proscribed magic would not be so dangerous except by the power of which it can avail itself in imitating them.

Religious observances are the Word in action. The man who performs them is, with or without his will, taken possession of by the doctrine whose rites he fulfils. If Julian could forsake Christianity, it was because he never practised it of his free will, and because also he was secretly addicted to the Hellenic ritual. The Church has full knowledge of this power, and it is for this reason that she less apparently concerns herself in interior sentiments than in exterior observances. Confess, she says, and go to Church, the rest will come of itself.

It is certain that the devotees of Black Magic evoked and saw the devil, thus giving form and actuality to the ideal of absurdity itself. The authentic reports of numerous magical prosecutions do not permit us to doubt this. The exaltation which produces vision is contagious, and propagates itself with the rapidity of electricity in all those whose mental strength does not protect them against this natural influence. Thus the so-called spiritual phenomena in America are to be accounted for. So also all serious theologians agree in declaring that a vision proves nothing in doctrinal matters. This declaration of the masters should warn the uninitiated against supernatural revelations and prophecies based on visions.* The great and unhappy Emperor Julian had the misfortune to believe sincerely in his gods on the faith of the apparitions procured him by Jamblichus and Maximus of Ephesus. This completely Jewish or Christian credulity placed him at the mercy of new enthusiasms, stronger and more widespread than his own, and he was overwhelmed and borne away by their current.

There is a story told of St Louis, the king, which does him infinite credit. He was sought out one day in great

* See Note 30.

haste and invited to witness a miracle occurring at that time in his chapel. Christ had become visible in the Host, and had manifested His presence before a multitude of witnesses. "Why should I go?" asked St Louis: "I believe in the real presence of Jesus Christ in the sacrament because I do not see it; if I saw it I should have to believe no longer."

A public miracle is a proof of exultation, and, consequently, of collective folly; it produces faith only as the pest produces the pest. The folly of the Cross, as St Paul calls it, has been merely a homeopathic remedy for the riotous and luxurious insanities of the age of the Caligulas and Neros. The fasts of the Stylites were only a deliberately unreasonable reaction from the suppers of Claudius and the feasts of Trimalcyon. St Anthony protested against Petronius, and the unclean animal which served him for a dog was the living satyr of Roman morals during the Decline. So Seneca, at the feasts of Nero, praised and envied the austerities of Diogenes, and St Anthony in his desert dreamed epics of intoxication and debauchery which shamed the inventions of Tigellinus. Harmony results from the analogy of contraries.

Exaltation is produced by physical means, which are— 1, Continued and periodical tension of the mind. 2, Fasting. 3, Images and pictures. 4, Music and chants analogous to the object of enthusiasm. 5, Fumigations and perfumes. Who then will be astonished if pious people are subject to revelations and ecstacies? But it is also true to say that by the same means we may attain to the intuitive vision of Kichatan, Pimpocan, or Parabavastu, see even the hideous phantom which is the synthesis of all false Gods, Satan. From this it follows that forms of worship are all essentially magical, as we have said, and that religious practices are a means of producing ecstacy; now the natural phenomena of ecstacy are what the vulgar habitually look on as miracles. These phenomena are—1, Insensibility to all pain and injury. 2, More or less lucid vision or somnambulism. 3, Extempore eloquence and knowledge infused by over-excitement and by direct communication with the common medium of the thoughts of others. 4, A fluidic superabundance capable of operating extraordinary effects, such as the immediate communication of ecstacy and all its phases, instantaneous cure of certain affections, apparent suspension of some natural laws, that of gravity, for example, which daily happens in America and elsewhere, when tables are seen to rise up and remain suspended in the air while no one is touching them. Similar phenomena are known to have been produced at the time of the convulsionaries of the cemetery of St Médard. Ecstatic women were lifted from the earth; even the foes of Jansenism bear witness to the fact, though they attribute the miracle to the devil, and cite in proof the immodesty of such aërial ascensions, where, as it is asserted in the controversies of the time, women's clothes were raised and tucked up of themselves, contrary to all physical laws, during the ascensional motion of the convulsionary's body. Does not this complication of the miraculous prove the presence of a natural agent, of a motive power brought into action by the over-excitement not only of one person but of a whole circle of enthusiasts? Nature is invariably the producer of miracles; fanaticism profits by them, science explains them; it is for wisdom to make use of them for the triumph of reason and progress.

KABBALISTIC CLASSICS.—THE TALMUD AND TALMUDISTS.

The importance of the Talmud, denied with derision by the ignorance of Christians and blindly sustained by the superstition of the vulgar among the Jews, rests entirely on the great and immutable truths of the sacred Kabbalah. The Talmud, whose name is composed of the sacred Tau and a Hebrew word which means instruction, contains seven distinct parts which science should be careful not to confound—The Mischna or Talmud of Jerusalem, the two Ghemara or Talmud of Babylon, the Thosphata or additions, the Berichta or appendices, the Maraschim or allegorical commentaries, and the Haggada or traditional histories.

The Talmudists, compilers of this multifarious work, belonged to three classes of Rabbins, whose successive authority has preserved, interpreted, and annotated the primitive texts. These were the Tenaimes or initiates, the Amoraimes or vulgar disciples of the former; then came the Massoretes and the Chachamines, blind preservers of texts, systematic calculators of signs, whose absolute value they did not know, doctors who no longer saw the Kabbalah, save in some mathematical diversions of a misunderstood Gematria and an inadequate Temurah. With the Jews, as with the Christians, the tendency of the official church or synagogue has always been directed towards the materialisation of signs, to substitute the hierarchy of temporal influence for the hierarchy of knowledge and virtue. Thus, previously to Christ's advent, prophecy, representing initiation and progress, had always been in open conflict or secret hostility with the priesthood; so also the pharisaism of the time of Jesus persecuted the new Essenian school of which He was the founder, and opposed itself later on to the more liberal teachings of the disciples of Hillel and Chamaï. Later still, the Kohanimes were again hostile to the initiated Israelites of the Alexandrian school, and the synagogue of Chachamines and Massoretes only left the Kohanimes or excellent masters in peace, thanks to an occultism which was doubtless one of the secret roots of Masonic institutions during the darkness of the Middle Ages. It is not, then, from the official synagogue that we must demand the keys of the supreme Kabbalah and the concealed sense of the Talmud; the present representatives of ancient Biblical theology will tell you that Maimonides, the great light of Israel, not only was no Kabbalist, but regarded the study of the Kabbalah as useless or dangerous. Maimonides, notwithstanding, venerated the Talmud, and thus resembled those Utopians in mysticism who reject Christianity while adoring the Gospel. Never at any period have inconsistencies dismayed the human mind!

If the Talmud had not been originally the great Kabbalistic key of Judaism, its existence, and the traditional veneration of which it is the object, would be incomprehensible. In fact, a text of the Israelite catechism imposes on all the Jewish faithful the consideration of the Talmud as the classical and authentic storehouse of Jehovah's secret laws, reserved by the wisdom of Moses for the traditional teaching of the sacerdotal tribe. We know, besides, that the body of this occult philosophy is positively what all serious initiates have considered the harmony of the Kabbalah. So the key of this science, which alone opens all the secret doors and enables us to penetrate all the profundities of the Bible, may be equally adapted to the mysteries of the Talmud—another conventional Bible fabricated only for testing the biblical keys. For this reason the Talmudists, anxious to show the allegorical sense of certain absurd passages in. the sacred books, surpassed this absurdity itself, and gave as the explanation of an improbable text a completely impossible commentary. Here is an example of their method :—

The author of the allegorical book of Job represents blind force under the emblem of two monsters, one of whom is terrestrial and the other marine, and which he names respectively Behemoth and Leviathan. Doubtless, it is not without a Kabbalistic meaning that he employs the number 2, or the duad, for blind force is always in competition with itself through the fatal or providential law of equilibrium, and just as in the eternal generation of things harmony results from the analogy of contraries, so in titanic excess of power, harmony is preserved or re-established by the antagonism of two equal forces. This is what the author of the book of Job intended to convey, and this is how the Talmudists surpassed his fiction.

"Elohim permitted the sea to produce a master for itself and the earth likewise a king. The sea brought forth Leviathan and the earth Behemoth from its lacerated womb. Leviathan was the great sea-serpent, and Behemoth the cherub with immense horns. But soon Leviathan so filled the sea that the waters cried out to Elohim, unable to find refuge. The earth lamented on her part, being ground under the feet of Behemoth and despoiled of all verdure. Elohim took pity on them, removing Leviathan from the sea and Behemoth from the earth. And He salted them to preserve them for the feast on the Last Day. Then shall the elect eat the flesh of Leviathan and of Behemoth, which will be found delicious because the Lord Himself hath preserved and prepared it."

Where is Voltaire to deride this monstrous salting, to laugh at this god-cook, and at this festal consumption of frightful mummies? We frankly grant him that rabbinical allegories often shock good taste and that fine flower of literary polish which they neither knew nor could divine. But what will scoffers say if by the fable of Leviathan and Behemoth they can be made to understand the solution of the enigma of evil? What would they answer were it said to them—The devil of Christianity represents the blind excesses of vital force, but Nature preserves and maintains equilibrium, monstrosities themselves have their cause and serve sooner or later for the nourishment of universal harmony. Fear not, therefore, phantoms; all that is above man must be more beautiful and better than man; below him is the beast, and the beast, however overgrown he may be, must be either the help or the pasturage of man! Cowardly children, fear no more that the devil will eat you! Be men, and it is you who will eat the devil, for the devil, that is, the spirit of absurdity and unintelligence, can never raise himself above the animal. This is what we are to understand by the final and Kabbalistic banquet of Behemoth and Leviathan!

Picture now, a Kohanimic or Massoretic commentator taking the Talmudic allegory on facts literally, establishing, for example, that the moon is the saltery of the Eternal Father, that He transported Leviathan and Behemoth thither after He had opened and salted them, and then you will have some notion of the Talmud's compilation, of its veiled lights and ingenuous errors.

The first Talmud, the only truly Kabbalistic one, was collected during the second century of the Christian era by the last chief of the Tenaims, Rabbi-Jehuda-Hakadosch-Hanassi, that is, Juda the most holy and the prince. The names of Kadosch and prince were given to the great initiates of the Kabbalah, and are preserved among adepts of occult Masonry and the Rose-Cross. R. Jehuda composed his book according to all the rules of supreme initiation; he wrote it within and without, as Ezekiel and St John have it, and he indicated its transcendental sense by the sacred letters and numbers corresponding to the Bereschit of the first six Sephiroths. The Mischna consists of six books, named Sederim, whose order and subject correspond to the absolute signs of Kabbalistic philosophy, as we are about to explain.

We have already said that the Kabbalists do not define God but adore Him in His manifestations, which are idea and form, intelligence and love; they suppose a supreme power based on two laws, which are stable wisdom and active intelligence, in other terms, necessity and liberty. It is thus that they form a primal triangle conceived in the following manner:—

Kether, the Crown.

Binah, *understanding.*　　　　　Chocmah, *wisdom.*

Then, as a reflection of this supreme conception in our own

ideality, they establish a second triangle in an inverted sense. Absolute justice, corresponding to supreme wisdom or necessity, absolute love, corresponding to active intelligence or liberty, and supreme beauty, which results from the harmonies of justice and love, corresponding to divine power.

Gedulah, *Love.*   Geburah, *Justice.*
Tiphereth, *Beauty.*

By joining and interlacing these two triangles there is formed the Burning Star or Solomon's Seal, that is, the complete expression of the theological philosophy of Bereschit, or universal Genesis.

On this basis R. Jehuda establishes the divisions of his work. The first book, or Sederim, corresponding to the notion of Kether, is entitled ZERAIM, the seeds, because in the notion of the Supreme Crown is contained that of the fructifying principle and of universal production. The second book corresponds to the Sephira of Chocmah; it is entitled MOED, and treats of sacred things in which nothing must be changed because they represent eternal order. The third book, in correspondence with Binah, liberty or creative power, treats of women and the family, and bears the name of NASCHIM. The fourth book, inspired by the idea of Geburah or justice, treats of crimes and their punishment; its title is NAZCHIM. The fifth book, corresponding to Gedulah, that is, to mercy and love, is entitled KADOSCHIM, and treats of consoling beliefs and things holy. Finally, the sixth book, analogous to the Sephira of Tiphereth, contains the most hidden secrets of life and the morality which concerns it; it treats of purifications, that is, of spiritual medicine, and bears the mysterious name of THAROTH or TAROT, expressing in itself alone all the concealed sense of the symbolic wheels of Ezekiel, and the name of Thorah, still given by the rabbins to the whole of Scripture. At the head of the Mischna, Rabbi Jehudah-Hakadosh-Hanassi, places the tradition of the old Jewish sages—the proverbs and maxims of Solomon's successors in the study of sovereign wisdom.

" By three things does the world subsist," said Simon the Just, " by the teaching of the law, the obligations of the cultus, and works of mercy." So we have once more the

Kabbalistic triangle, the fixed law, progressive religion, and charity, which is the common life and reason both of law and cultus.

Antigonous has said—" Be not as the servant who obeys for recompense ; let your reward be in your obedience itself, and be the respect of things above inherent in you." There is nothing superstitious in this, and it should be pondered over by a number of Catholics.

" The journey is short," said R. Tarphon, "the need is great, and the workmen are idle, but they will not gain less abundantly the meed of their day's labour; the Master answers for them, and his activity supplements their indolence." Promise of salvation to all, bold denial of sin and misery, responsibility of Providence, which excludes the notion of chastisement in the temporal necessity of suffering, suffering being looked on only as a spur to human indifference.

Akabiah said—" Know these three things well and thou wilt never sin—whence thou comest, whither thou goest, and unto whom thou art responsible." Here are three things which must be known in order to be never more guilty of deliberate sin. He who knows them will sin no more, otherwise he would be insane. He who does not yet know them cannot sin—how, in fact, can we fail over duties of which we are ignorant?

Such are the maxims collected by Judas the holy and princely at the head of the book of seeds or universal principles. He proceeds afterwards from the figurative to the positive, and treats of agriculture. Here Volney and Dupuis would discover the calendar in the highest mysteries of Judaistic religion, and why should not the calendar be found there? Does not the Crown of Kether correspond to the crown of the year, and are not religious festivals the visible jewels of that diadem of supreme belief? But the transcendent philosophy of the Talmud leaves far behind all the superstitions of materialised faiths. " He who says—I will sin and the day of pardon will absolve me, makes void the day of pardon, and will by no means be absolved from his wilful wickedness."

" Sins," say the Talmudists once more, " when they are between man and God can be absolved by God on the day of pardon, but when they are between man and man, that is, when they concern justice between brothers, man only can remit them by declaring before the law that restitution has been made." This is magnificent and needs no commentary.

Such is the wisdom which presides over the festivals of Israel described in the second book of the Talmud of Jerusalem, so closely connected with the first, since the one treats of the culture of fields and souls, the other of the cultus of God and of the symbolic calendar. The third book, or Sederim, is more particularly consecrated to women and the fundamental basis of the family. Talmudic jurisprudence does not divide man from woman, and does not seek, by irritating questions of respective equality or superiority, to establish antagonism in love; for Kabbalists, woman is neither the equal, nor servant, nor mistress, nor companion of man; she is man himself, conceived from the maternal or affectionate standpoint; woman possesses all the rights of man in man, and man respects himself in woman. "Never, therefore, let human folly divide those whom divine wisdom has pleased to unite, and woe to those who live single!" The questions of female emancipation and social equality are, in fact, the dreams of celibate women, and from the standpoint of natural law the celibate is a monstrosity. "O, soul of my soul, heart of my heart, and flesh of my flesh," said an initiate in the mysteries of the Mischna, with characteristic oriental pomposity, "you speak of becoming my equal! you would therefore become other than myself; you would tear your heart from mine, you would make two of those who are one; and just as God formed thee from the very bone and flesh of my body, you would draw something monstrous out of you to complete yourself and replace me in your nature. But when you are my rival in love, will you ever be my equal in desolation and regret?"

"The altar weeps," said a Talmudic rabbin, "when the husband and wife separate."

The fourth book of the Mischna, on injustice and compensation, is a collection of civil laws far superior to any code of the Middle Ages, and it is to the source of this secret legislation that the preservation of Israel through so many persecutions must be referred, as also its emancipation by industry, which is the final material term of civilisation, and the safeguard of all the political rights so painfully and completely recovered in our own days by the reinstated children of the old Jewish pariahs.

308   MYSTERIES OF MAGIC.

The books entitled Kadoschim and Tharoth complete by their details the body of the great Jewish traditions. Wide is the distance between this splendid work of initiation and the commentaries of the two Ghemara, or the Aristotelian legislation of Moses Maimonides, who was, nevertheless, an erudite doctor and great man, but he was prejudiced against the Kabbalistic keys of the Talmud by his horror of superstition and his reaction against mysticism. In his "Guide to the Lost," and in his "Eight Chapters," he directs Talmudic traditions to the common laws of nature and reason ; then in the *Jad Hacksaka* or "Assistance," he welds Jewish belief into a symbol of thirteen articles, which is a masterpiece of simplicity and reasonableness, but which, unconsciously to Maimonides himself, is so connected with pure Kabbalistic principles, that the first thirteen keys of the Tarot precisely correspond by their Kabbalistic signs to the thirteen fundamental articles of the symbol of Maimonides.

Masonic associations were formed in his time ; they collected the traditions lost to the Jews and proscribed by the Christians, for the very name and attributes of masonry have reference to the reconstruction of the Temple, that universal dream of the Kabbalah. "The reign of Messiah will come," said one of the fathers of the synagogue, "when the people shall be for ever delivered from the oppression of the kings of the earth."

"There is no true Israelite," said another master, "for whom the Temple is not an immediately realisable edifice, for he reconstructs it in his heart." The Temple was, therefore, a social Utopia, and a symbol of perfect government founded on the democratic hierarchy of merit and intelligence. The Templars, initiated in the East into this doctrine, were, therefore, real and dreadful conspirators, whom popes and kings were obliged to exterminate in order to secure their own existence. Then came the French Revolution, which confounded in a universal chaos the memories of the Amoraimes, the hopes of the Jesuits, and the initiations of Freemasonry. The spirit of the Ruins had breathed, and the rebuilders of the Temple left their plans, squares, and compasses in the débris.

The Temple, nevertheless, should and will be rebuilt, for human intelligence eventually attains its ends, and a perfect and rational Logos has never been articulated and repeated through the ages without creating, sooner or later, its realisation in proportion to the largeness of its aspirations and the exactitude of its calculations.

THAUMATURGICAL EXPERIENCES OF ÉLIPHAS LÉVI.

I.—Evocation of Apollonius of Tyana.

In the spring of the year 1854, I repaired to London to escape from internal disquietude, and to devote myself, without distraction, to study. I had letters of introduction to persons of distinction, and to those seeking communications from the supernatural world. Of the latter I met with several, and, amidst much affability, I discovered in them a fund of indifference and triviality. They immediately required of me the performance of prodigies, as from a charlatan. I was not a little discouraged, for, to speak truly, so far from being disposed to initiate others into the mysteries of ceremonial magic, I had always dreaded its delusions and weariness for myself. Moreover, such ceremonies require a paraphernalia which is expensive and difficult to collect. I immersed myself, therefore, in the study of the supreme Kabbalah, and thought no further of English adepts, when one day, on returning to my hotel, I found a note in my room. This note enclosed half of a card transversely divided, and on which I at once recognised the character of Solomon's seal, with a tiny slip of paper, on which was written in pencil: "To-morrow at 3 o'clock, in front of Westminster Abbey, the other half of this card will be given you." I kept this singular appointment. A carriage was waiting at the place; I held unaffectedly my portion of the card in my hand; a footman approached and made a sign to me, opening the carriage-door as he did so. Within there was a lady in black whose face was concealed by a thick veil; she motioned me to a seat beside her, displaying the other part of the card I had received. The door was shut, the carriage rolled away, and the lady raising her veil, I saw that my appointment was with an elderly person, who beneath her grey eyebrows had bright black eyes of preternatural fixity. "Sir," she began, with a strongly-marked English accent, "I am aware that the law of secrecy is rigorous among adepts; a friend of Sir B. L., who has seen you, knows that you have been asked for phenomena, and that you have declined to gratify curiosity. It is possible that you do not possess the necessary materials; I can show you a complete magical cabinet, but I must require of you, first of all, the most inviolable secrecy. If you do not guarantee this on your honour, I will give orders for you to be driven home." I made the required promise, and have kept it faithfully by not divulging the name, quality, or abode of the lady, whom I soon recognised as an initiate, not actually of the first degree, but still of a most exalted grade. We had several long conversations, during which she insisted always on the necessity of practical experiences to complete initiation. She showed me a collection of vestments and magical instruments, even lending me certain curious books which I was in want of; in a word, she determined me to attempt at her house the experience of a complete evocation, for which I prepared myself during twenty-one days, scrupulously observing the rules laid down in the Ritual.

All was completed on the 24th of July; it was proposed to evoke the phantom of the divine Apollonius, and to interrogate it about two secrets, one of which concerned myself, while the other interested the lady. The latter had at first counted on assisting at the evocation with a trustworthy person, but at the last moment this person proved timorous, and, as the triad or unity is rigorously prescribed in magical rites, I was left alone. The cabinet prepared for the evocation was situated in a turret; four concave mirrors were hung within it, and there was a kind of altar whose white marble top was surrounded with a chain of magnetic iron. On the marble the sign of the Pentagram was engraved and gilded; the same symbol was drawn on a new white sheep-skin stretched beneath the altar. In the middle of the marble slab there was a small copper brazier with charcoal of alder and laurel wood, while a second brazier was placed before me on a tripod. I was vested in a white robe very similar to those worn by Catholic priests, but longer and more ample, and I wore upon my head a chaplet of vervain leaves entwined about a golden chain. In one hand I held a new sword, and in the other the Ritual. I set alight the two fires with the requisite and prepared materials, and I began, at first in a low voice, but rising by degrees, the invocations of the Ritual; the flame invested every object with a wavering light, and finally went out. I set some more twigs and perfumes on the brazier, and when the flame started up again, I distinctly saw before the altar a human figure larger than life, which dissolved and disappeared. I recommenced the evocations, and placed myself in a circle which I had already traced between the altar and the tripod; I then saw the depth of the mirror which was in front of me, but behind the altar, grow brighter by degrees, and a pale form grew up there, dilating and seeming to approach gradually. Closing my eyes, I called three times on Apollonius, and, when I reopened them, a man stood before me wholly enveloped in a winding-sheet, which seemed to me more grey than white; his form was lean, melancholy, and beardless, which did not quite recall the picture I had formed to myself of Apollonius. I experienced a feeling of intense cold, and when I opened my lips to interrogate the apparition, I found it impossible to utter a sound. I therefore placed my hand on the sign of the Pentagram, and directed the point of the sword towards the figure, adjuring it mentally by that sign not to terrify me in any manner, but to obey me. The form thereupon became indistinct, and immediately after disappeared. I commanded it to return, and then felt, as it were, an air pass by me, and something having touched me on the hand which held the sword, the arm was immediately benumbed as far as the shoulder. Conjecturing that the weapon displeased the spirit, I set it by the point near me, and within the circle. The human figure at once reappeared, but I experienced such a complete enervation in all my limbs, and such a sudden exhaustion had taken possession of me, that I made two steps to sit down. I had scarcely done so when I fell into a deep coma, accompanied by dreams of which only a vague recollection remained when I recovered myself. My arm continued for several days benumbed and painful. The figure had not spoken, but it seemed to me that the questions I was to ask it had answered themselves in my mind. To that of the lady, an inner voice replied, "Dead!" (it concerned a man of whom she was seeking news). As for myself, I wished to learn whether reconciliation and forgiveness were possible between two persons who were in my thoughts, and the same interior echo impiteously answered, "Dead!"

Here I narrate facts as they actually occurred, I impose faith on no one. The effect of this experience on myself was incalculable. I was no more the same man; something from the world beyond had passed into me. I was neither gay nor depressed any longer, but I experienced a singular attraction towards death, without, at the same time, being in any way tempted to suicide. I carefully analysed what I had experienced, and, in spite of a keenly felt nervous antipathy, I twice repeated, at an interval of a few days only, the same experiment. The phenomena which then occurred differed too little from the former to require their addition to this narrative. But the consequence of these further evocations was for me the revelation of two Kabbalistic secrets, which, if universally known, might change in a short period the basis and laws of society at large.

Am I to conclude from this that I have really evoked, seen, and touched the great Apollonius Tyaneus? I am neither so far hallucinated as to believe it, nor sufficiently unserious as to affirm it. The effect of the preparations, the perfumes, the mirrors, the pantacles, is a veritable intoxication of the imagination, which must act strongly on a person already nervous and impressionable. I seek not to explain by what physiological laws I have seen and touched; I assert solely that I have seen and that I have touched, that I saw clearly and distinctly, without dreaming, which is sufficient ground for believing in the absolute efficacity of magical ceremonies. I look upon the practice, however, as dangerous and objectionable; health, both moral and physical, would not long withstand such operations, if once they become habitual. The old lady I speak of, and whom, subsequently, I had cause to complain of, was a case in point, for, in spite of her denials, I do not doubt that she continually practised necromancy and goëtic magic. She at times talked complete nonsense, at others yielded to insane fits of passion, whose object could be scarcely determined. I left London without revisiting her, but I shall faithfully keep my promise to say nothing whatsoever which may disclose her identity, or give even a hint about her practices, to which she doubtless devoted herself unknown to her family, which, as I believe, is numerous, and in a very honourable position.

II.—Ghosts in Paris — The Magician and the Medium—Éliphas Lévi and the Sect of Eugène Vintras.

THE other week Mr Home determined once more to leave Paris, that city where even angels and demons would not long pass for wonders, and would have no alternative but a speedy return to heaven or hell to escape oblivion and abandonment by mortals. Mr Home, with a dejected and disillusioned air, took leave of a lady of quality whose generous welcome had been one of his chief felicities in France. Madame B., hospitable on this day as always, wished to keep him to dinner; the mysterious being was on the point of accepting, when it was remarked that a Kabbalist, known in the world of occult sciences by the publication of a work entitled "The Doctrine and the Ritual of Transcendent Magic," was expected. Mr Home changed countenance at once, and declared, stammering and with visible anxiety, that he could not stay, and that the approach of this professor of magic caused him invincible fear. All that could be done to reassure him was useless. "I do not judge this man," he said, "I do not say that he is good or bad, I know nothing of him, but his atmosphere distresses me; near him I should feel deprived of strength and, as it were, of life." And after this explanation Mr Home hastened to take his leave.

This terror on the part of men of prestige in presence of the true initiates of science is no new fact in the annals of occultism. The history of a vampire who trembled at the approach of Apollonius may be found in Philostratus. We could not say whether Cagliostro would have worked miracles before Swedenborg, but he would have certainly dreaded the presence of Paracelsus or Henry Khunrath, had these great men been his contemporaries.

Be it far from us, notwithstanding, to denounce Mr Home as a low-class sorcerer, that is, as a charlatan. The celebrated American medium is as naïve and amiable as a child. He is an unfortunate being, alive with sensibility, unintriguing and defenceless; he is the sport of a terrible force whose nature he is unaware of, and his first dupe is undoubtedly himself.

The study of the phenomena produced in the presence of this young man are of the highest importance. On one occasion, a Polish gentleman, who was present at one of Mr Home's séances, placed a pencil and a sheet of paper between his feet on the ground, and requested some sign of the spirit's presence. For some moments nothing occurred; then suddenly the pencil was flung from one end of the room to the other. The gentleman stooped, picked up the paper, and found thereon three Kabbalistic signs which were understood by none present. Mr Home alone seemed to feel great annoyance at seeing them, and manifested a certain terror; but he refused to explain himself on the nature and meaning of the characters. They were, therefore, preserved and brought to that professor of magic whose approach was so dreaded by the medium. We have examined them, and their description is minutely as follows :—

They were scored deeply, and the pencil had almost torn the paper. They were drawn without order and not in a straight line. The first was the sign which the Egyptian initiates usually place in the hand of Typhon. A Tau with a double vertical line open in the form of a compass, a *crux ansata* with a circular ring above; below the ring a double horizontal line, and beneath this a double oblique line in the form of a V turned upside down.

The second character represented the cross of a grand hierophant with the three hierarchic transverse lines. This symbol, which belongs to the highest antiquity, is still the attribute of our sovereign pontiffs, and terminates the superior extremity of their pastoral crook. But the sign traced by the pencil had this peculiarity that the upper branch, the head of the cross, was double, and formed again the terrible Typhonian V, the sign of antagonism and separation, the symbol of hatred and eternal strife.

The third character was that which the Freemasons call the philosophic cross, a cross with four equal branches, with a point in each of the angles. But, instead of the four points, there were two only, placed in the two right hand angles, once more a sign of separation, strife, and negation.

The professor, whom it will be permitted us to distinguish

from the narrator, to avoid wearying our readers by an appearance of egotism, the professor then, Maître Éliphas Lévi, gave to those assembled in the drawing-room of Madame de B——, the scientific explanation of these three characters, in the following manner:—

"These three signs belong to the series of sacred and primitive hieroglyphs known only to initiates of the first order. The first is the signature of Typhon. It expresses the blasphemy of this evil spirit by establishing dualism in the creative cause. For the *crux ansata* of Osiris is an inverted lingam, and represents the paternal and active power of God—the vertical line issuing from the circle—fertilising the passive Nature—the horizontal line. To double the vertical line is to assert that nature has two fathers, it is the substitution of adultery in place of divine maternity, it is the affirmation of blind fatality, with the eternal conflict of appearances in the void as its result, instead of the affirmation of an intelligent first cause; it is, therefore, the most ancient, authentic, and terrible of the stigmata of hell. It signifies the *god atheist*, it is Satan's signature, and being of a hieratic character, it corresponds to the occult characters of the divine world.

"The second signature belongs to philosophical hieroglyphs; it represents the ascensional measure of the idea and the progressive extension of the form. It is a triple Tau inverted, it is human thought by turns affirming the absolute in the three worlds, and here this absolute is terminated by a fork, that is, by the sign of doubt and antagonism. So that if the first character means, *There is no God*, the rigorous signification of the second is that *There is no hierarchic truth*.

"The third, or philosophic cross, has been in all initiations the symbol of Nature and her four elementary forms; the four points represent the four inexpressible and incommunicable letters of the occult Tetragram, that eternal formula of the great Arcanum G∴ A∴ The two points on the right side represent power, those on the left love, and the four letters should be read from right to left, beginning at the top right-hand side, and thence proceeding to the bottom letter of the left, and so on for the others, making St Anthony's Cross. The suppression of the two points to the left signifies, therefore, the negation of the Cross, the negation of mercy and love;

the affirmation of the absolute reign of force, and its eternal antagonism, from above below, and from below above; the glorification of tyranny and revolt; the hieroglyphic sign of the nameless vice which rightly or wrongly was reproached against the Templars; the sign of eternal disorder and despair."

Such then are the first revelations of the hidden science of the Magi on these extra-natural manifestations. And now let us be permitted to compare other contemporary apparitions of phenomenal writings with these signatures, for it is a process which science should institute before appealing to the tribunal of public reason. No investigation and no indication should, therefore, be disdained.

At Tilly-sur-Seulles, in the vicinity of Caen, a series of inexplicable phenomena occurred some years ago, under the influence of a medium named Eugène Vintras. Certain ridiculous processes and a swindling law-suit caused this thaumaturge to fall speedily into oblivion and contempt; he was attacked besides with virulence in pamphlets whose authors were formerly admirers of his doctrines, for the medium Vintras meddles with dogmatism. One thing is, nevertheless, noteworthy in the invectives to which he is subject, that his adversaries, while seeking to defame him, acknowledge the truth of his miracles, and content themselves with ascribing them to the devil.

What, then, are these authenticated miracles of Vintras? On this point we are better informed than any one, as will presently be seen. Official reports signed by honourable witnesses, artists, doctors, priests, otherwise irreproachable, have been communicated to us; we have examined eye witnesses, and, better than all, we have seen for ourselves. The matters deserve to be related with some detail.

A writer who, to say the least, is eccentric, and whose name is M. Madrolle, now lives at Paris. He is an old man whose family and connections are reputable. He wrote formerly in the most exalted Catholic strain, and received the most flattering encouragements from ecclesiastical authority, even approbations emanating from the Apostolic Seat; finally, he saw Vintras, and drawn away by the prestige of his miracles, he has changed into an obstinate sectarian and an irreconcilable enemy of the hierarchy and priesthood.

At the period when Éliphas Lévi published his *Dogme et Rituel de la Haute Magie*, he received a broadside from M.

Madrolle which astounded him. The author maintained loudly therein the most unheard of paradoxes in the confused style of ecstatics. According to him, life was sufficient for the expiation of the greatest crimes, since these were the result of a death sentence. The most wicked men, being the most unfortunate of all, appear, in his eyes, to offer God a more sublime expiation. He declaimed against every check and every condemnation. "A religion which condemns is a condemned religion!" he cried, and subsequently preached the most complete licence under the pretence of charity, forgetting himself so far as to say that the most imperfect and apparently reprehensible act of love was of more value than the most perfect prayer. Finally, he denied the existence of the devil with a vehemence which was occasionally full of eloquence.

"Imagine to yourself," said he, "a devil tolerated by God, commissioned by God! Imagine, further, a God who has created the devil, and permits him to fall furiously on creatures so weak already and so quick to deceive themselves! A God of the devil, in fine, seconded, anticipated, and even surpassed by a Satanic God." The rest of the performance was of similar force. The professor of magic was almost frightened, and obtained the address of M. Madrolle. It was not without some trouble that he discovered this singular pamphleteer, and the conversation which then took place between them was very nearly as follows:—

Eliphas Lévi.—" Monsieur, I have received your *brochure;* I have come to thank you for your present, and venture at the same time to testify to you my astonishment and regret."

M. Madrolle.—" Your regret, Monsieur. Will you kindly explain yourself? I scarcely understand you."

" I regret poignantly, monsieur, to see you guilty of errors into which I fell formerly myself, but I had, at least, the excuse of youth and inexperience. Your brochure misses fire because it wants moderation. Your intention was, doubtless, to protest against errors in faith and abuses in morals, but it turns out that it is faith itself, and morality, that you attack. The exaltation which overflows in your little work must itself do you considerable wrong, and some of your best friends have been reasonably anxious about your health."

" I don't doubt it! They have said, and still say, that I

am mad, but it is not the first time that believers must experience the folly of the Cross. I am excited, monsieur, and you would be the same in my place, because it is impossible to be unmoved in the presence of prodigies."

"Ah! you speak of prodigies; this interests me. Come now, frankly and between ourselves, what wonders are in question?"

"What wonders indeed if not those of the great prophet Elias, returned to earth under the name of Pierre Michel!"

"I see, you are speaking of Vintras; I have heard his performances spoken of. But does he really work wonders?"

At this M. Madrolle leaped on his chair, lifted his eyes and hands to heaven, and ended by smiling with a condescension which was akin to profound piety.

"Does he work wonders, monsieur? Why, the greatest, the most astounding, the most incontestable, the most veritable miracles performed on earth since the days of Jesus Christ? . . . What! Thousands of Hosts appear on altars where there were none; wine rises in empty chalices, and it is no delusion, it is wine, a delicious wine; celestial music is heard; the fragrance of another world diffuses itself, and, finally, blood—true human blood which doctors have examined—oozes and sometimes flows copiously from the Hosts, leaving mysterious characters thereon. I tell you here what I have seen, what I have heard, what I have touched, what I have tasted! And you would have me keep cool in the face of an ecclesiastical authority which finds it easier to deny all than to examine the smallest thing."

"Allow me, monsieur; it is pre-eminently in matters of religion that authority can never be wrong. What is good in religion is the hierarchy, and what is evil is anarchy; to what, in fact, would sacerdotal influence be reduced if you assert as a principle that we must believe in the testimony of our senses rather than in the decisions of the Church? Is not the Church more visible than all your miracles? Those who behold miracles and do not see the Church are more to be pitied than the blind, for they have not even the resource of being led."

"Monsieur, I know all this as well as yourself, but God cannot contradict Himself; He will not allow sincerity to be deceived, and the Church herself cannot decide that I am blind when I have eyes. . . . Stay, here is what we read in the letters of John Hus, towards the end of the forty-third letter:—'A doctor told me that I should submit to the Council in all things, and then all would be well and legitimate for me. He added: If the Council said you had one eye though you have two, it must still be maintained that the Council is not wrong. I answered that if the universal world declared such a thing, so long as I had the use of my reason, I could not admit it without injuring my conscience.' With John Hus I reply to you that truth and reason existed before any Church and Council."

"I must interrupt you, my dear monsieur. Formerly you were a Catholic; you are such no longer, but consciences are free. I simply submit that the institution of hierarchic infallibility in matters of religion is far more reasonable and far more incontestable than all the miracles in the world. Besides, what should not be done to preserve peace? Do you think that John Hus would not have been a greater man had he sacrificed one of his eyes to universal concord instead of inundating Europe with blood? Oh, monsieur, let the Church decide when it pleases that I am blind of one eye, I beg but a single favour, it is to tell me of which one, that I may close it up henceforth, and see by the other only with irreproachable orthodoxy."

"I confess I am not orthodox after your fashion."

"I see that well; but let us return to the prodigies! You have then seen, touched, smelt, and tasted! But, exaltation apart, will you describe me something circumstantially and in detail, something which above all shall be evidently miraculous? Am I overbold in asking this?"

"Not the least in the world, but what shall I select? There are so many. . . . Stay!" he added, after a moment's reflection, and with a slight emotional tremor in his voice, "the prophet is in London and we are here. Very well; now if, mentally only, you should ask him to send you the Sacrament immediately, and if in a place closen by yourself, in your own house, say, in a cloth or in a book, you should find a Host on your return, what would you think?"

"I should declare the fact inexplicable by common critical methods."

"Well, sir," cried M. Madrolle triumphantly, "that is exactly what frequently happens to me! Yes, monsieur, when I wish it, that is, when I am prepared and trust that I am worthy of it, I find the Host where I ask for it, I find it really and palpably, though often ornamented with little miraculous hearts which might have been the work of Raphael."

Éliphas Lévi, who felt ill at ease during the discussion of facts with which a kind of profanation of the most sacred things was mixed up, took his leave of the former Catholic writer, and went away pondering on the strange influence of Vintras, who thus had turned this old-established faith and this old scholar's understanding.

Some days after, the Kabbalist Éliphas was aroused at an early hour in the morning by an unknown visitor. He was a white-haired man, dressed entirely in black, having the countenance of an extremely devout priest; in a word, he was of highly respectable appearance. This ecclesiastic was provided with a letter of introduction couched in the following terms:—

"DEAR MASTER,

"I present you an old scholar who would jabber with you the jargon of sorcery. Receive him as myself (that is, as I have myself received him), by getting rid of him as quickly as possible.

"Yours wholly in the sacred and saintly Kabbalah,
"AD. DESBARROLLES."

"Monsieur l'abbé," said Éliphas, smiling as he finished reading, "I am quite at your service, and can refuse nothing to the friend who has written to me. So you have seen my excellent pupil Desbarrolles?"

"Yes, monsieur, and have found him a most amiable and erudite man. I consider yourself and him to be worthy of the truth recently manifested by the astounding miracles and undoubted revelations of the archangel St Michael."

"Monsieur, you honour us. Has Desbarrolles astonished you by his knowledge?"

"Undoubtedly! He possesses in no common degree the secrets of chiromancy; on the mere inspection of my hand he told me nearly all the history of my life."

"He is quite able to; did he go into minute details?"

"Sufficiently minute to convince me of his extraordinary knowledge."

" Did he say that you were formerly curé of Saint-Louis, in the diocese of Tours, that you are the most zealous follower of the ecstatic Eugène Vintras, and that your name is Charvoz ? "

This was a perfect *coup de théâtre;* the old priest at each of these questions leaped on his chair; when he heard his name, he turned pale and started up as if a spring had been touched and impelled him.

"You are indeed a magician," he cried. "Charvoz is certainly my name, but it is not the one which I now pass under—I call myself La Paraz."

" I know it; La Paraz is your mother's name. You have left an enviable position, monsieur, that of a country curé with a most charming presbytery, to share the perturbed existence of a sectarian."

" Say, rather of a great prophet ! "

" Monsieur, I believe confidently in your own good faith, but you will permit me to examine slightly the character and mission of your prophet."

"Yes, Monsieur, investigation, broad daylight, the light of science, are precisely what we seek. Come to London and see for yourself—the miracles are permanent !"

"Monsieur, will you first give me some scrupulously exact details on these miracles ?"

"As many as you please." And thereupon the old priest began to narrate things which everyone would have considered impossible, but which in no way astonished the professor of transcendent magic. For instance, one day, in a paroxysm of enthusiasm, Vintras was preaching before his heterodox altar, twenty-five persons being present at his discourse. There was an empty chalice on the altar, one well known to the Abbé Charvoz, for he had brought it from his church at Mont Louis, and was absolutely certain that the sacred vessel had neither secret conduit nor double bottom.

"To prove," said Vintras, "that God Himself inspires me, He has revealed to me that the chalice is about to fill with drops of blood under the semblance of wine, that all of you may taste the juice of the vine of futurity, that wine which we shall drink with the Saviour in the kingdom of His Father."

"Seized with astonishment and fear," said the Abbé Charvoz, " I went up to the altar, took the chalice, looked into it, and found it quite empty. I turned it upside down before all, then descended to kneel at the foot of the altar, holding the chalice in my two hands. Suddenly, a slight noise, like a drop of water falling from the ceiling into the chalice, was distinctly audible, and a drop of wine appeared at the bottom of the cup. All eyes were turned towards me, and then to the ceiling, for our simple gathering was held in a poor room; the ceiling had neither break nor fissure, nothing was seen to fall, and, nevertheless, the sound of the drops as they descended increased in rapidity, while the wine rose towards the brim. When full, I passed it slowly under the eyes of all present, then the prophet wetted his lips with it, and all, one after another, tasted the miraculous wine. No recollection of delicious savour gave any idea of it. . . . And then what shall I tell you of the blood-prodigies which daily astonish us? Thousands of bleeding hosts fall on our altars. The sacred stigmata are manifested to those who desire it. Hosts, which at first were white, are slowly imprinted with characters and bleeding hearts. Must we believe that God would abandon the holiest of things to the wonder-working of the demon? Must we not rather adore and confess that the hour of the supreme and final revelation has arrived?"

While thus speaking, the Abbé Charvoz had the same kind of nervous tremor in his voice which Éliphas Lévi had already noticed in M. Madrolle. The magician bent his head thoughtfully, then all at once—"Monsieur," he said to the Abbé, "you have one or more of these miraculous hosts about you—be good enough to show me them!"

"Monsieur!"

"I am convinced that you have; why attempt to deny it?"

"I do not deny it," said the Abbé Charvoz, "but you will excuse me from exposing to the investigations of incredulity the objects of the most sincere and exalted faith."

"Monsieur Charvoz," said Éliphas gravely, "incredulity is the distrust of an ignorance almost certain to deceive itself. Science is not incredulous. In the first place, I believe in your conviction, since you have embraced a life of privation and even of reprobation for your unhappy opinion. Show me, therefore, your miraculous hosts, and be assured of my respect for the objects of a sincere adoration."

"Well," said the Abbé Charvoz, after some further demur, "I will do so," and he unbuttoned the top of his black waistcoat and took out a small silver reliquary, before which he knelt down with tears in his eyes and prayers on his lips. Éliphas knelt beside him, and the Abbé opened the reliquary, which contained three hosts, one whole and the others almost in a paste, and as if kneaded with blood. The whole host bore upon each side a heart in relief on the centre—a clot of blood in the shape of a heart, and which seemed formed within the host itself in an inexplicable manner. The blood could not have been applied from without, for the colouring by imbibing had left white the particles which adhered to the outer surface. The phenomenon had the same characteristics on both sides. The professor of magic was seized with involuntary trembling, which did not pass unnoticed by the old priest, who, having again venerated and locked his reliquary, took out an album from his pocket and silently placed it in the hands of Éliphas. It contained copies of all the bleeding characters which had been seen on the hosts from the beginning of the miracles and ecstacies of Vintras. There were hearts of all kinds, emblems of all sorts, but three above all excited the curiosity of Éliphas to the highest point.

"Monsieur l'Abbé," said he to Charvoz, "do you know these three signs?"

"No," answered the Abbé, frankly; "but the prophet assures us that they are of palmary importance, and that their secret significance is soon to be made known—that is, at the end of time."

"Well, monsieur," said the professor of magic, solemnly, "even before the end of time I will explain them to you; these three Kabbalistic signs are the devil's signature!"

"Impossible!" cried the old priest.

"It is true," replied Éliphas, with emphasis.

The signs were as follows:—1. The star of the microcosm, or the magic Pentagram, that star wherein the human figure was sketched by Agrippa, with the head in the ascending point and the four members in the four other points—the Burning Star which, when inverted, is the hieroglyphic sign of the goat of black magic whose head can then be sketched in the star with the two horns above, the ears on the right and left, and the beard below, sign of antagonism and blind fatality, the goat of lewdness assaulting heaven with its horns, a sign execrated even in the Sabbath by initiates of a superior order. 2. The two Hermetic serpents, but the heads and tails, instead of converging in two parallel semicircles, diverged, and there was no intermediate line representing the caduceus. Above the serpents' heads was the ominous V, the typhonian fork, the character of hell. On the right and left were the sacred numbers III. and VII. relegated to the horizontal line which represents passive and secondary things. This, therefore, was the significance of the character :—Antagonism is eternal; God is the strife of blind causes which perpetually create by destroying; religious things are passive and passing, boldness makes use of them, war profits by them, and discord is perpetuated by both. 3. Lastly, the Kabbalistic monogram of Jehovah, the Jod and He, but reversed, which forms, according to the doctors of occult science, the most frightful of blasphemies, meaning, in whatever way it might be read :—' Fatality alone exists, God and spirit do not exist. Matter is the grand totality, spirit the dream of demented matter. The form is more than the idea, the woman more than the man, pleasure more than thought, vice more than virtue, the multitude greater than its chiefs, children above their fathers, and madness more than reason.'"

This is what was hieroglyphically written in characters of blood on the pseudo-miraculous hosts of Vintras! We declare on our honour that all the facts above stated are such as we have described them, and that we ourselves have explained the characters according to true magical science and the true Kabbalistic keys.

The disciple of Vintras also imparted to us the description of the pontifical vestments given, said he, by Jesus Christ Himself to the pretended prophet in one of his ecstatic sleeps. Vintras caused the vestments to be made, and clothes himself in them to perform his miracles. Their colour is red; he must wear on his forehead the cross in the form of a lingam, and must have a pastoral crook, surmounted by a hand of which all the fingers are shut save the thumb and index. Now, all this is diabolical in the highest degree, and is not this intuition of the symbols of a lost science something truly marvellous, for it is transcendent magic which, basing the universe on the two pillars of Hermes and Solomon, has divided the metaphysical world into two intellectual zones, one white and luminous, comprising positive ideas, the other black and opaque, including those which are negative, and which has given to the synthetic notion of the first the name of God, and to the synthesis of the second the name of the devil, or Satan. The sign of the lingam borne on the forehead is, in India, the distinctive mark of the worshippers of Seeva, the destroyer; for this sign, being that of the Great Magic Arcanum, which is connected with the mystery of universal generation, to carry it on the forehead is to make a profession of doctrinal immodesty.* Now, say the Orientalists, on the day when modesty shall have ceased in the world, the world, abandoned to debauchery, which is barren, will soon come to an end for want of mothers. Modesty is the acceptation of maternity. The hand with three fingers closed expresses the negation of the triad and the assertion of purely material forces. A hand showing only the auricular is equivalent, in the sacred, symbolical language, to the exclusive affirmation of passion and *savoir-faire*. It is the scurrilous and materialistic version of the great words of St Augustine—" Love, and then do what you will." Now, compare this sign with M. Madrolle's doctrine :—" The most imperfect and apparently most culpable act of love is of greater value than the best of prayers." If it be asked, what is that force which independently of human will, and more or less of human knowledge (for Vintras is an illiterate and uneducated man), formulates its doctrines with signs buried in the ruins of the ancient world, unearths the mysteries of Thebes and Eleusis, and writes the most cultured of Indian reveries in the most secret Hermetic alphabet, we answer that these wonders are reproduced by magnetic intuition of the fluidic thought-pictures in the universal vital fluid.

* See Note 31.

III.—THE MAGICIAN AND THE SORCERER.—SECRET HISTORY OF THE ASSASSINATION OF THE ARCHBISHOP OF PARIS.

An artisan called one day on Éliphas Lévi. He was a man of some fifty years old, of impressive appearance, straightforward and rational in speech. Questioned on the object of his visit, he answered, "You should know well enough; I come to beg and entreat of you to return me what I have lost."

It must be owned in sincerity that Éliphas Lévi knew nothing of his visitor, nor of the object he was in search of, so he answered: "You suppose me a greater sorcerer than I am; I know not who you are nor what you seek, so if you think I can serve you, you must explain and define your request."

"Well, since you refuse to understand me, you will at least recognise this," said the unknown, taking from his pocket a little black, well-thumbed book. It was the Grimoire of Honorius, which consists of an apocryphal constitution of Honorius II. for the evocation and control of spirits, plus some superstitious recipes. The work was the manual of wicked priests who practised black magic during the darkest periods of the Middle Ages. Sanguinary rites, mixed with profanations of the Mass and the consecrated elements, formulæ for bewitchment and witchcraft, finally, practices which idiocy alone could permit and knavery counsel, are to be found therein. For the rest, the work is complete of its kind, and, being consequently scarce at the booksellers, is run up by amateurs to a high price at public auctions.

"Dear monsieur," said the workman, sighing, "from the age of ten years I have not once neglected to perform my office. This book never leaves my person, and I conform rigorously to all the prescriptions it contains. Why, then, have those who came to me deserted me? Eli, Eli, Lamma"——

"Stop!" cried Éliphas. "Do not caricature the most formidable words which agony ever caused to be uttered in the world. Who are the beings that come to you by the virtue of this horrible book? Do you know them? Have you promised them anything? Have you signed any compact?"

"No," interrupted the owner of the Grimoire, "I do not know them, and have entered into no bond with them; I know only that their leaders are good, the intermediaries alternately good and evil, the inferiors evil, but not blindly so, nor without the possibility of growing better. He whom I have evoked, and who has so often appeared to me, belongs to the most exalted hierarchy, for he is of comely appearance, well clad, and always gave me favourable answers. But I have lost the first page of my Grimoire, the most important, that which bears the autographic signature of the master spirit, and since then he has no longer appeared to me when I call him. I am a lost man, I am bereft like Job, I have no longer strength nor courage. Oh, master, I conjure you,—you who have only a word to say, but a sign to make, and the spirits will obey,—take pity on me, and recover for me what I have lost!"

"Lend me your Grimoire," said Éliphas. "What name do you give the spirit which appears to you?"

"I call him Adonaï."

"And in what language was his signature?"

"I do not know, but I suppose it was in Hebrew."

"Hold," said the professor of transcendental magic, tracing two Hebrew words at the beginning and end of the book, "here are two signatures that spirits of darkness will never counterfeit. Go in peace, sleep well, and evoke no more phantoms!"

The workman departed, and eight days after he returned to the scientist.

"You have restored hope and life to me," he said; "my strength has partially returned; by the signatures which you gave me, I can soothe those who are in pain and liberate the obsessed, but *him*, him I cannot see, and until I behold him I shall be sad unto death. Formerly, he was always near me; sometimes he touched me in the night and woke me to tell me everything I wished to know. Master, I entreat you, grant that I shall see him again!"

"Whom?"

"Adonaï."

"Do you know whom Adonaï is?"

"No; but I wish to behold him once more."

"Adonaï is invisible."

"I have seen him."

"He is without form."
"I have touched him."
"He is infinite."
"He is pretty much about my own height."
"The prophets tell us that the hem of his vestment sweeps away the stars of the morning."
"He has a very neat surcoat and the whitest linen."
"Holy Scripture, moreover, says that none can behold him without dying."
"He has a benevolent and jovial countenance."
"But how do you proceed to obtain these apparitions?"
"I perform all that is appointed in the great Grimoire."
"What! even the bloody sacrifice?"
"Certainly."
"Wretch! But what is the victim?"

At this question the artisan started slightly; he grew pale, and his look was disconcerted.

"Master, you know better than I do what it is," he said humbly, and in a low voice. "Oh, it cost me a hard struggle, above all the first time, to cut with one blow of the magic knife the throat of the innocent creature! One night I had just ended the mournful rites, I was seated within the circle on the inner threshold of my door, and the conflagration of the victim was being finished in a large fire of alder and cypress-wood. Suddenly, close at hand I again saw it, or rather felt it pass; a heartrending cry rang in my ears, and from that moment I seem to be hearing it always."

Éliphas rose and looked fixedly at his interlocutor. Was there a dangerous madman capable of renewing the atrocities of the Seigneur de Retz before him? The appearance of this person was, however, gentle and honest. No, it was not possible!

"But come now, this victim, say plainly what it is! You suppose that I know it already, and perhaps I do, but I have my reasons for wishing you to tell me."

"According to the magic ritual, it is a kid of a year old, virginal and unblemished."

"A real kid?"

"Certainly. Rest assured that it was neither a plaything nor a straw-stuffed dummy!"

Éliphas breathed freely.

"Come!" thought he, "this man is not a sorcerer worthy

of the stake. He knows not that when the abominable authors of the Grimoires speak of a virgin kid, they mean a young child." "Well," he continued, turning to his client, "give me the details of your visions; what you have related interests me in the highest degree."

The sorcerer, for he may well be called by this name, then recounted a series of strange facts, of which two families had been witnesses, and which were perfectly identical with those of the medium Home—hands issuing from walls, motions of furniture, phosphorescent apparitions, &c. One day, the rash novice in magic dared to call Astaroth, and beheld the apparition of a gigantic monster, with the body of a hog and the head taken from the skeleton of a colossal ox. All this was told with a truthful accent, with a certitude of having actually seen, which excluded any suspicion of the good faith and complete conviction of the narrator. Éliphas, as an æsthete in magic, was delighted at this lucky find. A true mediæval sorcerer, a sincere, undoubted sorcerer, in the nineteenth century! A sorcerer who had beheld Satan, under the name of Adonaï, dressed like a citizen; and Astaroth under his true, diabolical form! What an artistic object, what an archæological treasure!

"My friend," he said to his new pupil, "I am inclined to assist you in recovering what you have lost. Take my book, conform to the prescriptions in the Ritual, and come to see me again in eight days' time."

On the date appointed, a fresh conversation took place, and then the artisan declared that he was the inventor of a life-saving machine of great naval importance; one thing only was amiss in it, it would not work; there was an imperceptible defect in the movement. What this defect was the demon of perversity alone could reveal, and it was absolutely necessary to invoke him.

"Beware!" said Éliphas Lévi. "Try this Kabbalistic invocation instead for nine days," and he gave him a leaf in manuscript. "Begin this evening, and to-morrow let me know what you have seen, for to-night you will have a manifestation."

The next day our individual did not fail to appear.

"I was woke up suddenly, towards one in the morning," said he. "I saw a great light at the foot of my bed, and in this light *a phantom arm*, making passes in front of me as if to magnetize me. Then I again fell asleep, and a little time after, being woke up a second time, I saw the same light, but it had changed its place. It had passed from left to right, and in its luminous depth I distinguished the semblance of a man, who was looking at me with folded arms."

"What was he like?"

"Much of your size and appearance."

"'Tis well! Go and continue doing what I prescribed."

Nine days elapsed and then came a new visit from the adept, who this time was all radiance and animation. The moment he saw Éliphas, "Thanks, master!" he cried, "the machine works—some unknown persons have provided me with the necessary funds for the completion of my enterprise. I have regained peace and sleep — all thanks to your power!"

"Say rather, thanks to your own faith and docility. And now, farewell, I must study..... What now? Why do you assume that supplicating air? What more do you want?"

"Oh! if you would only"——

"Well, what? Have you not had all and more than you wanted, and there has been no question of remuneration?"

"Yes, truly," said the other, sighing; "but I long to see him again."

"Incorrigible!" exclaimed Éliphas.

Some weeks after, the professor of transcendent magic was roused about two in the morning by a severe pain in the head. For several moments he anticipated congestion of the brain; but he rose, lit his lamp, opened the window, walked up and down in his study, then, soothed by the fresh morning air, returned to bed, where he slept profoundly. Subsequently, he had a nightmare; he saw with terrific realism the ox-headed giant of the artisan-mechanist. This monster pursued and attacked him. When he awoke it was broad daylight, and some one was knocking at the door. Éliphas rose, threw a garment round him, and opened it. There was the workman!

"Master," said the latter, entering hastily, and with an alarmed aspect, "how are you?"

"Excellently well," answered Éliphas.

"But were you in no danger to-night about two o'clock?"

Éliphas was not under cross-examination, and no longer remembered his indisposition.

"In danger?" he repeated. "In none that I know of."

"Were you not attacked by a monstrous phantom, which tried to strangle you? Did you experience nothing?"

Éliphas recollected.

"Yes," said he, "I had truly an incipient apoplexy and a horrible dream. But how did you know of it?"

"At the same hour an invisible hand struck me roughly on the shoulder and woke me with a start. I then dreamed that I saw you in the clutches of Astaroth. I sat up in bed, and a voice cried in my ear, 'Get up and hasten to your master's help, he is in danger!' I rose hurriedly, but where should I run to first? What danger menaced you? The voice had told me nothing on these points. I determined, therefore, to wait till sunrise, and as soon as it was daylight I hastened to you, and here I am."

"Thank you, my friend," said the Magus, offering his hand. "Astaroth is a vicious jester, but I had merely a slight determination of blood to the head, and now I am perfectly well. You may be quite reassured and go back to your work."

Strange as the facts may be which have just been narrated, a still more extraordinary, and this time tragical, drama remains to be revealed. It is connected with the sanguinary event which, at the beginning of this year, plunged Paris and all Christendom in sorrow and stupefaction, an occurrence which no one suspected had black magic mixed up with it.

During the winter, at the beginning of last year, a bookseller informed the author of the *Dogme et Rituel de la Haute Magie* that an ecclesiastic had been inquiring for his address, and manifested a strong desire to see him. Éliphas Lévi did not feel himself inspired with such immediate confidence towards this stranger as to expose himself without precautions to his visits; he named a friend's house where he would be present with his faithful pupil Desbarrolles. On the appointed day he repaired to Madame A——'s, and found the ecclesiastic, who had already been awaiting him several minutes. He was a young, somewhat emaciated man, with a prominent pointed nose and dull blue eyes. His bony and projecting forehead had a breadth disproportioned to its height; his head was elongated behind, his smooth and short hair, parted at the side, was of grizzly flaxen, approaching light chestnut, but with a queer disagreeable tint about it. His mouth was sensual and combative; his manner, however, was affable, his voice gentle, and his utterance occasionally a little embarrassed. Questioned by Éliphas Lévi on the object of his visit, he answered that he was in search of the Grimoire of Honorius, and he desired information from the professor of occult science on the best way to procure the little book, now scarcely to be met with.

"I would give fully a hundred francs for a copy of this Grimoire," said he.

"The work in itself is worthless," answered Éliphas. "It is a pseudo-constitution of Honorius II. that you may have seen quoted by some learned collector of apocryphal constitutions."

"Not exactly, but I wish to fulfil a fancy; I have something to perform."

"I trust that something is not an evocation of black magic; you know, as I do, Monsieur l'Abbé, that the Church has always condemned, and still condemns severely, everything connected with those forbidden practices."

A slight smile, mingled with a kind of sarcastic irony, was the sole response of the abbé, and the conversation fell. The chiromancist Desbarrolles was, however, examining the priest's hand attentively; the latter perceived it, a natural explanation ensued, and the abbé cheerfully offered his hand to the experimentalist. Desbarrolles knitted his brows and seemed embarrassed. The hand was damp and cold, the fingers smooth and spatulated; the mountain of Venus, or that part of the palm which is connected with the thumb, was of unusual development, the line of life was short and broken; there were crosses in the centre of the hand and stars on the mountain of the moon.

"Monsieur l'Abbé," said Desbarrolles, "if you have not received solid religious instruction, you may easily become a dangerous sectarian, for you are drawn on the one hand towards the most exalted mysticism, and on the other to the most concentrated obstinacy and incommunicativeness in the world. You investigate much but imagine more, and as you confide your fancies to no one, they may well attain proportions which will make them your real enemies. Your habits are contemplative and a little indolent, but it is an indolence whose arousing is perhaps to be dreaded.

You are impelled towards a passion which your calling
. . . . but, your pardon, Monsieur l'Abbé, I think I have
passed the limits of discretion."

"Say all, Monsieur, I can hear, and wish to know, everything."

"Well, if, as I do not doubt, you turn to the profit of
charity all the restless activity which is caused you by the
desires of the heart, you must be blessed very often for
your good works."

The abbé gave once more that doubtful and ominous
smile, which lent his pale face such a singular expression.
He rose and took leave, without telling his name, and without it occurring to any one to ask it. Éliphas and Desbarrolles conducted him to the staircase out of respect for
his priestly dignity. Near the head of the stairs he turned
and said slowly, "Before long you will hear of something.
. . . . You will hear me spoken of," he added, emphasizing
each word. Then he bowed, waved his hand, and, turning
without another word, descended the staircase. The two
friends returned to Madame A——.

"There goes a most extraordinary person," said Éliphas.
"What he uttered at parting seemed very like a menace."

"You intimidated him," said Madame A——. "Before
you arrived he was beginning to speak out plainly, but you
talked of conscience and the commandments of the Church,
till he no longer dared to confess what he wanted."

"Pshaw! What did he want then?"

"To see the devil."

"Did he think I carried him in my pocket?"

"No, but he is aware you give lessons in the Kabbalah
and magic, and hoped you would help him in his enterprises. He informed my daughter and myself, that, in his
country presbytery, he had already performed an evocation
one evening by the help of a common Grimoire. He told us
that a sudden gust of wind seemed to shake the building,
the rafters groaned, timbers creaked, doors trembled, windows
were flung open with great noise, and hissing sounds were
heard in every corner of the house. He awaited the formidable vision, but saw nothing, no monster presented
itself; in a word, the devil refused to appear, and this is
the reason that he is in search of the Grimoire of Honorius,
where he hopes to find more powerful conjurations and
efficacious rites."

"But this man must be a monster or a madman."

"He may be madly in love," said Desbarrolles. "He is tormented by some passion, and absolutely looks for nothing less than that the devil should take interest in it."

"But then how shall we hear him talked about?"

"Who knows? Perhaps, he has planned the abduction of the Queen of England or the Sultana?"

Here the conversation ended, and an entire year elapsed without any intelligence concerning the strange young priest. On the night between the first and second of January 1857, Éliphas Lévi was awakened with a start of agitation consequent on a bizarre and ominous dream. He seemed to be in a dilapidated Gothic room, very like the deserted chapel of an old castle. A door concealed by black drapery opened out of this chamber; behind the drapery the ruddy light of candles could be just caught sight of, and it appeared to Éliphas that, prompted by a curiosity which was full of terror, he approached the black drapery, which parted thereupon, and an outstretched hand seized his arm. He beheld no one, but heard a low voice saying in his ear :—"Come and see thy father, who is about to die!"

The Magus woke with palpitating heart and brow bathed in perspiration. "What does this dream signify?" thought he. "My father is long since dead—why tell me that he is about to die?" The following night the same dream came to him, with the same circumstances, and Éliphas Lévi again woke up, hearing those words in his ear :—"Come and see thy father, who is about to die!"

This repetition of the nightmare painfully impressed Éliphas. He had accepted an invitation to dine, on the third of January, in some cheerful society, but he now wrote to excuse himself, finding that he was ill-disposed for the gaiety of an artist's banquet. He remained therefore in his study; the weather was cloudy; at noon he received a visit from one of his pupils in magic, M. le Vicomte de M——. The rain was then falling in such torrents that Éliphas offered the Vicomte his umbrella, which the latter would not accept. A courteous little dispute followed, which ended by Éliphas walking back with his pupil. Out of doors the rain stopped, the Vicomte found a coach, and Éliphas, instead of returning home, crossed the Luxembourg mechanically, issued by the gate which opens on the Rue d' Enfer, and found himself in front of the Panthéon. A double line of barriers improvised for the novena of St Geneviéve, showed pilgrims the way to St Etienne-du-Mont. Éliphas, whose heart was saddened and, therefore, disposed to prayer, followed this path and entered the Church. It might then have been four in the afternoon. The church was filled with the faithful, and the daily office was performed with great recollection and unusual solemnity. The banners belonging to the churches of the city and the suburbs bore witness to the public devotion towards the virgin who had saved Paris from famine and invasion. At the bottom of the church the tomb of St Geneviéve was ablaze with lights. Litanies were chanted, and the procession issued from the choir.

After the cross-bearer, accompanied by his acolytes and followed by the choir-boys, came the banner of St Geneviéve, and the Genevevan nuns in double file, clothed in black, with white veils on their heads, blue ribbons with the medal of the legend round their necks, and a taper in their hand, surmounted by a little Gothic lantern, as tradition gives to the images of that saint. After the nuns of St Geneviéve came the clergy, and finally the venerable Archbishop of Paris in a white mitre, and wearing a cope which on either side was held back by his two vicars-general. The prelate, leaning on his pastoral staff, proceeded slowly, and blessed to the right and left the crowd, which knelt down as he passed. Éliphas saw the Archbishop for the first time, and remarked that his features expressed goodness and mildness, but a look of great fatigue, and even a painfully concealed nervous suffering, were noticable. The procession passed to the end of the church, traversing the nave; it returned by the aisle to the left of the porch, and made a pause at the tomb of St Geneviéve, then it went back by the right aisle, continuing the chant of the Litany. A crowd of the faithful followed the procession, walking immediately behind the Archbishop. Quite pensive and affected by the pious solemnity, Éliphas mingled with this group, so as to pass more easily through the mass, which was closing up, and to regain the door of the church. The head of the procession had already returned into the choir, the Archbishop had reached the nave railing, where the passage was too narrow for three persons to walk abreast; the Archbishop was, therefore, in front and his two vicars-general were behind him, still holding the corners of his cope, which was thus open and drawn back, so that the prelate exhibited his breast protected only by the cross-ornamented embroideries of his stole.

It was then that those who were behind the Archbishop saw him stagger, and an out-call was heard, made in a loud voice, but without noisy clamour. What was uttered? It seemed to be—" Down with the goddesses!" but this was considered a mistake, so much did the words seem misplaced and senseless. The exclamation was nevertheless repeated two or three times, and some one cried, " Save the Archbishop!" while others vociferated, " To arms!" The crowd thereupon receded, overturning chairs and barriers and hurrying towards the door. There were shrieks from children, the clamours of women, and Éliphas, borne away by the crowd, was in a way carried out of the church, but the last glance he was able to cast therein fell on an awful and ineffaceable tableaux.

In the middle of a circle, increased by the terror of all who surrounded him, the prelate was standing alone, still supported by his crozier and sustained by the stiffness of the cope which his vicars-general had dropped, and which now hung down to the ground. The archbishop's head was slightly turned, his eyes, and disengaged hand, were raised towards Heaven; there was all the epic of the martyr in his mien; it was a submission and a holocaust, a prayer for his people and pardon to his murderer. The day was waning and the church had begun to darken; the archbishop, with his uplifted arms, illuminated by a last sunbeam which stole across the nave, stood out in relief against a black background, wherein could be dimly distinguished a pedestal without a statue, on which was inscribed these two words of the Passion of Christ, *Ecce homo*, and further still into the gloom an apocalyptic painting, representing the four last plagues about to be let loose on the world, and the whirlwinds of the abyss following the dusty train of the wan horse of death.

In front of the Archbishop an upraised arm, sketched in shadow like an infernal silhouette, was clutching and brandishing a knife, while, through all the uproar at the bottom of the church, the chant in the choir continued, as the harmony of the heavenly spheres is prolonged for ever regardless of our revolutions and anguish.

Éliphas Lévi had been borne outside by the crowd, and

had issued by the right door. At almost the same moment, the left opened violently, and an infuriated crowd poured out of the church, seething round a single man, who was held by fifty hands, and whom a hundred more strove to buffet. This individual, later on, complained of maltreatment at the hands of the police, but as soon as they could distinguish him in the tumult, they protected him against the rage of the mob.

Women followed him, crying " Kill him! "

" But what has he done? " was asked by other voices.

" The wretch! He has stabbed the Archbishop," answered the women. Other people, however, coming out of the church, contradictory statements multiplied.

" The Archbishop has been terrified and is ill," said some.

" He is dead," others declared.

" Did you see the knife? " asked a new speaker. " It is as large as a sword, and the blood streamed from the blade."

" Our poor monseigneur has lost one of his shoes!" ejaculated an old woman, clasping her hands.

" It is nothing, nothing at all," said a pew-opener thereupon. " You may go back into the church—monseigneur is not wounded, they are about to enthrone him."

At this the crowd made a motion to re-enter the church.

" Keep back! keep back! " uttered the solemn and mournful voice of a priest at this very moment. " The service cannot continue, the church is being closed, it has been profaned! "

" How is the Archbishop? " asked a man.

" Monsieur," answered the priest, " the Archbishop is dying, and perhaps even while I am speaking he may be dead."

The crowd dispersed in consternation to spread this disastrous news through all Paris. A bizarre circumstance took place in the case of Éliphas, and caused a certain distraction from his profound sorrow at what had taken place. In the midst of the tumult, an elderly lady of exceedingly respectable appearance took hold of his arm and claimed his protection. It was his duty to respond to this appeal, and when they were out of the crowd, she said: " How fortunate I am to have met with a man who laments this great crime, which so many wretches rejoice over at this moment! "

"What say you, Madam? How can any creature exist who is depraved enough to exult over such a calamity?"

"Silence!" the old lady enjoined, "perchance we are overheard. Yes," she continued, lowering her voice, "there are some who are delighted at this event; there was a sinister-looking man saying to the crowd, when interrogated as to what had taken place: 'Oh! it is nothing. A spider has fallen.'"

"No, Madam; you misunderstood. The crowd would never have endured such an abominable remark, the man would have been immediately arrested."

"Would to God that every one thought like you!" said the lady; then she added, "I commend myself to the charity of your prayers, for I see plainly that you are a godly man."

"That is not perhaps the verdict of the world at large," answered Éliphas.

"And what does the world signify to us?" asked the lady with animation. "It is lying, calumnious, impious! Perhaps it speaks ill of you, and I am not surprised; if you knew what it said of me, you would understand very well why I despise its opinion."

"Does the world speak evil of you, Madam?"

"The worst evil that can possibly be conceived."

"What is that?"

"It accuses me of sacrilege."

"You alarm me! And of what sacrilege, if you please?"

"Of a guilty farce which I am supposed to have played to deceive two children on Mount Salette."

"What! are you——?"

"I am Mademoiselle de la Merlière."

"I have heard your law-suit spoken of, Mademoiselle, and the scandal which it occasioned, but it seems to me that your age and respectability should have set you above the reach of such an accusation."

"Come and see me, Monsieur, and I will introduce you to my solicitor, M. Favre, a man of talent whom I am seeking to turn to God."

Thus conversing, the two speakers reached the Rue du Vieux-Colombier. The lady thanked her temporary escort, and renewed the invitation to visit her.

"I will endeavour to do so," said Éliphas, "and if I

come I shall ask at the door for Mademoiselle de la Merlière."

"Be sure that you don't, I am not known by that name —ask for Madam Dutruck."

"Dutruck, so be it, Madam! I humbly present you my respects," and they separated.

The trial of the assassin began, and Éliphas, reading in the newspapers that the accused was a priest, that he was of the society of St Germain l'Auxerroie, that he had been a country curé and that he seemed excited to the pitch of insanity, recollected the pallid priest who, a year before, had been in search of the Grimoire of Honorius. But the description of the criminal given in the public prints contradicted the suspicion of the magical professor, for most of them gave him black hair. "It is not he, then," thought Éliphas, "but there still rings in my ear, notwithstanding, the speech which this atrocious crime would now explain, 'You will not fail to learn something before long, and to hear me spoken of.'"

The trial took place with all the frightful circumstances universally known, and the accused was condemned to death. The next morning Éliphas read in a legal print the description of this scene unheard of in the annals of justice, and a mist passed over his eyes when he saw in the description of the criminal, "He is fair."

"It must be he," said the professor of magic.

A few days afterwards some one present at the trial, and who had contrived to sketch the profile of the accused, shewed it to Éliphas.

"Let me copy this design," said the latter, quite palpitating with terror.

He did so, and took it to his friend, Desbarrolles, asking, without previous explanation, "Do you know this face?"

"Yes," answered Desbarrolles, with animation, "it is that of the mysterious priest whom we saw at Madam A——'s, and who wished to perform magical evocations."

"Well, my friend, you confirm me in my sad conviction, That man whom we saw we shall never more see; the hand you examined has been imbrued in blood. We have indeed heard him talked of as he asserted, for do you know the name of this pale priest?"

"Oh, my God!" cried Desbarrolles, changing colour, "I fear that I do."

"It is true—he is the miserable Louis Verger."

Some weeks after, Éliphas Lévi was chatting with a bookseller whose speciality was old works on the occult sciences. The subject was the Grimoire of Honorius.

"It is seldom to be met with now," said the bookseller; "the last copy in my possession I disposed of to a young priest who offered me a hundred francs for it."

"A young priest! Can you recall his appearance?"

"Perfectly! But you must know it yourself, for he told me he had seen you, and indeed it was I who referred him to you."

Thus beyond doubt, the unhappy priest had obtained the fatal Grimoire, and had prepared himself for murder by a succession of sacrileges. The wretched man felt certain he would not die; he believed that the emperor would be forced to pardon him; some honourable exile awaited him; his crime had brought him immense notoriety; his musings would be worth their weight in gold at the booksellers; he would become fabulously rich, would attract the notice of some great lady, and would marry beyond the seas. By similar promises the phantom demon formerly prompted and drove on Gilles de Laval, lord of Retz, from crime to crime. A man capable of evoking the devil, according to the rites of the Grimoire of Honorius, is so far on the road to evil that he is inclined to all kinds of hallucinations and falsehoods; but the aberrations of perversity do not constitute madness, as the execution of this criminal proved. The desperate resistance he offered to his executioners is well known. "It is a deception," he cried; "I cannot die thus. An hour only—one hour—to write to the emperor; he would save me!"

Who, then, had deceived him? Who had promised him life? Who had assured him beforehand of an impossible clemency, for his reprieve would have outraged the public conscience? Ask all this of the Grimoire of Honorius!

Two things in this tragical history correspond with the phenomena of Home,—the stormy sound heard by the wicked priest during his first evocation, and the perturbation which prevented him speaking his mind in the presence of Éliphas Lévi. There may also be noticed the apparition of a sinister man rejoicing in the public sorrow, and making a truly diabolical speech in the middle of the dismayed crowd—an apparition seen only by the ecstatic of La Salette, the too notorious Mademoiselle de la Merlière, who has the aspect, notwithstanding, of a good and respectable person, though one strongly impressionable, and perhaps liable to talk and act unconsciously under the influence of a kind of ascetic somnambulism.

NOTES.

NOTE 1, The Sphinx (page 14).—This "eternal enigma" is elsewhere said to be the synthesis of ancient wisdom, as the Cross is the key of future wisdom. It is the law of mystery which guards the door of initiation to keep off the profane. It represents the Great Magic Mystery, whose elements are wholly expressed by the septenary, which, however, does not give the final word. Every man who thinks is an Œdipus called on to divine the enigma of the sphinx, or perish. The harmony of reason and faith, of science and religion, of liberty and authority, has become in modern times the true problem of the sphinx. Faith succeeding the daring dreams of antique initiation has been, in humanity, the voluntary blindness of the Theban king. The modern Œdipus has rebelled against the expiation of a crime which he has ceased to understand; he has sought to reopen his eyes, and the monstrous phantom of the sphinx has reappeared more menacing and terrible than ever. The empire of humanity is offered once more to him who can divine the enigma; we must reply to the human head and do battle with the lion's claws; intelligence henceforth is inseparable from power.

It will be seen that this interpretation is purely moral, and as such casts some light on the passage in the text. Eliphas Lévi's mystical version of the question propounded by the sphinx—how is the tetrad changed into the duad and explained by the triad?—has also some light cast on it by the statement that the material elements analogous to the divine elements are conceived as four, explained as two, and exist finally as three.

NOTE 2, Azoth (page 15).—Eliphas Lévi has censured the Indian hierophants for confusing the blind and dead light of the universal agent with the living and intellectual light of the creative, originating cause, and he has censured the Neo-Platonic initiates for confusing it with the body of the *protoplastes*. His own terminology, however, is likely to cause some embarrassment, at any rate to those unaccustomed to the tortuousness of mystical reasoning. Surely, if the God of the sages, "the efficient and final principle of the *magnum opus*," be denominated Azoth, this name should not be applied to the "universal seducer," the "monster to be overcome," that is, the Astral Light!

NOTES. 343

NOTE 3 (page 19).—The secret of the *Regnum Dei* or Kingdom of Jesus Christ is elsewhere said to be the discovery of the stable centre between the unopposed and unlimited power of sacerdotal autocracy on the one hand, and republican tyranny emancipated from all duties imposed and consecrated by the hierarchy on the other. This stable centre is declared to have been discovered by the Christian hierophants " who aspired to create a society dedicated to self-sacrifice by solemn vows, protected by rigorous rules, recruited by initiation, and which, itself the sole custodian of great religious and social secrets, would constitute kings and pontiffs without being exposed to the corruptions of power."

NOTE 4 (page 30).—The four sacred names are—JHVH, that is, Jehovah; ADNI, that is, Adonaï; AHIH, pronounced Eieie; and AGLA.

NOTE 5 (page 41).—Eliphas Lévi's whole theory on this subject originates in a sarcasm of Voltaire: " *Si Dieu a fait l'homme à son image, l'homme le lui a bien rendu.*"

NOTE 6 (page 63).—The received translation is—" The devil is the father of lies."

NOTE 7 (page 67).—But also two seek each other that they may become one. And the Nucterneron, according to the Hebrews, says that when Adam and Eve entered the nuptial couch they were two, but when they rose they were four.

NOTE 8 (page 76).—It should be noticed that while the Great Magic Agent is called the world's eye, imagination is characterised as the *eye of the soul*. Now the faculty of intuition is very closely connected, and in one sense identical with imagination, so that the Astral Light may be called the *intuition of Nature*.

NOTE 9 (page 83).—" Apollonius Tyaneus wholly enveloped himself in a mantle of fine wool, on which he set his feet, and which he drew over his head; then he bent his spinal column into a semicircle, and closed his eyes after performing certain rites, such as magnetic passes and sacramental words, whose object was to concentrate the imagination and determine the action of the will. The woollen mantle is of great use in magic, and is the usual vehicle of sorcerers when proceeding to the Sabbath, which proves that the sorcerers did not really go to the Sabbath but that the Sabbath came to the sorcerers when isolated in their mantle, and brought to their Translucid images analogous to their magical preoccupations, mixed with reflections of all similar acts accomplished previously in the world.".

NOTE 10 (page 89).—" All true initiates have recognised the immense utility of labour and suffering. Suffering, says a German poet, is the dog of that invisible shepherd who leads the flock of humanity. To learn how to suffer, to learn how to die, is the gymnastics of eternity, the noviciate of immortality. This is the moral of Dante's 'Divine Comedy,' sketched so early as the time of Plato in the allegorical picture of Cebes. This picture, whose description has come down to us, is at once a magical and philosophical monument. It is an extremely perfect moral synthesis, and at the same time the most audacious demonstration of the Great Arcanum, of that secret whose revelation would revolutionise heaven and earth. This secret is the royalty of the sage, the crown of the adept who in the beautiful allegory of Cebes is represented descending victorious from the summit of trials."—*Histoire de la Magie*, p. 147.

NOTE 11 (page 90).—The instrument of philosophical and moral alchemy which Eliphas Lévi here refers to is that faculty of the risen and emancipated mind—

> "By which from evil things,
> And things held worthless is the soul enrich'd."
> —*A Soul's Comedy*.

The light proceeding from the Translucid and investing the world, "the light that never was on land or sea," that light in which the "fairy-gifted poet beholds THE SAME THING EVERYWHERE," is the true alchemy which transmutes into gold "not only all metals, but also earth itself, and even the refuse of the earth." The province of supreme and divine magic is to perpetuate the transmutation of the poet.

NOTE 12 (page 97).—"There is not a people, and I may say there is not a man in possession of his true self, for whom the temporal universe is not a great allegory or fable which must give place to a GRAND MORALITY."—Louis Claude de Saint-Martin, *the philosophe inconnu*, in his *Tableau Naturel des Rapports qui existe entre Dieu l'Homme et l'Univers.*

NOTE 13 (page 105).—In utter contradiction to this express statement, and the occult tradition which it may be supposed to represent, Eliphas Lévi insists elsewhere that created spirits must be clothed with bodies, the limitation consequent on which alone making their existence possible. Otherwise, he says, the spirit would be everywhere, but everywhere in so imperceptible a degree that it would act nowhere. Even if it be correct that the Indian hierophants confuse the divine pneuma with the Astral Light, the blunder is not so ridiculous as this virtual identification of the intellectual and immortal essence with a tenuous vapour indefinitely diffused whenever the enclosing capsule is destroyed.

NOTE 14 (page 106).—How can this statement be harmonised with that in the chapter on the Kabbalah which says that the elect are invariably in a minority, because "the conditions of initiation can only be fulfilled by a small proportion of a vast multitude renewed from age to age, and which will continue *till the election and salvation of all?*" This passage is intelligible only on the supposition of successive reincarnations of the same soul in different generations of humanity, in some one of which it will receive the crown of the adept.

NOTE 15 (page 113).—The Generation of Spirits of the Air. "Lemures gignuntur per deperditiones æstaticas spermatis et sanguinis menstrualis. Sunt ephemeri et maximi mortales. Constant aere coagulato in vapore sanguinis vel spermatis, et quasi bullâ, quæ si ferro frangatur perit anima imperfecta lemurum. Quærunt simplices et credulos, fugiunt autem et doctos et ineptos insolentes ebriosos, &c. Timidi sunt et fugitivi sicut aves cœli et semper mori reformidant, quia bulla æris est vita eorum et statu facile corrumpitur."—PARACELSUS.

NOTE 16 (page 120).—It has just been remarked that these unemancipated spirits, these slaves of the elements, these beings devoid of free will, can only be incarnated as animals, and now we are told that they can be incarnated as vicious and imperfect men. Imperfection is common to the whole of humanity, even on the pinnacles of adeptship, and vice may degrade man below the level of the beast, but it cannot make him merely an animal.

NOTE 17 (page 144).—It is almost unnecessary to say that this pseudo-constitution is not the work of the pope to whom it is attributed. It is a production of the twelfth century; Leo III. was elected in 792. Those who believe it to be genuine, if there be any at the present day, would be rendering good service to occultism by tracing its history during the period which succeeded the pontificate of its pretended author. See on this question the *Dictionnaire des Sciences Occultes*, in Migne's *Première Encyclopédie Théologique*, article Léon III.

NOTE 18 (page 150).—Elsewhere the author tells us that the figures of the seven planets with their squares are found in the *Petit Albert*, but that these allegorial and mythological symbols have become too classical and commonplace to be successfully traced on talismans in these days, and that we must have recourse to more expressive and recondite *signs*. But the signs which he himself provides in addition to those in the text are certainly anything but vulgarised. The Kabbalistic signs of the seven spirits are—a lion-headed serpent for the Sun, a globe crossed by two crescents for the Moon, a dragon gnawing the hilt of a sword for Mars, a lingam for Venus, a hermetic caduceus and cynocephalous for Mercury, the burning pentagram in the claws or beak of an eagle for Jupiter, an old cripple or a serpent twined about the heliacal stone for Saturn. All these signs are found on archaic gems, and particularly on the Gnostic talismans known by the name of Abraxas. In the collection of talismans of Paracelsus, Jupiter is replaced by a priest in sacerdotal garb, a substitution which is not wanting in a well-defined mystical significance."

NOTE 19 (page 163).—In an interesting notice of this *Grimoire* found in his "History of Magic," Eliphas Lévi, with much appearance of plausibility, fixes its authorship on Cadulus, bishop of Parma, that is, the anti-pope set up by the emperor Henry IV., and a man who by his intrigues, debauchery, and simony, may be supposed to have been capable of every enormity. The argument, however ingenious, is of course entirely conjectural, and no proof is offered that the personage in question had any connection with the sorcery and diabolism of his century. What is certain in any case is this, that the saintly and eminent pontiff whose name it bears, neither was, nor could have been its author. By a typographical error, or an error in transcription, this Grimoire is occasionally attributed to Honorius III.

NOTE 20 (page 169).—But this moral disorder must not be necessarily attributed to the individual who pays its physical penalty; otherwise, what of hereditary diseases?

NOTE 21 (page 180).—And yet we have been told that the Astral Light is projected by the thumbs and palms of the hands, in which case magnetic passes are certainly more than signs; the will of the operator projects the vital fluid by means of them; but the eternal right of self-contradiction, formally claimed by Charles Baudelaire as an imprescriptible part of liberty, has ever been included among the rights of the Frenchman.

NOTE 22 (page 192).—We are distinctly and authoritatively told in the chapter devoted to Spiritual Transition that the divine and immortal spirit of a man who has lived viciously is held captive after death by its astral body, that in this envelope it torments dreaming girls, and haunts the places where the pleasures of its human life elapsed, in which case, in blank and utter contradiction to the statement made in the text, it is evident that souls can and do exist in the terrestrial atmosphere after they have departed this life, and that as vicious men are unhappily very numerous the air must be swarming with imprisoned spirits. Without being in any way committed to the spiritualistic hypothesis, which Eliphas Lévi was bent on disproving, and, it may be added, of vilifying, one is bound to confess that the animus thus gratified in the face of consistency and reason, is a triumph for the doctrine against which it is directed.

NOTE 23 (page 201).—This is apparently the *verbum inenarrabile* of the Alexandrian School, called Ararita by the Kabbalists. " All is enclosed in one word, and in a word of four letters—it is the Tetragram of the Hebrews, the Azoth of the Alchemists, the Thot of the Bohemians, and the Kabbalistic Tarot. This word expressed in such various ways signifies God for the profane, man for the philosophers, and gives to the adept the final word of human science and the key of divine power ; but he alone can avail himself of it who understands the necessity of never revealing it." (*Dogme de la Haute Magie*, p. 90.) This is undoubtedly that word referred to in the chapter on Divination, the occult name of the Great Arcanum, " of which the sacred Tetragram itself is only the equivalent and image." Those who are mystified by the childish puzzle in which it is there supposed to be enclosed will be gratified to learn that according to the *Histoire de la Magie* the *mot unique* hidden in every sanctuary is Agla. See chapter on "The Kabbalah," page 290 of this digest.

NOTE 24 (page 202).—That is, how can gold be produced from salt, sulphur, and mercury of the common and material kind ? But the gold of the philosophers can be, and is, produced from the salt, sulphur, and mercury of the philosophers. The so-called metallic transmutation, not being accomplished by the manipulation of ordinary metals and minerals, is not really the transmutation of metals, but the application of the adapting powers of the divine and immortal spirit to the dead exterior substances of the material world.

NOTE 25 (page 204).—The following mystification was appended as an "important note " on this subject in the second edition of the *Dogme et Rituel de la Haute Magie*. For the mineral work, the first matter is mineral exclusively, but it is not a metal ; it is a metallic salt. This matter is called vegetative, because it resembles a fruit, and animal, because it produces a species of milk and blood. It contains the fire used to dissolve it.

NOTE 26 (page 216).—And it is absolutely true that if a man be bidden to look for anything by another whose will dominates but perturbs his own, and whom he fears to displease, his anxiety to find it will sometimes so confuse him that he will not see the object, though it may be under his very eyes.

NOTE 27 (page 218).—This reasoning is ingenious but purely Machiavelian, and the legend itself represents the deliberate performance of a miracle to cover and, what is worse, to verify a falsehood. It should also be noticed that the falsehood was of the most inexcusable kind, being told not to conceal a good deed from those who would interfere to prevent it, but that the merit of the deed might be increased by its secrecy. It is a curious instance of human subtlety turning to evil even such a beautiful counsel as that which exhorts us not to let the right hand know the charitable actions of the left. And now, if we turn to Eliphas Lévi's *Histoire de la Magie*, we find him condemning, in Indian philosophy, the very principle which he has upheld—namely, that the wise man cannot lie. In the Oupnek'hat, a book of Indian occultism, the following passage occurs :—" God is truth, and in Him light and shadow are one only. Whoever knows this can never lie, for even when he tries to do so his falsehood becomes a truth." Again, the same work tells us that " it is permitted to lie in order to facilitate marriages, to exalt the virtues of a Brahman or the qualities of a cow." This is immoral, doubtless, but it does not surpass the spiritual wickedness of the Christian legend which, by representing a divine miracle covering a falsehood, practically teaches that it is allowable to lie in order to exalt the merits of a good work.

NOTE 28 (page 219).—There is no attempt to explain the suffering—the actual physical maltreatment—of the victims of were-wolves on this theory.

NOTE 29 (page 288.)—It is not to Pascal but to the mystical theology of the Seraphic Doctor, S. Bonaventura, that we owe this idea. In the sixth chapter of the *Itinerarium Mentis ad Deum* (a work which should be in the hands of every student of mysticism), he says :—" Russus revertentes dicamus, quia igitur esse purissimum et absolutum, quod est simpliciter esse, est primarium et novissimum, ideo est omnium origo et finis consummans.

Quia æternum et præsentissimum, ideo omnes durationes ambit et intrat, quasi simul existens earum centrum et circumferentia. Quia simplicissimum et maximum, ideo totum intra omnia, et totum extra omnia, ac per hoc est *sphæra intelligibilis, cujus centrum est ubique et circumferentia nusquam.*"

NOTE 30 (page 299).—In the chapter on Divination we were told that most religious revelations have been given in dreams, and that the patriarchs looked on dreams as "certain revelations." Are the *masters* in modern Israel, of whom Eliphas Lévi has made himself the uncommissioned and unaccredited spokesman, "greater than our father Abraham," and wiser than Joseph the diviner?

NOTE 31 (page 325).—And yet in the *Dogme et Rituel de la Haute Magie*, there is an engraving of ADDHANARI, the great Indian Pantacle, which is distinctly said to represent Religion and Truth, and to be analogous to the ADO-NAÏ of Ezekiel, but which bears upon its very forehead that *lingam* which is here declared to be a confession of doctrinal shamelessness. The contradiction is as complete as words can make it, and its object is obviously to discredit all magical marvels occurring outside the hierarchy of initiation or the authority of the Latin orthodoxy.

INDEX.

	PAGE
Astrology Theologised	32
Anatomy of Tobacco	17
Antiquarian Study	24
Astrologer's Guide	26
Archæology and Occultism	29
Adams, F. W. L.	32
Adams, Mrs. Davenport	34
Arundale, Miss	36
Baughan, Rosa	8, 14, 17
Blavatsky, H. P.	16, 21, 26
Burma	22
Batty, John	24
Bonatus	26
Browne, Hablôt K.	30
Betts, B. W.	31
Beauty and the Beast	34
Chirognomancy	17
Cosmo de' Medici	11
Curate's Wife (The)	14
Colman's Plays	19
Confessions of an English Hachish Eater	20
Cruikshank, George	25
Church, W. E.	25
Cardan	26
Cook, Miss Louisa S.	31
Collette, C. H.	35
Chatterji, Mohini M.	36
Dickens	5
Dickensiana	38
East Anglian	18
Eliphas Levi's Writings	30
Ellis, W. A.	36
Forlong, Major-General J. G. R.	12
Forty Vezirs	13
Folk-Songs	23
Geometrical Psychology	31
George, G. M.	7
Gibb, E. J. W.	13
Greville-Nugent, Hon. Mrs.	18
Hints to Collectors	5, 6
Hubbe-Schleiden, J. U.	35
Heptameron	10
Horne, R. H.	11
Hartmann, F.	10, 16
Hermes	33
Illumination	15
Ingram, John H.	21
Incidents in Life of H. P. Blavatsky	26
Johnson, C. P.	5, 6
Jones, Ebenezer	24
Jones, Sumner	24
Judge, W. Q.	33
Jennings, Hargrave	37
Keightley, B.	36
Kitton, F. G.	13, 30, 38
Kent, Charles	7
Kabala Denudata	27
Kingsford, Mrs. Anna, M.D.	32, 33
Lamb	34
Leech	13
Linton, W. J.	24
Lilly	26
Leolinus Siluriensis	17

	PAGE
Low Down	27
Literature of Occultism and Archæology	29
Leicester	32
Marchant, W. T.	9
Martinengo-Cesaresco, Countess	23
Mathers, S. L. M.	27
Maitland, E.	15
Machen, A.	10
Magic	10
Mountaineering Below the Snow-Line	10
Mysteries of Magic	30
Navy	36
Nesfield, H. W.	31
Northamptonshire Notes and Queries	30
Occult World Phenomena	16
Olcott, H. S.	28
Occultism and Archæology	29
"Phis"	30
Physiognomy	8
Primitive Symbolism	12
Palmistry	14
Panton, J. E.	14
Paracelsus	16
Pope Joan	35
Praise of Ale	9
Poe	11, 21
Paterson, M.	10
Path (The)	33
Phalliciem	37
Raven (The)	21
Regular Pickle (A)	31
Rideal, C. F.	17
Rueing of Gudrun	18
Salem Ben Uzair	12
Sphinx	35
Sultan Stork	3
Sheykh-Zada	13
Swinburne, A. C.	36
Sinnett, A. P.	15, 16, 26, 36
Sweeting, W. D.	30
Spiritual Hermeneutics	32
Sea Songs and River Rhymes	34
Shepherd, E. H.	11, 19, 24, 34
Swinburne Bibliography of	4
Sithron	12
Scott, J. G.	22
Studies of Sensation and Event	24
Serjeant, W. C. Eldon	26
Theosophy, Religion, and Occult Science	28
Tobacco Talk	8
Theosophist (The)	21
Two Tramps	27
Transactions L. L. T. S.	36
Thackeray	3, 6, 25
Tamerlane	11
United	15
Valley of Sorek	7
Virgin of the World	33
Walford's Antiquarian	20
Westropp, H. M.	12
Walford, E.	20
Wellerisms	7
White, C. H. Evelyn	18
Waite, A. E.	30
Word for the Navy	36

www.ingramcontent.com/pod-product-compliance
Lightning Source LLC
Chambersburg PA
CBHW031419150426
43191CB00006B/327